The education of the people

The education of the people

A history of primary education in England
and Wales in the nineteenth century

Mary Sturt

LONDON

ROUTLEDGE AND KEGAN PAUL

First published 1967
by Routledge & Kegan Paul Ltd
Broadway House, 68–74 Carter Lane
London, E.C.4

Printed in Great Britain
by Butler & Tanner Ltd
Frome and London

c/n :   07100 2161 5

Preface

This book is an attempt to show how, during the 19th century, the idea grew up that the provision of universal education was one of the functions of the state. It is also a history of that period of education, giving the chief events, and describing, as far as possible, the actual conditions in the schools.

The major part of the material is taken from official documents: the Reports of Commissions, Hansard, the Minutes of the Committee of Council, Inspectors' Reports, the Minutes of the greater School Boards, Acts of Parliament and Law Reports.

I have used periodicals of various kinds to show the changing views of different groups. The *Edinburgh* and *Quarterly Reviews*, *The Times* and the *Morning Chronicle*, the *School Board Chronicle* and the *School-master*, among others.

Scattered about the country, sometimes guarded by archivists, sometimes resting insecurely in the vicar's or headmaster's desk, are manuscript log-books of schools, Minutes of the smaller School Boards, papers dealing with attendance committees and Mechanics' Institutes. I have found and read some of these, but the total numbers are probably so large that I have seen only a very small fraction.

From country junk shops I have collected a few school text-books. They are not easy to find, and must be destroyed annually in thousands. They are out of date, and have not the halo of antiquity. They are hard to find in a big library, e.g. the Bodleian, as so many are anonymous, and others, if they were received, are not preserved. Yet these books, if they can be obtained, give a very clear picture of the actual content of the teaching.

For the later years of the century there are still personal memories.

M. S.

Contents

Illustrations

viii

Abbreviations

P.P.   Parliamentary Papers
Minutes   Minutes of the Committee of Council on Education
Report   Report of the Science and Art Department of the Committee
          of Council on Education

The references to the Minutes and the Reports are to the edition in
the Library of the Ministry of Education.

The efficacy of ignorance has long been tried, and has not produced the consequences expected.

Samuel Johnson

A system of National Education is necessarily of slow growth. In a country possessing representative institutions public opinion must first be convinced of the necessity and utility of so vast a creation as that of universally accessible and efficient elementary schools. In a mixed constitution, protecting all in the enjoyment of civil and religious freedom, the most difficult problem which can be proposed to a statesman is such a scheme, involving the civil rights and religious privileges of every class, yet in harmony with political justice, and being a full expression of national power.

Sir James Kay-Shuttleworth

Chapter One

The importance of subordination

The education of the people, which began in the early 19th century, was, for England, a new idea. The extent of literacy had varied at different periods; but there had never been any suggestion that universal literacy was either possible or desirable, or that there should not be at least part of the nation cut off from the pleasures and dangers of the written word. A traditional culture, a craftsman's skill, a dogmatic religion provided all that was necessary for the greater part of the nation.

The Reformation did not bring the idea of universal literacy to England. In Scotland the 17th century saw the spread of parochial schools drawing their energy partly from the need of each man to study the Bible for himself. England, less concerned with individual conscience, felt that the Church could still supply the guidance that was needed; and that salvation was not dependent on the power to read. Nor did the English feel that education was necessary for a man's advancement. Theory and social feeling were united in the belief that 'the Poor' should remain in the condition in which God had placed them, and that the stratification of society could not be disturbed without impiety and political danger. Samuel Johnson's table talk is full of the importance of due subordination in society.

This feeling was the stronger because, in the conditions of the times, the Poor must often have appeared as a different type of human being. The country labourer, perhaps stripped of his common land by the enclosures, or of his garden by the demand for arable land stimulated by the Corn Laws, was beset by the regulations of the Poor Law and the rigours of the Game Laws. The powers of the magistrates and the demands of the farmers gave little chance of physical health or moral

I

dignity. In the towns the overwhelming hours of work, the conditions in the factories and the appalling housing left those that did not die permanently enfeebled. The children caught into factories at five or seven had their bodies deformed and their minds stunted. These people were excluded from central or local government, the Church did not reach them: they were nobody's concern. Moreover, it was only necessary to consider what had happened in France to realize the importance of discipline at home.

This view of the Poor fitted very well with the facts of economic life. In an unmechanized age, when industry and domestic life were almost inconceivably inconvenient and laborious, a large part of the population inevitably spent their lives in simple and heavy work in order that things might be made, food grown and a minority live in comfort. The canals and railways of England were built with equipment hardly more developed than that used in constructing the pyramids; agriculture depended on the horse and the hoe; domestic life was a long round of carrying water or wood. If all this work was to go on, someone must be willing to do it, or be forced to do it by the impossibility of any other living. The Poor (and their status was so well defined that in the books of the period they almost always have a capital letter) were the necessary base of the whole social system. Without them and their work nothing could happen. It is comprehensible, then, that any attempt to take them out of their class, to make them too grand for their work, was regarded as dangerous in the extreme. Those whose minds did not go beyond the convenience of their own order, felt a hostility to the very suggestion of education. 'If a horse', says Mandeville in his treatise against Charity schools, 'knew as much as a man, I should not like to be his rider.'[1] This pamphlet and Archbishop Whately's rejoinder nearly a hundred years later show the strength and the persistence of the opposition to the education of the Poor. When work was so unpleasant, how could it be done except by people who were unable to imagine any other way of life?

When the matter was thought about philosophically there were two lines of approach, the economic and the religious. Adam Smith, who had written in the 18th century, became the gospel of the 19th. He explained that trade was a system of mutual service and exchange, and did good under the 'obvious and simple system of natural liberty'. This liberty was interpreted as freedom from any legal regulation of wages and conditions, and the absence of any protection for the Poor. By that convenient mental mechanism which prevents awkward facts from being brought into effective association, this doctrine of 'freedom' was not applied to such things as the Corn Laws or duties on various articles. Pitt could say that 'trade, industry and barter would always find their own level, and be impeded by regulations which violated their material operation and deranged their proper effect'. This meant that wages must be allowed to sink to their lowest levels; and the old laws which had regulated wages, and which were discovered still to exist in 1813, were immediately repealed as 'pernicious'.

Brougham stated the principle perfectly clearly:

Men should be employed and paid according to the demand for their labour, and its value to the employer. No doctrine is more *monstrous* than that all accumulation of capital is a grievance to them; that every man has a title to that which he renders valuable by his labour; that the amount of remuneration for his work must be ascertained, not by the competition in the market of labourers and employers, but by the personal wants and wishes of the former.

A second line of thought which appears frequently was that 'individual interest, properly understood, was also public interest'. The important words were 'properly understood'; and they were almost always omitted. Burke might argue that the interests of farmers and labourers were one. The farmer wanted his work well done and this was only possible with a well-fed, intelligent and happy labourer:

It is plainly more to the farmer's interest that his men should thrive, that his horses should be well fed, sleek, plump and fit for use, or that his waggon and ploughs should be strong, in good repair and fit for service.[2]

Unfortunately, while the country districts were 'overpopulated' and the influx of Irish labour continued in the towns, private interest saw no reason for preserving the labourer in the same comfort as a horse.

There was, moreover, a conviction that poverty, the abject, destructive poverty of the time, was necessary. Without 'vice and misery' the Poor would breed too fast. There was only a certain amount of food, only a certain fund to pay wages. The Poor would breed till they were on subsistence level. If numbers increased beyond that point, the surplus would die of starvation; if the workman grew comfortable, and his children survived, he would once more, by numbers, force himself back to starvation. It was a simple creed; and had a beautiful biological inevitability about it.

Besides political economy there was religion. The Church was a vast

3

property-owning corporation, and found its very essence involved in the maintenance of the present system. The duty of submitting to the Will of God was stressed on every occasion. A meek contentment was the chief virtue. Lowliness, humility, and a willingness to remain patiently in that state of life to which God had called you.

Kay-Shuttleworth sums up this whole philosophy:

There are men who believe that the labouring classes are condemned for ever, by an inexorable fate, to the unmitigated curse of toil, scarcely rewarded by the bare necessities of existence, and often visited by the horrors of hunger and disease—that the heritage of ignorance, labour and misery is entailed upon them as an eternal doom. Such an opinion might appear to receive a gloomy confirmation were we content with the evidence of fact.[3]

Obviously education had to be very carefully given if it was to fit into this scheme of things. As late as 1832 it could be said, 'Ministers and men in power, with nearly the whole body of those who are rich, dread the consequences of teaching the people more than they dread the effects of their ignorance'.

In the debate on the desirability of Education, which went on from about 1750 to 1833, when some, at least, of the 'ministers and men in power' had decided that education was inevitable and desirable, it is remarkable how little education was offered to the Poor, and how concerned everyone was with its effect on others rather than on the recipient. There is much talk about the way that education will improve morals, prevent social disturbance, and make servants better workers; but hardly anything about the greater happiness that it will bring to the scholar. It needed a revolutionary like Tom Paine to demand education as a simple function of government: 'A nation under a well-regulated government would permit none to remain uninstructed. It is monarchical and aristocratical government only that requires ignorance for its support.'[4]

In England there were many who saw dangers everywhere.

Industry [said a writer in the *Gentlemen's Magazine* in 1797] is the duty to impress on the lower classes. A little learning makes a man ambitious to rise, if he can't by fair means then he uses foul. . . . His ignorance is a balm that soothes his mind into stupidity and repose, and excludes every motion of discontent, pride and ambition. A man of no literature will seldom attempt to form insurrections, or form idle schemes for the reformation of the state.

4

Or, with more show of humanity, Mr Giddy in parliament opposed Whitbread's bill of 1807 for instructing pauper children:

The scheme would be found to be prejudicial to the morals and happiness of the labouring classes; it would teach them to despise their lot in life, instead of making them good servants in agriculture and other laborious employments to which their rank in society had destined them; instead of teaching them subordination it would render them factious and refractory, as was evident in the manufacturing counties; it would enable them to read seditious pamphlets, vicious books and publications against Christianity; it would render them insolent to their superiors.[5]

On the other hand there were those who hoped that some good would follow. Adam Smith thought that education might give a certain political stability:

Though the state was to derive no advantage from the instruction of the inferior ranks of the people, it would still deserve its attention that they should not be altogether uninstructed. The state, however, derives no inconsiderable advantage from their instruction. The more they are instructed the less liable they are to the delusions of enthusiasm and superstition, which, among ignorant nations, frequently occasion the most dreadful disorders.[6]

Just occasionally there is a hint that the pupil might have gained something from his instruction:

If we speak of education here it will naturally carry our Ideas to the Spade, the Plough or the Team. As early and constant Labour is the Province of this Class, there is but a small Share either of Time or Abilities for Instruction; still as they are by Nature susceptible of it, those who have Power cannot employ it better than bestowing it; so far as least as may open their Minds to distinguish Truth from Falsehood, Right from Wrong, Innocence from Guilt. If to this were added at least the Power of reading their Mother-tongue, it would at times be an Entertainment and a Consolation to them; and it would remove, in some Degree, that total Darkness and Ignorance they must otherwise remain in.[7]

Even Pestalozzi who has been hailed as the prophet of Education saw clearly the relation between learning and the child's way of life:

The child of the soil and the whole class of landless agricultural labourers must learn in their language lessons to express themselves accurately about everything that has to do with their calling. . . . But laborious toil is their lot in life, and their language lessons must not set up interests which would undermine the bases of their happiness and

5

well being. . . . Education should enable men to follow their particular calling with Godliness and honour. . . .

It should not enable them to change to anything better.[8]

The actual education offered to the Poor under these circumstances was, naturally, slight. The Charity[9] Schools were the characteristic educational effort of the early 18th century. They were supported by some endowments, private charity and church collections. Indeed a sermon in aid of a charity school was one of the standard exercises for every aspiring cleric. From these sermons we can learn how little education was, in fact, offered, and what a modest alleviation of human misery was intended. Bishop Butler said that the aim of Charity Schools 'was not in any sort to remove poor children out of the rank in which they were born, but, keeping them in it, to give them the assistance which their circumstances plainly called for, by educating them in the principles of religion as well as of civil life'.

Most of the time in the schools was taken up with 'industry'; that is, the mechanical performance of some task. The children might well work seven hours a day and be taught to read for a short period now and then. The movement, which was full of energy at the beginning of the century, was split after 1715 and even more after 1745 between the High Church party, which favoured the Stuarts, and the senior officials of the Church who had been appointed by the Hanoverians. Each faction accused the other of perverting youth, and the national effort was dissipated in sectarian competition.

Even under the aegis of the Society for the Promotion of Christian Knowledge the political element remained. In 1738 the Society received a patent enabling it to raise funds to set up spinning schools in suitable places for the 'breeding up of young people in handy labour, trades and manufactures' which would be of benefit not only to themselves 'but likewise to the nation in general and better answer to the inclination of the contributors for promoting piety and virtue'. Even more explicitly, the Society was setting up schools in the Highlands after 1745 to promote 'the Protestant Religion, Good Government, Industry and Manufactures and the Principles of Duty and Loyalty to His Majesty, His Heirs and Successors and to no other use or purpose whatever'.[10] The Society was grieved that the schools did not seem to suit the character of the Highlanders.

The Charity children appeared in their uniforms in church on the day of appeal, and made a pleasing sight for the well-to-do middle class,

6

who satisfied their need for alms-giving in such an affecting way. But the reality of the children's lives was often shocking.

It was difficult to find teachers. The superintendents of the Charity Schools were seldom people of honesty or humanity, and it was only occasionally that a founder could discover 'a person who had known brighter days, but whose change of situation was not unaccompanied by a change of heart'. The normal arrangements were to pay the superintendent so much a head for boarding the children, and to allow him to take in addition 'the profits of the children's work'. When, moreover, the schools were generally left without supervision, the temptation was altogether too great. The children were starved, ill-treated and condemned to exhausting hours of work for the profit of the teacher. At one school in York, when the ladies of the committee actually visited the place, the conditions were found to be so bad that a complete reorganization was undertaken at once.[11] The greater number of these schools were never investigated. Even if they had done what they were supposed to do, little impression would have been made on the general ignorance. They failed to do even that.

The curriculum, in so far as it existed, was the same as that of any other school for the Poor at that time. John Foster maintained that schools for the Poor should be 'as little as possible scholastic; to be kept down to the lowest level of the workshop, excepting perhaps in one particular—that of working hard; for the scholars were to throw away time rather than be occupied with anything beyond the merest rudiments'.

Reading was often taught on the ground that it was a good basis for religious training. Hannah More said, 'I know of no way of teaching morals but by infusing principles of Christianity, nor of teaching Christianity without a thorough knowledge of the Scripture.' But reading was not to go beyond this religious purpose, nor were other arts to be taught. Jonas Hanway summed up this position more briefly: 'Reading will help to mend people's morals, but writing is not necessary.'

As the driving force of the Charity School movement waned under political disagreements, the energy was transferred to the foundation of Sunday Schools. Once they had been thought of, they seemed the perfect type of education. They would give a little safe instruction without disrupting the economic pattern.

The Rev. Charles Moore pleading in Rochester in 1795 for Sunday Schools thought that they were desirable because

they seek to furnish opportunities of instruction to the children of the

7

poor without interfering with any weekly industry; to infuse into the tender minds of infancy ideas of decency, sobriety and industry; to inure them early to habits of regularity in their attendance at church, and to teach them how to spend the leisure hours of Sunday to their own improvement, advantage and happiness, which are now almost universally consumed in idleness, profanation and riot. [Also] the children are to be taught to read, and to be instructed in the plain duties of the Christian religion, with a particular view to their good and industrious behaviour in their future character of Labourers and Servants.[12]

Raikes when founding his Gloucester Sunday Schools had the convenience of the well-to-do almost equally in mind. The children of Gloucester were employed in the pin factories all the week. On Sunday they were free, but no provision of any kind was made for their occupation or amusement.

'Farmers and other inhabitants of the towns and villages receive more injury to their property on the Sabbath than in all the week besides; this in a great measure proceeds from the lawless state of the younger class who are allowed to run wild on that day free from every restraint.' So he conceived the idea of penning up the children on Sunday also.[13]

The schools kept almost factory hours. Children assembled at 8 in the morning, were instructed till church time and then escorted there; sent home to dinner, reassembled at 2 and 'continued in school till 7 o'clock when daylight will permit, and in winter till 6 o'clock'. After three years of this he felt he had been successful: 'The behaviour of the children is much civilized, and Gloucester is quite a heaven on Sundays compared to what it used to be.'

Sunday Schools were convenient; they were not ambitious to teach too much; and they were firmly under the control of a religious body. This attitude is made quite clear by the rules of a York Sunday School drawn up in 1786:

1. The objects of this charity shall be poor persons of each sex and any age, who shall be taught to read at such times and in such places as the committee shall appoint.
2. The teachers shall take care that all who are committed to their charge shall attend public worship every Sunday, unless prevented by illness or any other sufficient cause.
3. The religious observance of the Christian Sabbath being an essential object with the society, the exercises of the scholars on that day will be restricted to reading in the Old and New Testaments, and to spelling as a preparation for it.

8

It was rare for these schools to attempt to teach anything more than reading, and that reading would be confined to the Scriptures. But they answered a demand. Their pupils were by no means all children, and they did contribute a great deal towards the literacy of the radical leaders of the next century. This is clear from a passage in Samuel Bamford describing the growth of radicalism just after 1815:

The Sunday Schools of the preceding 30 years had produced many working men of sufficient talent to become readers, writers and speakers in the village meetings for parliamentary reform: some also were found to possess a rude poetic talent, which rendered their effusions popular and bestowed an additional charm on their assemblages.

Every year the numbers of schools increased, and the scholars on the books ran into thousands.[14]

Sunday Schools had another advantage. Potential teachers were rather easier to find than those for day schools. They could combine teaching with their ordinary work. In Martha More's *Mendip Annals*:

The spiritual improvement of the parish was left entirely to the care and management of Tommy Jones and Johnny Hart, as the two young miners are called, but a Higher Power not only presided over, but greatly blessed these two poor youths, who are concealed from all human sight in the bowels of the earth six days out of seven, and on the seventh day they emerge, like two young apostles, to instruct and enlighten the rising generation.[15]

Men in all walks of life became Sunday School teachers, sometimes for a small fee, increasingly often voluntarily. At the beginning of the 19th century it became fashionable for young ladies to have a Sunday School class, and make small presents to their children, and thus they got to know something of their lives. As the schools developed, they trained their own teachers, and became self-perpetuating. In numbers, and in the effort that the organizing of such numbers involved, the achievements of the Sunday Schools were impressive.

But, once again, political considerations produced discord, and the Dissenting schools were accused of Jacobinism and of failing to teach the 'laws of subordination'; while the Church was thought to be too rigid.

When other schools for the Poor were founded they were usually thought of as appendages to the Church rather than as independent institutions with separate, if related, functions to perform. Martha More

9

when she recounts the success of her schools, tends to stress the increase in church attendance as her chief glory:

> Cheddar we found more prosperous than we had ever seen before—one hundred and sixty children in the school. To see all these poor children in one room crowding together, to hear the din of voices, to know what was going on, and the positive certainty that they were all training in the knowledge of the Scriptures, was a magnificent sight, though the children were ragged, and produced glorious feelings, though the expression fails. One of the oldest and most creditable farmers assured us that three years ago four or five women, and fourteen or fifteen men comprised a common congregation; and that now, in the forenoon, they had often five hundred.

Though, as attendance at church implied a decent standard of dress, and an ordered way of life, the fact has a wider significance.

Often the school was founded and maintained by the local clergyman. If a humble man he did the teaching himself. There is a record of one, at Nayland in Suffolk, who, before the school was built, took classes in the church, using his spinning wheel at the same time. The school was suspended in very cold weather.

On other occasions the master was supplied by the holder of some existing office. The office of Clerk to the Parish was often of some value, and he was required to teach in addition to his other work. This was an arrangement favoured by the S.P.C.K. It is recorded of Spofforth 'Five children are likewise taught gratis by the schoolmaster of Spofforth in consideration of him being chosen clerk to the parish'. And at Skipton there was 'a school called a song school, where all the boys of the town are taught to sing psalms by the parish clerk who has a salary for that purpose besides his parish dues'. This appeared to many to be the best arrangement. Southey, writing in the *Quarterly* in 1811, could say definitely, 'The parish priest should be the superintendent of the parish school, and, when a race of men have been educated for the purpose, it would be well if the clerk were always the school master.'

Where there was a separate schoolmaster he was often appointed for qualities other than scholarship and teaching ability. These are the qualifications set out in York in the 18th century for a Charity Schoolmaster:

> He must be a member of the established Church of England;
> a frequenter of Holy Communion;
> master of his passions;

of meek temper and humble behaviour;
of a good genious for teaching;
one that understands the grounds and principles of the Christian religion;
can write a good hand and understands the grounds of arithmetic.

As a more extreme example of this tendency, a church choir in Suffolk in 1789 required a counter tenor, and an advertisement appeared:

Wanted to take charge of a school in populous village where boys and girls are taught reading, writing, and arithmetic. A youth not exceeding 16, accommodating in his disposition, with a good voice, a genius for music, capable of teaching psalmody will be acceptable.

No other particular qualifications.

N.B. No objection to a Eunuch.[16]

The advertisement produced the right man, for when the youth died three years later, a most handsome stone tablet was put up in the church porch commemorating his merits.

M. S.
Thomas Smith
Quem pium, placidum,
Sacrorum docilem,
Philomelae aemulum,
Pater chori coelestis
In Coetus Angalorum transtulit
Anno aetatis 19
MDCCXCL

Under all these disadvantages the Poor did not show themselves very apt scholars; but their betters were not well instructed either. Among the gentry the men would have usually had some slight classical education, and the women would know how to read and write, the latter often imperfectly. The lower middle classes in the towns would have such rudiments of literacy as they needed for their trade or occupation; in the country the farmers were mainly illiterate. It was the upper middle class and a few of the nobility who maintained the highly intellectual society of the age.

All these points, so far as concerns the country, are illustrated in Martha More's *Mendip Annals*, an account of the attempt made by her and her sister Hannah to establish schools in the area. The original impulse was given by Wilberforce, who was so shocked by the condition of Cheddar that he offered to provide the money if Hannah would do the work of helping the district. As a former teacher, Hannah's mind turned to education, and she set out to found schools in a district which was remote, ill-served by roads and off the beaten track, yet possessing some industry, and probably not more unfortunate than many parts of England.

She introduces us to the abandoned villages:

We have one large parish of miners so poor that there is not one creature in it that can give a cup of broth if it would save a life. Of course they have nothing human to look to but us. The clergyman, a poor saint, told me, when we set up our schools there twenty-five years ago, that eighteen had perished that winter of putrid fever, and he could not raise sixpence to save a life.

We see the non-resident clergy: 'The Rector', she says tartly on one occasion, 'now made his annual appearance, the first since the school was opened. . . . He went to the house, examined the children, left them half-a-guinea, received his tithes and marched off.' Of another she records:

The incumbent is a Mr R., who has something to do, but I cannot find out what, in the University of Oxford where he resides. The curate lives at Wells, twelve miles distant. They have service only once a week, and there is scarcely an instance of a poor person being visited or prayed with.

The villagers, though without help, were not without discipline. The Poor Law Overseers held terrible powers. One farmer's wife discounted the necessity of a school:

Her husband said to another person a Sabbath school was not wanted, for that when they played games or rioted in the churchyard on Sundays, he sometimes went and cursed and swore among them a little, and, as he was Overseer, they then dispersed: and what did people wish for more?

There were worse terrors. A single magistrate could inflict a severe flogging, even on a child, for a petty theft, and any too overt discontent would bring death:

There is a little hamlet, called Charter House, on the top of Mendip, so wicked and lawless that they report thieving to have been handed down from father to son for the last forty years. The poor woman under sentence of death (for attempting to begin a riot and purloining some butter from a man who offered it for sale at a price they thought unreasonable) was an inhabitant of this place.

The farmers, who supplied the real ruling class of such districts—

the landlords were mainly non-resident—were completely opposed to education. Their view, expressed in various ways, was: 'The lower class were fated to be poor and ignorant and wicked; and that, wise as we were, we could not alter what was decreed.'

The farmers were themselves illiterate, and that sharpened their hostility to Hannah. The clergy had no such excuse, but they joined with the farmers and raised the cry of Methodism, and petitioned the Dean whenever the schools appeared to be going too well.

And yet this dangerous education was on the level of the age:

Let me add that my plan for instructing the poor is very limited and strict. They learn of week-days such coarse work as may fit them for servants. I allow of no writing. My object has not been to teach dogmas and opinions, but to form the lower class in habits of industry and virtue.[17]

In her work Hannah gave her sympathy and devotion to her people:

I have devoted the remnants of my life to the poor, and to those that have no helper; and if I can do them little good, I can at least sympathize with them, and I know it is some comfort for a forlorn creature to be able to say, 'There is somebody that cares for me.' That simple idea of being cared for has always appeared to me a very cheering one.

Yet in social conception she was at one with her age. Every year she gave a great picnic to each of her villages, and after the meal and the junketings she made a speech to the gathering, setting out their duties of hard work and submission:

I can never omit a short exhortation on the indispensable duty of *industry*. The Christian will be industrious that he may please God.

Let the men and women of Shipham and Rowbarrow become honest and good graziers and hoglers. They were placed in this spot by Almighty direction. The very ground you walk upon points out your daily labour. Excel in that, and an honest hogler is as good in the eyes of the Almighty as an honest squire; therefore we wish to recommend you to do your duty in that state of life where God has placed and called you. Every disposition to rebellion against the higher powers would prove how little you are changed in your hearts, after all that has been done for you; and remember that rebellion against rulers first brought on the troubles in France.

Even this carefully limited help was too much for the age. All the forces of society united against her—'hard-hearted farmers, little cold country gentry, a supercilious and ignorant corporation' and the hostile Church. The Journal of the schools ends sadly:

Yatton closed. And if, during the years we have been at Yatton, some children may hereafter, in the hours of sorrow and distress, recall to mind one useful sentence, or recollect one text of Scripture learned and explained at school, surely it has not been carried on for nought.

Such was the climate of thought at the end of the 18th century, and it was among people with these ideas that the belief in popular education had to make its way.

Notes

1. B. Mandeville, *Essay on Charity and Charity Schools* (1723), p. 331. Dr Whately, *Sermon on the Duty of the Education of the Poor* (1830).
2. E. Burke, *Thoughts and Details on Scarcity* (1800), In Collection of Tracts, printed by Lord Overstone (1859), p. 469.
3. M.S. 1877.
4. T. Paine, *Rights of Man* (1792), pt II, ch. 5.
5. Hansard, 1807, IX, 798.
6. Adam Smith, *Wealth of Nations* (1838 ed.), Bk V, ch. 1, art. ii, p. 352.
7. James Nelson, *Essay on the Education of Children* (1753).
8. J. H. Pestalozzi, *Swansong*, p. 54.
9. For the general history and achievement of Charity schools, see G. M. Jones, *The Charity School Movement* (1938); Mrs Trimmer, *Oeconomy of Charity* (1801), and *Reflections on educating children in Charity Schools* (1792), pp. 11–12.
10. G. M. Jones, op. cit., p. 202.
11. For this and other facts about Education in York, see Edward Benson, 'A History of Education in York, 1780–1902' (Ph.D. thesis in Public Library, York).
12. Charles Moore, *Sermon preached at Rochester* (1795), p. 18.
13. For a general account of these Sunday Schools, see G. Webster, *Robert Raikes* (1873), Alfred Gregory, *Robert Raikes* (1877), pp. 43 ff. and Arnold Broadbent, *First Hundred Years of the Sunday School Association* (1933).
14. Samuel Bamford, *Passages in the Life of a Radical*, p. 8.
15. Martha More, *Mendip Annals* (2nd ed., 1859). The whole account is full of interest on the subject of the attitude towards education.
16. Information from the Vicar, Nayland.
17. R. Brimley Johnson, *Letters of Hannah More* (1925), p. 183.

Chapter Two

The Humanitarians

The beginning of the 19th century saw a remarkable development of private benevolence throughout the country. Individuals and tiny groups were, in many different ways, trying to do something to decrease the mass of misery which suddenly seemed to have become shameful and almost unnecessary. Without imagining any change in the structure of society they tried—as had Hannah and Martha More—to help a few children here—a few women there. They looked at the condition of the agricultural labourers and thought of plans for providing them with milk. They ran a village shop that sold honest goods at fair prices. They devised a new type of grate for cottages to economize fuel and diminish draughts; they taught six poor children to do straw plait, and fed and clothed them on the proceeds. Their activities were infinitely small, and yet in total they accomplished much.

The Society for Bettering the Condition of the Poor acted as a forum in which these attempts could have due publicity. The Reports that it published told these scattered reformers what was being done. The range was wide. There were accounts of vaccination, of water purification in Paisley, of the management of bees on Mount Hymettus, or of the lack of amusements for the poor in Spain. There is a report on an institution for the aged near Paris, and a paper of admonitions addressed to Foundling children when they are apprenticed. The Society was active for about the first ten years of the 19th century and it is interesting to see the change that comes over the palliatives that are suggested. The earlier volumes are full of soup kitchens and the profit to the cottagers of keeping a pig, or the advantages of a female Overseer of the Poor. If a school is mentioned it is a place where children spin for ten hours a day or where, in Tortola, they make cheap shirts for seamen. In the later volumes there is a definite change of emphasis. There are reports on Scottish education, on the findings of the Irish Board of Education, and on the school in the Borough Road.

These philanthropists were driven almost inevitably to pay more and more attention to education. Children in need of care made more appeal to sympathy than their elders; and there was more hope of establishing them in good ways. The work that was done was so modest that it is hard to believe in its importance. In the reports for the year 1802 there is an account of a school for poor children near Bath. They would be received at two years old and might stay till twelve. They learnt sewing, and left when they were able to make a shirt. The comment which accompanies this account is most enlightening because it shows the motives, as well as the hopeless weakness of such work:

The union of any 3 ladies in this work of pious charity at the expense of £4 a year to each of them will afford education to 20 children, will give comfort, relief and attachment to almost as many poor families; will assist the present and improve the rising generation, and will at the same time provide for some poor and honest widow those means of occupation and livelihood without which she might have been compelled to be a burthen to herself and the parish.

The employment of children in these schools of private charity was natural and inevitable. They were being educated for their place in life and the resources of the founders were limited. What these good ladies did was to organize the children's work so that they could support themselves; and if they learnt anything academic it was in their odd moments of leisure.[1] In 1813, the minutes of the managers of the British Girls' School of York recorded the resolution.

That the additional time which is required for reading and writing be taken from that allotted to knitting, and that the whole of the forenoon be employed in needlework.

The great problem was to find work for the children to do—especially the boys. In the 18th century the insatiable demand for thread kept the children busy. The activity of spinning was entirely brainless, and the trick of doing it was one that could be learnt by quite small children. With the development of mechanical methods, the demand for handspun yarn almost disappeared. The promoters of these schools looked round for other ways of helping the children to earn their keep. One school in Birmingham set the boys to putting heads on pins and sticking them in paper. Another, a rather later one, ran a printing business, where the boys worked the presses while the girls boiled potatoes and rice which they later ate, with treacle, for dinner. It was rather easier for the girls. Straw plaiting had not yet been mechanized, and it was an activity that could be learned sufficiently easily for their ability, and the pay was good.[2] They might even, one philanthropist feared, earn as much as £1 a week; and such high wages might be dangerous. However, he consoles himself with the thought that, as the supply of plait increased, the price was sure to fall. In a school at Seven Dials they did straw plait and learned reading. For an extra 3d. a week they could learn writing. The school fees were deducted from the children's earnings. The schools with the most material hope of success were those based, like Lady Noel Byron's on horticulture.[3] The extraordinary thing is that there were so few that chose this most obvious and beneficial of activities. Partly it was that schools sprang up mainly in towns where land was not available, but also that the promoters were not in touch with the land. In the country the prejudice against even agricultural labourers having gardens was overwhelming, so that, when a country pursuit was engaged in, it was the making of nets—to be used instead of hurdles—and not the production of the so much needed food.

A further weakness of these schools, and one fatal to any real progress, was their evanescent nature. Entirely dependent on private benevolence and personal interest, few of them can have existed long. An outstanding personality could maintain them for a time; but not even a permanent endowment was safe from neglect and dishonesty as soon as the directing mind was withdrawn. It was only the very small minority of philanthropists who were able to become leaders—or eponymous heroes —of a sect.

The interest in education as a power for social amelioration was not confined to England. Europe was as full of misery—and better supplied with ideas. The English philanthropist looked abroad, with that tendency to admire what is done beyond the Channel so characteristic of him at all ages.

The prophet of humanitarian educational reform was Pestalozzi, and the keenness of the reformers for help and ideas is shown by the processions of distinguished men who went to Switzerland to learn how to bring up a couple of dozen orphan children in kindness and virtue. The idea that the wretched starveling children who shrank into doorways at the approach of men, or lived on garbage like dogs, could be trained and taught and made happy, useful members of the community shone on well-intentioned Europe like a beacon light. Pestalozzi with his tiny school, which he ran for only a short time, seemed to those, who were appalled at the misery of the age, the hope of mankind. When in his old age he came to summarize his underlying philosophy he said something which echoed in the hearts of reformers—though for a hundred years or more the teachers were sadly unable to put it into practice:

Every philosophical investigator of human nature is [he declared] compelled to admit that the sole aim of education is the harmonious development of faculties and dispositions which, under God's grace, make up a personality.

It is not possible to think of making a human child what he ought to be by any other means than solicitude for the development in him of love and all round intellectual activity, and finally bringing the two into harmony.

He is constitutionally perfectly adapted to the achievement of his lofty destiny and to the performance of his duty, because his manhood disposes him towards these high aims, coming as they do from love, based as they are on activity, and allied as they are with freedom.[4]

This noble sentiment was kept in tune with the times by the fact that his children worked, and were prepared for the life of peasants. At Hofwyl where Wehrli, himself a peasant, led his boys out to the fields for a ten-hour working day, visitors from England could see an amelioration of life for the poor without any danger to the structure of society. The ideal fired them.

When Robert Owen, somewhat more radical, showed, in far-off New Lanark, how factory children could be kept out of the mills till the age of twelve and allowed opportunities for reasonable development, it was worth the long and uncomfortable journey to study his methods. When Wilderspin collected small children into school and gave them a little physical exercise and singing, it became a cult. It is not therefore so very surprising that a school, kept in a shed off the Borough Road, London, should have become a matter of national importance.

The two fundamental problems facing those who wished to use education to help the poor were the cost of schools and the lack of teachers. Money to supply the schools, teachers to instruct in them were the essential conditions of education—and both were lacking. The revelation that burst on Europe from the Borough Road was that you could do without both, and still give a full-time literary education.

Joseph Lancaster was the son of an old soldier who eked out a living

19

by making cane sieves. He was a passionate, eager lad, full of high ideals, and with a burning thirst for knowledge. 'I soon learned to read,' he says, 'soon read with delight; my book became my meat, drink and diversion.' He also had the gift of words; and later in life says of himself on one of his money-raising tours, 'Every word thrilled through my veins like the vital fluid in its course. I felt all I said, and every body felt it too.' His natural field of work would have been the Church, or the dissenting ministry which he preferred; but he early became connected with the Quakers, and later joined the Society. As there was no paid ministry among them, he turned to teaching; and in 1798 opened his school in an outhouse of his father's premises.

Lancaster was one of the great schoolmasters, and his understanding of children, his humanity, his zest and his most unquakerlike love of jollity, display, and even extravagance, must have made his school very different from others of similar pretensions. When, in addition, he evolved a system which promised to solve the problem of popular education, the Borough Road became a place of pilgrimage.

A notice outside the school read:

'All who will may send their children to have them educated freely. (The expenses of writing books excepted.) And those, to whom the above offer may not prove acceptable, may pay for them at a very modest price.' The fees were 4d. a week and those who could not pay were taken free.

Three years before Lancaster opened his school the Rev. Andrew Bell returned to England from Madras, having amassed, in nine years, a competence of some £27,000. During those years he had managed to hold eight army chaplaincies, to give a number of courses of philosophical lectures, which were well rewarded, and, probably, to engage in trade under the favourable conditions which were arranged for Britons by the East India Company. The only thing which he did without official salary was to act as Superintendent of the Military Male Asylum at Madras. This was a school for the sons of soldiers, and was doubtless in a very bad condition. Many of the boys, naturally, had Indian mothers, and no one took much care of them. The teaching was deplorable, and the food, clothing and treatment were bad. Bell seems to have worked hard at the school. He made various reforms in the boys' way of life, took them out swimming in the warm ocean, and resolved to reform the teaching. In this he was opposed by the masters, who had no intention of changing their methods, or taking the smallest trouble over their work. Bell got rid of them, and decided to use the older boys to teach the younger, as being a method cheaper than the other, and probably more effective.

This was easier for him than for his imitators. The boys were boarders and, therefore, under his hand for instruction; and he could keep them till they were old enough to be of use. Moreover in day-to-day intercourse he could acquire a real hold of their minds and form their characters. In his list of monitors, two are fourteen, two are twelve and two over eleven years. They were soldiers' sons, and had grown up in the ordered life of the army.

On his return to England Bell felt that the Directors of the Company ought to give him a pension, so he published a pamphlet on his work at the Asylum. Much the largest part of the work was taken up with testimonials to his work, and fulsome letters of dedication; but he did explain his use of children as teachers, and told how, one morning, when on his ride, he had seen a Malabar school with the children writing their letters in sand, and had brought back and made use of the idea. The pamphlet, called *An Experiment in Education,* was published in October 1797 and brought a pension of £200 a year.

These two men, Bell and Lancaster, dominated the educational scene for the next thirty years, and the results of their work and rivalry endured beyond that. The Scot from St Andrews, who had taken orders as a speculation and become the figurehead of a great Anglican crusade, was buried in Westminster Abbey; the flamboyant, extravagant Quaker, who could create but not conserve, and who could charm the nation into generosity, died, penniless, in a street accident in New York. They might have worked together, but for the religious rivalry that occupied so much of the thought and energy of the age, and which was triggered off by the indefatigable Mrs Trimmer, who was so prominent a figure in Sunday Schools and other Church education.

Lancaster, struggling with his ever-growing school (in times of difficulty he added free dinners to its other attractions), found himself compelled to use the older boys to teach the younger, and thus through necessity arrived at the same methods as Bell. Bell had found it cheaper to use a sand tray for early writing instead of paper; Lancaster found that slates from a demolished house made a good writing surface, and thus gave to 19th-century education one of its most characteristic symbols. In 1800 Lancaster came across Bell's *Experiment,* found some of the ideas helpful, particularly the sand writing, and was encouraged in his work. He had progressed far enough by 1803 to publish *Improvements in Education, as it respects the Industrious Classes of the Community*.

His school was not yet known to any but a few fellow-Quakers, and the only one who helped him was Mrs Elizabeth Fry, who visited him in 1801; but in the course of the two years after 1803 it became almost the most important educational institution in the world. His book, his speeches, the hope that he held out of solving the problem of popular education, brought visitors and subscribers from far and near. The list of subscribers to the third edition of the *Improvements* contained the names of three dukes, three duchesses, four marquesses, nine earls, twelve countesses, two viscounts, fourteen 'lords', twenty-three 'ladies', fifteen 'sirs', thirty-six members of Parliament, two archbishops and nine bishops as well as such foreigners as a prince, a baron, an ambassador and a general. This list is important because of the magnitude of the support, but more for the presence of the leaders of the Church. Lancaster had not then been discovered to be dangerous. His visitors included 'foreign princes, ambassadors, peers, commoners, ladies of distinction, bishops and archbishops, Jews and Turks'. The crown of it all came when in August 1805 he had an audience with George III, at Weymouth. The King said that he highly approved of the system and gave a subscription of £100 for himself and suitably graduated ones for the rest of the family. Lancaster had also been to see Bell and had a very cordial interview with him at his comfortable rectory at Swanage (stipend £600 a year). At this point, in September 1805, Mrs Trimmer intervened. To explain her action it is necessary to give Lancaster's views on the teaching of religion.

As a Quaker he wished to avoid sectarian teaching. 'Above all things, Education ought not to be subservient to the propagation of the particular tenets of any sect, beyond its own members', and he imagined a teaching which was grounded in the Bible, 'established in general Christian principles', and should have as its basis 'glory to God, and the increase of peace and good will among men'. It was this unsectarianism, this attempt to base education on the common ground of Christianity, which so enraged Mrs Trimmer—especially when its upholder had received royal approval and seemed likely to become a power in Education. Lancaster had mentioned Bell's work with appreciation in his *Improvements*, and Mrs Trimmer followed up the idea. Writing to Bell:

From the time, Sir, that I read Mr Joseph Lancaster's *Improvements in Education* in the first edition, I conceived an idea that there was something in his plan that was inimical to the interests of the Established Church, and, when I read your *Experiment in Education,* to which he referred, I plainly perceived that he had been building on your foundation. . . . Engaged as I have long been in striving to promote the interests of the Church. . . . I cannot see this 'Goliath of Schismatics' bearing down all before him, and engrossing the instruction of the common people, without attempting to give him a little check.[5]

A little later she writes, 'Of all the plans that have appeared in this kingdom likely to supplant the Church, Mr Lancaster's seems to me the most formidable. . . . Mr Lancaster's school is, in my estimation, a direct philanthropine.'

Dr Bell was quite ready to agree that Lancaster was a plagiarist and a knave. 'I observed his consummate front, his importunate solicitation of subscriptions in any and every shape, his plausible and ostentatious guise, and, in his third edition, I think I can see something which indicated that he can now stand alone, basking in the sunshine of royal countenance and popular applause.' So he was not unwilling to quit the calm country of Dorset (on receipt of a sinecure worth £1200 a year), and lead the crusade for the monitorial system under the aegis of the Established Church.

The quarrel which continued for so many years for the control first of the schools, and then, in the 1840s, for the control of the training colleges, provokes wry laughter today. But it was not without its uses, though it prevented the establishment of a state system of education, and so gave to English education its curious haphazard character.

'A general state education', wrote J. S. Mill, 'is merely a contrivance for moulding people to be exactly like each other, and as the mould in which it casts them is that which pleases the predominant power in the government it establishes a despotism over the mind, leading by natural tendency to one over the body.'[6]

The sectarian quarrel preserved us from this danger. It also engendered an enormous amount of energy which was directed, competitively, into the building of schools. Best of all, the battle was never won. In Belgium, as Kay-Shuttleworth pointed out later, the Church won the right to be the controlling force in education, and used its exclusive position to neglect and close the schools. The Church of England never won the right to control education by closing its opponents' schools. It had to open its own to compete. So that out of the fury, out of the jealousies and disingenuous arguments, came two strong societies each working for the spread of education; and, in fact, in the end offering very much the same instruction.

The essential mechanism of the system common to both sects was the subdivision of the matter of instruction in such a way that each section should be completely simple; and the corresponding division of the children into groups, each group learning the same thing under the tuition of one of the older or more advanced pupils. The groups varied in size from ten to fifteen, and a child on admission was assigned to the group that fitted his attainments. As the teachers were children, all the work to be done in the group was reduced to its elements and written on a card from which they worked. They were not required or expected to go beyond the words on the card. In fact, it was claimed as a merit of the system that, as the children knew nothing beyond what was on their card, they could not digress or waste time. Each child worked in his squad until he had learnt that particular piece of work, he was then promoted. Bell had thought of little more than this basic organization. Lancaster, with real insight and humanity, went much farther.

It was part of this insight that there were inspecting monitors who examined the different squads to see who was ready for promotion; and that promotion should be an important occasion for child and teacher. 'When a boy is removed from one class to another, he had permission to choose a prize, of a stated value, for himself, as a reward for his diligence; and the monitor is entitled to one of the same value for his care in improving his scholar.'

While in the group, there was the same desire to make things interesting. There was an order of precedence, and each child had a number suspended from his button and changed it as he went up or down in class. The top boy had a leather ticket saying *Merit*, or *Merit in Reading*. He also had 'a picture pasted on pasteboard and suspended on his breast' which he had to give up when he lost his top place. There were also money prizes, up to 6*d*. for twelve cards of excellence in writing with the pen.

The monitors who taught these squads were selected for their superior ability and character, but the position also had a psychological value.

I believe that many lads of genius are unknown in the schools they attend, even to the masters themselves, because they have no stimulus to exertion, no opportunity of distinguishing themselves. Whenever superior merit shows itself in the schools it should always be honoured, rewarded and distinguished: one or two lads of this description influence the whole school by their beneficial example. I generally reward such by gifts of some of the most valuable books and other prizes—silver pens and sometimes silver medals.

The chief offences committed by youth at school arrive from the liveliness of their active disposition. I have ever found the surest way to cure a mischievous boy was to make him a monitor. I never knew anything succeed much better, if so well.

Monitors not only taught squads and inspected for promotion, they were also responsible for the whole order and cleanliness of the school; for ruling the copy books, preparing the pens, making enquiries for absentees, giving out the books. They were, at least in theory, always in charge, always present, always vigilant. If by any chance disorder or ill behaviour occurred, and it did not happen often, the culprit was held up to ridicule. As a Quaker, Lancaster disapproved of corporal punishment. He would fasten a piece of wood round a child's neck, the wood not heavy or painful but inconvenient. He would send a dirty boy to have his face washed by the girls. If he kept a child in, being a practical man, he would tie him to a desk so that the teacher did not have to stay with him. Worst of all, a persistent offender was seated in a basket and hauled up some feet above the floor. 'Occasionally boys are put in a sack, or in a basket suspended to the roof of the school, in the sight of all the pupils, who frequently smile at "the birds in the cage". This punishment is one of the most terrible that can be inflicted on boys of sense and ability. Above all it is dreaded by the monitors.'[7]

To further decrease the chances of trouble, Lancaster needed a playground for his children, as the space gave them the opportunities of exercise away from the streets, and the existence of a playground 'attaches the children to the school'.

If this system inevitably made the early stages of learning mechanical and limited, Lancaster looked far beyond them. 'It has been found', he said, 'beneficial to vary the class books, that sameness may not tire or disgust the juvenile mind.' We can contrast the pronouncement of Dr Bell that 'Writers, ancient and modern, have observed that children do not *tire*, like men, of perpetual attention to minute points'—and whereas the National Schools rapidly settled down to a state in which the Bible was the *only* book in use, Lancaster has quite an impressive list, far longer and more various than in any other school of the period. He used: Watt's *Hymns for Children, Instructive Hints* ('Which fully answers its title'), Barbauld's *Hymns, Pastoral Lessons*, Trimmer's *Introduction to*

the Knowledge of Nature and The Use of the Scriptures, Martinet's
Catechism of Nature, or rather of natural history, Turner's *Arts and
Sciences* ('an instructive book, read, with the exception of the heathen
mythology, by a class of the senior boys'), A. J. Freame's *Scripture
Instruction* and Priscilla Wakefield's *Mental Improvement*.

He also provided a library, for which in one year he bought 30
volumes. In all, the library had about 330 books, and Lancaster valued
it highly. 'The library is very useful, the books being lent out gratis to
those who merit the privilege; it at once affords the means of instruction, in a very cheap, extensive way, and is conducive to emulation in
learning at the same time.'

We can contrast this with what was considered adequate provision
elsewhere: '52 short tracts of a religious and moral nature furnish a
year's reading. They are read loud after service and then lent out to be
read over again at home.'

Some idea of what he achieved with his best pupils can be gained
from his account of a boy who wanted to write. This child was always
writing. In turn he composed paragraphs for newspapers, a collection
of anecdotes, a sermon, an answer to Paine's *Rights of Man*, and a
defence of revealed religion.

In all these attempts [says Lancaster] he wasted many quires of paper,
rose in the morning early, neglected his meals, and was often wholly
swallowed up in the subject with which his mind was engaged. What was
the result of all these laughable attempts? He insensibly acquired the art
of thinking intensely and clearly on any subject on which his mind was
engaged; and, in the end, attained a concise, familiar style of writing,
which, it is probable, he never would have acquired by any other means.

Possibly the best impression of the merits of Lancaster and his school
can be got from his accounts of expenses for 1802 when he was struggling alone with such scanty resources and subscriptions as he could
raise.

School expenses:	£	s.	d.
25 thousand pinions [for pens] at 7/6 a thousand	9	7	6
Two reams of paper for 160 books, gifts to those unable to pay for them	2	3	0
Seven dozen slates	1	8	0
Five thousand toys	16	16	0
Seven dozen (old) children's books	1	9	0
25 French half-crowns engraved. A reward for Merit	4	17	6

Three star medals	18	0
Eight silver pens at 3/- each	1 4	0
36 purses	12	6
Books		
12 Walkingame's Tutors		
6 Trimmer's *Introduction*		
30 vols. additions to the library and books for use in school	4 1	0
300 loads of rubbish for raising the playground	5 0	0
20 leather tickets (attention to reading, etc.)	10	6

In the next year's accounts he has an item of £4 6s. for sundries for 'encouragement of children', as 'gingerbread, nuts, apples, oranges, cherries etc, for scrambles'. And he also has spent £4 5s. on six excursions to Clapham, Wandsworth, Richmond, etc., with select companies of 30, 40 or 50 boys.

Nearly all the pioneers of education, as of other causes, found themselves in the same condition. With good ideas and no funds to draw on they were always extending their work, and increasing their debts. After 1840 they were often rescued by grants from the Committee of Council, but at the beginning of the century there was no resource but private benevolence; and this was not very reliable. As Lancaster's school grew, as he put up new buildings, so did his debts; and like many other enthusiasts, he had no idea how to deal with them. He was no business man, and the strain of ostentation in his character laid him open to personal extravagance. Gradually his Quaker friends stepped in, to a large extent removed Lancaster from control, and sent him off on propaganda tours; while they systematized his methods and probably destroyed the individual features of the school. Joseph Fox, William Allen, a manufacturing chemist, and Joseph Foster formed the nucleus of a Society which grew rapidly. The ecclesiastical support was withdrawn, but the leaders of humanitarian and radical thought remained. Such men as Brougham, Whitbread, Wilberforce, Joseph Fry were all active members; and in May 1811 the first anniversary dinner was held, presided over by the Duke of Kent. The Society was later named the British and Foreign School Society because already the principles were spreading to other countries, and among the young men who came to be trained in the system were some from the West Indies or even farther afield.

It was necessary, if the Church was to make any effective answer to Lancaster, to organize a society on the same model, but with different principles; and in October of the same year the National Society for promoting the *Education of the Poor in the Doctrine and Discipline of the Established Church* came into being. The aim was strictly sectarian, and the mind behind the movement far less liberal and imaginative than Lancaster's.

It is not proposed [Bell had said in 1805, in a statement that was later to prove very inconvenient to his followers], that the children of the poor be educated in an expensive manner, or even taught to write and cypher. There is a risk of elevation, by an indiscriminate education, of the minds of those doomed to the drudgery of daily labour above their condition, and thereby render them discontented and unhappy in their lot. It may suffice to teach the generality, on an economical plan, to read their Bible, and understand the doctrines of our Holy Religion.[8]

Although the Society found it convenient to disclaim that it was ever proposed to deny writing and arithmetic to the poor, they never wavered from their determination to give a strictly denominational education. In the first place they derided the idea that there was a body of belief common to all Christians that could be taught in school without offence to any particular sect. (The idea of complete tolerance, even for Jews, as in Holland, did not occur to anyone.) But even supposing there were such a common body of belief, it would be very dangerous to allow a child to grow up without ensuring his eternal future by making him a member of some sect.

I consider myself not only entitled but bound to say that the system of religious instruction proposed by Mr Lancaster is highly objectionable in a religious, a moral and a political view. For, with regard to great numbers, youth is the only period of existence in this world, and who that is a Christian can reconcile himself to the thought that this period should pass without any knowledge of the fundamental doctrines of the Gospel.

The Committee of the Society took its stand firmly on the Establishment and on the present organization of society.

The Committee looks for farther support to those who are attached to the constitution in Church and State; the sole object in view being to communicate to the Poor generally by the means of a summary mode of education, lately brought into practice, such knowledge and habits, as are sufficient to guide them through life, in their proper stations, especially to teach the doctrines of Religion, according to the principles of the Established Church, and to train them in the performance of their religious duties by early discipline.

They would also learn their place in society.

One of the most important lessons impressed upon them will be the duty of resignation to their lot; and common sense, experience and Scripture will unite in assuring them that 'he who will not work, neither shall he eat'. Where dissent from this doctrine is so unwise, so unreasonable, and indeed so impracticable, it is not very likely to arise. By the very constitution of society the Poor are destined to labour, and to this supreme and beneficial arrangement of Providence they must of necessity submit.

All sections of society, church, landowners, manufacturers, could co-operate with a society conducted on these principles.

There was also a sense of urgency.

These efforts should not only be universal but immediate [says a pamphleteer of 1815]. The first reason, the danger of being anticipated by the zealous activity of those who entertain views and sentiments hostile to the Established Church. Unless therefore a similar spirit of energy and industry *now* animate the members of the Church of England, they may soon have to lament, that where prevention might once have been easy, it was afterwards impracticable.

The Committee shared this view and the movement spread like wildfire through the dioceses. Meetings were held, committees appointed, subscriptions collected, and sets of rules drawn up. Those of Colchester, for example, say

That in what ever way the said subscriptions may be applied, particular care should be taken that all the children reaping the benefits of this most charitable institution shall, without exception, be instructed in the excellent Liturgy and Catechism of the Church of England, shall constantly attend Divine Service in their parish church, or in some chapel under the Establishment, on the Lord's Day, unless such reason for their non-attendance be given as shall be satisfactory to the parochial members of the committee.

This enforced conformity to the Established Church caused many difficulties all through the century. In most places the landowners and works managers would provide a National School, but not a British one; so that non-conformist parents were in a sad dilemma. One of the early inspectors commenting on this situation says:

The masters, to increase their slender pittance, are induced to connive at the infringement of the rules which require conformity in religion, and allow the parents to purchase exemption for a small gratuity; those who cannot afford it being compelled to conform, or expelled in case of refusal.

Where, however, the rules are impartially enforced, or the parents too poor to purchase exemption, a compromise follows. The children are allowed to learn the church catechism and to attend church, so long as they remain at school, but are cautioned by their parents not to believe the Catechism, and to return to their parental chapels so soon as they have finished schooling. The desired object is attained by both parties. Outward conformity is effected for the time, and the children return in after life to the creed and usages of their parents.

If parents had slightly more money or more scruples, the children were sent to private venture schools which were expensive, where the teaching was worse, and no attempt was made to teach even the fundamentals of religion.

Such an attitude contrasted strongly with that of the British schools which accepted teachers and children of any denomination without question, merely hoping that they would attend a place of worship of their own choice on Sunday.

The school in the Borough Road early developed a training department where men came to learn the system, and the National Society opened a large Model School in Westminster in emulation. Dr Bell was appointed General Director, and the Rev. Johnson of Grassmere as Headmaster. Here the system was practised, and here intending teachers could be trained. Schools were being founded so rapidly that the supply of trained teachers was never adequate; but there was a steady, if small, output of teachers every year.

Once Lancaster's unconventional and vivifying influence was withdrawn, the schools, in spite of their rivalry and sectarian differences, rapidly approximated. In the teaching methods employed there were no real differences, and the dogmatic adherence to such distinguishing details as whether the squads under instruction stood in a hollow square or a semicircle was mere jealousy. If one reads only the books written by the advocates of the system one gets a picture of conveyor-belt instruction proceeding in perfect order and due succession. The monitors who were the agents of this process are thus described by Dr Bell:

A few good boys selected for the purpose who have not begun their career of pleasure, ambition, or interest; who have no other occupation, no other pursuit, nothing to call forth their attention, but this single object; and whose minds you can lead and command at pleasure, form the whole school; they teach the scholars to think rightly, and, mixing in all their little amusements and diversions, secure them against the contagion of ill example, and, by seeing that they treat one another kindly, render them contented and happy in their condition.[9]

Equally unrealistic was the description of the schools, common to both authors, as for ever quiet, for ever diligent under the unwavering attention of the little teachers. Where there was such close continuous supervision there could be no idleness or misbehaviour:

It is the great boast of this system, that, by the perpetual presence of our teachers, it prevents the offence, and establishes such habits of industry, morality and religion as have a tendency to form good scholars, good men, good subjects and good Christians.

In a word, it gives, as it were, to the master the hundred hands of Briareus, the hundred eyes of Argus, and the wings of Mercury.

Even Lancaster, who really knew better, could say:

'The assistant sees, at every instant, how every boy in his class is employed, and hears every word uttered.'

The system of instruction became continuously more elaborate and more inhuman. Its details have some importance because they were the norm to which the most instructed practice was supposed to conform. The ideal remained unchallenged for some thirty years or more, and remnants of it lingered in the incredibly tenacious memory of educationalists till this century. Owing to the method of teaching, everything must be reduced to its elements and presented in the simplest and most mechanical way. Reading began with making letters in a sand tray under the eyes of the monitor. Then they went on to the spelling and writing of two-letter syllables. Here is the account of how it was done, using slates instead of sand.

'The class stand or sit in a square, the teacher occupying one side of it. The teacher says "Show cards". At the word "Show", each child puts the right hand to the card placed under the left arm, and at the word "Cards", draws it forth.' The class then copy from the cards.

The teacher gives out the page as 'Page 1'. A figure 1 is written at the right-hand top corner of the slate.

The teacher gives out the first word as 2nd line from top.

The cards are placed under the slates so as to see the word and line attended to.

The teacher points to a child to begin and the others follow. 1st child, 2nd child, 3rd child, 4th child, 5th child, 6th child.

1 . . . a . . . la,   1 . . . e . . . le, etc.

The children should be directed to drop the right hand from the slate to the side of the body after each letter is written. The readiness to catch the signal for this will soon discover the most proficient child in the class.

These elaborate methods for destroying meaning were held to be a virtue. Reading was learnt by spelling all the *monosyllabic words in English,* and any word later encountered with more syllables was broken up and read syllabically.

Mrs Trimmer has prepared a spelling book contrived to instruct, rivet, and confirm the scholar in this elementary process, which I have said is not only the groundwork, but the actual anticipation of all that follows.

This Monosyllabic Spelling-book consists of all the syllables which most usually occur in the English language in a regulated succession from short and simple to long and difficult. It contains no reading which the child can either comprehend or readily learn by memory, or repeat by rote.

As the child progresses to polysyllabic words he learns to resolve the words into their constituent parts and to read those as monosyllables. Each word is read separately.

There is no other difference between his reading now and in monosyllables, than that he is taught to pause somewhat longer at the end of a word than between the syllables of which the word is composed.

Thus — he — pro-ceeds — through — the — child's — book — part — first — and — se-cond — Mis-tress — Trim-mer's — spel-ling — book — part — se-cond — and — is — ne-ver — al-low-ed — to — pro-nounce — two — syl-la-bles — to-ge-ther — till — he — can — thus — read — syl-la-ble — by — syl-la-ble — and — spell — e-ve-ry — word — dis-tinct-ly.

The great majority of children never really arrived at reading anything. One of the early Inspectors records:

With the best intentions, those who have adopted the system of the National School Society, have, in many cases admitted into their schools, nothing for the elder children except the Bible, small volumes of extracts from it and the catechism; and the effects seem to me most unfortunate. All the books on subjects with which the children are most familiar being excluded from the school, that thirst for variety which for wisest purposes has been implanted by the Creator in the minds of children, finding no gratification, their faculties are stunted in their growth, and they sink into an inert listlessness.

In many of the schools the children did nothing more than pronounce the words in the book. No attempt was made to see if they understood them or to fix them in the memory. A little later 'questioning' became fashionable. This is how it was conducted according to the standard prescribed method:

Mode of Reading and Questioning.

Every scholar pointing with the forefinger of the R. hand to the lesson, the teacher is to read it, and each scholar to repeat it, in a low voice, after the teacher. The teacher is then to point to the scholar who is to begin. The first reading to be according to the sense thus; 1st scholar The way; 2nd of God; 3rd is; 4th a good way

reading the lesson thus, till perfect. Next the class is to read according to the stops; then to examine on book, that is the class being divided into two parts, and all the scholars looking at their books one half is to question the other successively as follows: *Q.* What is the way of God? *A.* A good way. *Q.* What is a good way? *A.* The way of God.

Next the class is to examine off book; that is one half of the class put their hands with their books behind them, and are questioned in rotation by the other half; who retain their books in their hands before them. And so vice versa.

In Arithmetic the method was as mechanical and even more meaningless. After the figures had been learnt and written in the sand tray they proceeded to sums. The sums were written on a card given to the monitor.

In the first place, when his class are seated, the monitor takes the book of sums—suppose the first sum is as follows:

$$
\begin{array}{r}
\text{lbs.} \\
27935 \\
3963 \\
8679 \\
\underline{14327} \\
\underline{54904}
\end{array}
$$

He repeats audibly the figures 27,935, and each boy in the class writes them; they are then inspected, and if done correct, he dictates the figures 3963 which are written and inspected in like manner, and thus he proceeds till every boy in the class has the sum finished on his slate.

He then takes the key and reads as follows:

First Column

7 and 9 are 16, and 3 are 19, and 5 are 24. Set down 4 under the 7, and carry 2 to the next.

So it goes on for each line, with dictation and inspection till all have the sum correctly on their slates.

By this means, any boy of eight years old, who can barely read writing and numerate well, is, by means of the guide containing the sums, and by the key there to, qualified to teach the 1st four rules of arithmetic, simple and compound,—if the key is correct,—with as much accuracy as mathematicians who have kept school for 20 years.

Naturally the problem of order was as great as that of teaching material. The noise must in any case have been considerable, even though many of the routine commands were given by signs. Children stood for the greater part of the day, 'toeing the line' of their semicircle or rectangle. Now and then they went to a group of desks to sit while others stood—there were not, of course, seats for everyone—and in Sunday Schools there were no seats at all before 1853. But it was not only economy that kept children on their feet. It was felt to be a good thing.

The classes do not go to their seats but once in five or six lessons, or rather after an hour's exercise on the floor; as it is found that they can best learn them by rehearsing them to their teacher, under the stimulus arising from their competition for places.

In the minds of the promoters of these schools the supreme advantage was that they were economical—in money and man power. Instead of many books there was only one copy, printed large on cards and hung on the wall or held by the monitor. Instead of paper and pens and ink there were sand or slates capable of being used over and over again. There was only one teacher—and that saved more than the salary of his assistants. Teachers were the educational commodity in the shortest supply, and any method which extended the influence of the teacher was a help. It did seem that a method so suitable *must* be good, and all the educational enthusiasm of the age was poured into work for the two societies. Moreover, as they were societies with funds, organization and officials there was some hope of permanence; and the short-lived schools of isolated philanthropists were absorbed into the greater body.

Unfortunately everything turned out differently. The schools may have been cheap, but they were bad, and it was all too soon found that children do not make good teachers. In the first place they were ignorant. Instead of the post of monitor being a coveted honour, any clever child wanted to learn himself and hated the work; and, further, a child's attention is naturally so unstable, he becomes so easily bored, that he was unlikely to attend to his duties. Furthermore the supply even of such monitors was most uncertain. Few families were able or willing to leave a child at school when it was at an age to earn, and ten or eleven was probably the greatest age at which any number of children would be available.

In the 1840s when the first inspectors were visiting the schools the Monitorial System receives nothing but condemnation. A few extracts from reports will show the general state of the schools.

I believe the system to be essentially faulty, and that it is an impediment to discipline, a hindrance to the proficiency of the best scholars in the school, who are doomed to the drudgery of teaching the alphabet and the primer instead of making progress in the higher branches of instruction themselves. The monitors may usually be described as the unfittest of teachers. If education involves mental and moral culture, and requires skill, gentleness, patience and kindness in order to gain access to and mastery over the minds it is designed to inform and mould, how is it to be reconciled with common sense that children should be chosen for that office? And yet, where ever they are employed, no inconsiderable amount of the entire instruction given is entrusted to them. I have seen even the use of the cane delegated to them. They teach miserably. They are, almost without an exception, wholly and manifestly incompetent for the work.

Or with perhaps more individual detail:

Thirty-one girls read Mark 12 to the monitor. The noise in the school was so great that as I sat by the monitor I could not hear the girl who was reading in the class. Several children were laughing to each other, others were inattentive; and the only symptom of reverence in the whole class was that every time the name of our Lord was pronounced the whole class made a short rapid curtsey, occasioning along the whole class an irregular popping down, the effect of which, combined with their undisguised levity, was exceedingly unpleasant. The mistress was occupied in another part of the school.[10]

Or more touchingly the plaint of the clever child in a Welsh school excusing her ignorance:

Since I came I have done nothing but teach these unpleasant little children.
(Dw i ddim wedi gwneud dim ond dysgu' r hen blant bach annifyr yma.)

The difficulties did not end with the monitors. The teacher's lot was very hard.

To organize a school of this kind satisfactorily a man required almost

35

superhuman organizing and supervisory powers. So far from being able just to watch others work, as is suggested, he must be eternally busy, 'animating and directing the whole'. The instructions say, 'Begin by arranging the school into classes'. As the classes were arranged by proficiency, and might well be changed for different subjects, every child, ideally, should be tested; and a careful check made to see exactly which class he would fit. How difficult that is to do every careful teacher knows. In all probability it was simpler in practice because so many children would know nothing. Then monitors had to be selected, and perhaps trained. Then, if the school was on the National system, the children of each class had to be paired off, the best with the worst, so that they could help each other. Next the lessons for each day must be determined. 'In each class the teacher's book is marked with the day of the month, where the lesson begins in the morning, and each lesson for that day with a score. No lesson should, with the lower classes, occupy more than a quarter of an hour.' So the marking of some fifteen lessons for each class might well consume the large part of an evening. In addition there was the task of seeing that the children actually learnt their work, that they were promoted when they knew it, and of recording daily progress. Naturally this was impossible under actual conditions, and an approximation to it depended on having trained and efficient monitors. This is the report of a school conducted by a master who had trained for six months at Borough Road:

It is impossible in a school so recently established to have monitors competent to teach, yet 9 monitors are employed in the school, all of whom were found to be incompetent. Upon these monitors and the master aged 21 depends the education of 267 children. The master is necessarily inexperienced, and it is difficult to imagine a school where more experience would be required. Though he appears anxious to do his best, he does not, and cannot control the school, which is not only numerous, but consists of children who, being altogether uncivilized, appear to require discipline more than instruction.

What taking over a school was actually like—and how indispensable its monitors were—bad or good—can be seen from this account by Robert Roberts of his struggles in 1850:

I went over to Amlwch and commenced work. The first sight of my new pupils made me regret having ever come there, but it was too late to retract. When the school door was opened in the morning, in rushed a crowd of boys such as I never saw except in the gutter; half of them had

1   Joseph Lancaster

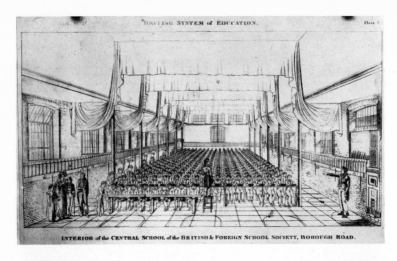

2a *Above* Interior of the Central School of the British and
Foreign School Society, Borough Road. Built about 1825
2b *Below* Stow's Glasgow Normal Seminary

no shoes and stockings, most of them had evidently not been washed for some days past, and all were unruly as wild colts. There being no pupil teacher or assistant, I picked out three or four of the most likely looking boys to assist me in bringing some kind of order out of this chaos. After two or three failures, I succeeded at last in getting myself heard, but it was useless to give out any orders in English—that language was utterly unknown to all except two or three English boys. How the late master managed was then a mystery to me. I afterwards learned that he was an easy going man, case hardened to noise and confusion, who spent more hours at the 'Ship' than at the school, and left the teaching to take care of itself.

There was a great deal to fight against at Amlwch. Big boys, thoroughly ignorant, brutal in their manners, and disgusting in their habits; parents as ignorant and as brutal who looked upon the schoolmaster as their natural enemy and resented his attempts at correcting their children's evil habits; no encouragement from outside, not one of the better classes ever entering the school, or taking the slightest interest in it; the clergyman despondent; the laiety indifferent or hostile.[11]

Few of the teachers of the period were as intelligent or as well educated as Robert Roberts—and few were willing to make as much effort. The difficulties were too much for them and there was no direct stimulus to efficiency. The pay was so low that no one would do the work unless he was incapable of any other, and such training as a man might get by watching the conduct of one of the big schools was enjoyed by few. Even those few, in the month or so that training lasted, learnt little except the tricks of the trade, and their pristine ignorance of all subjects was left undisturbed.

Yet bad as many of the monitorial schools inevitably were, they represented a very considerable advance. They set out to give children an education, though a very simple one; they were not just places, as their predecessors in charity had been, whose proudest boast was that they had 'Supplied the neighbourhood with some good female servants, and have preserved several hundreds of children from ignorance and profligacy.' If they absorbed the energies that had previously gone into these charity schools and gave them a new and more permanent expression, they stood out in honourable relief from the private venture schools which had previously been the only means of education for the vast mass of the people. We have accounts of these schools from various sources from about 1832 when the Manchester Statistical Society started collecting evidence, and our knowledge continues into the 1840s with the reports of the early Inspectors who were charged with surveys of different districts. The schools fell into two groups. Dame schools for very small children, and common day schools for those rather older. Nearly all of them were bad—some almost incredibly so.

The Dame Schools are described in the Report of the Committee of the Manchester Statistical Society 1834 as

in the most deplorable condition. The greater part of them are kept by females, but some by old men whose only qualification for this employment seems to be their unfitness for every other. Many of these teachers are engaged at the same time in other employments, such as shopkeeping, sewing, washing, etc. which renders any regular instruction among the scholars absolutely impossible. Indeed neither parents nor teachers seem to consider this as the principal object in sending their children to these schools, but generally say that they go there to be taken care of and to be out of the way at home.

These schools are generally found in very dirty unwholesome rooms— frequently in close damp cellars, or old dilapidated garrets. In one of these schools eleven children were found in a small room in which one of the children of the mistress was lying in bed ill of the measles. Another child had died in the same room of the same complaint a few days ago, and no less than 30 of the usual scholars were then confined at home with the same disease.

In another school all the children, to the number of 20, were squatted on the bare floor, there being no benches, chairs or furniture of any kind in the room. The master said his terms would not allow him to provide forms.

There were hardly ever any books, unless a child could bring one, or part of one from home.

Occasionally, in some of the more respectable districts there are still to be found one or two of the old primitive Dame Schools, kept by a tidy, elderly female, whose school has an appearance of neatness and order, which strongly distinguishes it from this class of schools. The terms, however, are here somewhat higher, and the children evidently belong to a more respectable class of parents. The terms of the Dame School vary from 2*d*. to 7*d*. a week, and average 4*d*. The average yearly receipts of each mistress are about £17 10*s*. The number of children attending these schools is 4722; but it appears to the committee that no instruction really deserving the name is received in them.

The Rev. John Allen reporting on schools in Durham and Northumberland has much the same account to give:

The dame schools appeared to me to be divisible generally into two classes; those kept by persons fond of children, and of clean and orderly habits,—and these, however scanty may be their means of imparting instruction, cannot altogether fail of attaining some of the highest ends of education, as far as regards the formation of character,—and those kept by widows and others who are compelled by necessity to seek some employment by which they may eke out their scanty means of subsistence, without any real feelings of interest in their work. Many of this latter class presented a most melancholy aspect; the room commonly used as a living room, and filled with a very unwholesome atmosphere; the mistress apparently one whose kindly feelings had been long since frozen up, and who was regarded with terror by several rows of children, more than half of whom were in many cases without any means whatever of employing their time.[12]

In fact they were 'not so much places of instruction, as of periodical confinement for children whose parents were at work during the day'.

In the worst of these schools the door was always kept firmly fastened, because if it were opened for a moment an uncontrollable torrent of children would make a dash for air, light and space; so unendurable was the dungeon existence of dark and inactivity.

The Common Day Schools which received slightly older children were almost equally bad.

They are in rather better condition but are still very little fitted to give a really useful education to the children of the lower classes. The masters are generally in no way qualified for their occupation, take little interest in it, and show very little inclination or disposition to adopt any of the improvements that have elsewhere been made in the system of instruction. The terms are generally low; and it is no uncommon thing to find the master professing to regulate his exertions by the rate of payment he receives from his pupils—that he gives enough for 4*d.*, 6*d.* or 8*d.* a week, but that if the scholars would pay higher he would teach them more.

This is an Inspector's account of one Lancashire school:

It was a room on the ground floor, up a dark and narrow entry, and about 12 ft. square. Here 43 boys and girls were assembled, of all ages from 5 to 14. Patches of paper were pasted over the broken panes of one small window, before which also sat the master intercepting the few rays of light which would otherwise have crept into the gloom. Although it was August, the window was closed, and a fire added to the animal heat, which radiated from every part of the crowded chamber. In front of the fire, and as near to it as a joint on the spit, a row of children sat with their faces towards the master, and their backs to the furnace. By this living screen the master, though still perspiring copiously, was somewhat sheltered from the intolerable heat; as another measure of relief, amidst the oppression of the steaming atmosphere, he had also laid aside his coat. In this undress he was the better able to wield the three canes, two of which, like the weapons of an old soldier, hung conspicuously on the wall, while the third was on the table ready for service. When questioned as to the necessity of this triple instrumentality, he assured us that the children were 'abrupt and rash in their tempers', that he generally reasoned with them respecting their indiscretion, but that when reasoning failed he had recourse to a little severity.

There was no classification of the children; and the few books in the school were such as the parents chose to send. Under such circumstances the poor man had an arduous task to accomplish; and not knowing what situations might not be in our gift, he informed us that he would gladly avail himself of any opportunity of quitting an employment to which extravagance alone had caused him to descend.[13]

In fact the schools had every vice. The teachers were unfit, the buildings were deplorable, the children wretched, and attended for the briefest time and quite irregularly. The people who took up teaching did so because they were unfit physically or mentally for anything else. Some were labourers who through illness or accident became incapacitated for work, others were shopkeepers who had failed in business, incompetent craftsmen, or men so lazy that teaching seemed the only calling that would demand nothing of them. Lancaster had said in 1803 that 'the drunkenness of a schoolmaster is almost proverbial' and these men kept the proverb true.

In various districts investigations were carried out to discover the age at which most people started teaching and what they had done before they started. Of one district it is reported:

Of the 47 common day schools, five are under the care of females.

Of the masters of the remaining 42—

16 had been unsuccessful in some retail trade.

11 had been miners or labouring men who had lost their health or met with accidents in the works, and had subsequently 'got a little learning' to enable them to keep school.

10 had received some instruction, with a view to adopt the profession of teaching.

4 were ministers of dissenting places of worship.

1 was the clerk of the parish church.

In another district there was an even wider scatter of trades, including a 'musical wire drawer', several mariners, a butler, barber and cowman. The women had been milliners, and maids. In both districts 30 was the average at which they had started teaching. When, in the 1840s, some sort of training was available not one in eight had received any, and any instruction that had been received lasted, perhaps, a week or two.

Nor did the teachers give all their time to teaching. Large numbers of them had a second occupation. The commonest was sexton, or parish clerk, or assistant to the overseers of the Poor Law (that is supposing the teacher could read and write, which was often beyond the power of the farmers who were the overseers). Others were book-binders, bonnet-makers, turnpike men, one managed to be a drover in summer, when probably the children were employed in the fields, and one was a layer-out-of-corpses at the workhouse.[14]

The low quality of the teachers and their pursuit of other occupations were directly due to the difficulty of making even the poorest living by teaching. The teacher lived by his fees, and these were low, corresponding to the poverty of the parents. There was no standard. One man reported that he had to

make separate bargains with his scholars; some paid weekly, some quarterly, some yearly, all irregularly. He had as much as £30 owing. The people who paid the most regularly were the poorest; he had, however, never in his life turned a child from his school; he always trusted to be paid some time.

Another poor woman complained:

Her school hardly yielded her 1/- a week; she could not get paid by the parents of her pupils. 'A great many,' said she, 'are very poor, and I am poor myself. They owe me money, some as much as 4/- and 5/- which I shall never get, and which are large sums to me.'[15]

Sometimes, of course, it was a wife who earned a little, perhaps £7 a year, to supplement her husband's inadequate earnings, and in these cases the school may have been of the better class; but it is clear from the records that good schools hardly existed, and that those that were not very bad were rare.

If these were the schools of the day it is clear that the monitorial schools of the two societies really had something to offer, and that the enthusiasm that they aroused was not entirely misplaced.

Notes

1. Cf. Mrs Trimmer, *Reflections upon the Education of Children in Charity Schools* (1792), pp. 25, 29.
2. William Corston, *English Leghorn—a new source of Industry* (1810).
3. Report on the school by Tremenheere, Minutes, 1842, p. 555.
4. Pestalozzi, *Swansong*. Conclusion.
5. Mrs Trimmer, *Comparative view of the Means of Education promulgated by Mr Joseph Lancaster* (1805).
6. J. S. Mill, *Essay on Liberty* (1859), p. 190.
7. The punishment was in use and apparently had retained its terrors at Marlborough in the 1920s. J. Betjeman, *Summoned by Bells*, p. 69.
8. Andrew Bell, *Experiment in Education* (1805).
9. Joseph Lancaster, *British System of Education* (1810), Ralph Wardlaw, *Essay on Joseph Lancaster's Improvements in Education* (1810), Andrew Bell, *Mutual Tuition and Moral Discipline* (1823), Rev. Frederick Iremonger, *Bell's System of Instruction* (1827) and Sir Thomas Bernard, *The Barrington School* (1812).
10. Minutes, 1840–1, p. 185.
11. Robert Roberts, *Life and Opinions of Robert Roberts* (ed. J. M. Davies. Cardiff, 1833), p. 311.
12. Minutes, 1840–1, p. 126. See also 1840–1, p. 162.
13. Minutes, 1840–1, p. 163.
14. Minutes, 1842, p. 37; P.P., 1847, XXVII, pt 1, pp. 32, 33, 34.
15. P.P., 1847, XXVII, pt 1, 33.

Chapter Three

The challenge of pauperism

The political history of education, that is the history of the acceptance
of education as one of the duties of the state, runs through the early
years of the century parallel with, but distinct from, the history of education as a humanitarian ideal. The first field in which it seemed that
education was the concern of the state was in the administration of the
Poor Law.

The end of the 18th century saw the organization of the pauper as a
distinct class, and the growth of the belief that, though he was scarcely
human, he was a necessary part of the social order. Without him, tire-
some as he was, society would have no base and be liable to topple over.
Swift, looking at Irish society in the earlier part of the century, wrote his
bitter pamphlet *A Modest Proposal for preventing the Children of poor
people in Ireland from being a burden to their parents or country and for
making them beneficial to the Public*. He suggested that the best use to
make of the children of the poor was to sell them for food at the age of
one year, when the upper classes could probably be induced to pay 10*s*.
a head for them, and treat them as a delicacy. The mother would make a
profit of 8*s*. on each one, and the babies would be saved from the pains
of life.

I desire those politicians who dislike my overture that they will first
ask the parents of these mortals, whether they would not at this day think
it great happiness to have been sold for food at a year old in the manner
I describe, and thereby have avoided such a perpetual scene of misfor-
tunes as they have since gone through by the oppression of landlords,
the impossibility of paying rent without money or trade, the want of
common sustenance, with neither house nor clothes to cover them from

43

the inclemencies of the weather, and the almost inevitable prospect of entailing the like or greater miseries upon their breed for ever.

The state of mind and society that he satirizes still existed more than half a century later: and this time it is cruel fact. It is revealed in a paper published by the Society for Bettering the Condition of the Poor in 1804. Presumably the document had been sent to the Society by the same man who had revolted against the proposals of his parish, and had insisted on their being referred to higher authority. The parish therefore took counsel's opinion, and the questions and answers are set out in the paper. These are the two most important:

There has been no provision made in the aforesaid parish for the employment and instruction of the children of the poor. This is alleged by some to be one reason that the parish is infested by about 230 idle and profligate children. The friends of the parish have received a proposal from a settler in one of His Majesties newly discovered islands to take them all as apprentices under the Act . . . and to allow the parish a noble for each child. . . .

They add that 'something like this has been largely practised upon a very great scale: affording relief and emolument to some very considerable parishes, while it has contributed to people those invaluable schools of morality, the cotton mills'.

The answer was that the act expected parishes to spend money on apprenticing the children, not to sell them.

The second question is even more scandalous.

Certain wealthy farmers have suggested that we shall erect a *prison* in the parish and then give notice in the neighbourhood that if any persons are disposed *to farm* the poor of this parish, they do give in sealed propositions of the lowest price at which they will take them off our hands; and that they be authorized to refuse relief to any one unless he will be shut up in the aforesaid prison. The proposers of this plan conceive that there will be found in the adjoining counties persons, who, being unwilling to labour, and not possessing substance or credit to take a farm or shop so as to live without labour, may be induced to make a very advantageous offer to the parish. If any of the poor perish under the contractor's care the sin will lie at his door, as the parish will have done their duty by them.

The reply was a firm negative. If any one votes for or promotes this proposal 'They will be answerable in conscience not only for every poor person who may die, but also for every instance of suffering or depravity in consequence of it.'

This attitude to the pauper coexisted with a continual and alarming increase in his numbers. The system of poor relief later known as Speenhamland, from its supposed place of origin, which used the rates to supplement wages, spread pauperism ever farther into the body of society. It is hard now to imagine the condition of things, or the vast expense of keeping a large part of the population in semi-idleness and utter misery. The figures for two counties show the way the cost increased.

Assessments for the relief of the poor

	1816	*1817*	*1818*	*1819*
Oxford	£114,000	135,000	152,000	147,000
Anglesey	£10,000	11,000	13,000	15,000

Over a longer period the cost rose from ¾ million pounds in 1750 to more than 7 million[1] in 1834.

The proportion of paupers in the population was also terribly high. The returns for Sussex in 1827 show that about a third of the population were receiving relief, and Sussex was not one of the worst counties.

Numbers relieved in 1827

Sussex

Parish	*Population*	*Relieved*
Ashurst	394	161
Northiam	1358	532
Great Horwood	584	156

In Manchester a little later, during six months, 3883 Irish were relieved at a cost to the community of £4027, and 6993 English at a cost of £9664. Over the country as a whole it was reckoned, in 1807, that there were 1,234,000 persons receiving poor relief out of a population of 8,870,000 and that the total cost to the nation was £4,267,000 a year.

The terrible thing about pauperism, to those who considered it seriously, was not only its effect on the happiness and wealth of the community, but its hopelessness. There appeared to be no prospect of improvement, no way to which man could look and say 'there lies the path of salvation'. Miserable parents brought up miserable children, without hope or skill or the training which gives the impulse to work.

It was, naturally, the children who most attracted the attention of philanthropists and reformers. Some, abandoned by their parents, were left to the Overseers of the Poor, and after a period in the confused squalor and degradation of the mixed poor house, were sent as apprentices to the cotton mills. More unhappy, perhaps, were the children who were handed over to the smallest and basest of employers. Thousands of children died of cruel treatment, overwork and starvation in every kind of slum and cottage occupation. In the 18th century their deaths were too common to be considered. In the 19th one Commission after another uncovered the conditions of their lives; and slowly the various Boards of Guardians began to take some slight precautions. They banned the most notorious trades. For example we find one London Board resolving to 'apprentice' no more children to the silk weavers.

Other children, slightly more fortunate, remained untended but free with their parents. In the manufacturing districts their work found a ready market. In other places they were unemployed, and mainly unemployable, and were sent out to beg. As an example it is recorded that 'in the 50 parishes of the Hundred of Ongar 581 children of 12 years and upwards were left unoccupied and supported by the rates'. Doubtless after the manner of children in this state, they did as much damage as their half-starved condition provided energy for. The need for education as the first step in the reformation of the poor must have seemed clear.

The conviction would be strengthened by example at home as well as abroad. Pestalozzi and Wehrli had shown that it was possible to reclaim at least some of these lost children;[2] the Quakers, Scotland and parts of the North of England showed that pauperism on this scale need never arise. The Quakers by care, help and education, prevented it altogether among their members: 'A Quaker beggar is an impossibility.' The Scottish parochial schools figure largely in every discussion of the period. The evidence that the Lord Register of Scotland gave to the Committee in 1818 shows that parochial schools existed in all country parishes. Some dated from Charles I, others from 1695, and others were quite recent. The Heritors (landed proprietors) were required to provide the school-house and land, and half the master's salary. They might ask their tenants to provide the rest, but often did not. The schools were managed by the Presbytery and the landowners—most harmoniously. The control was real. Every year some schoolmasters were dismissed for drunkenness, immorality, excessive severity to the children or taking work outside their office. No religious demands were made. Dissenters and even Roman Catholics attended without trouble.[3]

In the big towns there were public schools established by big corporations or subscriptions, or private schools.

In Scotland the number of people receiving poor relief was far smaller than in most of England. It was confidently asserted that this was due to the superior educational provision. This was a telling argument. Unfortunately it overlooked a most important fact. At this time in Scotland the Poor Law, in the English sense, hardly existed. There was no poor rate (it was not introduced till 1844 to deal with massive distress) and all the money for relief came from church collections and charitable endowments. This money was administered by the kirk-session with personal visits; and the shortage of funds and the strict supervision must have prevented anything like the wholesale pauperism in the South. On the other hand a large part of the destitution simply went unrelieved. In towns, especially in those with a large Irish population, conditions were as bad or worse than those in Manchester or Liverpool; and even in the country there was great unhelped suffering. Undoubtedly the schools did much; they provided for the respectable poor an education and a path of advancement, which encouraged all those with energy and ambition. But they were not the sole cause of the comparative freedom of Scotland from pauperism.

When the educationalists quoted English figures there was perhaps more substance in their argument. Certain of the Northern counties in England had parochial schools, almost on the Scottish pattern, and in these counties the proportion of paupers was much lower. At the time when a third of the inhabitants of districts in Sussex were paupers, only 138 persons out of a population of 3769 at Kirkby Lonsdale, which was in the parochial schools area, were relieved. With this fact before them, reformers in England began to consider what they might do to provide schools.

On 10 January 1804 the Society for Bettering the Condition of the Poor proposed an enquiry into the present state of schools for the Education of the Poor. They wished to find out:

Where there were adequate schools, and where insufficient?
Where new schools were wanted?
In relation to charity schools (excepting the great foundations):
What was their income?
How many children educated or clothed?
When and by whom were they founded?
and What can be done to extend their benefits?

47

The returns to be made (preferably) to and reported on by a Special Committee of the Privy Council.

It is proposed, in the light of the report,

To open charity schools to all the original objects of the founder.

To engraft on charity schools day schools where the children pay *3d.* a week.

To open parochial schools, where wanted on the same terms.

To make official applications to the Lord Chancellor to correct abuses where found.

To enable the magistrates to pay a child's school fees where necessary.

They add:

The whole system of education in this country may be thus completed with a trifling alteration of the mode, and none of the principle of the present system, and with very little, if any increase in parochial charges.

The General Committee of the Society was, at this time, a very influential one; with Sir Robert Peel, Lord Sidmouth, Wilberforce, a suitable complement of Bishops and Earls, and the King as patron. Nevertheless the suggestions for an enquiry remained unnoticed. It was left for the indefatigable Brougham, with his passion for notoriety and scandal, to investigate the matter in 1818.

Meanwhile it was clear to everyone that the number of paupers was growing and that something must be done. The revolting phrase 'pauper management' suggests the attitude of mind of most of those concerned; but in 1807 Whitbread, a wealthy and convinced philanthropist, thought of something more constructive. He brought in a Poor Law bill which, however much he might protest his reasonableness and understanding of the facts of life, yet contained enough new ideas to frighten both Houses of Parliament.

The preamble of his speech when introducing it, after setting out the magnitude of the problem, and reviewing some remedies which had been suggested by Malthus and others, goes on:

My wish is not to get rid of the Poor Laws, but, I think, by taking proper steps they may hereafter become almost obsolete. The principles on which I would proceed to effect this most desirable object are these: to exalt the character of the labouring classes of the community; to excite him to acquire property; to mitigate restraints that now confine and cramp his sphere of action; and to hold out a hope of reward to his patient industry.

The first stage in all this is education.

In the front of my plan for the exaltation of the character of the labourer must appear a scheme for general national education. I propose a general system of national education by the establishment of parochial schools; not compulsory upon the poor, but voluntary; and I am confident that it will soon so work its way that every man in England and Wales will, as in Scotland, feel it a disgrace not to have his children instructed.[4]

References to Scotland appeared at every stage of the debate. It was the firm opinion of all parties that the Scottish schools had conquered pauperism, freed the country of beggars, civilized the inhabitants, and sent the Scots out to govern England and cultivate the gardens of its aristocracy.

As one man declared,

The influence of the schools' establishment of Scotland on the peasantry of that country seems to have decided by experience a question of legislation of the utmost importance: Whether a system of national instruction for the poor is favourable to morals and good government.

The schools as imagined by Mr Whitbread were to be established in the parishes by a democratic committee, and children were to attend for two years between the ages of seven and fourteen.

Besides schools he proposed a savings bank for the labouring classes, probably worked through the Post Office; some relief of the Law of Settlement; improvements in ratings; and certificates and rewards for those who shall have brought up six or more children to a certain age without recourse to parish relief.

This was altogether too much for Parliament to swallow. It was suggested that the proposals should be divided into four bills—and they were then defeated in detail. The debates on the Schools bill, which was taken first, show the general temper. The Commons complain that they have been rushed (the bill had lain on the table from 22 February to 27 April); they think that it would be better to found charity schools near the sea to train boys for a naval life, and let them earn their living by fishing; then the schools would only cost half what similar ones did inland. Schools might have had a very beneficial effect in Scotland, but would it be the same in England?

In the Lords the battle was more fairly joined.[5] There were two main points. Are the schools to be democratic in foundation, and are they to be handmaids of the Established Church? Lord Hawkesbury (later Lord Liverpool) dealt with the first point. He opposed the measure because 'The institution of schools was to be at the sole discretion of the majority of the Parishioners in number, without any reasonable discrimination of rank and property.'

The Lord Chancellor supported him: 'He would never agree to any plan that left matters of this nature to be judged of and decided by the majority of the inhabitants of a parish.'

The Archbishop of Canterbury, among others, dealt with the second point:

The provisions of the bill left little or no control to the minister in his parish. This would go to subvert the first principle of education in this country, which had hitherto been, and he trusted would continue to be, under the control and auspices of the Establishment. Their Lordships' wisdom and prudence would, no doubt, guard against innovation that might shake the foundations of our religion, and it would be the chief object of their vigilance and care *ut castra maneant in religione nepotes*.

It foreshadowed the struggles to come that he did not go unopposed. Earl Stanhope protested, a lone voice, against what he called 'the abominable principle that no part of the population of this country ought to receive education unless in the tenets of the Established Church'.

His speech anticipated a later jibe in the *Edinburgh Review* that 'the alphabet was still among the mysteries which the English Church concealed from her catechumens'.

The failure of this attempt to impose a system of education by law did not halt the spread of schools. The beneficial rivalry of the two Societies was beginning, and political events and pressures were making the power to read ever more important. The war with France was bringing hardship at home and troubles abroad; but however much the propaganda posters might represent Napoleon as a tyrant, however many countries he might conquer, the total effect of the French victories was to send a wind of liberty through Europe.

In 1792 Condorcet had set out before the National Convention a plan of universal education which he recommended as the one means by which Liberty might be preserved and Equality attained. He was listened to respectfully, but the nation was engaged in a struggle that left no thought or money for education. It was left to the subject neighbours of France to carry out the ideas.

Under French tutelage a minister of Arts and Sciences was appointed in Switzerland in 1798 who produced a scheme for cantonal schools with Inspectors and local committees. The plan was stillborn, but the idea lived.

In Holland, as early as 1784, the Society for the Public Good had started improving education, and its schools had spread even to the Cape of Good Hope. The Society published books, cheap and easy to understand, on morals, domestic economy, mechanical science, agriculture, vaccination and the training of midwives.

When Napoleon occupied the country, he left the Dutch in control of their education, and in 1796 the National Assembly asked the Society for facts and figures about education. The result was a series of Laws of 1801, 1803, and 1806 setting up a National system that was democratic and liberal. In 1808 Van den Ende, as Inspector General for Primary Schools, gave Holland Europe's first system of popular education. Schools were built where they were required; they were controlled, flexibly, by Inspectors, who were chosen with the greatest care for their liberality and humanity; and they were undenominational and completely tolerant. By 1816 there were two training colleges and a system of pupil teachers. Foreigners visiting Holland were struck by the cleanliness and order of the schools, the absence of corporal punishment, and the fact that they were co-educational. The absence of religious friction was wonderful. Special arrangements were made for Jews; while Roman Catholics and Lutherans received general religious teaching in the schools and were expected to attend a place of worship of their own choice on Sundays.

If Holland adopted education as an expression of the ideals of liberty and equality, Prussia followed Napoleon in the creation of a state system that riveted the child to the Government. The French child might be taught that 'to honour our Emperor and to serve him is therefore to honour and serve God himself' and the Prussian learnt much the same thing with a change of words. In 1802 the organization of French education began—half-heartedly—with the expression of the hope that the Departments would concern themselves with primary education; and ended triumphantly in 1806 with the creation of the University of France, and the schools of higher education, wherein all teachers were state servants.

Prussia in 1809 imitated its conquerors. Smarting under the defeat at Jena and the French occupation, the country seized the opportunity created by the sweeping away of the old schools and the clerical domination. The men of culture, with a new future before them, began building up the great German myth in which learning was to play so large a part. As Fichte explained, Education was the only domain in which the French had left them free to act; and through education the noble, pure and dominant nature of the German people must be realized. True to the model and their own nature, organization started at the top, with the founding of Berlin University in 1810, and proceeded to the gymnasium and higher schools, where the teachers too had the character of state functionaries. Primary education was left to follow, as best it might, a long way behind.

All this, of course, worked less vigorously in England. No French armies had fought on English soil, and no French governor had swept away the long-established abuses—less bad than many on the Continent, but bad enough. On the contrary, the rulers, as a whole, were determined to keep things as they were; and, as the danger that reform would come by force of arms from outside diminished, so the determination that it should not be started by ideas at home hardened. So long as Castlereagh and Sidmouth were in power, and the constitution gave complete control to the landed classes whom they represented, every effort was made to repress the spread of ideas and to contain the growing forces of radicalism.

Whilst the war was still on, the shortages of food and consumer goods brought great misery, and the accumulated pain of life was growing more than people could bear. There was not the hate which in France had sharpened the guillotine, but there was a conviction that the poor must help themselves, and do it by union and common measures. They began to band themselves together and ask for higher wages. The Government did not hesitate. The Combination Acts of 1799 and 1800 speeded up the process of law against trade unions, long illegal under the common law of conspiracy. When the peaceful means envisaged by the incipient trades unions were denied them, sporadic rioting broke out, conducted for the most part with a scrupulous regard for life, and most types of property. After the wars, still more violent repressive measures were taken. The troops were ordered out, informers and *agents provocateur* were employed, the Habeas Corpus Act was suspended, taxes were put on periodicals.

This was not altogether untimely. Political journalism had been born, and was already playing its part in moulding the thought of the mass of the nation. Cobbett's *Political Register* had been published (at first as an anti-Jacobin paper) since 1802. In the long run, its insistence on *constitutional* reform as the key to economic progress was to do much to keep the country free from violence; but it is not surprising that the idea that working men had a right to discuss and criticize the way their

3 Sir James Kay-Shuttleworth

4a *Above* National School at Llanfairfechan, Caerns. Built according to plans of 1840. Note the ventilators in the roof
4b *Below* Chester Training College in 1892

betters ran the country was at first disliked. No one could tell how dangerous such a thing might be.

The end of the war with France in 1815 brought a shock to the whole nation. It was not only disappointment that the hardships which had been borne had brought so little benefit; it was also the gigantic upheaval, economically, which the post-war slump brought to the manufacturers, and the sudden drop in the price of wheat, due to the re-establishment of trade, which staggered the landowners and farmers.

Cobbett ironically congratulated his working-class readers on the failure of their hopes of reform:

The war which began in 1793, is now over. The troops are not all come home, the ships are not all paid off, the account is not wound up; but the war is over. Social Order is restored; the French are again in the power of the Bourbons; the Revolution is at an end; no change has been effected in England; our Boroughs, and our Church, and Nobility and all have been preserved; our government tells us that we have covered ourselves with glory. . . .

The richer classes made what arrangements they could. The manufacturers covered their losses by dismissing their workpeople, and the landlords passed the Corn Laws. Viewed from the standpoint of the House of Lords the Corn Laws were inevitable:

In the panic created by the sudden fall of corn prices after the war, farmers threw up their farms in multitudes, and became bankrupts aed village paupers. The landlords themselves, who had unwisely launched out into expenses on the expectation of perpetual high prices, had often mortgaged their estates, and were now in great difficulties. Rents had fallen. In 1816 it was believed by as much as nine million.[6]

In this general panic, when the whole agricultural economy of the country seemed to be in dissolution, the Corn Laws, which aimed at keeping the price of wheat at 80s. the quarter, were passed. They were intended to save agriculture and the country; they did only harm.

In the renewed agitation that disappointment and misery caused, Cobbett and his *Political Register* once more became the leading influence. In 1816 he reduced the price to 2d., and thus placed before all men the chance to study the condition of the country.

At this time [says Bamford], the writings of William Cobbett suddenly became of great authority. They were read on nearly every cottage hearth in the manufacturing districts of South Lancashire, in those of Leicester, Derby and Nottingham; also in many of the Scottish manufacturing towns. Their influence was speedily visible. He directed his readers to the true cause of their sufferings, misgovernment, and to its proper corrective, Parliamentary Reform. Riots soon became scarce, and from that time they have never obtained their ancient vogue with the labourers of this country.

Hampden Clubs were established in many of our large towns and the villages and districts round them. Cobbett's books were printed in a cheap form; the labourers read them, and henceforward became deliberate and systematic in their proceedings. Nor were there wanting men of their own class to encourage and direct the new converts.[7]

At first, though violence was abandoned, the Radicals thought in terms of protest and monster meetings. This phase ended in one of the saddest episodes of that sad time, when a Manchester meeting, conceived in terms of Cleanliness, Sobriety and Order 'to which was added Peace', was broken up by an unprovoked charge of dragoons.

The shock that this Peterloo 'massacre' gave to the whole country was profound. Shelley in Italy broke into doggerel invective; the shops showed cartoons of the dragoons cutting down shrieking women; and the students at Cambridge, including young Macaulay, burnt with generous indignation. Thus the event became an epoch. Never again did the Government behave with such senseless ferocity; the Radical party redoubled its parliamentary activity; and its greatest leader, Place, developed the technique of pressure, through the marvellously economical instrument of a single private member, Joseph Hume, which enabled him to get the Combination Acts repealed in 1824.

In this belief, that peaceful parliamentary reform, and not riots and revolution, was the way to progress, the group of new Radical leaders grew up. These were men of great ability and force, who were born sons of craftsmen, small farmers or tradesmen. William Cobbett had been a plough boy, but he worked on his father's farm. Francis Place had been a leather breeches maker, and later a tailor. His father had kept a sponging house, before becoming a publican. William Lovett was a cabinet-maker by trade; his father the captain of a small trading vessel who died at his birth, his mother the daughter of a blacksmith. Samuel Bamford, a weaver, was the son of an unusually skilful weaver who was later governor of the Manchester workhouse. His mother was the daughter of the best bootmaker in the district who worked for all the best families. Robert Owen was the son of a saddler. Such men could obtain some education and had the health and strength to profit by it.

54

These men organized the working-class and Radical movements, and they organized it on the basis of adult education. In consequence the next ten years was a period of continual unofficial agitation, as more and more people tried to fit themselves to take an intelligent part in political life. Partly this work was done by small groups meeting together for discussion and passing the books, that they were too poor to buy, from hand to hand. William Lovett who was born in 1800 and spent his childhood and youth at Newlyn gives an account of his ignorance and the revelation that his discussion group brought him when he went to London.

I was fond of reading as a boy, but found great difficulty in procuring instructive books. There was no bookshop in the town—scarcely a newspaper taken in—and there was at that period a considerable number of the adult population who could not read. To the best of my recollection there was only one bookseller's shop in the market town, and, with the exception of Bibles and Prayer Books, spelling books and a few religious works, the only books in circulation for the masses were a few story books and romances filled with absurdities about giants, spirits, goblins and supernatural horrors. The price of these, however, precluded me from purchasing any. . . . A young man of my own age was my companion of an evening very frequently during my apprenticeship, but he too like myself was ignorant. Of the causes of day and night, of the seasons and of the common phenomena of nature we knew nothing, and curious were our speculations concerning them. We had heard of 'the sun ruling by day and the moon by night' but how or in what way they ruled was a mystery we could never solve.

That which first stimulated me to intellectual enquiry was my being introduced to a small literary association, entitled the Liberals which met in Gerrard Street, Newport Market. It was composed chiefly of working men, who paid a small weekly subscription towards the formation of a select library of books for circulation among one another. They met together on two evenings in the week, on one of which occasions they had generally some question for discussion, either literary, political or metaphysical.

He began to read and join in the debates.

My mind seemed to be awakened to a new mental existence; new feelings, new hopes and aspirations sprang up within me, and every spare moment was devoted to the acquisition of some kind of useful knowledge.[8]

This personal experience led the Radical leaders to set education high among the aims of their movement, and the desire for personal development was reinforced by the demands of industry which became increasingly complex technically. There was a growing demand for skilled mechanics, and a corresponding demand for the knowledge on which this skill depended. Dr Birkbeck, feeling the need, started lecturing in Glasgow in the early 1820s, and when he moved to London continued his work. Mechanics' Institutes, with libraries, reading-rooms and lectures sprang up behind him. Ten years later the employers were beginning to glimpse the value of such work. 'The directors of a Railway Co. have asked for evening lectures in mechanics for engine drivers, stokers and others. This is to keep them from the tavern, for accidents are always occurring because the men have drink taken.' If these lectures were effective in keeping the men from their accustomed potations they must have themselves wished to be instructed.

The most ambitious of these schemes was the foundation of London University in 1827 which threw open knowledge, not to the working man, but to the many who were prevented by their religious views, or their comparative poverty from going to Oxford or Cambridge, and so breached the wall of Ecclesiastical privilege.

These activities were not unopposed. The *St James' Chronicle* intemperately remarked about the London Mechanics' Institute in 1825, 'A scheme more completely adapted for the destruction of the Empire could not have been invented by the author of evil himself than that which the depraved ambition of some men and the vanity of others and the supineness of a third and more important class has so nearly perfected.'

With all this in men's minds it is natural that popular education should once more become of public interest. Henry Brougham, the Scottish lawyer, who had entered English politics with such vigour, was in 1816 agitating for a select committee to enquire into the Education of the Lower Orders in the Metropolis. This was known to be very defective. In 1807 it had been stated that in one district '5000 children, the offspring of the labouring Irish, were daily advancing in ignorance to maturity'. In another there were '1000 children imbibing, in all probability, early habits of idleness and profligate companionship'. It was very desirable that the nation should know just how badly the poor fared. It is also possible that Brougham thought it would be well to expose the deficiencies of his adoptive country. In any case the committee having produced many sad facts about the lack of education in the Metropolis, proceeded to show that the rest of the country was no better provided.[9]

In the light of these extensive enquiries and the deficiencies they disclosed, the proceedings of the committee that sat, under Brougham's chairmanship, in 1818 are slightly ridiculous.[10] The Committee heard evidence from the Lord Register of Scotland on his national system, from two representatives of the National Society, one being mainly concerned with town schools and one country; from Mr Millar of the British and Foreign Schools Society, and from Mr W. F. Lloyd of the Sunday School Union. The evidence was brief and the questions perfunctory, and it all went into fourteen pages of the printed report which ran in all to 500 pages. All the rest of the report is occupied with showing how grossly educational charities were mismanaged, and the Committee settled down to the congenial task of baiting the representatives of the major educational endowments.

The Committee treated the representatives of such famous schools as Eton, Winchester or St Bees very roughly. Their questions ranged over the whole field of administration, and show that a great deal of preparatory work has been done in uncovering abuses. They wanted to know, for example, why the eminent Porson had not been given a scholarship to Kings; and how it came about that Lord Lonsdale had been able to acquire, for a trifling payment, the right to dig coal under the Manor of St Bees, and the adjacent property, which belonged to the school. There is no mistaking the glee with which Brougham exposed the absences, evasions and ignorances of his victims.

The idea behind all this should have been to show that existing educational endowments, if properly used, could have done much to supply the needs of the nation; and the enquiry should have linked up with the proposals of 1804. In fact, they were so interested in the abundant scandals which education provided that they had no thought for anything else; and their final conclusion that they 'recommend the bringing in of a bill for appointing commissioners to enquire into the abuse of charities connected with the Education of the Poor' was not likely to produce any result.

Far more important was the subsequent survey taken, parish by parish (at a cost of about £1000 and with permission to use the Post free), of the schools of England, Scotland and Wales. This survey gives us our first real picture of the *quantity* of education available in Britain. They were not yet concerned with the *quality* of the education given.

At this date a school was a school; and presumably it did what was required of it, which was, at most, to teach children to read.[11]

Thus in their questionnaire they asked what endowed schools existed in the parish, what other schools there were, and whether there were adequate means of instructing the poor children. The results are most interesting. In the first place the record shows clearly the extent to which the grammar schools had decayed. Up and down the country there are accounts of foundations where three boys attend, or where the master has £100 a year but has not taken any pupils for the past five years. At Lincoln there was 'A school in which sons of freemen of the city and the members of the cathedral church may be taught classics free. Master £60 with house and garden, and undermaster £50. Six boys taught.'

At York the two endowments of St Peter and Archbishop Holgate had between them thirty boys. The larger, St Peter's, was housed in the ruined church of St Andrew; the other fared worse, it had a room by the master's house, and had nearly fallen into disuse 'from his neglect, or his inability, in consequence of indisposition'. Violence played a part in this decay as well as idleness.

In the free Grammar School at Lichfield, the master of which is, unhappily, a clergyman, the premises have been valued at £50, and the whole value of the situation was for some years £129-14-4. During the last 7 years no boys have received instruction at the school. The decay of this school seems mainly attributable to the violent conduct of the master. His treatment of two boys, on two separate occasions, subjected his modes of punishment to investigation before the magistrates; one boy having been subsequently confined to bed under surgical advice for a fortnight.[12]

Sometimes the school had perished entirely.[13] 'It is reported that formerly there was an endowed school at Newport, but all trace of it are lost.' It is almost unique to find a school, as at Brentford, which was receiving and using its endowments.

A school at Brentford founded and endowed by Sir Anthony Browne in 1557. The children must be 8 years of age and able to read and write before they are admitted. At present 70 are educated. The master receives £384 from land and Dagenham tithes at £1115 a year. Out of which he pays a classical master £150, two english masters one 50 guineas, and the other 30 guineas, and gives 5 almspeople £10 a year each, and keeps the school and alms houses in repair.

In general the Committee could say of the grammar schools 'The intention of the donor seems entirely perverted.'

On the other hand, the tiny endowments for primary education seem to have fared better; they were less tempting to 18th-century rapacity.

Up and down England there were hundreds or even thousands of these small charities. A typical entry in the survey of 1818 reads: 'Topperfield. A school in which 20 children are educated by a teacher who has £10 a year left by the will of Mr Robert Edwards; in addition the parish have given this year a house and garden rent free, and the teacher has about 50 other children whose parents pay for their education.' Or, for a rather later date, from Levisham in Yorkshire: 'One school, belonging to the church, has £11 per annum left by will for the benefit of 12 poor children. The children are chosen every year on Easter Tuesday.'

How numerous these small endowments were it is impossible to say. If one looks through the lists of schools arranged by counties it is clear that some districts were better off than others. Cheshire and Yorkshire were well supplied; perhaps half or a third of the parishes had some provision. Westmorland and parts of the northern counties did even better with their parochial schools. Essex had many fewer, and when we get to Herefordshire or Monmouth there are hardly any, and parish after parish has the sad entry, 'The poor are completely destitute of the means of education, and are in general desirous of possessing them.'

In the cities there is more diversity of provision. It is impossible to give figures for the country at large, but one or two examples will show the types and numbers of schools that existed.

The returns for the city of Oxford show what existed in a town better provided than the average.[14]

From the returns it seems that the city had a population of nearly 12,000, there were endowed school places for 59 children and there was the National school taking 300. On the usual calculation of the period, of a quarter of the population being of school age, Oxford was at least 2500 places short.

By contrast Bangor in North Wales was already a scholastic centre. Its population was 2383 and it had

a free grammar school founded about 150 years hence at which about 100 children are instructed free. There are two classical masters and a writing master. The upper master's salary is £60 per annum, and the under master's £30 with a house and garden each. The funds arise from lands

which yield a very small sum, not adequate to meet repairs etc. but they
have all been applied to the school; and the remainder of the expense is
defrayed by voluntary contributions by which the present school house
and houses were built.

It also had other schools:

A National school for boys and one for girls, both supported by voluntary contributions, and the former containing 100 boys and the latter 70
girls: also two schools containing 80 boys and girls in connection with
the above.

A school at which 80 boys are taught at the expense of their parents and
the scholars are a degree above paupers. Three Dames schools for girls
attended by 70 children. A Sunday school belonging to the Dissenters.
A lady's boarding school. In Pentir a school for boys and girls containing
40, partly supported by the Bishop of the diocese and his family.

In Bangor there is a great desire for education with the majority of the
parents, and there is ample provision for them.

The poorer classes of Pentir are desirous of possessing more sufficient
means of education.[15]

Even in Penmachno, lost among the hills, and the last haunt of
brigands, with 893 inhabitants, there was 'a school endowed with £10
per a. from the tythes of the parish to which £9 are added from the
poor rates, and in which about 60 children are instructed, who only pay
a trifling quarterage to the master'.

On the other hand in all Merioneth with a population of 30,854 there
were 10 endowed schools educating 339 children on an income of
£239 10s., and 15 unendowed ones with 495 children—a total for the
county of 832 or about 1 in 38 of the population. It is no wonder that at
Llanfawr, population 1962, 'the poorer classes have no means whatever
of educating their children, and the minister states the parish is in so
ruinous a state it would be necessary to clothe and feed the children
before they could attend school, and they live at present by begging'.

This great enquiry produced only Brougham's Parochial Schools
Bill of 1820,[16] which never had the slightest chance of being passed;
and which he recommended in an interminable speech full of the most
irrelevant erudition.[17]

Notes

1. *First Report of Commissioners for Enquiry into the Poor Law*, 1834, XXVII, p. 46.
2. Henry Brougham's account, P.P., 1818, IV, 194.
3. P.P., 1818, IV, 1.
4. Hansard, 1807, VIII, 865; 24 April, IX, 538.
5. Hansard, 1807, IX, 1174.
6. G. M. Trevelyan, *British History in the 19th Century*, p. 152.
7. Samuel Bamford, *Passages in the Life of a Radical*, p. 7.
8. William Lovett, *Life and Struggles* (1876), pp. 21, 35.
9. P.P., 1816, IV; 1818, IV.
10. P.P., 1818, IV.
11. P.P., 1819, IX, A, B, C.
12. Minutes, 1842, p. 39.
13. P.P., 1840, XL, 25. *Report on Berkhamsted School.*
14. P.P., 1819, IX, B, 728.
15. P.P., 1819, IX, C, 1197.
16. P.P., 1820, I, 471 and 493.
17. Hansard, 1820, II, 49.

Chapter Four

The beginnings of state control

For the next twelve years events were too exciting for the generality of the nation to have much thought for education, however eagerly Mill and the Benthamites discussed it.[1] During this period there were no debates on English Education in either house of Parliament, though education in Ireland received a little notice from time to time. These were the years in which South America was freed from Spain and opened to English trade; when Greece cast off the Turks; when the disabilities were removed from Dissenters and Catholics; years of the building of the first railways; and of the agitations which led to the freeing of the slaves, and the reform of the Poor Law. Above all and dominating all was the massive movement for Parliamentary Reform.

The demand for Reform had been part of the Radical programme for many years. Cobbett had taught his working-class readers long ago that parliamentary reform would be a necessary step to economic improvement; now the cause was taken up by the new middle class, the men who had built up the industries of England. These industrialists, who were pushing themselves into wealth and prominence, were mainly of working-class origin. There were a few aristocrats, like the Duke of Bridgwater, who took part in the transformation of the country, or who were leaders in the agricultural revolution, like Coke of Norfolk; but the millowners, the men who worked the mines, who devised and made the machinery and built the railways were mainly workmen who, by ability, force, determination, and often brutality, had made their own way. Many had bought themselves country properties and played the lord, diverting roads and rebuilding villages; others merely inhabited large and seemly houses on the edges of Birmingham or Liverpool. They gave their children the education that they themselves had missed. The young Peel, whose father was a calico printer, was sent to Harrow and Christchurch, where he was a gentleman commoner. Robert Dale Owen was sent to de Fellenberg's school for gentlemen at Hofwyl at the extremely high cost of £300 a year.

These were the 'new men' of the 1820s, and on them the fate of the nation depended. These were the men behind the series of law reforms which during the forty years from 1820 were sweeping away the bloody and unintelligent code that Eldon loved. They benefited from the repeal of the Test Acts in 1828, and sympathized with Catholic Emancipation in 1829. The Church of England had been their enemy, and they were pleased to see her absolutism decreased. It was becoming possible to think in terms of fundamental reform.

Such men knew what they wanted in economics and politics; and, though voteless and without opportunities of representation in Parliament, they began to make their influence felt. Napoleon's Continental System had led to retaliatory Orders in Council which attempted to prevent neutrals, in particular the United States, trading with Europe. This in turn had a bad effect on our trade with them. In 1812, unfortunately just too late to avoid the war with America, the manufacturers forced the withdrawal of the Orders, thus giving a foretaste of what they would accomplish in 1832.

But they were not the only advocates of Parliamentary Reform. The Radicals and the working classes were equally determined and were rapidly learning the techniques of making their wishes felt. In fact the passage of the Reform Bill in 1832 was the greatest demonstration that the united national will could not be resisted.

Lord John Russell said, 'It is impossible that the whisper of a faction should prevail against the voice of a nation.' And the voice of the nation was strong.

The Reform Bill did not enfranchise the proletariat. More than 200 pocket boroughs were deprived of their representatives, and the seats given to the new cities which had grown up. In the boroughs the right to vote was fixed at the Ten Pound rating franchise. In the counties the vote, formerly confined to the Forty Shilling freeholders, was extended to tenant farmers. As there was not the protection of secret ballot, this vote rather increased than diminished the landlord's power. Thus in the towns, the upper middle class and the tradesmen and superior artisans got the vote, but the poorer workmen were left without it; and in the country all labourers were voteless, and the tenant farmers were under an extra compulsion. This restricted franchise explains the partial nature of the spread of education in the next forty years.

The new Parliament, in spite of the limited franchise, and the fact that almost all its members were still country gentlemen, began its work in a completely new spirit. For one thing the manufacturers were represented and could oppose their interests to those of the landlords; for another, the nation knew, and Parliament knew it knew, that it was able to force its will even on the House of Lords. Reform *was* possible; there were ways in which obstinacy could be overcome and obscurantism circumvented.

The two greatest influences in the beginnings of state education in England came from Ireland, and the New Poor Law. The example of Ireland supplied the political technique and the forms of organization; the experience of the New Poor Law, the men, a consciousness of the need and the methods. When the two streams of thought joined the state-control of education began.

As early as the 16th century it had been realized that 'Irishmen will never be conquered by vigorous war; they must be instructed and become the king's true subjects, obedient to his laws, forsaking their Irish laws, habits and customs, and setting their children to learn English'. From then on England had tried to tame her reluctant partner by education as well as the sword. Her two main endeavours had been to free the tongues of the Irish from their 'barbarous language', and their minds from their 'dangerous superstitions'.

Very large sums of money were, therefore, expended in founding schools which were English speaking and Protestant. At a time when not a penny of public money was being spent on education in England, education and culture in Ireland were receiving something like £60,000 a year from the state

The Appropriation Act of 1829 shows that about £9000 was given for the support of the Roman Catholic Seminary at Maynooth, and about £45,000 for schools of different types, £25,000 of this being given to the Kildare Place Society, which the Government used as its chief agent (as it used the England Societies later) in spreading popular education.

Unfortunately almost all the money given for schools was wasted. The schools were scandalously and hopelessly inefficient, and their religious bias made them hated by the vast majority of the population. The Kildare Place schools were mainly in Ulster, and made little contribution to the education of the country as a whole; the Society for the Discountenance of Vice which received £9000, the proceeds of fines on unlicensed stills in Dublin, did practically nothing; and the Charter schools, boarding schools which received £10,000, were merely hells in which a few wretched children starved and shivered.

This educational failure was not a matter of concern to the English Parliament so long as the great majority of the Irish were disenfranchised.

The Catholic Relief Bill of 1829 made an immediate difference. On 9 April, the day before the Lords finally passed the third reading, a petition was presented from the Irish Roman Catholic Bishops asking for the institution of a national system of education 'calculated to benefit the community, without interfering with their religious opinions'.[2]

The Commons were quite uninterested in the *subject* of the petition; but a nice little wrangle took place, led by General Gascoyne and Mr Banks, the member for Corfe Castle, as to whether men who were Bishops, professing the Roman Catholic religion, residing in Ireland, were Irish Roman Catholic Bishops, or not. The point was not pressed, and the petition was allowed to lie on the table; while the Government, as the first step in the desired reform, provided that all the Irish education grants might 'be issued, suspended or granted upon condition at the absolute will and discretion of the Lord Lieutenant'.

It was now clear that there would have to be changes, and for the next year there were petitions for and against the Kildare Place Society. Nobody took much interest in them. On 9 September 1831 Edward Stanley, Chief Secretary for Ireland,[3] on a vote of supply, set out his scheme for a complete reform of education in Ireland. He prefaced his speech by saying that it was not a question of what sum of money should be given, 'but they had this important and delicate problem to solve, namely, how the sum granted could best be applied in promoting the welfare, prosperity and happiness of the people for whose benefit it was intended'. He then proposed a scheme by which under an Order in Council the whole conduct of Irish education should be in the hands of a Board appointed by the Government. This Board should receive and administer all the moneys granted for education; and the other agencies, the Kildare Place Society in particular, should be left without funds and allowed to die. The Board was to be composed of eminent persons of different religious persuasions, Bishops among them, and its function was to ensure that an education was offered free from even the suspicion

65

of proselytism. The House, rather scantily attended, was not much moved. One or two people said they had been supporters of the Kildare Place Society all their working lives and would be sorry to see it die; but these regrets were not very strong, and the money was granted and the Board agreed to without a division.

This having been settled, and as soon as the summer holidays were over, Stanley wrote to the Duke of Leinster asking him if he would become President of the new Board.

He set out the principles on which the Board was to act.[4] It must be composed 'of men of the highest character, including individuals of exalted station in the church, and it should contain persons professing different religious opinions'.

The Board was to have 'complete control over the various schools which may be erected under its auspices, or which, having been already established, may hereinafter place themselves under its management and submit to its regulations'.

It was to grant money for the building and support of schools where there was local support to the extent of about one-third the cost. It was to appoint Inspectors, establish and maintain a Model School in Dublin, edit and print text-books and sell them at half price or give them free; it was to have power to 'fine, suspend or remove altogether' unsatisfactory teachers, and to give gratuities and pensions to good ones. It was to receive applications from any Christian group who might wish to found a school, and who could give reasonable security for its permanence, but it must especially welcome applications when they were sponsored by clergymen of *different* persuasions.

The religious and literary teaching were to be distinguished. The literary teaching was to be common to all, the religious was to be specific, and given on certain days in the week, or before or after the literary teaching of the day. Everything was to be done to ensure that harmony between different denominations was maintained.

This little piece of Irish history is noteworthy because it completely rehearses the history of English educational advance—the same problems, the same tactics, the same stages. But England was not ready to begin immediately. The agitation for the Reform Bill was at its height, and till that question had been settled nothing else could be considered.

The Reformed Parliament met early in 1833 and by the summer the reforming party were ready to try their strength. The preliminary trial of opinion was made by Roebuck, the radical member for Bath. On

66

30 July he rose to move a resolution that 'the House would, with the smallest possible delay, consider the means of establishing a system of National Education'.[5]

The speech in favour of this motion is interesting as showing how far progressive thought on education had gone. He begins by apologizing for taking up the time of the House with so uninteresting a topic as education—and then makes a speech that must have lasted an hour or more. After recommending education on the common grounds that it would promote political tranquillity and public virtue, he propounds his scheme.

At the head of the whole there would be a minister of Public Instruction. He should be 'among the highest in the State, indeed, a member of the Cabinet'. He should have complete oversight of the schools, determine what were needed, apportion the money, advise on methods of instruction, take complete charge of teacher training, and encourage the production of text-books. Under him the country would be divided into School Districts, and in each district there would be a School Committee of five, elected by all the heads of families in the district, or by all those who contributed to the funds. The Committee would appoint the teachers, determine the nature of the schools, and be responsible for their management.

Education was to be compulsory from about six to twelve or fourteen, and those who were able should pay something towards it; for the rest of the funds 'a general tax must be laid on the people for that end'. There should be a division of schools. The infant schools should be common to all, and it was much to be hoped that the children of rich and poor would attend together.

In infancy all children, no matter what their after-destination in life, require the same treatment. All that we can do at that tender age, is to provide for the due development of the body, prepare the mind for culture, and lay the foundations of habits of application, and self-government and kindly sympathies. As far as regards moral training this age is all-important; as regards the mental, comparatively less.

At the next stage, reading, writing and numbers were to be taught. It was most important, at this stage, that reading should really be mastered. It was impossible to understand what was read if the reading was not easy. A mere acquaintance was almost useless. These two stages could be called primary education.

At this point the education of the rich and poor might divide. For the poor there should be schools of Industry, but they should be very different from the schools of that name that had stunted and blighted children in the past. In addition to learning a trade, the child was to receive a general intellectual education with special emphasis on economics and politics; training in art and in music; in natural history and 'our own physical system'. After this there might be part-time evening education for those who could find time and energy.

The Normal Schools were to take pupils at fourteen and educate them till the age of twenty. Admission was to be by examination and those who completed the course satisfactorily would receive a certificate, which entitled them to teach. 'These masters, when chosen by the people, would become an order of the State endowed with a great trust, which, if fulfilling that trust with fidelity, would render them worthy of the highest respect and consideration of the people.' In old age they should be protected from want.

All the schools should give teaching in the common elements of religion, and provision should be made for sectarian education as desired. In populous districts there could be denominational schools, and the elective nature of the School committees would ensure that each district obtained the education it wanted. He fortified his argument by quoting the practice in France and Prussia, and, more interestingly, in New York and Massachusetts.

In the debate which followed, the most significant remark was made by Lord Althorp, the Chancellor of the Exchequer: 'He was sure that he did not address one gentleman who did not feel anxiously desirous that the education of the people should be increased and improved in the utmost possible manner. The question was as to the best means by which that object could be effected', and he deprecated state control, and praised the progress made by voluntary effort.

Nothing further was heard of the motion, but the trial of opinion had gone well: Lord Althorp could go on to the next stage.

Just eighteen days later, when the session was so near its end that most of the members had gone away, the Report of the Committee of Supply was read. In it there was provision of £20,000 for Education. As this was a Money bill the chance of it being interfered with by the Lords was less. Even so it was generally attacked, even by those who might have been expected to welcome it. Joseph Hume thought the amount offered was enough to discourage private benevolence, and not enough to do any good of itself.[6] Cobbett saw no good in teaching a ploughman to

68

read, it did not improve his ploughing. Mr Shaw, from Ireland, could not vote for anything till he knew all the details of how it would be used; Mr Murray, from Scotland, thought there might be something in it, and was almost tempted to vote for it; but decided in the end to oppose it. Lord Althorp answered patiently. By 50 votes to 26 the Report passed, and it was decided 'that a sum, not exceeding £20,000, be granted to His Majesty, to be issued in aid of private subscriptions for the erection of school houses for the education of the children of the poorer classes in Great Britain, to the 31st day of March, 1834, and that the said sum be issued and paid without any fee or other deduction whatever'.

The money had been granted, but the Government had no machinery for spending it in its own person. So it adopted the method that had been already adopted in Ireland, made the denominational Societies its agents, and issued the money to them to spend on the development of their work. It was perhaps a little more cautious than it had been over Ireland, and the Treasury drew up a set of rules which would govern the distribution of the grant.

My Lords read the act of the last session by which the sum of £20,000 is granted to His Majesty to be issued in aid of private subscriptions for the erection of schools for the education of children of the poorer classes in Great Britain.

The Chancellor of the Exchequer feeling it absolutely necessary that certain fixed rules should be laid down by the Treasury for their guidance in this matter, so as to render this sum most generally useful for the purposes contemplated by the grant, submits the following arrangements for the consideration of the Board.

1. That no portion of this sum be applied to any purpose whatever except for the erection of New School Houses; and that in the definition of a school house, the residence of the master or attendants be not included.

2. That no application be entertained unless a sum be received by private contribution equal at the least to half of the total estimated expenditure.

3. That the amount of private subscriptions be received, expended and accounted for before any issue of public money for such school be directed.

4. That no application be complied with unless upon the consideration of such a report, either from the National School Society, or the British and Foreign School Society, as shall satisfy this Board that the case is one deserving of attention, and there is a reasonable expectation that the school may be permanently supplied.

5. That the applicants whose cases are favourably entertained be required

to bind themselves to submit to any audit of their accounts which the Board may direct, as well as to such periodical reports respecting the state of their schools, and the number of scholars educated, as may be called for.

6. That in considering all applications made to the Board a preference be given to such applications as come from large cities and towns, in which the necessity of assisting in the erection of schools is most pressing, and that due enquiries should also be made before any such application is acceded to, whether there may not be charitable funds, or public or private endowments, that might render any farther grants inexpedient or unnecessary.[7]

These regulations governed the distribution of the grant for the next six years, but they were increasingly felt to be unsatisfactory. The Treasury gave the money, and *could* ask for an audit. It had the *right* to ask for reports and make enquiries. But it had no machinery for doing so. It had no experts to guide, and no inspectors to supervise the founders of schools. Many of the buildings put up with the help of public money were quite unsuitable for their purpose; in perhaps the majority of cases the accounts were confused and improperly audited; in a few cases there was serious peculation and fraud. The Treasury, secluded in London, was in no position to deal even with this. The really serious defect lay in the teaching. There was as yet no conception of the qualities needed in a teacher, or of the standards that might be expected. The Treasury could do nothing to help. In fact the promoters of schools did as they pleased, and all too often sought an end that was far from educational.

At first, however, the arrangements appeared satisfactory. The report at the end of the year stated:

In reviewing the practical operation of the grant, which must in the first instance have been considered experimental, My Lords feel that they may safely recommend to Parliament to grant a farther sum of £20,000 for this service in the ensuing year.

The grant might now be considered established and public policy required that it should be used to the best advantage. Enquiries became a regular part of Government activity. In 1834, 1835 and 1838 committees considered English education, and parallel but separate ones considered Irish. The character of the two sets of committees was totally different. While the Irish were engaged in trying to devise a scheme of national education, the English had few hopes or ideas.

The Committee of 1834 was the best—lively and really trying to understand the problems. They heard evidence on the Scottish, Irish, French and Prussian systems; they had the Clerical Superintendent and the Secretary of the National Society; the Secretary and Treasurer of the British and Foreign Society; the headmaster of the Borough Road school; Mr Lloyd and another to talk on Sunday schools; the head of a school for the criminal and outcast children of London; the Chaplain of the Military Asylum at Chelsea; the Bishop of London; and they ended up with the Lord Chancellor.[8]

The evidence from abroad stressed the importance of state organization and the training of teachers; the Scottish and Irish representatives assured the Committee that if there was good will there need not be any religious difficulty. It only arose when fomented by the clergymen.

Q: Have you found that any obstacles have been interposed to the practical efficiency of the Board (of Commissioners for Education in Ireland) by the circumstances that the members of it are of different religious persuasions?

A: None in the least. We have never had a division on any subject.

And when the question was pressed:

Very little difficulty with regard to the teachers and the children. The difficulties are chiefly with the jealousy of the clergymen with regard to their influence and authority in the school.

One matter which was discussed at length was the pay of teachers, and methods of keeping them in the schools if they were trained, and therefore able to aspire to a better position. Mr Lloyd, among others, spoke very clearly on the subject. When asked what improvements he would like to see in schools he said:

The first improvement would be the training up of suitable persons to be teachers, and that these teachers should have adequate encouragement, i.e. £100 a year. Next in importance to the system of training would be a system of inspection. There should be, with regard to education, a vigilant eye everywhere; and many schools have, for want of that, sunk very materially indeed. Schools cannot be too much inspected and examined.

He thought they should be visited five or six times a year for a teaching session. He thought, too, that in poor districts the Government should pay part of the teacher's salary.

'If teachers are to have the wages of porters or ploughmen you will never get fit persons for teachers.'

'How will you *keep* good teachers?'

'The only way is by increasing the remuneration to teachers, and elevating the teachers rather in the scale of society. One of the great benefits of the system in Scotland, with regard to the teachers, has been that they range in a very different station of society from the teachers in England. The teachers in Scotland are the companions of clergymen and associates of the respectable classes.'

Another witness went farther. He thought £120 a fit salary for an able teacher: '£120 a year would always command talent, and give you sufficient influence over him.' At present, able men find other methods of making money, and take less and less interest in their schools. With an adequate salary outside work could be forbidden.

The Committee tried to find out what was the actual, or desirable curriculum in the schools. Mr Trimmer, who had succeeded to his mother's school, had the most restricted views:

Q. What proportion of children are taught writing as well as reading?
A. The greatest proportion.
Q. The greatest proportion are taught reading, writing and accounts?
A. Yes.
Q. Are they taught needlework?
A. Yes. They used to have a manufacture of soldiers' shirts during the war, which helped to support the school.

And when pressed on the matter of books he thought that the books for the National schools did not require any particular additions; his mother's were quite satisfactory.

On the other hand the Bishop of London and the Lord Chancellor held far more liberal views:

Mere reading, writing and ciphering is not enough; the elements of historical and geographical knowledge, a little natural history and drawing, with grammar and singing, I regard as essentially necessary in even the most elementary education.

On the proper duration of school life the most eminent were also the most liberal. 'Till boys', said the Bishop, 'are thirteen years of age, generally speaking, their minds are not sufficiently expanded and informed to understand clearly what they are about, and to know the use and application of that which they have learnt before mechanically.'

And the Bishop while agreeing with the expanded range of subjects added, 'It is found that the children are not at all less interested in the religious part of their education in consequence of their attention being occasionally directed to other branches of knowledge.'

Lastly the Committee asked the Lord Chancellor his opinion on the most important matter of all.

Q. Do you consider that the aid or interference of the legislature is required for promoting general education in this country?
A. I am of opinion that much good may be done by judicious assistance; but legislative interference is in many respects to be altogether avoided, or very cautiously employed because it may produce mischievous effects.
Q. Do you think that a system of primary education established by law would be beneficial?
A. I think that it is wholly inapplicable to the present condition of the country, and the actual state of education.
Q. Do you consider that a compulsory system of education would be justified either on principles of public utility or expediency?
A. I am decidedly of opinion that it is justified upon neither.[9]

He would in fact leave things as they were. Any general system, even of teacher training, would be too expensive, and the flow of private benevolence should not be diverted.

As in 1818, the sittings of the Committee were followed by an educational survey of the country. This time the forms were sent to the Poor Law overseers, instead of the clergy, and the opinion was that they were well filled up.

It is of course quite impossible to calculate what was the overall expansion of education between the two dates, but for Oxford, to take one example, we can see that there are many more schools. Eight are actually noted as having been started since 1830, but there seem to be at least 42 more than were entered in 1818. Many of these were private and small. The big National school has changed its site; but it is larger than ever and now has a library. It is still supported entirely by 'gentlemen of the University'.

The Committee of 1835 was frivolous.[10] They did not even bother to make any recommendations. 'At the present late period of the session they find themselves unable to report their opinion to the House.'

They contented themselves with giving the evidence they had heard. Wilderspin was examined on his infant schools, and Frances Place gave a very amusing account of the life of a London apprentice in his youth. By far the most serious part of its work was an extended examination of James Simpson, an advocate of the Scottish bar, who lived in Edinburgh and had written a book on *The Necessity of Popular Education as a National Object*. The book was clearly thought to be of great importance.

73

The Committee, under the guise of an examination, allowed him to expound his system for seven days and the evidence runs to eighty pages. Many of his ideas are not new, they had already been expressed by Roebuck; others, though not adopted in his exact form, clearly influenced the suggestions put forward in the next few years.

He begins his exposition by setting out his educational philosophy:

When I speak of education I mean physical and moral as well as intellectual. Physical is the improvement, by proper exercise of the several systems of the body. Moral the practical exercise of the pupil's moral feelings in the society of his fellows, where, and where alone, such moral exercise can have an adequate field. Intellectual education is the training, exercising and improving of the intellectual faculties, to the increase of knowledge and wisdom. Education is distinguished from instruction. Instruction is addressed to the intellect only, education includes training physical and moral.

He believed in free compulsory education from infancy to the age of fourteen for both boys and girls, and such an education could only be given by the state. To achieve this he proposed a scheme, strongly influenced by the Scottish system of parochial schools. There should be a central Board of Education, appointed by the Crown, charged with the superintendence of schools; with building and equipping them; inspecting them; training and appointing teachers to them. It was to be matched by a local committee which had the duty of watching over its particular school and providing running expenses and the teacher's salary from a local rate. This rate would be analogous to the charge that in Scotland fell on the landowners, but here it would be more widely spread. 'The first power and duty of this local board would be the raising and apportionment of the assessment. The only other duty which occurs to me, which it would be safe or expedient to commit to this parish or district board would be observation and attention to what goes on in the school.'

His last proposal followed the Irish method and was to separate completely secular from religious teaching, and, to ensure that the separation was complete, to forbid the secular teacher to give any specifically religious teaching. He might point out the wonders of nature and teach the moral law, but the religious teaching was to be given by ministers of religion at stated times to their own adherents.

When asked 'Do you think that the arrangement you propose ought to satisfy the different sects?' he was not hopeful. 'When the object is the supporting of a dominant establishment I do not think it will be satisfactory:—it will satisfy no sect who court power and predominance.'

These ideas appeared to have no effect on the minds of the Committee on English education which reported in 1838 and which was completely defeatist. They reported:[11]

1. That in the Metropolis and the great towns of England and Wales there exists a want of education among the children of the working classes.
2. That it is desirable that there should be means of suitable daily education (within the reach of the working classes) for a proportion of not less than $\frac{1}{8}$th of the population.
3. That the amount of assistance afforded by Government should be regulated as heretofore, subject to modification of these rules in cases where the poverty of the district was proved to require it, the special grounds being reported in each case.
4. That under existing circumstances, and under the difficulties which beset the question, your committee are not prepared to propose any means for meeting the deficiency beyond the continuance and extension of the grants which are at present made by the Treasury for the promotion of education through the medium of the National and British and Foreign School Societies.

The resolutions which were proposed to give help to Roman Catholic schools, and to establish a Board of Education to 'enquire and digest' and lay down rules were defeated.

On the other hand the Irish Committee, which reported at the same time, had a complete scheme for extending and improving the Irish system.[12] The Central Board was to continue giving grants for establishing *and* maintaining schools to the extent of two-thirds of the total cost. The local committee, to be called at first a School Meeting, was to ask for a school, form an estimate of the cost, and then assess themselves for supplying the part which fell to their share. This School Presentment would be sent up in the same way as other local assessments for roads, bridges, fishery piers, workhouses or prisons. It would be a normal part of the machinery of local government. The schools would not be free, except in some cases of extreme need. In general, religious teaching was to be separated from secular and to be given denominationally. Only when the scholars were all of one denomination could the religious teaching form part of the ordinary school teaching.

The teachers were to be paid by salary and fees. It was felt that some revenue from fees would encourage effort. There were also to be provided a teacher's house, and some special rewards for good work. The

75

aim was to make the post of schoolmaster attractive to a man of ability and character. This was to be done by providing him with a 'fixed and reasonable income, comfortable residence, hope of promotion, certainty of reward for honest and long continued discharge of duty'.

In appointing teachers a list was to be kept by the Board of approved 'candidates', and the local committees were to make their selection from that list. If complaints were made about the teacher it was the Board's duty to investigate, and, if necessary, remove him.

The reports of Inspectors were to be collected and presented annually to the Lord Lieutenant and laid before Parliament.

On the matter of teacher training the question was raised whether it were better to have separate Normal Colleges (on a site in the country, but near the town; with a numerous body of professors qualified to conduct it; of exemplary discipline and with as little disturbance as possible) or whether Professorships and courses on the art and science of teaching should be started in the Universities. The latter course gives the intending teacher a wider view, the former a more specialized training. They come to the sensible conclusion that both modes of training have their place—but perhaps for primary teachers the Normal College is the better.

The Irish Committee had, in fact, faced and dealt with all the main problems of education: central and local control; the division of finance; a supply of schools adequate for local needs; the recruitment and training of teachers; their payment and status; inspection. The thorny question of religion had already been settled by mutual tolerance. The English Committee apparently considered none of these things. The reason was certainly political. The House of Lords would reject any measure on education that was sent up to it; and it was very unlikely that the government of the day would introduce an Education bill. Melbourne, though a Whig, had the greatest dislike of any social legislation, especially of education. He thought it a pity 'to bother the poor'. They were much better left alone. His various pronouncements on education were all hostile to it. To those who suggested that education might be a cure for crime he retorted, 'Recollect that crime has existed in all ages, all attempts at eradication have hitherto proved useless. Education will not help, for education is knowledge; which may be good or bad.' Or, indulging in a well-merited jibe at his more enthusiastic followers, 'All are agreed about the benefits of Education, but are unable to agree as to the means of carrying them into effect.' To Queen Victoria he said, 'I do not know why there is all this fuss about Education. None of the Paget family can read or write, and they do very well.' His greatest scorn was for Normal Schools: 'You will see they will breed the most conceited set of blockheads ever known.' With such a prime minister it was hardly profitable for a committee to bring in recommendations for a state system of education.

Nevertheless, public opinion was in favour of it. As Lord Howick remarked to his chief, 'Thank God, there are some things that even you can't stop'—and this was one of them.

The reformers meant to have education, and again Ireland provided the example. It was decided to create, by Order in Council, a body to superintend education, in the manner of the Irish Board; but this was to be a Committee of the Privy Council, composed of great officers of state, and, a most significant variation, was not to contain any ecclesiastics.

The choice of the Privy Council to be the guardian of the infant department was perhaps a wise one; and it was in accordance with pre-cedent. The Board of Trade had been a branch of the Privy Council in former times, and so had the Colonial Office. It was not, of course, expected that the Lord President of the Council would really concern himself with the details of the education of little boys and girls; and a purely advisory body had no affinity to an executive department, yet the arrangement had its advantages. 'It was fortunate', said the *Edinburgh Review* in 1861, 'that the cause of liberal education was then, in some measure, sheltered from the attacks of the Church and the Tories by the dignity and authority of the Privy Council, and that the Privy Council was at that time presided over by a minister of consummate prudence and moderation.'

The scheme was artful. An Order in Council was effective by virtue of the Queen's prerogative and could not be reversed by Parliament; and the money which was needed for its functioning would be provided on a vote of supply.

Lord John Russell, who had taken over the leadership of the House of Commons when Althorp went to the Lords, now took charge of education, from the rather unlikely position of Colonial Secretary. On 4 February 1839, as a preliminary test of opinion, he wrote to Lord Lansdowne.[13]

My Lord,

I have received her Majesty's Commands to make a communication to Your Lordship on a subject of the greatest importance. Her Majesty has observed with deep concern the want of instruction which is still observable among the poorer classes of her subjects. All the enquiries which have been made show a deficiency in the general education of the people which is not in accordance with the character of a civilized and Christian nation. . . .

It is some consolation to Her Majesty to perceive that of late years the zeal for popular education has increased, that the Established Church has made great efforts to promote the building of schools, and that the National and British and Foreign Schools Societies have actively endeavoured to stimulate the liberality of the benevolent friends of general Education.

Still much remains to be done; and among the chief defects yet subsisting may be reckoned the insufficient number of qualified schoolmasters; the imperfect method of teaching that prevails in perhaps the greater number of schools; the absence of any sufficient inspection of the schools, and examination of the nature of the instruction given; the want of a Model School which might serve for the example of those societies and committees which anxiously seek to improve their own methods of teaching and, finally, the neglect of this great subject among the enactments of our voluminous Legislation.

As a result of these considerations her Majesty 'desired that there should be a Committee for the consideration of all matters affecting the Education of the People', the Committee to consist of—The Lord President of the Council, the Lord Privy Seal, the Chancellor of the Exchequer, and the Home Secretary. There were difficulties, and the letter goes on to set out the religious problem:

With respect to religious instruction there is, as your Lordship is aware, a wide or apparently wide difference of opinion among those who have been most forward in promoting education.

The National Society, supported by the Established Church, contend that the schoolmaster should be invariably a Churchman; that the Church Catechism should be taught in the school to all the scholars; that all should be required to attend church on Sundays, and that the schools should be in every case under the superintendence of the clergyman of the parish.

The British and Foreign School Society, on the other hand, admit churchmen and dissenters equally as schoolmasters, require that the Bible should be taught in their schools, but insist that no catechism should be admitted.

Others again contend that secular instruction should be the business of the school, and that the ministers of different persuasions should each instruct separately the children of their own followers.

In the midst of these conflicting opinions there is not, practically, that exclusiveness among the Church Societies, nor that indifference to Religion among those who exclude dogmatic instruction from the school, which their mutual accusations would lead bystanders to suppose.

Much, therefore may be effected by a temperate attention to the fair claims of the Established Church, and the religious freedom sanctioned by law.

Lord Lansdowne replied accepting office; there were no protests; the way was clear for the publication of the Order in Council on 10 April creating the new Committee on Education.[14]

Its intentions were also made known. It had two major proposals and two minor; and these went no farther, if as far, as arrangements which admittedly worked well in Ireland. The two minor proposals were that the Committee claimed the freedom to make grants, in special circumstances, to schools which were not in association with either of the Societies, and to give gratuities to deserving teachers. Of the major proposals one was to appoint Inspectors who would visit and report on schools which received grant, and the other was to found a training college and model school which would supply teachers to all types of schools, but in the first place to the Poor-Law and other Government schools. As this model school and training college were to serve the whole nation, it was thought right to arrange that in it, as in the Poor-Law schools themselves, religious instruction should be divided into general and special. The general religious instruction should form part of the general instruction of the college, while the special should be given by ministers of different denominations in accordance with the wishes of the students or their parents.[15] This was a far less radical treatment of the religious difficulty than had been accepted in Ireland, and it followed arrangements that were being made increasingly in England. At first there was no hostile reaction.

It was a time when political problems were at their most bitter. There was trouble in Ireland; there were anti-corn law meetings; the Chartists were threatening open rebellion and the troops were out; the Government was torn by the necessity of liberalizing the constitution of Jamaica; the penny post and vote by ballot were demanded on every hand; imprisonment for debt was liable to be abolished, and the Church was fighting a furious battle to preserve the right to throw householders into prison for an indefinite period for failure to pay Church rates.[16] This question of Church rates engendered the bitterest feelings in both parties, and was partly responsible for the attitudes of both those who supported and those who opposed the Establishment.

On Saturday, 27 April there was token opposition in the Lords to the new Committee. The *Morning Chronicle* reported it briefly and contemptuously: 'The Bishop of Chester presented a petition, we did not collect whence, against any system of national education not in connection with the Established Church.'

On 1 May Lord Stanley, who had been the architect of the Irish system, but who had now crossed the House and was in opposition, asked, remembering his own tactics, that the vote of supply for the education grant should be taken separately from the other votes of supply, and should come fairly early in the session so that there should be adequate opportunity for debate. This was at once granted.

On 4 May petitions were presented in both Houses against the educational proposals; and then there was a pause. A greater crisis supervened. Lord Melbourne's government, distracted and weak, succeeded in carrying its Jamaica Bill by a majority of only five. It at once resigned. Two days later they were back in power again; and the country and newspapers were full of loyal addresses to the Queen and abuse of Peel for having insulted and attempted to browbeat a gentle lady.

After this set-back the Tory party changed its tactics. Some months later the *Edinburgh Review*[17] celebrated the victory of the Committee on Education by an article accusing the Tory party of bad faith. It called the article 'Church and Tory Misrepresentation', and declared that an active partizan of Sir Robert Peel's had said: 'Only one chance remains to us. We must appeal to the clergy and the people, we must raise the Church cry.' In consequence everything was perverted to this end. Church interests were found to be involved in everything from Canada to Australia, from prisons to usury, and 'to complete the cycle of absurdity, the London and Blackwall Railway Bill was opposed by the Bishop of London as dangerous to church interests'. The article continues,

the Tory party judged rightly that the proposition for the education of the people might advantageously be converted into a church question; and being convinced that it was only by the agitation of church questions, and the active propagation of a most unfounded alarm that party objects could be compassed, every engine was at once set in motion to counteract the intention of the government:—to prevent not only now, but for ever, the establishment of a national system of education.

It is necessary to accept some such political explanation—or to attribute to the Church leaders a degree of stupidity and bigotry which is hardly conceivable.

On 24 May *The Times* opened the main campaign with a leader on *Church Rates and Education*. Though, in fact, it could not show that the two topics were really connected, it was a most ingenious juxtaposition; for if only the passion engendered by the rate question could contaminate the outlook on education all might be well. The article ends by quoting the Bishop of London: 'Under such a system of religious instruction children will be brought up in the wildest latitudinarianism, and left in doubt as to what religion they ought to practice', and he could only reprobate 'a system necessarily and inevitably leading to indifference, ultra-liberalism and lastly to infidelity'.

On the next day, with a magnificent disregard of consistency, *The Times* saw in the Bill the threat of Popery. 'The attempt of the Queen's ministers is a downright fraud, it is to smuggle Popery into England as an item in Mr Spring Rice's budget, to pass the overthrow of our church as a clause in a money bill.'

Two days later there is another inflammatory leader. Then there is a pause, for the election of a new Speaker. But this pause for parliamentary business is not all loss. In a well-placed paragraph it is suggested that although the education debate is adjourned 'there is an equal necessity for petitions from all parts of the country—the interval may be turned to immense advantage'. In the same issue it gives a whole page to a protest meeting in Willis's Rooms, St James.

The *Morning Chronicle* ignored the matter as far as it could; but by 28 May it sees danger. 'National education is, it appears, to be made a party question. The primary step towards it will have to encounter the determined and fierce opposition of a portion of the clergy, backed by the Tory faction.' It mentions with scorn a pamphlet by the Rev. Robert Wilberforce, vicar of East Farleigh. 'His father spent his life in freeing black slaves. Does the son desire to establish a mental slavery of the whites by way of balancing the account?' The passage in the pamphlet which most provoked the *Chronicle*'s contempt ran 'By laying down that your training institution shall admit persons of every form of faith, you adopt in reality a principle at variance with the rules of every church in Christendom.' As comment on this, the *Chronicle* points out that, if merely to be a fellow-student with someone of a different Christian sect is so corrupting, how can anyone hope to be safe.

The *Chronicle*'s contempt was unavailing. The meetings continued, the petitions poured in. The *Chronicle* reports on 31 May: 'Mr Speaker desired that such Hon. Members as had petitions respecting National Education should forthwith present them. The House instantly became a scene of extraordinary confusion. About twenty members ran simultaneously to the table, and the noise was so great that for some minutes none of them could be heard.' Possibly some of these petitions were sincere; many were patently absurd or dishonest. What could be thought of a petition from 439 schoolmasters saying that they 'would rather see the children die in ignorance than be educated under the proposed plan'? Or of the handbill offered to one of Mr Hawes' constituents as an official pronouncement? 'We the undersigned Churchwardens, take the liberty of directing the attention of the parishioners to a scheme which has for its ultimate object the introduction of mutilated bibles and Romish and Socinian catechisms into every National School in the country.'

The great mass of this opposition was nominally directed against the model school and training college, and on 4 June Lord John Russell, when he announced that the debate would take place on 14th, said that the Government had dropped the suggestion for the training college: 'Owing to the difficulties which they experienced in reconciling conflicting views, they were reserving their original design for farther consideration, and postponing taking farther steps until greater concurrence of opinion is found to prevail.'[18]

It was when the main debate opened on the 14th that the dishonesty of the whole opposition becomes apparent.[19] The training college is gone, there is not a vestige of religious teaching proposed in any part of the scheme; but yet the charges of destroying religion were repeated from speaker to speaker. The most uncompromising was the Bishop of London:

If a system of national religious education were to be based on the principle of giving to the members of every different sect the same advantages as were enjoyed by those in connection with the Established Church, then the Church of England might as well at once abdicate its functions.

He thought it was the duty of the clergy and especially the Bishops, to protest against all attempts to raise all dissenting sects to a level with the Church in the estimation of the people.

He would not then enter into the question whether dissenters ought to be assisted by the state in the education of their children.

(But he rather implied that they should not; though when challenged he withdrew it.)

The rather more rational opponents, such as Disraeli, saw in government control of education the instrument of a new tyranny. Mr Dunn, of the British and Foreign School Society, asked 'Why should we thus toss at the feet of any Government an amount of moral influence the possession of which, in some circumstances, might lead to the destruction of our liberties.'

Then there was Lord Stanley, who certainly should have known, asserting 'So long as that Board or Committee was allowed to exist, so long they would find scheme after scheme produced for abstracting money from the public funds in furtherance of a system of education which the majority of the country condemned and which was completely at variance with the constitutional principles which he and those on his side of the house supported.'

The Government side had it all ways in logic. Mr Hawes laid down the Liberal view:

Of all the great questions which had been debated since he was in the House he did not consider that there was one of them which involved a principle of higher importance than that which was then before them. The vital principle of religious liberty was now at stake. All who were determined to abide by this principle of equality and impartiality of religious liberty throughout the country should give a hearty and steady support to the proposition of the Government.

Lord Brougham, as became his profession, took his stand on the law.

If the Church of England attempted to maintain the claim to the superintendence by a National Church of the public education of the youth of the country, the people of this country would not submit to pay for such a system, and he would be the first to counsel them to resist it.

The law had not said that the people of England should not be taught secular learning without the superintendence and control of the Church. That was not the law of England.

O'Connell pointed out that the money to be voted for education came from the common revenues to which all sects were forced to contribute, and was in no way the property of the Established Church.

In fact the Radicals could only believe that the Church was 'influenced with the design of maintaining the present state of ignorance throughout the country' and that there was 'a determined and unconquerable hostility to the general education of all classes and sects of the people of England'.

To make it still more absurd £50,000 was granted that very year, without trouble, for Irish education, under conditions far less favourable to the Church of England than even the most energetic opponents could have feared at home.

No wonder Lord John Russell complained that 'the most excessive eagerness had been manifested in opposition to the system, and the zeal of the opponents of it had been carried to an extent he couldn't account for'.

The debate lasted the 14, 19, and 20 June and the arguments were repeated with nauseating monotony. The Rule of Procedure which forbade the discussion of the general principle of a bill on each occasion of debate had not yet been passed; and nothing checked the claims and counter-claims of Church and Education. But, as *The Times* picturesquely said, 'Though the craft is burnt to the very water's edge—yet it still continues to float.'

At last it was carried by five votes 'that the order of the day for a committee of supply be read'. The actual vote on the £30,000, which was necessary to supply the Committee, followed on the 24th, and this time the Government's majority was only two. The *Chronicle* explains, or excuses, this result by saying that the vote had been taken unexpectedly early, and some Liberals were shut out. Still, two were enough to give the victory.

The proceedings in the Lords, being really meaningless, were less protracted—and the conclusion certain.[20] Their Lordships had other things on their minds over which they had more control. They were, in particular, much concerned about a Bill which threatened to limit the unregulated proliferation of Beer Houses; but they found time to agree to a petition to the Queen, which the Archbishop of Canterbury proposed, protesting against the 'entrusting to any public authority, without the consent of Parliament, of the important functions committed by the Order in Council of 10 April to the Committee of the Council on Education'. In his speech the Archbishop repeated the oft-told tale of the threat to the Church and the Realm. We can sympathize with Lord Melbourne's weary comment as he summed up the debate: 'They never knew what was likely to create alarm and raise a cry, but he must say that this was one of the most idle and unfounded cries that was ever raised, and he was extremely sorry that it had been taken up as it had been.'

84

The Lords took no notice. The address to the Queen was carried by 229 votes to 118, and, in a procession of carriages, the Noble Lords moved off up the Mall to present their protest in person. The Queen received them, but she stood firm. Making use of the, by now, traditional phrase that all would be done with 'due respect to the freedom of conscience granted by law, and with a faithful attention to the security of the Established Church', she dismissed them back to their legislative duties.[21]

If Ireland had thus shown the way for the central organization of education, the techniques, the men and the passion required to make it work were the results of the New Poor Law. The scandals of the system of outdoor relief had become so outrageous, the degradation it inflicted on some quarter of the population so profound; and the annoyance and expense which it caused to the middle classes so intolerable that one of the earliest acts of the Reformed Parliament was to implement the report of the Royal Commission and appoint three Commissioners, with Edwin Chadwick as Secretary, to institute a new system.

Poor relief—from the Middle Ages—had been organized on the basis of parishes, and these small units were hopelessly inefficient and corrupt. It was now proposed to form centres of parishes grouped about their market town; to provide a workhouse for each Union, and to refuse all outdoor relief—compelling those in need of help to reside in the house and do a stated amount of work in return for their keep. To encourage self-help and effort it was the considered policy to make the work in the house more unpleasant and the living worse than the poorest labourer (short of starvation) could earn outside. No attempt was made to force employers to pay a minimum wage, and no provision was made for periods of bad trade or poor harvests. To the habitual pauper, this scheme brought bewilderment; to the labourer fury and despair, a further fall in the standard of living and the terrible necessity of sending wives and children to work in the agricultural 'gangs'; to the Overseers of the Poor and to all the petty officials, who drew power and profit from the system, it brought indignation. The Assistant Commissioners who were sent out to persuade the authorities and organize the Unions had to be men of great tact and intelligence and force of character. The most important of them, for the history of education, was Dr James Kay (he later took the name Kay-Shuttleworth and this is used throughout this book). Kay-Shuttleworth had trained as a doctor in Edinburgh and worked in the slums there. He had gone to Dublin and then to Manchester; and his papers on the conditions in the cholera-ridden courts and cellars, published in 1832, did much to turn men's minds to the need for reform. He appears as a man fearless and compassionate; practical and idealistic. He took an active part in the agitation for the Reform Bill, and in 1835 he became one of the Assistant Commissioners for the Poor Law, working at first in the Eastern District and later in the Metropolitan. His friend, Mr E. C. Tufnell, was also an Assistant Commissioner, and together they brought trained minds and established sympathy to bear on problems that had never been considered before.

In all the parishes there had inevitably been people who needed care; the sick, the old, orphans or the children of criminals. They were too few in numbers to be given separate accommodation, and were herded together in squalor and misery, the children learning nothing good, and growing up to a life of helpless dependence. When the Unions were formed, the problem of the children became more obvious, and the Assistant Commissioners were brought most vividly face to face with the problem of the uneducated child. In the workhouses of the country there were some 40,000 to 50,000 children who were orphans, deserted children or the offspring of idiots, invalids or felons. They were dependent on the state for their upbringing and training; and, what the state made them, they would become. As things were, the state made them idlers, thieves and lifelong paupers. It was these children who were the educational challenge to the Commissioners. They saw the problem quite clearly: 'Whether the state acknowledge its interest in the education of the masses or not, the consequence of the neglect of the pauper class evidently was prolonged dependence and subsequent chargeability as criminals in the prisons and penal colonies', wrote Kay-Shuttleworth in 1838. He continues to argue that if all these children went into the Army or Navy the state would consider that it was well worth bringing them up healthy, intelligent and well instructed. People must realize 'that there is an indirect as well as a direct service in return for education'. 'The duty of rearing these children in religion and industry and of imparting to them such an amount of secular knowledge as may fit them to discharge the duties of their station, cannot be denied.'[22]

The difficulties in carrying out this duty were many. First there was the theory of 'less eligibility'. The man in the workhouse was to be worse off than the poorest labourer outside. Many people thought his child should be so also. In pursuance of this policy one Board of Guar-

dians at Bedford wrote in 1836 asking for authority to cut off the teaching of writing from its pauper school because some children outside did
not learn it. This they said was not 'economy' but a desire to 'avoid
greater advantage to the inmates of the workhouse than to the poor
children out of it'. To their honour the Commissioners refused to sanction the curtailment of instruction.[23] The idea however was strong, and
it was necessary to argue that education was in a different category from
all other advantages. Food, clothes and other things might be kept to the
lowest level, but education should not be based on any standard of the
lowest parental care: it should be superior. 'Education is to be regarded
as the most important means of eradicating the germs of pauperism
from the rising generation, and of securing in the minds and in the
morals of the people the best protection for the institutions of society.'
Or as another Commissioner reported:

I cannot avoid coming to the conclusion that education among the lower
classes is connected with the development of those virtues which we
desire to see them possess and exert for the sake of the public weal, as well
as of their own happiness, and which the Poor Laws have done so much to
destroy. . . . Some scheme of education should accompany the plan which
the Commission now propose for healing the wounds which the Poor
Laws have inflicted upon the morals and habits of the labouring classes.

Even Chadwick, who was universally—though wrongly—regarded as
the most soulless of bureaucrats, advocated a training for all children
in the hands of the Poor Law.

Oliver Twist, which was published in 1839, deals with the problem of
the education of pauper children in Dickens's propaganda manner. It is
interesting to see the points that are made. Oliver was brought up in an
establishment separated from the adult paupers, but, as he was farmed
out for $7\frac{1}{2}d$. a week, and as there was no selection of his guardian and no
supervision, he was maltreated and starved. He received no education,
with the result that at the age of nine years, when the workhouse wanted
to get rid of him, no one wished to be burdened with a child lacking all
skill and power of work. They were compelled to 'apprentice' him; that
is pay someone to take him away. The 'gentlemen' who presided over
his fate were not ill-intentioned, but old, largely indifferent, and concerned with other matters; and the officials were men of low character
and ability, corrupted by petty power. Kay-Shuttleworth, Tufnell and
the other Commissioners were determined to bring this state of affairs
to an end.

If the children were to be educated, how was it to be done? Even when the parishes had been grouped into Unions there were often too few children in any one workhouse to make a tolerable school. The Commissioners suggested that there should be central schools serving several Unions. Then there could be considerable numbers of children in their own establishments quite removed from the contamination of adults. This was fiercely resisted; each workhouse clamouring to keep 'its own' children and refusing to be merged, even partially, with its neighbours. So the small school remained, and the education in them varied 'through the gradations "very bad" to "tolerable", and the difference arose from the different capacities of the teachers, the schools being similar in all other circumstances'. It was, then, the teachers to which the Commissioners turned their eyes. There were hardly any. They were sought from the Central School, Westminster, the Borough Road, Edinburgh Sessional School, Glasgow Normal Seminary, and were 'procured with great difficulty'. The pay the workhouses offered was but some £20 a year, with board and lodging inside the workhouse; but yet some men, and good men too, were found to accept it.

Some of the London boroughs had adopted the method of farming their children out, for about 6*d.* a day, to contractors who had big establishments in the suburbs. These places were very far from good, but there were large numbers of children, round about 1000, in some of them; and the Mr Aubin who ran the one at Norwood was well disposed and willing to let Kay-Shuttleworth experiment. It was in this school that the basic plan of education was worked out. The children were not prepossessing. As Kay-Shuttleworth said later,

The pauper children assembled at Norwood from the garrets, cellars and wretched rooms of alleys and courts in the dense part of London are often sent thither in a low state of destitution, covered only with rags and vermin; often the victims of chronic disease; almost universally stunted in their growth and sometimes emaciated with want. The low-browed and inexpressive physiognomy or malign aspect of the boys is a true index of the mental darkness, the stubborn tempers, the hopeless spirits, and the vicious habits on which the master had to work. This is the seed from which the elementary school grew.[24]

With this unpromising material he started. The school as he found it was taught on the monitorial system, and a large part of the children's time was occupied with the lowest kind of repetitive work. They sorted bristles and senna, made hooks and eyes and fastened them to cards.

88

'Occupations', says Kay-Shuttleworth, 'of the most cheerless description, incapable of exercising the ingenuity of children, useless in preparing them for any farther duties, and pernicious because it disgusts them with labour.'

In preparation for their duties on the Poor Law Commission Kay-Shuttleworth and Tufnell had already made the Educational Grand Tour which, for them, included Scotland as well as Switzerland, France and Holland, and they came back full of ideas. With Pestalozzi they had seen the regeneration of children as hopeless as the orphans of Norwood; with Wehrli the training of peasant schoolmasters who went out to educate their own class without taking them away from their traditional way of life; in Scotland they saw the use of class teaching and the organization of a training college that was predominantly interested in academic subjects and in 'method'. From Holland came the idea of pupil teachers and the government of schools through inspectors. They at once set to work at Norwood.

As a first step they banished all industrial work that was not meaningful and varied. For half the school time the boys worked as tailors, shoemakers, blacksmiths, tinmen, ostlers, carpenters and were trained as mariners. Those under eight were taught straw-plaiting and basket-making. A field was provided for outdoor work, a mast set up with its rigging for instruction in seamanship, and gymnastic apparatus erected in the playground. The girls learnt general housework, to look after young children, to do simple cookery, laundry and needlework. To milk the cows, manage the dairy and nurse the sick. The aim was general, not to train children for some special employment.

By setting the children early to work as a part of the moral training of the school, you have announced [so Kay-Shuttleworth informed the Commissioners], that you do not intend that the children shall be prepared for some particular handicraft or service, and you do not expect that such instruction is in any case to supersede the necessity of farther training. You desire only that the education of this class of labourers should have a direct relation to their condition in life, and you expect that they may be taught the use of various tools, by which they may be enabled to increase the comfort of their households in later life, or obtain better wages by superior usefulness.

On the academic side the matter was more difficult. The monitorial system was already in disrepute; and if it was ineffective as a means of imparting knowledge, it was utterly useless as a source of moral influence.

89

The 'simultaneous' method of class teaching, which was practised in Scotland, was far better. He managed to get one or two teachers who understood the new methods, and he organized his school in classes of 50. He could not provide them with separate rooms, but he curtained off parts of the big hall. The aim, when the organization should be complete, was to have one candidate teacher, one pupil teacher, and one monitor to each group of 50 children, and one fully qualified teacher to every 100. Then the teacher would instruct the groups alternately as a class, while the group not being taught by him would be with the inferior instructors doing lessons such as writing or sums 'in which moral training forms no element'.

The monitors were to be selected in the ordinary way from the brightest of the older children. They would take care of the mechanical work of assembling the classes, keeping silence, giving out books, slates, pencils and so forth. The pupil teachers were boys slightly older who had been gathered from other workhouse schools and were distinguished by 'zeal, skill, attainments and gentleness of disposition' and were considered fit to be 'apprenticed and reared as teachers'. The candidate teachers were older still and might have been sent from outside by people who wished to found a school on the new methods.

The selection and training of the teachers was a matter of the first importance.

The moral discipline of the school is thus dependent, in a great degree, on the method of instruction; and when it is proposed that religion shall mingle with the whole tissue of internal discipline, the regulation of that discipline, so as by paternal kindness and wisdom to inspire confidence and regard, becomes one of the most important objects of solicitude.

With this in view, it was important to see that the learning process was meaningful.

To hope to rear the children in the practice of mutual forbearance and good will and in respect and love of their instructor, while the teaching is such as to require the memory to be loaded with what is not understood, is vain; because the teacher by such method strips knowledge of its attractions, and encounters the necessity of enforcing application by the fear of punishment and the hope of reward.

The children learnt to read and write and do sums. They were encouraged to keep accounts of the work they did. They were taught some history and geography, drawing and singing. The Scriptures were read

90

daily and there were morning prayers. Sectarian teaching was allowed. On that very vexed question Kay-Shuttleworth comments, 'The difficulties arising from differences in religious belief are happily scarcely even incidentally found to operate; and the means adopted for affording them religious instruction apparently obtain universal acquiescence.'

The school was a success.

The children now at least display in their features evidence of happiness; they have confidence in the kindness of all by whom they are surrounded: their days pass in a cheerful succession of instruction, recreation, work and domestic and religious duties in which it is not necessary to employ coercion to secure order. Punishment, in its ordinary sense, has been banished from the school, and such slight distinctions as are necessary to mark the teacher's disapproval of what is wrong are found effective.

Petty thieving, which was the daily and almost universal vice of the school is at an end.

Strangers are approached with confidence and respect; a rule of mutual forebearance and goodwill is established among the children, conversation is correct, their demeanour decent.

The industrial training of the children has already had the effect of reducing the age at which they are received into service and of rendering premiums and apprenticeships unnecessary: not however in consequence of their skill in a particular handicraft, but because the children have acquired industrious habits.

Norwood became one of those institutions that those interested in education *had* to visit; and Kay-Shuttleworth even managed to get a grant of £500 a year from the Treasury to pay for his expensive imported teachers.

It was Kay-Shuttleworth, fresh from his successes at Norwood, and full of the importance of training Poor-Law teachers that the infant Committee of Council chose for their secretary. It was a good choice. Kay-Shuttleworth was a dedicated man. He knew the life of the poor more intimately than any one, other than a doctor, could, and he understood that the path of true advance lay only through education and knowledge. And he had other qualifications. As an Assistant Commissioner of the Poor Law he had seen the effects of lack of education and had had the task of carrying through an unpopular reform by persuasion alone, without the backing of power. He had seen what could be done, and how to do it, and this knowledge must have directed much of his later work. Matthew Arnold, who clearly did not like but respected him, has given this description. 'He was not a man of high cultivation, and he was not a good writer. As an administrator he did not attract by person or manner; his temper was not smooth and genial, and he left on many persons the impression of a man managing and designing, if not an intriguer. But the faith in popular education which animated him was no intriguer's passion. It was heroic.'

It was in this faith that Kay-Shuttleworth took office.

Notes

1. See Brian Simon, *Studies in the History of Education, 1780–1870* (1960), ch. II.
2. Hansard, 1829, XXI, 608.
3. Hansard, 1831, VI, 1249.
4. P.P., 1831–2, XXIX, 757.
5. Hansard, 1833, XX, 139.
6. Hansard, 1833, XX, 732.
7. P.P., 1837–8, VII, 165, repeating Treasury Minutes, 30 August 1833, 11 July 1834.
8. P.P., 1834, IX, 1.
9. P.P., 1834, IX, 220.
10. P.P., 1835, VII.
11. P.P., 1837, VII, p. x.
12. P.P., 1837–8, VII, 363.
13. P.P., 1839, XLI, 265.
14. Kay-Shuttleworth, *The School in relation to the State, the Church and the Congregation* (1847), chs. I and II.
15. P.P., 1839, XLI, 259.
16. P.P., 1839, XLI, 13, 15. Petition presented during Education Debate on Thorogood of Chelmsford. He was a poor man, a dissenter, and he objected, on conscientious grounds, to paying a 5s. 6d. church rate. He discussed the matter with the Churchwardens and no decision was reached. He was then summoned to appear before the Consistorial Court of the Bishop of London. He was unable to leave his business, and he feared the costs of the journey, so he did not go. Without any further word he was arrested; put into prison in close confinement; not allowed to see his wife on Sunday, the only time she was free, and had now been there four months with no prospect of release. Many other similar petitions are recorded in Hansard at this time.
17. *Edinburgh Review*, October 1839, p. 149.
18. P.P., 1839, XLI, 263.
19. Hansard, 1839, XLVIII, 227.
20. Hansard, 1839, XLVIII, 1234.
21. Hansard, 1839, XLIX, 128.
22. Frank Smith, *Life of Kay-Shuttleworth* (1923), p. 47, quoting from the MS of 1877.
23. Poor Law Commission, 2nd Annual Report, p. 529.
24. Poor Law Commission, 5th Annual Report, pp. 145–60: Training and Education of Pauper Children, 1841; Minutes, 1842–3, p. 598; 1844, II, p. 376; Reports on Mr Aubin's Schools of Industry at Norwood.

Chapter Five

First acts of the Committee of Council

Of course, those who saw in the new Committee of Council a threat to the dominance of the Church in education were quite right. The omission of any ecclesiastics from the Committee had not been accidental; it typified the new spirit which the Committee intended to show. In describing the thought of the period Kay-Shuttleworh said, 'The school, it is probable, was, in the conception of the majority of the clergy and laity, simply a means of spreading Christian truth, and of establishing the discipline and ceremonials of the Church in the conviction and sympathies of the great mass of the population.' If this was the aim, secular learning was of little importance; and the academic qualifications of the teacher were largely immaterial when compared with his regularity of church attendance. The intention of the Committee was to change this.

As far back as 1839 [he records in another place], the Government requested me to give my attention to the organization of a system of Public instruction; and I had received from the chief ministers of the Crown a special injunction, and that was to assert the civil influence in Education. They did not intend leaving it simply to the Church or the religious bodies; they felt that, if it was to become national, the State must have something to do with it. They intended to assert the civil power in the interest of the great masses of the people, because, without that power, mere voluntary zeal would not master the whole of the difficulty of the case.[1]

It was to be a hard fight. He described it later as 'almost mortal', and he would never have been victorious if he had not possessed a peculiar combination of zeal and experience.

94

When after his summer holiday in 1839 he returned to his desk as Secretary to the Committee of Council, all was before him. 'When I returned with my friend Mr Tufnell from the continent I found in my office—no grant to be received, no business done and an absolute deadlock.' He said, 'In the interest of the great masses of the people of this country this must not go on', and he set to work to get things established.

The two main items in the original plan of the Committee had been the foundation of a government training college, and the establishment of a system of inspection in the schools. The government college had been abandoned, and Kay-Shuttleworth and his friend Tufnell determined to supply the lack by their private efforts. This will be described later. As an official, he therefore turned his attention to the task of establishing an inspectorate and forcing it upon the schools.

The Government's intention was perfectly clear. By a piece of almost defiant timing, on the very day that Lord John Russell announced that the Government had abandoned the idea of a training college, he also announced that for the future all schools that received grants must submit to inspection.[2] It was ordered 'that no further grant be made, now or hereafter, for the establishment and support of Normal schools, or of any other schools, unless the right of inspection be retained, in order to secure a conformity to the regulations and discipline established in the several schools with such improvements as may from time to time be suggested by the Committee'.[3]

Inspectors were just becoming a recognized agency of government. Earlier Factory Acts had omitted to appoint any; it was only in 1833, when they were provided, that the regulations were to any extent observed. Those who wished to ignore regulations might well be wary of them.

The idea of using inspectors in schools was not new. They had been working in Ireland for some time; and on the Continent they had long been established as the supreme method of controlling education. In the evidence given before various committees, the British and Foreign Society had clearly expressed its view in favour of inspection. In 1837 both William Allen, the chairman of the society, and Henry Dunn, the secretary, spoke in favour of it.

'A vigorous system of school inspection,' said Allen, 'carried out with the consent of parties, but under the authority of the Board, might be added, and they are satisfied that the result would not be less favourable to the extension of Education than to its improvement.' And Dunn said,

It appears highly desirable to the Committee that the schools aided by parliament should be inspected, and full reports published concerning them, but in the opinion of the Committee no enquiry as to the way in which the public money has been applied could prove satisfactory to the country which was not carried out by persons unconnected with the societies whose schools they are to visit to report on.[4]

These views were shared by the new Committee of the Privy Council; they were not shared by the National Society. Its representatives before the different committees had made no mention of inspection; and when it was introduced they were prepared to resist it.

If the true function of the school was but to be the gateway to the Church, what had Government inspectors to do with it? To placate this party, the proposals for the appointment of Inspectors was modified by the Minute of 24 September.

Inspectors, authorized by H.M. in council, will be appointed from time to time to visit schools to be henceforth aided by public money. The Inspectors will not interfere with the religious instruction, or discipline, or management of the school, it being their object to collect facts and information and to report the results of their inspection to the Committee of Council.[5]

Even this did not calm the fears of the High Church party. When it became clear that the Committee meant what it said, and that all grants for school buildings would be accompanied by a demand for inspection, the schools, at least in the first year, preferred to refuse the grant. Detailed accounts of the manner in which the £30,000 voted for education in 1839 was spent show that of the £19,895 offered to the National Society, only £5369 was accepted. In all the other cases, even when the grant offered was all that had been asked for, the money was refused. The British and Foreign School Society only rejected £325 of their much smaller share.[6] In later years the reluctance to accept help with inspection declined, but for two or three years some grants were still refused.

This was not at all what the Committee wanted, and attempts were made to effect a compromise. Lord John Russell, who was firmly behind his Secretary, and Kay-Shuttleworth himself were prepared to be so completely reasonable and accommodating that their adversaries would be put to shame before all sensible people. In July 1840 the famous Concordat was negotiated between Lord Lansdowne, Lord John Russell, the Archbishop of Canterbury and the Bishops of London and

Salisbury. The Church was given everything—except freedom from inspection. It was agreed that

before any person is recommended to the Queen in Council to be appointed to inspect schools receiving aid from the public, the promoters of which state themselves to be in connection with the National Society or the Church of England, the Archbishops of Canterbury and York be consulted by the Committee of the Privy Council, each with regard to his Province, and that they be at liberty to suggest any person or persons for the office of inspector, and that no person be appointed without their concurrence.

That the inspectors of such schools shall be appointed during pleasure, and that it shall be in the power of the Archbishop at all times, with regard to his own Province, to withdraw his concurrence in such appointment, whereupon the appointment of the Inspector shall cease, and a fresh appointment take place.[7]

Moreover the instructions with regard to religious teaching were to be framed by the Archbishop; and copies of the reports were to be sent to the Archbishop, and the Bishop of the diocese, as well as to the Committee of Council.

It is noteworthy that, in spite of the extremely undignified terms of appointment, good, able men were willing to accept the office of inspector; and still more noteworthy that they do not seem to have served their Church rather than their Queen, by finding all the schools of the National Society good. In the reports, praise and blame, but generally blame, seem very impartially awarded. The general impression from reading many reports is that those of the Church inspectors are superior in thought and more truly critical than those of other denominations. Nor is there evidence that the Bishops abused their power.

The inspectors went forth armed with instructions as to their behaviour, and forms to fill up of the most extraordinary minuteness. If their manners were to be mild and conciliatory, the information they were to gather was to be exhaustive. The forms on which details of buildings, equipment, etc. were to be entered are too long to quote, but here is part of the code of behaviour.

They must see that grants are duly spent, and report on discipline, management and methods of instruction in their schools.

In superintending the application of the Parliamentary grant for public education in Great Britain, my Lords have in view the encouragement of local efforts for the improvement and extention of elementary education. The employment of Inspectors is therefore intended to advance this object, by affording to the promoters of schools an opportunity of ascertaining, at the periodical visits of inspection, what improvements in the apparatus and internal arrangements of schools, in school management and discipline, and in the method of teaching have been sanctioned by the most extensive experience.

The inspection of schools aided by public grants, is, in this respect, a means of co-operation between the Government and the committees and superintendents of schools by which information respecting all remarkable improvements may be diffused where ever it is sought; you will therefore be careful, at visits of inspection, to communicate with the parochial clergyman or other minister of religion connected with the school or with the promoters, and will explain to them that one main object of your visit is to afford them your assistance in all efforts for improvement in which they may desire your aid; but you are in no respect to interfere with the instruction, management, or discipline of the school, or to press upon them any suggestions which they may be disinclined to receive.

. . . It is of the utmost consequence you should bear in mind that this inspection is not intended as a means of exercising control, but of affording assistance; that it is not to be regarded as operating in restraint of local efforts, but for their encouragement; and that its chief objects will not be attained without the co-operation of the school committees;—the Inspector having no power to interfere, and not being instructed to offer any advice or information excepting where it is invited.

In adopting the regulations in the enclosed minutes respecting religious instruction the committee have refrained from enjoining any report on this head, in order to allay unfounded apprehensions, and to afford the strongest security that no interference with the duties peculiar to spiritual teachers is intended by the Inspector of Schools.[8]

They were, however, gladly to take the opportunity of examining the religious instruction if invited to do so.

It had been suggested by the Central Society for Education in evidence to the Commission of 1838 that the inspectors should be of two kinds, central and local. The duties of the former would be to collect information of a general kind which would show the needs and educational provision of a district, while the latter class would conduct detailed inspections and examinations of schools. Something rather like this did happen, though the classes of inspectors were not distinct.

In Kay-Shuttleworth's scheme the inspectors were to be the key men in the development of a proper attitude to education. They were to act by persuasion and by gradually educating public opinion. In their reports they were to set out the facts, and, by an appeal to the good intentions of some and the self-interest of the many, they were to build up a body of opinion that would welcome education and develop it. They must make the rich give, and encourage the poor to receive. The first two inspectors to be appointed to the difficult task were the Rev. John Allen and Hugh Seymour Tremenheere. Hugh Seymour Tremenheere was a Cornishman who had been educated at Winchester and New College and called to the bar. He entered public service, and his first official task was to investigate, in 1839, the circumstances of John Frost's rebellion at Newport, where a Chartist mob had clashed with the military. For two years after that he was inspector for the Committee of Council on Education and his reports are the most interesting of those submitted. In 1842, after a dispute which involved his right of free comment, he resigned his post under the Committee, but remained in public service; reporting on a large number of matters as a prelude to reforming legislation. He had a hand in at least fourteen Acts of Parliament, all for the betterment of the poor.

Practically the first task given to the new inspector was to make a survey of the educational provision in the manufacturing and mining district of South Wales. The choice of the district and of Tremenheere to write the report underlined Kay-Shuttleworth's views on the part education should play in preserving order.

This report,[9] like the others that Tremenheere wrote, is of the greatest interest as a social as well as an educational document. He not only considered schools and the standard of literacy, he discussed wages, savings banks, religion and the effects of early work in the mines. His vision of education as an integral part of the social pattern, and not as something separate and self-contained, is most valuable; and the understanding that the whole life of the people must be raised before they are even able to accept the education offered, points the way to true educational progress.

As might be expected he found in his district widespread illiteracy, complicated by the two languages; with less than half the children of school age attending school. Out of a sample of twenty-five children only five could read and none could write. The schools were bad, they were frequently Anglican when the population was Nonconformist, and the pull of early employment made any prolonged attendance at school impossible. The parents were glad enough to have their little children cared for, and the infant schools were well attended; but after six or seven a child became useful, and learning appeared unnecessary.

It is perceived by them that their children are sure of being able to gain an ample livelihood at an early age without the aid of 'learning'. The parents are therefore apt to believe that their superiors are actuated by some selfish motive in endeavouring to induce them to send their children to school. They are averse to the trouble of making their children clean every day in cases where they are sent to schools where cleanliness is enforced. The boys are taken into the coal mine at 8 or 9 years old, often earlier. The value of the labour of the youngest is about 6*d.* a day. Their occupation consists in opening and shutting air doors, in throwing small pieces of coal or ironstone into the trams, or in handing implements to the men at work. A boy thus learns early to become a good miner. It is not improbable, however, that not much skill in that respect would be lost by his beginning somewhat later; and it is certain that from the time he enters the mine he learns nothing else. A mother stated that her husband wanted to take one of her boys, then only 7 years old into the mine. She said 'that her others had gone there young enough at 8; and after they went there, they turned stupid and blind like, and would not learn anything, and did not know what was right; and now they were like the rest, they went to the public-houses like men'.

Even had the children attended, the schools had little to offer.

It is manifest that, under the most favourable circumstances, the instruction offered to the children of the labouring classes in the day schools of this district could not be expected to have much permanent effect in disciplining the mind, raising the tastes and habits, and correcting the disposition. But when it is also remembered that the small amount actually sought for is spread irregularly over a period seldom exceeding two or three years, the great and general deficiency in the extent and value of such elementary education as is obtained in these schools will be the more evident.

On the receipt of this report, Kay-Shuttleworth, rather optimistically, thought that he might use it to quicken the pace of reform.

Over these early years of educational effort hung the grim shadow of Chartism. Kay-Shuttleworth was speaking for many moderate men when he said,

We are far from being alarmists; we write neither under the influence of undue fear, nor with a wish to inspire undue fear in others. . . . We confess that we cannot contemplate with unconcern the vast physical force which is now moved by men so ignorant and so unprincipled as the Chartist leaders. . . .

His remedy was an education which would lead the workers to recognize that their advantage lay in accepting the conditions of society.

It is astonishing to us, that the party calling themselves Conservative should not lead the van in promoting the diffusion of that knowledge among the working classes which tends beyond anything else to promote the security of property and the maintenance of public order. To restore the working classes to their former state of incurious and contented apathy is impossible, if it were desirable. If they are to have knowledge, surely it is the part of a wise and virtuous Government to do all in its power to secure them useful knowledge, and to guard them against pernicious opinions.[10]

This rather egoistic conception of the aim of education could be held up to scorn by men like William Lovett, who saw things from the other side. This is his comment on educational matters at the time.

The hawks and owls of society were seeking to perpetuate that state of mental darkness most favourable to the security of their prey; while another portion, with more cunning, were for admitting a sufficient amount of mental glimmer to cause the multitude to walk quietly and contentedly in the paths they, in their wisdom, had prescribed for them.

Whichever be the juster formulation, the cry among moderate men was that education was the way to tranquillity; and it was common form to set out the cost of police, jails, legal process and execution, and contrast that with the modest sums necessary to educate children in virtue.

Holding these views, Kay-Shuttleworth sent off a letter[11] to twenty-nine mining proprietors in Monmouthshire explaining what he felt to be for the public good. Enlightened self-interest was the contemporary substitute for morality, and to this he appealed.

The Committee of Council, being anxious to give immediate effect to their wish to provide the means of efficient elementary education for this population, are desirous to encourage the erection of school houses, and the settlement of well-instructed and religious men as teachers of elementary schools throughout this district, and feeling assured that you concur with them in considering such measures as highly important to the future welfare of the labouring population by which you are surrounded, and not less to the security of property, and to the peace of society, are disposed to offer you and the other persons locally interested, their assistance for the establishment of a school in your immediate neighbourhood.

The mining proprietors did not respond at all well. In the preserved correspondence there is only one reply, and that does not come for six months. Then Sir Thomas Phillips of Newport writes to say that he would like to found a school, and that the cost of the buildings, in a district where labour is dear, will exceed £600.

With a haste most unusual in a bureaucrat, Kay-Shuttleworth wrote by return of post offering him half the cost of the school building, adding a homily to explain why a school is so necessary:

Already the imminent danger of a great public calamity has proved that the security of property and the peace of society are liable to disturbance in that district; and their Lordships conceive that it is consequently apparent that it cannot be the interest of a great body of wealthy proprietors that the labourers should continue the prey of low moral habits, to a large extent without religion, in gross ignorance, and consequently the easy victims of the disaffected and of the emissaries of disorganizing doctrines. My Lords conceive that the same motives which induce merchants and manufacturers to devote a portion of their annual profits to the insurance of the capital they employ in trade ought to be sufficient (even without any reference to moral considerations of much greater dignity and importance) to deter sagacious men from leaving their wealth exposed to the dangers of popular tumults and secret violence, when a comparatively small annual expenditure, judiciously employed in introducing the elements of civilization and religion would render society harmonious and secure.

In the same letter Kay-Shuttleworth sets out another part of his educational philosophy. He meant to improve schools, not only to assist their foundation.

I am to remind you that, in holding out the prospect of more liberal aid in the erection of schools in this district, my Lords expressed their desire that the plans of school houses selected should be consistent with the most recent improvements in elementary education, as confirmed by the experience of those parts of Europe where the greatest attention has been paid to the discipline and management of schools. They were not less solicitous that the steps taken in the selection of the schoolmaster and his assistants should be such as to warrant their unqualified approbation. Their Lordships express their anxiety on these subjects, because they are convinced that mere instruction in the rudiments of elementary knowledge (which is too commonly the limit of the usefulness of an elementary school) contains within it no element efficacious for the redemption of the people from semi-barbarism to the enjoyments of the benefits of a Christian civilization. . . .

We have no report of the teachers actually appointed.

This first attempt, then, to accelerate and guide the growth of educa-

tion was not very successful; and there is no evidence that the attempt
was repeated. Public opinion was left to do its work unaided.

This is the period when the great reports on the conditions of women's
and children's work in mines, factories and agriculture were being prepared, as well as the reports on the sanitary conditions of large towns.
Kay-Shuttleworth's inspectors followed much the same routes. Tremenheere went to the tin-mining districts of Cornwall, and thence to
the tragic districts of Norfolk and Norwich where the starving hand-
loom weavers were matched by a peasantry as wretched as any in the
country. Baptist Noel went to the Midland towns, from Birmingham to
Lancashire, and John Allen to Chester, Derby and the mining districts
of Durham and Northumberland.

One of the functions of these early reports was thus to present a
general picture of the state of education in the country and to try to
show how it was associated with wider social problems. From the instructions the inspectors received it is clear that they were also expected
to deal with the schools individually and exhaustively, in the hope that
managers and patrons might be led to adopt new standards; that is if
they were allowed to make the necessary enquiries. Actually, their legal
rights ended with an inspection of the buildings and the accounts to see
if the Treasury grant had been properly spent: 'You will not fail to avail
yourself of every facility freely afforded you; you will carefully avoid
acting in the presumption that you are invested with any authority to
enter or inspect any schools without the express permission of the
managers, or to require from any individual facts or information which
they are unwilling to communicate to you.'[12]

In all too many cases the managers stood to their rights, as Walkins,
one of the inspectors, found.

My duties consisted mainly in driving a gig from point to point of a
projected tour, with the schools, greater or less (many more of the latter)
at longer or shorter intervals. Many of them were schools aided by grants
from the Treasury where no examination of the scholars was allowed by
the Managers, but the premises only were inspected and the accounts
audited. Day after day I have driven in this way through the agricultural
districts of the North of England with little more to do than looking at
ill arranged and insufficient buildings, and trying to methodize half kept
and confused accounts.

Yet enough was revealed to show that the promoters of schools
needed instruction, quite as much as the general public. In many cases

they were perfectly content with a standard of accommodation and teaching far below the minimum permissible; and frequently thought that the mere fact of having provided a room, of any sort, and called it a 'school', completed their obligations.

'Of the 136 schools that I have visited in this district,' says Mr Allen, 'only in 33 do trustees of the school meet regularly to observe its progress.' 'Benevolent persons,' he points out, 'pay teachers and have no concern with results. In one school under rich patronage, not one child could tell its letters.' In another case there was an endowment, a wealthy landowner who was anxious to do what was best for his tenants, and a clergyman who was proud of his school. The inspector was shown the school; this is what he found.

A room in the rear of a shop about 10′ × 12′ in which, with my hat on, I could hardly stand upright: the floor was crowded with benches on which some two dozen children were sitting in ranks closely packed, without any visible means of occupying their time. The mistress was in the shop, having left the children in the care of a girl who was standing amid the crowd with an infant in her arms. The atmosphere was so oppressive and disagreeable that I could not wonder at the teacher finding excuses for being absent from her work.[13]

The British and Foreign School Society had a deplorable habit of building their schools into the basement of chapels. The children reached them by going down steep steps to a narrow area, and the rooms within were very short of light or air, unless some floor boards were taken up in the chapel above to admit it. In addition they either failed to provide any sanitation at all; or set a privy in the area in such a way that decency and smell were alike outraged.[14]

Even where the buildings were satisfactory the qualifications of the teacher were ignored.

In one school, the mere structure of which had cost above £300, and in which more than 70 children were assembled on the day of my visit, the Mistress (a good worker) was unable either to write or to detect the most gross errors in spelling, and a large portion of the children were sitting wholly unoccupied.

A teacher's post was regularly regarded as the best means of providing for the otherwise destitute: and, once a man was appointed, what were people to do? In one school 'a poor lame creature, apparently disabled by paralysis, 'kept precarious order by hitting the boys on the head with a Testament which he held in his hand'.[15] He had been appointed before the present vicar came, and no one knew what to do. If the man were dismissed, he would become a charge on the parish; or starve, painfully, in the sight of all. Even where the master could fend for himself, and where the conduct of the school was clearly unsatisfactory, a committee of nine managers might refuse to face reality unanimously. What for instance was to be done about a school where 'the master made a practice of hiring himself out as a day labourer at harvest time and at other seasons of the year, *during school hours*, and sent the children to gather sticks for him, or to collect manure from the public roads'?[16]

In the then state of general knowledge and thought, these examples did not seem very shocking. The farmers were still largely illiterate, and the Poor made few demands. Of the attitude in Cambridgeshire the Rev. J. Allen writes:[17]

One thing that caused me considerable pain during my tour in these counties was the avowal in conversation from persons, who were themselves blessed with every advantage of early education, of the opinion that schools were but of doubtful good, so that even where pains were taken towards their maintenance, I found instances of persons speaking as if they chose the establishment of a school as the least of two evils, under the impression that if a teacher were not set to work subject to their influence, others, subject to worse, would find employment in the district. Until I went into this part of England, I think I never had official intercourse with any that maintained such a position, and judging from the apathy exhibited in some cases as to how little really valuable instruction was supplied in a school, I certainly have never elsewhere met with such practical evidence of the sincerity with which these opinions were held.

He had not, it seems, visited Oxfordshire, which must have been as allergic to education as its sister shire. In the returns of the sums expended by the Committee of Council on Education arranged by shires for one year, Oxfordshire received the lowest of any, getting only £281, when Lancaster had £11,694 and Middlesex £10,366. The significance of these figures is that grants were in aid of local contributions, so that where grants were low there was neither interest nor money locally to call them forth.

In the towns the attitude was the same.

Francis Place, giving evidence before the Commission of 1835 makes two points from his own experience. The first was the scanty knowledge that a tradesman thought suitable for his son, and the second the fury that a gentleman could feel when he found his inferiors presuming to be educated.

'The instruction my father gave to my schoolmaster,' said Place, 'was that when I got to the end of the Rule of Three I was to be taken away; as that was, he thought, a complete education for his class of person' —and of a later occasion, when he was in business as a tailor and had built up a large library:

The prejudice against a man having books was very great. I was so well aware of the feeling that I suffered no one of my customers to know that I had a book, as far as I could avoid it. The person alluded to was un-advisedly let into my room in my absence by my foreman. When he discovered that I, a common tradesman, presumed to collect books, he took pains to take away the whole of his connection. If I had been a sot, he would have had no complaint against me, but he could not endure that his tradesmen should presume to acquire knowledge, should presume, as he thought I intended, to put myself on a level with himself.[18]

As an employer, too, the richer citizen doubted the value of literacy for his workmen or servants. The power to read made it possible to study religious or political books that were not at all conducive to social acceptance. Reading could be such a waste of time, and could lead to such awkward discoveries. The housewife dreaded a maidservant who could read. The phrase was 'she will only spend her time writing her own letters and reading yours'. It is only in 1860 that it was suggested that now people were ashamed to say it openly—however much they might mutter it in private. In many cases, therefore, it may be supposed that the badness of the schools and the inefficiency of the teachers were not altogether unwelcome to the local middle classes; even if they now and then contributed to their support, from motives of social prestige.

When the inspectors had been started on their task of surveying and commenting, setting out the wider implications for society and the narrower needs of the village school, one part of the secretary's work was under way.

The other, unofficial, matter to which Kay-Shuttleworth gave his mind in that September of 1839 was the training college. Among the plans for schools which were published in 1840 is one for an Orphan House and School of Industry.[19] It is placed last among the plans, and is by far the largest and most elaborate building shown. It is accom-panied by a long explanatory text in Kay-Shuttleworth's unmistakable style. He undoubtedly attached great importance to the scheme; and before we describe what he did privately at Battersea, it is worth considering what he would have liked the state or some other powerful body to do publicly.

The Orphan House was to provide a model school for 300 boys and girls and 150 infants. It was to serve also as a 'seminary for teachers of Elementary schools' and to house and instruct 100 pupil teachers aged from thirteen to seventeen and 100 candidate teachers who would be older. Some might be married, and there were rooms set aside for them. The institution was to be presided over by a Rector who had handsome accommodation on the premises; and there was a staff of resident teachers, both for ordinary subjects and also for industry. The plans show a building rising to four stories in the centre with lower wings half enclosing a courtyard; a handsome front entrance, which leads to a 'hall and museum and large lecture theatre'. From the hall an impressive double stone stairway leads up to the Rector's rooms and library on the first floor.

Behind, a range of lower buildings, dividing the boys' and girls' playgrounds, contains classrooms and rooms for industrial training. Behind this is the chapel, and behind again is the hospital block, parallel to the front range of buildings. This block contained reception wards for any children who might arrive in a dirty or diseased state, and sick bays for any inmates who fell ill. The industrial training provided for was various. The boys had workshops for netting, tinmen, tailors, and shoemakers. The girls had laundry, washhouse, kitchen and needlework room. The industrial teachers had special accommodation allotted to them. The classrooms were separate from the hall and each other, and held forty children each. They were large enough to allow a row of candidate teachers to sit at the back and observe. The big lecture theatre was intended not only for use by the college but as a place where 'teachers, resident in the surrounding neighbourhood and having charge of schools, could attend courses of instruction'.

Kay-Shuttleworth attached great importance to the residential part of the life. A boarding school in the first place had great advantages. 'An orphan or military asylum for children is preferable to an ordinary day school as an institution for a model school, because the art of instruction can be exhibited with much greater success' since, under these conditions, the children are kept for long periods 'removed from the influence of all other associations'. From among the children resident, the most promising would be selected for training. 'Every child showing sufficient natural talent and application, of good natural disposition, being uncorrupted by vice, and of good promise in his natural qualities and reverence for religion would be apprenticed to the head master' and could hope, in time, to rise to be the master of an independent school.

The older men, married or single, were to be equally carefully looked after. They would attend for one, two or three years the

course of instruction given by the Rector and his assistants, and would practise the art of teaching in the elementary school under the direction of the Rector. The right regulation of their habits during the course of instruction renders it extremely important that they should reside at the Normal School in order that they may be constantly under the eye of the Rector, be aided by his counsels and improved by his example and separated from every injurious influence.

Each of these students was given a room about twelve feet square to 'serve as bedroom and study. The room is warmed by a thermometer stove, and opposite the stove is placed the bed, having on one side of it drawers for his linen and clothes, surmounted by a small bookcase, and on the other a chest containing a wash hand stand and under it a cupboard for shoes etc.'

There is a long essay on heating and ventilation. For health, as the doctor points out, air must be fresh as well as warm. Kay-Shuttleworth advocated underfloor ducts with their outlets as near the stove as possible, and corresponding ventilators in the ceiling. The windows were to have their upper part hinged and might be opened with good effect in summer; and in times of great heat no harm would follow from leaving the door open as well.

No elevation is given of the building, and there are no building specifications, as with the schools whose realization is more probable; but, if we may imagine the same mind at work on this as on the others, the walls would have been of brick, with the doors and windows framed in stone. From the plan it appears that there would have been a pillared portico.

'To this form,' says Kay-Shuttleworth, 'large orphan schools or military schools or schools of industry might be converted', and a little later, 'Such asylums may be converted into important institutions for the education of children in religion and industry, and for preparing a considerable number of them to fulfil the duties of school master in after life.'

Had the Government training college come into existence it would probably have assumed this form. It fitted well with Kay-Shuttleworth's thought, and represented an idea that recurred later and was not finally abandoned for many years.[20] These plans may even have been part of the actual Minute that he presented to the Cabinet. Yet, although Kay-Shuttleworth must have spent much time and thought on the plan, he had never been hopeful about the Government College. 'A scheme was devised,' he said later, 'and put before the public, with a conviction on my part that it would fail; a scheme for a Training College purely civil. I prepared the minute, and presented it to the Government; I attended the Cabinet council, and it passed; and when they asked my opinion I said it would ignominiously fail.'

When he returned that September to the final ruin of the plan, he was undismayed. 'I did not consult any Minister of State or any Churchmen, or any other person than my friend Mr Tufnell', and together, from their own private resources, they set to work to do what the Government was unable to accomplish.

The aim at first was to carry the work begun at Norwood a stage farther, and to train up teachers specifically for the Poor-Law schools which they hoped would develop into the first instalment of a true state system of education. 'The Battersea Training Schools were founded in the hope that they would be employed to assist the executive Government in supplying masters to the schools of industry for pauper children, to the prisons for juvenile offenders, to the schools of Royal Foundation for the army and navy, to the schools of the dock yards and men-of-war, and to the colonies.'[21] His inspiration, as he explained later, was the school at Hofwyl presided over by Wehrli. On one of the tours he had stayed there, and the school had made the deepest impression on his mind. He had seen an institution for peasants run by one whose boast was that he too was a peasant's son. The young men gathered there lived by their eight hours' daily labour in the fields, eating the food they grew, and learning improved methods of agriculture as they did so. They were also trained in modest learning, in art and music, and, above all, were taught a philosophy of cheerful content and an eagerness to spread enlightenment and knowledge among their own class. They were trained as village teachers, as that and nothing more; and they went forth, it was hoped, in a spirit of glad service. One of Kay-Shuttleworth's most cherished memories was of standing outside the building on a tranquil summer evening and hearing the men singing one traditional

109

song after another, while they peeled the potatoes and prepared the vegetables for the next day's dinner.

With this in mind, he and Tufnell bought a house at Battersea standing in five acres of ground, and proceeded to adapt it to their purpose. They entered into close relations with the Hon. and Rev. Robert Eden, vicar of Battersea, who offered them the use of his village schools for teaching practice, and agreed to become chaplain to the college.

They followed the methods of the Swiss humanitarians and built up the school slowly. At first there were eight boys from Norwood.

Our first step on founding the institution at Battersea was to remove from the schools which had been under our immediate superintendence some of the most promising pupils. We were not indifferent to the impression that, in selecting the destitute children of pauper parents as the subjects of a trial of the transforming influences of a religious training, our success would not fail to increase the confidence of the public in the ameliorative tendency of national education. We hoped that a more active sympathy might be inspired for the 50,000 pauper children who await the legislative interference of Parliament for their efficient education in religion and industry. But our chief design was to ascertain whether, by training youths for a series of years in the strict regimen, the exact and comprehensive instruction, the industrious and self denying habits and the peculiar duties of a Normal School, we should not be able to procure more efficient instruments for the instruction of the children of the poor than by any other means.

After six months there were twenty-four of the Poor-Law boys, and added to these nine older men, twenty years of age and over, who had been sent by patrons to train for a shorter time so that they might take charge of a projected school.

The boys from Norwood came at thirteen years of age and were bound apprentice till the age of twenty-one, the first three years to be spent at Battersea, and after that, if their progress had been satisfactory, they were to finish their time as an assistant master at some approved school.

Still following the Swiss ideal, the school was thought of firstly as a family and a family bound together by the natural ties of love and respect. 'A family can only subsist harmoniously by mutual love, confidence, and respect. We did not seek to put the tutors into situations of inaccessible authority, but to place them on the parental seat.' In consequence of this aim, the tutors spent the day with the boys and shared their meals, sitting among them at table. Kay-Shuttleworth, still a bachelor, lived in part of the building, and mingled with the boys in the evening when he was free from his official work. He also took them out for excursions on foot to see things of interest and visit schools. A large part of the time was spent in manual work in the house or garden. It had its advantages, physical and financial. The outdoor work of digging the large, derelict garden, at first found exhausting by lads, who had had no experience of such toil, soon contributed to their health and spirits. No servants were kept, except a matron who acted as cook. All the housework was done by the boys; scouring the floors, cleaning shoes, grates and yard; waiting at table, and preparing the vegetables for the cook. Out of doors a small farm, cows, goats and poultry was managed by the boys. At first they did one hour of housework each day and four hours of gardening. Because of their lack of trained strength the gardening was done in one-hour periods at intervals through the day. There were seven hours of class work. The day stretched with unbroken occupation, mental and physical from 5.30 a.m. to 9 p.m.

This was of course the common policy of the time. The much less ambitious system of training offered at the Borough Road school aimed at keeping the students 'incessantly occupied from 5 in the morning till 9 or 10 at night': even to the detriment of their health. Kay-Shuttleworth, as became a doctor, was more careful; but he too believed in constant, directed activity.

A period of recreation employed according to the discretion of the students would be liable to abuse. It might often be spent in listless sauntering or in violent exertion. Or if a portion of the day were thus withdrawn from the observation of the masters of the school, it would prove a period in which associations might be formed among the students inconsistent with the discipline. In so brief a period of training it is necessary that the entire conduct of the student should be guided by a superior mind.

'The formation of correct habits,' he says elsewhere, 'and the growth of right sentiments, ought to precede such confidence in the pupils' powers of self-direction as is implied in leaving him either much time unoccupied, or in which his labours are not under the immediate superintendence of a teacher.'

It is the problem of moral training that fills his thought. It was a great adventure at the time to take pauper orphans and give them an education, not only in a trade but of a literary character. They might be puffed up by their superior knowledge when compared with their fellows. It had been remarked that when knowledge was universal it would be safe. Its diffusion was still far too narrow for it to seem anything but perilous; and the humble life to which the teacher was destined required very careful preparation.

The main object of a Normal School is the formation of the character of the schoolmaster, as an intelligent, Christian man entering on the instruction of the poor, with religious devotion to his work.

How easy it would be for him to form an overweening estimate of his knowledge and ability must be apparent when it is remembered that he will measure his learning by the standard of that possessed by his own friends and neighbours. He will find himself suddenly raised by a brief course of training to the position of a teacher and example. If his mind were not thoroughly penetrated by a religious principle, or if a presumptuous or mercenary tone had been given to his character, he might go forth to bring discredit upon education by exhibiting a precocious vanity, an insubordinate spirit, or a selfish ambition. He might become not the gentle and pious guide to the children of the poor, but a hireling into whose mind has sunk the doubt of the sceptic; in whose heart was the worm of social discontent; and who had exchanged the docility of ignorance and dullness, for the restless impatience of a vulgar and conceited sciolist.

In the formation of the character of the schoolmaster the discipline of the Training School should be so devised as to prepare him for the modest respectability of his lot.

Not only the way of life, but the dress had a moral significance.

For the younger pupils we had prepared a plain dark dress of rifle green, and a working dress of fustian cord. . . . As respects adults, we have felt the importance of checking the slightest tendency to peculiarity of dress lest it degenerate into foppery. We have endeavoured to impress on the students that the dress and the manners of a master of a school for the poor should be decorous, but that the prudence of his life should likewise find expression in their simplicity. There should be no habit or external sign of self-indulgence or vanity.

The learning that was felt to be so dangerous was of a very modest kind. To begin with the course was merely preparatory. The boys knew very little and the young men often less. Hardly any of them were able to write easily, read fluently or go beyond the rudiments of arithmetic. They were taught English, grammar, etymology and literature; arithmetic was taught with an eye to carpentry or simple surveying;

mechanics to explain the steam engine, which was the wonder of the age; physical geography with reference to agriculture and coal mining; history was treated as a story lesson; music and art had their place, and scriptural teaching occurred for one or more periods every day.

The aim in all the teaching was to awaken in the pupil a 'lively interest in truth' and to show him how it related to his life now or in the future. He must learn from practical observation and be led from the known to the unknown by gentle steps. Nothing should be learned by rote which could be apprehended by direct experience. It was hoped that as time went on and the students passed through the stages of their course greater liberty and independence of work would become possible, but in the beginning all was controlled.[22]

The three men that Kay-Shuttleworth chose to help him in the work were all Scotsmen, trained by Stow at Glasgow. Tate had charge of the senior boys, Horne, who had already served as organizing master in the Poor-Law schools, had the juniors, and Mcleod was put in charge of the village school. The training that they had received in Scotland was very different from the kind of family life that Kay-Shuttleworth had imagined for Battersea; and it was perhaps due, at least partly, to their influence that things changed so much in the short time that the college existed in independence. In Glasgow the students were older, and often better prepared. Some had been ministers, others university students. The period of training was shorter and more than half of it was spent in teaching and the giving of demonstration or criticism lessons. There was no industrial training and the academic subjects taught, which included physics, natural history and sacred history, gave a smattering of knowledge which lacked an honest sense of its limitations. Moreover the students were going to be masters in village day schools, and the elaborate training which Kay-Shuttleworth envisaged as the proper preparation for life in a residential school was inappropriate.

If the teachers were inclined to a concept of training different from that of the founder there was also the pressure of demand. The nine older men who had been admitted as a favour had multiplied into a much larger group. All the people who were eager to start schools wished to send youths to be trained for the task; and there was a steady pressure on Kay-Shuttleworth to accept nominees. They were not always very much to his taste.

There was yet another difficulty. The Poor-Law lads, who had been bred in a workhouse and lived a secluded life at Battersea, were to be sent out to hold school posts at the age of about sixteen or seventeen. They were ill prepared for the changed life of independence in a town. They might, Kay-Shuttleworth felt, be able to manage in a village, but the change to town life was too sudden. He therefore came to believe that the Dutch method was the right one, and that these pupil teachers should live at home, and come to college when they had served the early part of their apprenticeship.

For all these reasons Battersea was a very different place after two years. The romantic humanitarianism of Hofwyl is gone. The students still rose at 5.30 and proceeded to light the fire, but instead of work in the garden they had reports presented by the Superintendent and a lecture on the 'theory and art of school teaching and discipline'. There is only one period in the day when they feed the animals and one for physical exercises. Instead of ending the day with reading the *History of England* or singing, they now have an hour of 'Bible readings and lessons on the manners and customs of the Jews'. The numbers moreover are greater, we hear no more of the boys from Norwood.[23]

In 1843 Kay-Shuttleworth felt that the time had come to withdraw from the school at Battersea. He was now married and could no longer live in. A new principal would be an additional expense, and the venture had cost him and his friend some £2500 of their own money. The Committee of Council had given one grant of £1000 and promised another of £2200 if the future of the college could be firmly established. Kay-Shuttleworth had always regarded it as an essentially Anglican institution, though preserving the right of religious freedom, and he offered it, as a going concern, to the National Society, which accepted it.

In the formal minute which he wrote to the Privy Council announcing the transfer of the college there is a note of wistfulness showing clearly through his formal prose.[24] He had not exactly failed; but he had not done what he set out to do. He had had two main objects in mind, to give an example of Normal Education for schoolmasters 'comprising the formation of character, the development of the intelligence, appropriate technical instruction and the acquisition of method and practical skill in conducting an Elementary school'. This aim might have been achieved in the college as he had at first organized it, with lads to be trained over a period of three years in a simple and diversified curriculum; it was very unlikely to be possible to achieve so much with the students and the period of training that he passed on to his successors.

The second aim had been to show that it was possible to have an institution essentially religious and in association with the Church without violating the rights of conscience. He had indeed demonstrated this; but a demonstration is of no effect if it is unheeded. When he surrendered the college to the National Society he confessed that a college that was not denominational in a fairly narrow sense was not viable in the religious climate of the day. There was a strong body of opinion which agreed with him on religious freedom in an Anglican setting, but it was not organized and capable of maintaining an institution as expensive as a training college. The British Society might have been prepared to continue the college with that religious freedom in which Kay-Shuttleworth believed—but he was by persuasion an Anglican, and he gave his child for adoption to the body with which he felt the closest ties.

In his third aim he had completely failed—the scheme of 'devoting this establishment to the supply of masters to schools connected with the executive government and especially to the great schools of Industry for Pauper children'. Why he had been 'unable to fulfill his original design' he does not say. But we can imagine.

When he looked at the state of the labouring poor as shown in the reports that had been recently published, he felt that the need for Christian teachers was more urgent than ever, and that the best thing that he could do was to transfer the college to the Church to use for that great purpose.

Notes

1. Frank Smith, *Life of Kay Shuttleworth* (1923), p. 90, quoting the MS of 1877.
2. June 1839, Hansard, XLVII, 1377.
3. Minutes, 1838, p. 2.
4. P.P., 1834, IX, 219, 1331, 2055; 1837, VII, 451, 723.
5. Minutes, 1839, p. ix.
6. P.P., 1840, XL, 1.
7. Minutes, 1839, p. ix.
8. Minutes, 1839, p. 22.
9. Minutes, 1839, p. 175.
10. Kay-Shuttleworth, *Four Periods of Public Education* (1862), p. 231.
11. Minutes, 1840, pp. 28 ff.
12. Minutes, 1839, p. 22.
13. Minutes, 1844, II, pp. 8, 9.
14. Minutes, 1842, p. 464.
15. Minutes, 1842, p. 55.
16. Minutes, 1842, p. 54.
17. Minutes, 1844, II, pp. 6, 10.
18. P.P., 1935, VII, 793, 796.
19. Minutes, 1839, II.
20. Minutes, 1839, p. viii.
21. *Four Periods of Public Education*, pp. 294 ff.
22. Minutes, 1842, p. 60.
23. Minutes, 1842, p. 189.
24. *Four Periods of Public Education*, pp. 387 ff.; Minutes, 1843, p. 275.

Chapter Six

The early schools

From 1840 we have in the inspectors' reports their first hasty, and horrified views of the schools as they had grown up without regulation or supervision. The two fundamental difficulties were bad buildings and bad teachers. The reports for the first few years at least are full of examples of both. It would be nauseating to quote more than a few. Baptist Noel's thumbnail sketches of Birmingham have a certain vividness.[1]

Present 170 boys; the room will hold 400. Since Jan. 1 there have been 66 boys admitted. The average time during which the scholars stay is about 1 year. There was not one boy in the school 12 years old. The only book in use for the upper classes was the Bible, nor were there Bibles or Testaments enough to afford one to each of the boys who were reading them. There were no maps in the school. The children were taught nothing either of History or Geography. Indeed the master, occupied with the superintendence of 170 little boys, one-third of whom had been admitted within six months, could scarcely find time to give any direct instruction to the school, but was obliged to depend on his little monitors, not one of whom was 12 years old. Three out of the six classes into which the school is divided, were sitting, when I entered, without books in their hands, and doing nothing, and so continued for above half an hour.

Another school:

Fifty girls were present; room for 100. The books in use were those of the National School Society. The writing was bad. The mistress said she thought girls should not learn beyond compound addition in arithmetic, and she taught them no farther. Eighteen of the best readers then read to the monitor, making various mistakes which were not noticed by the monitor or mistress. Several times when a girl hesitated in reading the mistress called out 'Go on, go on, shout out.' When several words were wrongly spelt, and nine girls had successively mis-spelt the word *righteous*, the poor teacher exclaimed in a sort of scholastic agony, 'Girls, girls, don't be giddy, don't be giddy.' But when various simple questions had been put to the class which they were unable to answer her dismay became complete, and with ineffable anxiety she repeated, 'Girls, girls, O girls, shout out, shout out.'

Infant schools at this period were generally better than those for older children, and they filled a real need. Baptist Noel finds them worthy of quiet praise.

Infant schools, if they only rescued young children from an exhausted atmosphere and a wearisome confinement, from their own fretfulness and the irritation of their gaolers, if they were only safe and comfortable asylums when their parents were obliged to leave home for their daily employments—would be most merciful institutions: but they do much more than this; since many of their little inmates learn the first rudiments of arithmetic, acquire the art of reading, are taught to observe and reason on what is around them, and receive the first lessons of religion and morality.[2]

Sometimes, particularly in the country districts, the buildings were deplorable. Schools were held in hovels with the rain coming through the roof, in attics, in parts of churches so dark that the children had to go outside to see to read or write. They were grossly overcrowded.

A school in Wales:

This school is held in the mistress's house. I shall never forget the hot sickening smell which struck me on opening the door of that low dark room, in which 30 girls and 20 boys were huddled together. It more nearly resembled the smell of the engine on board a steamer, such as it is felt by a sea-sick voyager in passing near the funnel. Everything in the room (i.e. a few benches of various heights and sizes, and a couple of tables) was hidden under and overlaid with children.[3]

Or more moderately:

The rooms were for the most part, dirty and close. A rudely constructed desk for the master often occupied one corner; forms and desks for the children were ranged along the walls and from side to side. The books being provided by the parents, mere fragments, consisting of a few soiled leaves, appeared to be generally deemed sufficient to answer the purpose for which the children were sent to school. A pile of detached covers, and leaves too black for farther use, often occupied another corner, betokening

118

the result of long struggles with unmeaning rows of spelling, with confinement and constrained positions, and the other adversities of elementary learning. In many, silence was only maintained, for a few moments at a time, by loud exclamations and threats. In some the room was also appropriated to the domestic purposes of the household. In one, a deserted chapel, half the space was occupied with hay piled up to the roof. In a few only did the size and cleanliness of the room, and the demeanour and apparent qualifications of the master, afford a probability that the instruction sought to be given would be imparted with effect. But even in those of the highest pretensions, the amount of instruction was very scanty.[4]

At other times the teachers made no attempt to teach, and the children played with such abandon that the noise could be heard afar; and the visiting inspector was guided to the school without the need of enquiries. Sometimes the teacher did not attend at all.

I found the school room empty and locked at 11.00 in the morning, and was credibly informed that it was no uncommon thing for the teacher to be away for days together, and that once in particular, during a long frost, he absented himself 30 days in succession, under the plea that having but one leg, he was afraid to venture along the road from his house to the school room until the ice should be dissolved by a thaw.[5]

When the master was present, and keeping some kind of order, he did not appear to take his duties very seriously. 'It is singular,' remarked Jelinger C. Symons, 'that in three or four instances only have I found a schoolmaster occupied in teaching on suddenly entering a school of the common class. I have far oftener found them reading an old newspaper, writing a letter or a bill, probably for some other person, reading a magazine or doing nothing of any sort.'

At its best the instruction was not very efficient.

With few exceptions, there is no system of teaching in the schools in my district. The general plan is precisely that of the old fashioned village schools. The children sit in rows on forms, and save the master all sorts of trouble by 'reading their books'; and in order that he may assure himself of their industry, they all read aloud. Thus a Babel of tongues is kept going on all subjects, from Leviticus to the alphabet, in which any attempt to correct, or even to distinguish individual performances would be perfectly hopeless. One by one the more forward children are brought up to the master to 'say their lesson', which generally consists of a long column in Vyse's Spelling Book, to be said and spelt by heart, which is performed frequently with a wonderful accuracy and rapidity, and in a screech which seems expressly devised to annihilate all chance of expression or modulation of tone in reading. The Bible and Testament classes are generally once a day called up to read to the master. The Holy Scriptures are the standard reading book; and the great ambition of both master and scholar and parents is that the greatest possible number should be reading in the *Old* Testament. It is a sort of *premium diligentiae* awarded to the children who could gabble the most glibly.[6]

This custom, general by principle in National Schools, and probably almost as general, in spite of Lancaster's example, in the British ones—is often mentioned and deplored by the inspectors. It was not only that the exclusive use of the Bible unnaturally restricted the curriculum and offered children material incomprehensible in thought and language, but the miserable hours spent with it spelling out Acts or Genesis were calculated to make them avoid the Scriptures for the rest of their lives.

Nevertheless, as the inspectors went up and down the country they found some good schools. In one:

The exercise of the understanding was constantly kept in view. There were maps, and books illustrative of scripture. Occasional lessons were given on geography, anatomy, physiology, minerals and flowers. There was a lending library, a blackboard for drawing, and singing was well taught and there was ground for a garden. The school was supported by a noble lady.

Heywood, one of the more deplorable industrial towns, seemed, by its very nature, to drive the well-intentioned to greater efforts.

The infant school, attached to St. James Church in Heywood, appeared to me an exceedingly good school. The Master (a Scotch episcopalian trained under Mr Stow) aided by his sister, was more successful in bringing into action the intellectual faculties of the children than any other paid teacher that I saw in Lancashire. Here also I found a border of flowers round the playground, perfectly neat and free from weeds; this, which is always an agreeable sight as connected with a school, is most precious in a town like Heywood where the pleasurable feelings excited by flowers and other good gifts of the Author of Nature have but few opportunities of being called into action. Moreover a flower garden is a place where self denial may be very early taught,'

and hardly a flower had been picked.[7]

There was one school that would probably be outstanding, even today.

At Ockham the buildings and arrangement of the school seemed to me full of interest. The Nobleman, at whose expense the school is maintained, has got together a number of curious specimens of forest trees and 2 acres of the school garden are laid out as a nursery. The teacher who has been trained in Scotland, has considerable skill in Chemistry and other matters. The school was furnished with some chemical apparatus, a printing press with which the boys print their own regulations and a number of contrivances for the instruction and amusement of the pupils. On the ceiling is a draft of the solar system. Some of the tables are marked out as chess boards. There is an organ, a pair of globes, a magic lantern, and round the walls some busts and a barometer. Great attention is paid to the formation of habits of order. The boys are very intelligently taught, notebooks are kept, and they spontaneously made great use of the school library. School hours are from 9-11 and 2-4, the rest, except the dinner hour, is spent in the garden or the shop. The erection of a shed has witnessed to the skill of the boys as bricklayers and carpenters. About 3½ acres are enclosed for spade husbandry. The cheerful way in which they appeared to live together pleased me much.[8]

These schools, in their diversity, were essentially individual creations. Perhaps the majority were founded by ministers of religion, others by the gentry or aristocracy, a few by mine owners or manufacturers, of which the most famous were the schools that Robert Owen ran at New Lanark and in which his son Robert Dale Owen regularly taught.

We find a school in Yorkshire containing sixty boys and seventy girls and infants that was supported by the Misses Roberts of Sheffield; another was the private property of a Mr Nustler, a local tyrant, who refused to let the clergyman set foot in it—much to that gentleman's annoyance. Lords and ladies are frequently mentioned as maintaining schools or country gentlemen like Major S. Lyon and Sir Thomas W. White, Bt, who supported a school at Firbeck for many years.[9]

Some of these schools, when they were founded by local effort were opened with pomp and ceremony, and in Wales generally with song.

On that occasion the children, in number exceeding 400 assembled in the schoolroom, from whence after prayer and preliminary arrangement they walked in order to the Cathedral, preceded by a band of music, with flags bearing appropriate devices. After Divine Service, the procession on returning to the school, assumed a more imposing appearance, as had been previously arranged, in the following order—Boys, Girls, Band, Tradesmen, Gentlemen, Ladies, Churchwardens and Clergy, the two vergers in their gowns closing the whole. Bishop Majendie having previously entered the schoolroom, then received the procession.[10]

A nonconformist school could be opened with the same pomp.

The foundation stone of the building, intended for the education of 160 boys and 160 girls upon the British system of education, was laid on Thursday 21st inst. The day was highly favourable. At 1 o'clock the singers, from all the chapels, in one united band, proceeded through the streets, singing some well selected sacred tunes. At half past one the procession moved on in the following order:—the singers, the gentlemen's committee, the ladies' committee, the boys, the girls, and other friends of the cause, altogether forming a most imposing sight. At 4 o'clock the tea party commenced when about 900 sat down to partake of the refreshments, the Calvanistic Methodists having kindly lent their chapel for the occasion.

There were the usual speeches, some in Welsh.[11]

At the other end of the scale a silent struggle just kept the school alive.

At Bratton Fleming, from want of being able to meet with a suitable teacher, the Rector was himself acting as schoolmaster. At Beenham the writing is wholly taught by the clergyman, to whom the pens are sent each evening to be mended, and the copybooks to have lessons set.

There is a passage on the work of a clergyman at Heywood that is worth quoting to show what the best men could do.

Within the last thirty years the population of Heywood has increased from a few hundreds to more than double as many thousands, and these consist almost entirely of two classes, the operatives and their immediate superintendents, there are no gentry; and the bad arrangements of the more recent manufacturing towns of Lancashire here appear in their most disgusting forms; the clergyman with a flock of 8000 is not so well paid as an ordinary curate; but within the three years that he has held the appointment he has established an efficient day school, attended by a considerable number of factory children, and the best infant school that I have seen out of the immediate neighbourhood of London, with three night schools for such as are at work during the day. A daily school, supported by a factory master, has been placed under his superintendence, and in a short time two more day schools will be opened along the line of his population. On Mondays, Wednesdays and Fridays himself and his wife and their two female servants leave the house with the key in their pocket to spend the evening in a room given up to their use in a manufactory two miles distant. Here some sixty young persons who have been in the mill during the day are assembled; some of the girls are taught sewing and knitting; the rest with the boys learn writing and accounts; the evening's work is concluded with a short catechetical lecture out of the Bible, and prayer.[12]

One aspect of the personal nature of these schools was their impermanence. With no organization behind them, chance and mortality determined their existence. And, often, the harder a teacher worked the earlier he died. For many, teaching was a very dangerous profession.

Here is an account, from the pupil's side, of a school in Wales:[13]

In the course of a few months, the promised school was opened. There were many difficulties to encounter—difficulties so many and so formidable as to baffle the designs of the worthy promoters of the enterprise, but they were at last overcome. There were no Government grants in those days. The landowners did not care to encourage a Dissenting school, and no grant of land could be obtained for it; there was no resident clergyman to encourage the faint-hearted, or to rouse the apathetic; all had to be done by a small band of poor farmers. The only place where a school could be kept was in the chapel, all fitted with its square pews—not a very fit place for the trial of the new system. School fees were low—in that poor district they could not be otherwise, and the teacher's income must be supplemented by various dodges, collections in chapel, subscriptions among the farmers and tea meetings. But the farmers struggled bravely with the work, and greatly to their credit continued to battle more or less successfully with their difficulties, pecuniary and otherwise, till the Government came to their assistance.

The going to school for the first time was to me a great event. I had been to the Church school three or four years previously, before we left Havod, but it was only for a few weeks. The measles sent me home before I could derive much benefit from the school, and soon afterwards our departure from Havod removed me out of reach of school altogether.

But now I was eleven years old, had read a good deal in such books as were within my reach, and had a strong desire to learn more. Of course all the little information I gathered was from Welsh books, for I knew no English, and had never heard a dozen words spoken.

It would have utterly disheartened most schoolmasters to examine the fifty boys and girls who appeared at school on the first day. In age we ranged from six to twenty and upwards. Stalwart young farmers and grown up girls stood side by side with the small urchin just breeched. But, however unequal we were in size, we were pretty equal in ignorance. Some half dozen could read, indifferently, and in a phonic Welsh way, words of one syllable, and could make some lame attempt at forming letters. None understood the simplest sentence in English—we must be addressed in Welsh if we were to understand at all. Fortunately for us, our master was an enthusiast. He was fresh from the Borough Road British Training College and burned to make trial on the unpromising mass before him of the system of Joseph Lancaster. And it was astonishing what success followed his teaching, all things considered. Most of the instruction was superficial no doubt, and it is probable that the mass of children did not carry away with them much out of school that could be called directly a benefit to them. But this was rather the fault of the system than the teacher. John Davies was a hard-working teacher and inspired his pupils with a liking for hard work. In the two years I spent with him, I managed to attain a fair knowledge of English, made fair progress in the subjects usually taught in elementary schools, and picked up some acquaintance with algebra and geometry. . . .

At the end of that period, our worthy teacher, whose health had long been declining, was obliged to resign the school. After his death we were indeed as sheep without a shepherd; the school was closed and most of us rapidly forgot the little we had learned.

The Committee of Council was faced with the apparently hopeless task of bringing some order into this multitude of impermanent schools and of raising the standard. Kay-Shuttleworth in London with a few clerks; some five or six inspectors scattered through the country; no money to spend except on school buildings; no engine of control. It needed an heroic faith in education to attempt it. It needed before anything else the development of the means of training teachers. But that was a long-term policy. As the money he had to spend was specifically for school buildings it was easier to start by trying to control these.

With the Minutes of 1840, the secretary sent out to his inspectors forms of questions that they were to answer when considering the proposed site for a school. He also, following the example of the Irish Board, gave plans and specifications of approved types of buildings and draft conveyances to assist those who were proposing to found schools. He must have wasted no time in getting his architects and lawyers to work.[14]

The two Societies had been giving their thought to building schools since 1815, or earlier, and they had formed opinions of the type of building that would give satisfactory results at the lowest cost. Some of the earlier buildings had been elaborate. An early example was the school room opened in 1822 with such pomp by the enthusiastic Dean Cotton; where nothing, that benevolence and delicacy could suggest, had been omitted.

The building gave six square feet of floor space per child. It had a screen down the middle to separate the sexes, which could be easily withdrawn; it had ventilators both in the windows and roof; no windows to the exposed aspect; there were back doors to each of the courts, covered with porches and double doors; 'an entrance is also provided at one angle by which the ladies who visit the female school may enter in without passing either through the boys or the back courts. Large drains also pass through the building; a foot pavement around it and an excellent road made on the best principles leads to the main street.'

The published recommendations described a more modest building. The National Society in its 'General Observations on the Construction and Arrangement of School Rooms' states:

Form of room—should be oblong, a barn furnished no bad model, and a good one may be easily converted into a school room.

Benches and desks are best placed close to the side walls so that the writer may sit or stand with his face towards them. The classes which are writing or ciphering being thus arranged along the sides of the room, the middle will be left open for the classes to stand out while reading or under examination.

The benches of the classes are arranged on the floor without any desks. The number of children to one monitor varies from 12 to 30.

In the classes, even when large, the method of instruction is individual and successive, not simultaneous, and is conducted by a monitor.

The British and Foreign Society varied the geometric description of its room, and places the children who are writing in the centre, otherwise it is the same building.[15]

The form of room best adapted to the system is a parallelogram. The centre of the room should be occupied by desks and forms, a clear passage of from 6–8 ft being reserved for the reading stations. The windows should be either in the roof or elevated at least 6 ft from the ground. At 4–6 ft from the ground rails should be fixed against the walls from which lesson boards should be suspended. The ground space between the desks and the wall ought to have curved lines traced on it of nearly semicircular form, to make the station of each reading or spelling draft. The desks and forms should be so arranged that when all the pupils are seated each one may front the master.

The forms and desks must stand on cast iron legs and be firmly anchored to the floor.

The space and passage between a form and the next desk is 12"; the horizontal space between a desk and its form is 3". The breadth of a desk is 9". The breadth of a form is 6". Each child being seated upon his form occupies a space of 18" in length of the desk.

This large, blind room remained the standard provision for many years, even after the methods of instruction had changed. The noise of so many children and so many instructors assembled together had not apparently been recognized as an evil. In the great school at The Hague, that so impressed Kay-Shuttleworth, six teachers and 1000 children worked together in one room. At Norwood, a long, rather narrow room took 400 children in conditions that even Kay-Shuttleworth admitted were inconvenient. But, as long as the instruction was of the monitorial type, it was essential for the master to have the whole school continually under his eye.

In 1840, then, the Committee accepted this standard type of school building and sought to give it decency and dignity by good workmanship and a façade in accordance with the taste of the day.

In the published forms the inspector is instructed first to enquire into the site of the projected school.[16]

Are any vitriol works, tanneries, size manufactories, slaughter houses or other noxious trades situated near the site? . . . Is it in the neighbourhood of any undrained marsh, swampy ground, large uncovered drain or large stagnant pool?

If the site is satisfactory the land must be bought freehold and held in trust for the education of children. The legal form of the conveyance is provided.

Then follow plans for the buildings.[17] All sizes of schools are given, from the small village school of 30 children to the large town one of 224 children and 110 infants. The elevations are all similar with arched doorways, square headed windows with stone mullions and some with drip stones; a bell turret in the front gable; knockers, and iron scrapers let into the stone at all the doors. In the specification it is imagined that the buildings will be of brick with stone trimmings, but naturally the materials varied with the locality. At Llanfairfechen in Caernarvonshire, North Wales, there is a school still in use built almost exactly to these plans, but using the local granite instead of brick. Its windows seem to have the original diamond panes. Unsuitable as it is for modern use, it must have been a very fine school in its day, and the outer structure has taken no harm from time.

The construction of the building was to be of the best, and many of the specifications have almost the ring of poetry:

The whole of the timber to be the best yellow Memel, Riga or Dantzig fir; the deals are to be the best yellow Christiana; the oak to be English, hearty and well seasoned.

The slating to be stout Bangor Countess, to be laid and cut close and to overlap $2\frac{1}{2}''$ at the least.

All the stone used in the mason's work is to be of the best quality, free from shakes, flaws, vents and all other defects, and laid to be compressed according to its natural bed.

When benevolence and local patriotism combined with wealth, the results might be very handsome. This is the description of the school at Tiverton, the gift of Mr. John Heathcoat the local M.P.

The building, which is a fine specimen of the Tudor style, consists of a centre and two wings, with an elegant screen to form the entrance from the principal front. . . . The beautiful rooms are lit by large and very elegant windows, glazed in iron framing of a gothic filigree pattern. The floors of the two largest rooms are laid with a composition of artificial asphalt. The walls are built of the quarry stones of the neighbourhood, squared and hewn in a style much more highly finished than has hitherto been attempted. The dressings and ornamental parts are of Bath stone, the whole forming an harmonious mass of warm red or purple colour, which the light tints of the Bath stone beautifully relieve.[18]

So good was the work that we still have much of it with us. All schools were to have separate playgrounds for boys, girls and infants. The influence of David Stow of Glasgow was strong here, and also in the provision of the circular swings that he had advocated. From his teaching, too, came the idea of providing galleries in the main classroom. The collective lesson as a means of imparting information, as well as achieving moral improvement was becoming more widely used, and to be modern the schools must have this arrangement. The children, so that they could see and be seen were placed at desks that rose in steps like a lecture theatre. This gallery appeared first in Infant schools, but it was so great a feature of the instruction at the Training College in Glasgow that it was spreading into England with the imported teachers. This gallery appeared in the plans for the bigger schools in 1840 and led to delicate problems.

One point that exercised the mind of the planners was whether the teacher ought to have a desk, particularly if the simultaneous rather than the monitorial method is employed.

In many schools taught on the simultaneous method the teacher has no seat or desk provided: this is invariably the case in Holland. In Scotland, a small moveable desk, without any seat is used by the teachers in all the schools which have emanated from the Glasgow Normal Seminary.

This is a convenient form of desk. The teacher is not tempted to lounge, but is always, when in school, actively engaged in the duties of his profession.[19]

The heating and ventilation of the rooms was carefully described, and, as a final refinement, it was decreed that a thermometer should be kept in every classroom . . . so that there should be 'some more certain means of regulating the temperature than the sense of heat and cold experienced by the master'.

The regulations of the time expressly excluded the master's house from grant, and this was not changed till 1843, but, undeterred by this, Kay-Shuttleworth in the plans showed the master's house as an integral part of the building. The size of the dwelling was nicely graded according to the size of the school, and it is stated the 'arrangements for the dwelling of the master should be limited to the strictest simplicity'. Yet, even in the smallest schools, it could be a real home. At the least he had a sitting-room, bedroom and kitchen. By the time there were 100 children he had two bedrooms, and when the numbers reached 300 he had a flat of about six rooms with separate rooms for the assistant master. He had his own yard and his own 'offices'.

In essence all these schools were single-room buildings. The room might be divided between the girls and the boys under a separate teacher, or there might be a semi-permanent screen allowing the girls to be cut off to some extent when they were sewing, but the separate classroom was not shown except as a small room where a few children could be assembled for a special purpose. The idea of separate classrooms was slow in establishing itself. It is not surprising when there was only one adult in charge of a school that he hesitated to send groups of children off to engage in no one knew what activities. But the inspectors had already begun to comment on the inconvenience of the single-room school.[20]

The want of an additional classroom for the younger children, and of an enclosed and spacious play-ground to which they, in fine weather, and after the constrained positions and intellectual exertion of the school room have prepared them for relaxation, might be prudently and safely sent, almost necessitates the confinement during the whole day of those who are not actually under instruction more than a $\frac{1}{4}$ part of the time they spend in the schoolroom.

Or, as another phrased it, 'Teachers are compelled to conduct in one apartment and at the same time the various branches of an elementary

Education.' And he explained that this was difficult and the results unsatisfactory.

Kay-Shuttleworth maintained that every school should be divided into four classes, and in a school of 160 there should be four classes of 40 each. But it is clear from the plans, that, in most cases, these classes did not have separate rooms till the school reached something like 150.

These schools in the hopeful mind of Kay-Shuttleworth were intended to play a wider part in the life of the village. We could compare them to village colleges today; and their construction was to be an element in civilizing the district.[21]

The parochial or village library can nowhere be so conveniently kept as at the school house under the charge of the schoolmaster; and the buildings afford abundant facilities for this purpose. The office of secretary to the Benefit Society of the parish or village would in no respect injuriously interfere with the schoolmaster's duties; the meetings of the soceity would probably be held in the evenings. The schoolroom is, in all respects, conveniently arranged for such meetings, and would be a place of assemblage for the working classes, preferable to the tavern, where these meetings are too commonly held.

Notes

1. Minutes, 1840–1, pp. 182, 186.
2. Minutes, 1840, p. 166.
3 & 4. P.P., 1847, XXVII, pt I, pp. 16 ff., 238 ff.
5. Minutes, 1844, II, p. 9.
6. P.P., 1847, XXVII, pt II, p. 29.
7. Minutes, 1840, p. 319.
8. Minutes, 1841, p. 174.
9. Visitation Returns, Diocese of York, 1865, R. VI, A. 49; 1868, R. VI, A. 50. Borthwick Institute of Historical Research, York.
10. William Hughes, *Life and Speeches of Dean Cotton* (1874), pp. 18 ff.
11. Minutes of the British and Foreign School Society.
12. Minutes, 1842, pp. 319 ff.
13. Robert Roberts, *Life and Opinions*, p. 105.
14. Minutes, 1839, pt II.
15. *Manual of the System of Primary Instruction pursued in the Model Schools of the British and Foreign Schools Society.*
16. Minutes, 1839–40, p. 4.
17. Minutes, 1839, pt II.
18. Minutes of the British and Foreign School Society.
19. Minutes, 1842–3, p. i.
20. Yet even in 1885 separate classrooms are considered a doubtful luxury. Cf. F. J. Gladman, *School Work* (1885).
21. Minutes, 1839–40, pp. 46–92.

Chapter Seven

The early training colleges

As with so many things at the beginning of early English education, the formative ideas of the training colleges came from outside. Kay-Shuttleworth brought back with him the paternalism of Pestalozzi and tried to establish it at Battersea, but the major influence came from Scotland.

The two English Societies had for many years given some sort of training in their central schools, the British and Foreign at the Borough Road, and the National at Westminster. This training was normally a matter of a few weeks, and did little more than familiarize the pupils with the technical details of the monitorial system; and, perhaps, decrease their general ignorance to some small extent. The training institution in Glasgow was very different.

The Glasgow Educational Society was the creation of David Stow, who, from a well-to-do background, had come into Education moved by pity for the waifs of the Glasgow Salt Market. For some years he ran a school and training centre for infant teachers, and in 1832 he extended his work to children and teachers of junior school age. In 1838, conscious of the merit of its work, and hoping that the Lord would provide, the Society launched out into a large establishment 'with school and classrooms for the infant and junior school, and with 16 or 18 classrooms, or miniature schools, for training the students in the management of a class'.

The building in which Stow housed his institution was of a most impressive kind, and still stands on a corner of the New City Road. It houses today the Dundas Vale School. It has lasted well, as it should, for it was very expensive. At the time of its building, trade was bad and subscriptions were scant. Even a church collection did not yield much.

The Society was at least £2500 in debt. In this crisis they appealed to the Committee of Council asking for a share of the new grants.[1]

One can imagine that Kay-Shuttleworth was delighted at this request. He knew and admired the institution, and had drawn many of his most valued teachers from it. He was now offered an opportunity of encouraging its work, of making it better known, of setting it on a firmer base, and obtaining some hold over it, in case of difficulty in the future. He could also demonstrate to the English Societies, who had so far failed even to accept the grants that had been offered them, how he proposed to deal with training colleges. At almost the same time, the training college at Edinburgh, which was under the control of the Education Committee of the General Assembly of the Church of Scotland, also asked for a grant. As it seemed impossible that the Glasgow school should ever be efficiently managed, financially, under its present committee, the Government proposed that it should be taken over by the Church of Scotland. Then to these two institutions—in Edinburgh and Glasgow—a £10,000 capital grant should be made, and £1000 a year given for maintenance. It was this maintenance grant, the first of its kind, that was so important. As a condition of the maintenance grant the Committee demanded not only the usual inspection, but added that the grant would stop—in whole or part—if 'at any time hereafter it shall appear to the Committee of Council on Education that the schools are not satisfactorily maintained and conducted'.

The General Assembly wrote back saying that this was a new requirement, and that they had not known that it would be demanded. The reply was that a maintenance grant was also new and that it should reasonably be associated with an inspection which assured the continued efficient running of the institution. With a good grace the new control was accepted, and the Assembly also agreed to submit for approval the name of the Rector chosen.

The Glasgow Educational Society mirrored the educational philosophy of its founder.[2] David Stow saw in schools 'an antidote to the demoralizing influence of large towns and manufacturing villages'. He saw in the life of the streets the greatest threat to virtue. 'When example, precept and sympathy combine, as in boys of the same age, an influence is in operation compared with which the example and precept of parents and guardians are rendered comparatively powerless.' He thought that this natural sympathy of numbers can be taken by the school and used for good. The children must be taught for at least some of the time in

5 'St. Martin's National School. Built by Subscription on
Ground The Gift of His Majesty King George IV'

6a   *Above*   National School, Hatherley, Devon. Built in 1838
6b   *Below*   Gateway of National School, Okehampton, Devon.
The school, built in 1837, has now perished

large groups, and the group must be encouraged to develop a common opinion. The playground is as important as the classroom, for in it children act freely, and a watching teacher can observe and later correct their conduct. The primary function of the teacher is to train the children, and Stow preferred his students to be known as trainers. Physical exercise was most important. There were circular swings, of a maypole type, in the playgrounds, and in class the periods of work were to be broken up by 'clapping hands, stretching arms, simultaneously rising up and sitting down'. It was for the purpose of these lessons to large groups that Stow introduced the 'gallery', and it was he who developed the simultaneous lesson, on scripture or some other topic. As he did not believe in books, these lessons were almost the only way the children had of acquiring knowledge. Stow's two contributions to the form of the lesson were the system of 'picturing out' and 'ellipsis'. Picturing out was giving a description of some object or scene in words and indicating what points were of importance to the coming lesson. Ellipsis was one of the most dreary devices ever inflicted on children. It consisted in stopping half-way through a sentence and waiting till the class supplied the key words, shouting them all together. In his book he gives many examples of how the method works, such as:

The Potter's Wheel

You see this large wheel and this thing like a . . . *belt*? That belt goes round the . . . *wheel*, and when it is drawn over this small wheel, what will it do? *It will turn it*. The large wheel will . . . *wheel round*.

These ideas were impressed on the students by an elaborate training. Before Kay-Shuttleworth acceded to the request for grant he sent his Scottish inspector, John Gibson, to report.[3]

The report gives a very thorough and clear account of the system, and thus made available in England the results of the experiments in the North.

The students, as was customary in Scotland, were non-resident, and lived in carefully chosen lodgings where the most complete decorum was required. They generally attended for six months, usually supporting themselves during their attendance. On admission the attainments of the students were very varied.

Some have the advantages of a regular collegiate education, some only the ordinary burg and parochial schools. In a few instances there is knowledge of the Classics and Mathematics, but for the most part confined to the Evidences of Christianity, the Doctrines of Scripture, Bible

History, such a knowledge of Grammar as to enable them to parse with tolerable correctness, a general acquaintance with Geography and a knowledge of Arithmetic as far as vulgar and decimal fractions.

Of those admitted during the last year, 1 is a preacher of the Church of Scotland, 21 had been teachers in small adventure schools, 1 carpenter, 1 teacher of dancing, 1 portrait painter, 1 baker, 3 shopmen, 5 students at college.

During their training they were occupied partly in the continuance of their own education, and partly in practical teaching. The subjects taught were physics, natural history, geography, arithmetic and algebra, English grammar and sacred history. They also had 4 hours' music in the week, and an hour each of drawing, elocution and gymnastics. In all $16\frac{1}{2}$ hours were spent in this education. On the whole John Gibson thought their instruction rather misguided.

'The intellectual teaching', he says, 'seems to me to render their instruction as teachers superficial and desultory, and so to divert their attention from those subjects which, if not imparted to the children of our poorer population when young, will, in all probability, never be imparted at all.'

He does not actually object to physics, natural history and chemistry, but thinks they are too prominent.

They 'excite and gratify the curiosity without systematically strengthening and training the higher faculties of the mind'.

The work in practical education took up a larger part of the students' time—24 hours a week. This part of the work was most elaborately organized into four sections:

A. 8 hours in school, watching and helping.
B. $11\frac{1}{2}$ giving lessons in hall.
C. 1 in giving each other Bible lessons.
D. $3\frac{1}{2}$ public criticism.

A. Observes, teaches under observation, writes a journal and record of observations, which must be 'submitted weekly to the Rector for his perusal and criticism'.

B. Gallery lessons, and in miniature classrooms.

C. The class of students pretends to be a certain age and are taught. 'It is supposed that this exercise is attended with peculiar advantage. It is obvious, that, in consequence of the business being conducted while the students alone are present, ample and unrestrained scope is furnished to the Rector for the purpose of offering remarks on the process while in progress, and of showing in what respect either the questions put or answers given are injudicious and improper.'

D. The gallery lesson was Stow's special contribution. The time and attention given to it were, therefore, very considerable.

One half of the students are assembled in the hall and while one of them is employed in giving to the children in the gallery a lesson, with the subject of which he had previously been made acquainted, and for the examination and elucidation of which he is expected sedulously to prepare himself, the others sit as spectators and auditors, critically observing and jotting down for future use in their note books any peculiarities or defects of manner (such as awkwardness of movement, monotony of tone, want of animation, want of success in securing and riveting the attention) and at the same time watching for any inaccuracy or deficiency or superfluity of statement, any infelicity of illustration and analogy, any inaptitude in eliciting information of which the children had previously been in possession, in short any want of skill in communicating and vividly presenting to the mind that of which they were ignorant.

The lesson having been given, the student reads out slowly, and with a full, distinct Articulation, a Verse or Two of a Psalm or Hymn, which the Children sing; after which another student takes his place before the Gallery, and having by means of simple physical Exercises, refreshed the Children, and prepared them for renewed intellectual Exertion, he proceeds to give in the same Manner as above a Lesson on the Subject which has been previously prescribed to him.

Four such lessons are given, each occupying Fifteen Minutes.

These lessons serve the double purpose of training the Students to Skill in the Art of Teaching, and of furnishing the minds of the children with interesting and useful information.

Others meanwhile teach the rest of the children in small groups in the 'miniature classrooms'. The public criticism is conducted in the following manner:

. . . Every Wednesday at half past three the whole of the students retire to the hall, when, in the presence of the Rector and secretary, and occasionally the heads of the various departments, they state their opinions of the manner in which the business of the gallery had been conducted. Mr Stow then delivers, more or less in detail, his views, the masters of the model schools give the results of their observations, and the whole is wound up by the remarks of the Rector.

The female students take no active share in this exercise; they sit attentive and interested auditors.

It is not surprising that the inspector thought these gallery lessons rather overdone. They were in themselves good but 'the students had been led to attach an undue prominence and value to them', while their routine teaching was 'not characterized by even an ordinary amount of vigour'. In fact what they needed was more 'skill in the organization, general management and technical instruction of a school' and less concentration on the individual display of a single disconnected lesson.

There were thus before the English educational world two exemplars of teacher training, Battersea and Glasgow. In their conception the two institutions were very far apart and offered many contrasts. The English colleges which sprang up in considerable numbers in the next ten years varied widely as they selected different elements to copy, or added features of their own. There were certain common features, but individuality was very strong.[4]

They all drew their candidates from the same section of society— lower middle class or artisan. They did not even get the best of these. There were no government grants to students, and the rewards and honours of the teaching profession did not encourage recruitment. Teaching was looked upon as the last refuge of the incompetent; and whether the lads were sent by parents or patrons a common type was selected.

'No man', said an inspector, 'who can pay £25 a year to educate his son is likely to send a likely lad to be a teacher. A farmer or a tradesman may send a youth weak in mind or body, while good men of poorer families are excluded. If the Government would pay for them there would be far more applicants of better quality.'

Or as another realist phrased it to explain the difficulty in extending the course beyond a few months: 'The amount of time that men are prepared to spend preparing for an occupation is proportionate to the rewards expected from it. Teaching is a profession which has no prizes. Therefore in our "commercial country" no one will spend much time training for it.'

Kay-Shuttleworth explains the matter clearly:[5]

The Normal schools are at present supported partly by funds contributed by the Central Societies and Diocesan boards and partly by the sums paid by the patrons or friends of students to procure their settlement in the profession.

As the Central Society contributes for the most part only half the requisite funds, the selection of the candidates for admission is narrowed to the class who are able and willing to pay.

Unfortunately the tendency is to select young men wanting in those natural energies, physical or mental, requisite for success in an independent career in life.

Ill adapted as this class of students is for success in the Normal school, the number of candidates presented by patrons and friends, on the terms of payment required by the Normal schools, is barely sufficient to keep those schools in activity. There is therefore no opportunity for selection; and unless other sources be developed, even this imperfect supply is precarious, and liable soon to fail.

Too often the students were physically defective, and they were almost all deplorably ignorant.

It is reported that a great number of the candidates and students of the Normal schools show signs of scrofula, and that generally their physical temperament is sluggish and inert.

The Scottish students at Glasgow were well qualified by English standards. The reports of the English inspectors are full of comments on the ignorance and incompetence of the students at entry, and sometimes on their weakness when they leave. Of the girls at Whitelands it was said: 'Their state of ignorance is not owing to any want of sufficient instruction in the training school, but to the deplorable neglect of sound elementary education in the families of those who are raised a little above the poorest classes.' Of the men at Chester: 'On entry, out of 13, the papers of only 2 or 3 seemed adequate. 7 could scarcely write, 7 could not spell a simple sentence, 6 knew only the first four rules of arithmetic.' In general: 'The candidates have not been grounded in ordinary knowledge. They have too often had no further instruction than what can be obtained in an elementary school of average character, during the usual period of attendance, till 13 years of age.'

A few of the students came straight from school, the greater number had worked at other occupations. This added to the difficulty of their poor education. They were not ready to learn. 'The process by which a labourer or mechanic is converted at once into a student is a moral violence. It involves a disruption of a regimen of mind and body.'

Moreover, 'They do not for the most part enter the profession from inclination, and it is therefore proportionately difficult to give the right moral direction to their minds, and to kindle in them energies equal to the difficulties they must encounter.'

To these weaklings the colleges, with one accord, offered a life of unremitting activity.

The master is to be prepared for a life of laborious exertion. He must, therefore, form habits of early rising, and of activity and persevering industry. . . . The day is filled with the claims of duty requiring the constant exertion of mind and body.

In pursuit of this aim they all got their students up at 5.30 or 6 in the morning and kept them incessantly occupied till 9.30 or 10 at night. In one college there was a conventual half-hour of 'Recreation' twice a day after meals, in some others there was no provision for any release of tension—unless scrubbing the floor could be so thought of. This activity was not sweetened by the phantasies of ambition. The student was to be 'prepared for a humble and subordinate position, and though master of his school, to his scholars he is a parent, and to his superiors an intelligent servant and minister'.

The dietry provided was in accord with this prospect. There was a common pattern. Breakfast at 8 consisted of tea and bread and butter. There was a substantial dinner at one, with meat, pudding, potatoes, and, frequently, half a pint of small beer. Tea was some time between 5 and 7 and again consisted of tea and bread and butter.

By contrast the academic subjects were bewildering in their variety. They fell into several groups. Among the religious subjects were scripture, evidences of Christianity, church catechism, church services, Thirty-nine Articles, church history, history of the Reformation. Among the general, English grammar and reading, etymology, geography, history, writing, arithmetic, book-keeping, psalmody. Some might be taught Latin, Greek, natural history, trigonometry, navigation, linear drawing and mapping, French, geometry and algebra. All must study theory and practice of teaching, and teach in the school.

The average period of attendance was somewhat less than a year.

There was another characteristic that the men's colleges shared, though it did not extend to the women's. They were housed in a somewhat grandiose manner. The example here had probably been set by Stow, but his building, though large and expensive, was comparatively restrained. It is described, in the List of Buildings of Historical merit, as 'a two-story block with tower—Renaissance 1837'. The English architects sought an earlier model. Chester College was 'a structure of grave and massive yet picturesque character, and of the Tudor style of architecture, to which its irregular outline is well adapted. It presents a combination of great merit with a very appropriate character. It stands upon groined arches, the space under which was used as a model schoolroom, but now as a workshop.' Its material was brickwork with red sandstone facings.

York was a 'spacious building of Elizabethan architecture, whose design might, with no enormous additional expense, have been made to present a considerable degree of beauty'. Saltley went a little farther back in history: 'The site of the building is at Saltley, near Birmingham, and it is in the style of the domestic architecture of the time of Edward III.' Chelsea had a fine house and quadrangle 'in one of the Italian styles', and they had built themselves an octagonal practising school.

Inside these period shells the custom was to give each student a private room, so that he might have proper privacy for saying his prayers. One thrifty inspector commented that it was expensive in window tax and the colleges should get themselves classed as 'charity schools' and avoid it.

These buildings were financed from the funds of the Societies with considerable help from the Committee of Council. The standard building grants were £50 a place—in contrast to the 10s. a place customary for schools—and York received £3500 as capital grant. On the other hand the regulations expressly forbade annual maintenance grants, so that the students could not be helped; and at least two of the colleges were driven to devising special means of keeping themselves in funds.

With these general similarities, the individual colleges were very different. The college which most nearly followed Kay-Shuttleworth's original idea was St Mark's, Chelsea. It occupied a handsome house standing in eleven acres of ground, with a good water supply, a healthy situation and surrounded by a wall. The college, under the control of the National Society, admitted students between the ages of fourteen and eighteen: fifteen or sixteen was the preferred age. 'On admission the candidate is expected to read English with propriety, to spell correctly from dictation, to write a good hand, and be well acquainted with the outlines of scripture history, and to show considerable readiness in working the fundamental rules of arithmetic.' Any knowledge was welcome, and 'a talent for vocal music and drawing are particularly desirable'. Although most of the boys laid claim to these accomplishments, too often they were found 'to be merely nominal'. When the student was accepted he was apprenticed to the National Society and remained in their charge till he was twenty-one. They were responsible for his 'education, clothing and maintenance', and might 'make use of his services as a schoolmaster at any time and in any way that they might think proper'. He was expected to remain in the college for three years, after which time he was placed as an assistant or in charge of a school. He was required to make three annual payments of £25 and provide himself with an outfit of clothes. This £75 was provided by parents, patrons or Diocesan Boards.

The college thus continued Kay-Shuttleworth's idea of a place where boys grew up and were gradually trained for their future duties in a special moral atmosphere, severed from the corruption of the world. They were also to be taught small-scale farming. There were 3½ acres of garden and potatoes, 3 of meadow, flower garden and pleasance. The students spent about three hours a day on the garden work, the pigs, cows and poultry. It was also, the Principal felt, desirable that a village schoolmaster should add the talent of horticulturist to his other qualifications, and his own flower-beds were the very place to practise.

In the same spirit the future duties of the students and their position in life was continually stressed.

The object being to produce schoolmasters for the poor, the endeavour must be on the one hand to raise the students morally and intellectually to a certain standard, while, on the other hand, to train them in lowly service, not merely to teach them hardihood and inure them to the duties of a humble and laborious office, but to make them practically acquainted with the condition of that class of the community among whom they have to labour. . . .

The labours of the house, the field and the garden are intended to elevate, not depress; the studies of the schoolroom, not to exalt, but to humble.

The first principal, the Rev. Derwent Coleridge, son of the poet, who held office from 1841 to 1864, was a remarkable man and gave the college a very definite character. A zealous high churchman, he believed that it was 'the right and privilege of the Church to be the teacher of the nation. We can do nothing without training the young in Christian principles. The country schoolmaster must stand as clergyman's assistant.' Coleridge was also one of the best linguists in England. Besides a knowledge of all the ordinary European languages, ancient and modern, he knew Arabic and was an admiring reader of Welsh poetry. Among his more unusual languages were Hungarian, Coptic, Zulu and Hawaiian.

140

He came to St Mark's after being the master of the Grammar School at Helston.

In accordance with his first interest he set out to make 'the chapel service the keystone of the arch' of his college. Every morning, from 9 to 10, there was a full choral service on the cathedral pattern. As such services were then rare, St Mark's became an object of pilgrimage to those who were interested.

In accordance with his second, he made Latin a subject for all students. As he explained, 'I know of no way so *direct* to strengthen the memory, to teach the difference between words and their meaning, to supply them with a vocabulary adequate to the requirements of their new position, as the repetition of the Latin grammar, followed by the construction and analysis of easy Latin sentences.' In consequence all the college did Latin before breakfast. As a result of this teaching one or two students knew enough to do a fairly difficult unseen, but in the junior classes there was a good deal of confusion. In fact the 'majority of people were not carried beyond the accidence of the Eton Latin Grammar'.

The Rev. H. Moseley, the inspector, was perhaps justified in commenting, 'It will suggest itself that the careful study of English Literature of the highest class offers all those advantages, as a mental discipline, without some contingent evils.'

When the college had been open somewhat over a year Moseley gave an account of the staff and their duties. There were fifty students. The staff consisted of:

The Principal. He teaches Latin before breakfast; shares in reading the services, and is occupied in the mornings with correspondence and college business.

The Vice-principal. He teaches Latin; is responsible for the musical part of the services; lectures till 12 on Theology, History and Geography. From 5–6 he lectures again, and often lectures 6–7 on music.

H. W. Crank is mathematical, writing and general master. During all the school hours he is in attendance on the pupils, remaining with them after evening prayers until 9 p.m. To him the instruction in Latin of the Lower classes, subject to the periodic examination of the Principal, is entrusted.

The complicated duties of the last member of the staff, the industrial master, can best be given in the Principal's own words:

It is his duty to maintain order and enforce discipline by the influence of his character and the force of his personality; to live among them and to lead them on, as well by precept as by occasionally sharing their occupations, to simple, industrious and strictly regular habits; to correct personal conceit and even the least approach to a love of show and finery; to recommend (and this not by words only) a humble and dutiful industriousness, setting forth the religious obligation and beneficial tendency— not merely of labour in general, but of bodily labour in particular, as a blessing growing out of, and, in the case of those by whom it is rightly used, superseding, if I may so speak, the penal character of toil, through Him by whom, after an ineffable manner, it has been rendered holy, honourable and of good report in the church—all this with a reference to the special aim of the institution, as an instrument for elevating and ameliorating the lot of the labouring poor.

In addition to Latin the curriculum was bewilderingly wide. There was scripture, doctrine, arithmetic, algebra, Euclid, trigomometry, church history, geography, English history, English language. Certain of the subjects were, at least in theory, considered in great detail. The Vice-principal, when dealing with the history of the early Church, dealt with heresies. Among the heretics, the gnostics. These were subdivided into Jewish gnostics and Gentile gnostics, and the latter into those of Alexandria and Syria. He ended with a consideration of Marcion, Montanion and Tation.

The Principal clearly lectured in accordance with his interests rather than the capacities of the students. For the first inspection he set a paper, which he marked himself; and the questions are given in the report, with some selection from the best answers. Some of the questions are comparatively simple:

'a. Explain the nature and uses of language.

b. What is a word, as distinguished from a vocable?'

To the second part one of the best students answered:

'A word is the emblem of a thought. A vocable is the sign contemplated in its orthographical structure, without reference to any thought connected with it.'

Other questions were more difficult: 'What relation does grammar bear to logic, rhetoric and poetry? Illustrate by reference to the poetry of the Hebrews, of the Greeks and Romans, of the Anglo-saxons and of the modern English.'

Most of the students wisely left this unanswered.

The College had built itself a most ingenious octagonal practising school, and there eight of the older students taught for some time every day. Unfortunately they did not do it well, and the lessons given for the inspector were poor. 'I should doubt whether their *hearts* were sufficiently in the matter, whether teaching were an occupation in which they took an adequate interest, and the study of it familiar or, indeed, altogether congenial to them.'

Widely different was the new Battersea. It would not take men till they were nearly twenty, and it could seldom keep them more than a year. As compared with the others, the curriculum, except in etymology, was comparatively realistic. And the teaching was good. 'The great merit of this college is that teaching is studied as an art.'

If Chelsea thought of itself as sending out youths who would make their lives in the country, willing assistants to the clergy, Battersea thought that its older men, more formed and experienced, would find their place in the schools of the manufacturing and mining districts. The older men had, of course, been away from even the most modest schooling for longer, and the work of the tutors was correspondingly more arduous.

The discipline of an institution where the inmates are men of mature years, brought together for a common object from different callings, and from different motives, cannot but be difficult. . . . Those vagrant thoughts, to contend with which these men, unaccustomed to give a voluntary attention, would find, if left to themselves, almost a hopeless task, are effectually combated by the zealous watchfulness of their lecturers and the perpetual oral examination to which they are subjected.

All the lecturers were experienced teachers, and they kept the aim of the institution firmly before them: to make men teachers.

Perhaps because of their age, the college trusted its students, with the large amount of eight hours' leisure a week. It had also used part of its grounds for the plantation of forest trees, which had name plates with common and botanical names, and a botanic garden with plants which the students had gathered on their excursions. Indoors, as an inspiration to effort or emulation, 'busts of eminent men have been placed in conspicuous positions in the hall, lecture rooms and passages. The walls are covered with historical prints, tracings from monumental brasses, philosophical diagrams and architectural models.' This decoration was felt to be an 'unobtrusive motive to self-improvement'.

At St John's College, York, a different pattern appeared. There, in order to help with the college finances, a middle-class school, a yeoman school, had been started, and it rapidly appeared that the school was engulfing the college. There were thus 137 boys, 86 of them boarders, and only about 50 students. Students could come at seventeen, and, if they did, were expected to stay three years, but there were older men who only wanted a short course to fit them for 'inferior posts' in teaching and those, already teaching, who wanted a refresher course during harvest.

The first class of students paid £20 a year, but almost all had exhibitions of £10 given by the Diocesan Board or friends. The short-term people paid 10s. 6d. a week.

The staff was the Principal, who spent most of his time teaching the top class of the yeoman school; the Vice-principal, who was usually occupied with the middle school; Mr Field who was master of the middle school; Mr Want 'who has charge of the yeoman boys out of school hours and teaches in the upper school'. There was also a music master who helped; and Mr Hardcastle, an ex-student, who had been made an assistant. Into this pattern the students had to fit. They and the most advanced yeoman boys formed the upper school.

Not much oral teaching is possible. The students prepare the lessons beforehand, and the teaching is almost entirely catechetical. In their third year, if they stay so long, students do some teaching in the Middle school, but they are not required to prepare lessons, nor are they criticized.

The domestic life of the college was bleak. Students were excluded from their bed-rooms during the day, and a lavatory, dressing-room and shoe-room provided downstairs. These did 'not seem adequate in size or fitting for their purpose'. The reason why the students might not use their own rooms was to save fitting them out better. 'I missed greatly the comfortable appearance which they present in some other establishments of this nature—the well-chosen collection of neatly arranged books and the other little property in which the possessor seems to rejoice; there are civilizing influences of no little value connected with such things.'

According to the time-table there was no free period for the students during the day.

Chester again was different. Its students had perhaps the lowest academic attainments of the four, but they were active men, a large proportion of whom had been craftsmen in the local trades. 'They were generally robust and athletic men, four of whom would, I should think, weigh as much as five at Battersea or six at St Mark's.' The staff consisted only of the Principal and Vice-principal, and there was a strong emphasis on industrial work. They were engaged largely on building their own college. The living- and lecture-rooms had been put up, but the students did the decorating; the site had been left rough, and they levelled it; most important of all they were building their own chapel. They quarried the stone, built the walls, worked in wood and metal. Much of the material they begged. The list of crafts pursued is remarkable: carpentry, cabinet making, brass working, bookbinding, painting and graining, turning in wood and metal, stone cutting, lithography, filing and chipping, practical chemistry, varnishing and map mounting, gardening, excavating and transporting earth. The Principal was everywhere animating and directing.

The industrial occupation to be pursued by each student is assigned to him by the Principal, and it is carried on under his immediate and active supervision. In many cases it is that which the student had been accustomed to before his admission, and which he follows with practiced skill—often to the great benefit of the institution in the construction of apparatus, the decoration and repairs to the edifice and the laying out and cultivation of the grounds.

The Rev. Arthur Rigg devoted himself to these duties and the management of the college with an assiduity which made the inspector fear for his health.

The Principal has the general management of affairs, and he conducts the correspondence, exercises constant vigilance over its domestic affairs and the administration of discipline, and presides not only at the studies of the students, but at their industrial occupations. So much work is hardly to be borne.

In addition there was a commercial school which made a contribution to the finances of the college, but had not developed to the same overwhelming extent as at York.

The discipline was good. 'There was much order and decorum in the College, and complete silence during the hours of study.' Unlike the other early men's colleges there were long dormitories with cubicles fifteen feet by eight. This made ventilation easier, but the dormitories were not allowed to become noisy.

'Entire silence is enjoined from the time when they separate after evening prayers, and an officer, called an orderly, remains in the centre of the transept of each dormitory for ¾ hour after they have retired to rest.'

More use seems to have been made of student officials than at other colleges. There was a *Scholar* whose duty it was to see that all was neat and clean, ring the bell and collect the post. He had to ensure that all shoes were on at least five minutes before prayers (Thursdays and Saturdays excepted) and receive all articles for the shoemaker and tailor before 5 p.m. on Thursday. There was also an *Orderly* whose duty was to keep silence. 'Not to allow any student to make a noise or talk before morning prayers or at meals. To see that the industrial work is well done. To provide a towel every Saturday night for the use of the students in the yard.'

Here, as in most colleges, one of the students' daily tasks was to pump water into the building, and to pump the sewage out.

As a last variant we can take the training college in the Borough Road which had continued from the days of Lancaster. This maintained its organization with pious conservatism. Now, and for some years to come, the average time that the student spent in college was 3–4 months. During this time he spent $4\frac{1}{2}$ hours every day in the model school. His work there approximated to that of the Glasgow students. Stage by stage he went through the whole school, teaching each class in turn; in addition there were the gallery criticism lessons, and the lessons in which the students taught each other. Every day from 4 to 5 p.m. there was a lecture on pedagogy. For the rest,

The upper class consists of students of not less than 3 months' standing. Their attention has been directed to the following subjects: English Language, Mathematics, Natural Philosophy and Natural History. Their studies have been pursued with me from 6–8.30 during three evenings in the week. As much information has been afforded as the students have been supposed to be able to master by study in the early morning of the following day, either privately or in class.

The girls' colleges fared much worse. The early reports on White-lands and Salisbury show that for them there were no new buildings of Gothic grandure and inconvenience; nor was there even the dream of a varied culture. Of Whitelands it is reported:

The whole extent of the ground is about $\frac{1}{2}$ acre. The front, on which the buildings are erected, is in the Kings Rd, Chelsea. The premises generally are unworthy of and unsuitable for the great objects for which they are used. The rooms are badly situated for their purpose; they are, with few exceptions, low, ill lighted, and insufficiently ventilated; they are deficient in number, and inconvenient in size. The dining room is most inconveniently situated, placed at the end of a long wooden passage, and at the top of a flight of rickety stairs. It is low, dark, ill ventilated and ill shaped. . . . The laundry and scullery are altogether inadequate for their purpose, and are overrun with rats, from which it is hardly possible to keep the premises free, as there is a range of low, old buildings connecting the two houses occupied by the institution. . . .

When there are new buildings there will be even less space in the garden which is already overlooked.

Salisbury was a little more fortunate in its buildings. 'The house, originally rented and then purchased, is in the close, and may be generally described as a commodious residence for a large family. It is in good substantial repair.' There were 12 bedrooms for 32 pupils, there was no infirmary and the dining-room was much too small, it looked out on the street, and was a long way from the kitchen. The inspector thought it might make a good committee room.

On the academic side Whitelands had the advantage. There was a reasonably adequate staff. Mrs Field was in charge, assisted by Miss Lowman who gave the chief secular instruction with the help of Miss Cuckow and Miss Murphy. There was a resident chaplain to teach religious knowledge, and Mr Tate from Battersea came to teach arithmetic twice a week. As Mr Tate was the foremost exponent of arithmetic teaching in London the girls were lucky.

The main books in use were:

Latham *Small Grammar*, Arnold, *Exercises*, Sullivan, *Geography*, Gleig, *School History*, Mrs Markham, *History and conversations*.

But the main interest of the institution lay outside academic work:

They are carefully instructed in the art of plain needlework, knitting, marking and darning. To give them practice and experience in this department they are expected to cut out and make up the various articles of clothing secured to the poor children of the schools by their clothing clubs. They are also required to cut out and make their own clothes, as well as to undertake all other plain needlework which may be sent to the institution.

Pupils have also been in the habit of making themselves useful in the laundry; but owing to the crowded state of the Institution it has been found impracticable during the last few months to enforce this regulation.

It says in the prospectus: 'Their attention will not be confined to the studies of the schoolroom. Whatever skill or knowledge may be of use to a poor man's family, this will be diligently imparted.'

All this was liberal in comparison with Salisbury:

For some years Mrs Duncan not only superintended all the details of the Institution, but was the sole instructress of the pupils. Since Michaelmas 1845 she had had the assistance of Miss Bolland who was trained under her, but she still devotes the greater portion of her time to the work of teaching. . . .

One servant only is employed, a plain cook. The pupils, who, according to the rules, are to assist in doing the work of the house as the governess shall direct, do, in fact, act as housemaids. It was intended that they should acquire the habits of industrious and well trained domestics, so far as should be found possible without interfering with their prescribed course of studies. Of course due care is taken to instruct the pupils in every department of needlework. . . .

The library contains few books, and is strikingly deficient in works of reference. The supply of apparatus is proportionately scanty. . . .

The Time Table gives a complete account of the distribution of lessons. But the interruptions to which the governess is exposed on account of domestic affairs and frequent visits of enquiry must render it a matter of extreme difficulty to adhere to this system. . . .

'It is said, and doubtless with great truth, that occasional employment in even such work as scrubbing, cleaning shoes, etc. has a beneficial tendency in correcting faults of vanity, indolence, etc. and in giving a practical lesson in humility; and I should be far from wishing to abolish it. But . . .' it would be far more use to learn catering and various modes of housekeeping, and if there were good arrangements they might also learn to keep accounts.

Even their teaching practice was difficult. They taught in the National School but the 'schoolroom is unfortunately at too great a distance from the Training College (nearly $\frac{1}{2}$ mile) and by no means a model as regards arrangements and organization'.

They worked as long a day as the men, and probably had harder physical labour on worse food. The trouble was that they died, or showed such signs of a 'weak constitution' as made it necessary for them to leave. And this in spite of a medical examination on admission. At Salisbury, in the year before the report, two had died, and five been compelled to give up the course.

Perhaps the humblest of the women's colleges, though almost the most useful, was the college in the Gray's Inn Road run by the Home and Colonial Infant School Society. Infant schools were popular with parents, and are almost universally praised by inspectors. The demand

7 Schools of the 1860s and 1870s
a *Above* Educational dreariness. Town school built about 1860
b *Below* Village School, Hinton, Hants

8 Village Schools of the 1860s and 1870s
a *Above* National School, Moreton, Dorset
b *Below* National School, Owermoigue, Dorset. Built 1873 by
the Rev. J. R. Cree, squire and rector

for teachers was insatiable. The college gave a 20-week course at a cost of 8*s.* a week, and could take 36 students. Of the intake over recent years the inspector found that 88 were unemployed, 32 in business, 26 had been engaged in millinery or needlework, 15 in service, 39 in teaching. As the inspector comments, 'A single woman could often scrape together £6 which besides giving her a qualification, would keep her in reasonable comfort for 20 weeks.' When they came they knew practically nothing, and the course was devoted as much to their general improvement as to practice in teaching.

Of the course Tremenheere dryly observes: We must note 'that a distinct profession is made to inform the teacher in the principles of the art of teaching; that the range of study in this and the various points of general information, though of an elementary character, is extensive; and that the time in which all this is done is remarkably short'.

Some of the instruction that they received, and that they wrote out afterwards, was slightly absurd. When asked to 'Sketch a lesson on butterflies for children 2 years old', the answer was:

The point of the lesson would be to lead the children to distinguish the parts, and the uses of each of these parts to the animal; and also to try and cultivate humane and benevolent feelings towards the butterfly.

Yet these women did go out to do most valuable work, and to establish what an inspector described as 'a fragment of a more perfect system of Education'.

What, in fact, did the students learn under these conditions? The girls very little, except in a few cases. It was hardly possible that they should. In the early days, both they, and the men, came without any but the most rudimentary early training, with practically the whole world of knowledge closed to them. In the colleges the time at their disposal was deplorably short, and it was extremely difficult to employ even that to full advantage. By their very constitution, the Anglican colleges were committed to long periods of chapel services, and teaching on a variety of Church topics. There was also industrial work of various kinds. At Chelsea, at least $9\frac{1}{2}$ hours a week (not counting Sunday) were spent in chapel, and $4\frac{1}{2}$ in scripture and Church history. Industrial occupations took 15 hours a week, Latin 6 and all the other literary subjects about 7. The proportions were not so very different in the others.

Even in the time available how could a wide general knowledge be provided? If the aim was to 'elevate' the students and make them fit to co-operate with the clergyman, surely they must know something. The inspectors were always complaining of the lack of general knowledge, of English and of general culture. These are attainments which require years of early training to achieve, and there was little hope that, whatever the colleges did, their students would attain them. Perhaps they did their best by imparting scraps of information which were learned by heart.

The specimens of question and answer that are given in the early reports show something of the standard achieved. Of course the answers quoted are the best.[6]

In English history the type of question was: 'To what reigns would you attribute the introduction of the feudal system; the making courts of justice stationary and open to all; trial by jury?' The answer which was quoted as of first quality ran:

The feudal system was introduced into Britain by William the Conqueror, but the making courts of justice stationary and open to all was extorted from John when he signed the Magna Charta, because they had, before this time, followed the person of the king, and justice was not faithfully administered, the advantage being gained by those who could pay the greater sum of money. Trial by jury was founded as early as the reign of Alfred, but it may be said to have been revived with full force in the reign of John.

The best answers in geography are too long to quote, and on the whole that seemed to be the most successful subject.

In arithmetic all could 'Find the value of 137 at $£1. 7. 6\frac{1}{4}$', but none could 'Write down the equation of a circle, taking $2a$ for the diameter, and making the extremity of the diameter the origin of coordinates'.

When asked to construct a triangle the sides of which should equal three given straight lines, almost all failed; and no one could explain how a paper kite rises in the air.

When Moseley was examining Chelsea he was so anxious to be unbiased that he submitted the trigonometry paper to one of his friends, a professor at King's College. The report was not very encouraging.

I cannot report great excellence in any of the papers sent me. Four questions were simply examples of the simplest case of oblique angled triangles. The particular questions were thus answered. One which involved a slight knowledge of the theory of logarithms was generally

150

solved erroneously, and the other which demanded the numerical value of sin 30° was not done by any of the pupils. . . . They would have known much more of trigonometry if they had been taught systematically.

The subject which was dearest to the hearts of the colleges, and through them later to the schools, was etymology. And it was the one in which success was least possible. With students who barely knew English and no other language it could not be otherwise.

One college instructed its unlettered students, who hardly stayed four months, in the 'Structure of English Language including Greek, Latin and Saxon derivations'.

At Battersea no Latin was taught, but these are questions and answers in the test paper: '*Q*. From what Latin roots are the words accent, curry, carnage, success derived?'

Wisely ignoring 'curry', the candidate derived two (cum laude) as follows: 'Carnage: from carnis, flesh: whence also, incarnate, carnivorous, carnival.

Success: from sub, under and cedo, to yield: whence also accede, recede, concede, proceed, cede.'

A second answer is also quoted, and is practically identical—down to the errors.

How arid this teaching could be is shown by the report of a lecture given by one of the tutors at the Borough Road to impress an inspector: 'Mr Curtis gave a very exhaustive lecture on the grammatical termination -ing, drawing out the various significations and tracing back the termination to the primitive Saxon.'

Among the students there must inevitably have been a few of outstanding mental ability, natural scholars who could learn all and more that was offered to them. If we look down the lists of students' marks it is possible to pick out a youth with abilities in mathematics, or another in literature. For them the intellectual fare must have been as painfully inadequate as it was beyond the abilities of the majority. It was only later, when the students entered college with an appreciable amount of knowledge, that anything like a reasonable course could be evolved.

The students were training as teachers, and instruction in the art should have held a large place in the course. It clearly did at Battersea and at the Borough Road. York, Chester and Chelsea all seem, for various reasons, to have rather neglected it. At Battersea under Kay-Shuttleworth one of the first college activities was to start the production of a set of school text-books. His tutors were actively engaged in devising methods of teaching the different school subjects, and preparing text-books on the methods. This part of the work was very eclectic. Reading was to be taught on the Phonic Method as in Germany, Prussia and Holland. The system of writing came from Geneva, and of arithmetic from Pestalozzi via Ireland. The method of drawing from models was invented by M. Dupuis and that of singing popularized by Mr Hullah.

There was at this time no comprehensive book on Education in English, though, naturally, the Germans had already produced some. They had already reduced it to a system comprising three parts, *pedagogik*, the philosophy of education; *didaktik*, the art of communication; and *methodik*, school and class management. G. B. Denzel of Esslingen had produced a particularly full work which was referred to with respect by the inspectors. He ranged far over psychology and theology as well as dealing with problems of schools—but, unfortunately, it had not been translated.

At the beginning of the period, English students had only a little book by Henry Dunn, secretary of the British and Foreign Schools Society, on the *Principles of Teaching*.[7] It is written in the traditional, humble form of Letters to a Friend, and it could be spoken of with scorn when compared to the German work. Yet it is full of good sense and humanity. Much of it is still said in every course of education lectures; and the latest theories of teaching merely repeat many of his aphorisms. The first chapter on 'the Pleasantness of Teaching' analyses well the rewards of the constitutional teacher. 'The exercise of this kind of power, or what we call *influence* is universally grateful; the intensity, the exquisiteness of the enjoyment depending on the number of minds that can be influenced.' He finds the final justification of the calling in an 'unflinching faith in the efficacy of early instruction as a means of moral regeneration'. We still find the benevolent—and intelligent—despot the most valuable member of the profession.

He is absolutely opposed to any harsh government in the schools. A teacher must have the power to interest children, that is 'to make them happy in the performance of duty'. He must pick out the natural leaders in his school and rely on them. 'Since they *will* be leaders, pre-occupy their talent for command, and employ it on the side of order and industry.' Trust them and you will in this way create the virtue for which you give them credit. Disorder will only arise if the children are insufficiently or improperly occupied.

'Take care that every pupil shall at all times have something useful to do and a motive for doing it.' And when judging the children's work and behaviour give praise for the good rather than blame for the bad. Above all, remember that children are children, and adapt yourself and your methods to their state. 'Do not be found among those who foolishly complain that children are *childish*—they ought to be so.'

On the moral side there must be religious teaching, but the great work is to build up moral habits. These will never come except in an atmosphere of affection. 'To accomplish any good at all the affection of your pupils must be secured. If they do not love you, they will repel all your attempts to do them good. There must be sympathy between you and them, or all your efforts to influence them will be in vain.'

It was felt that such unpretentious good advice was hardly sufficient, and that a more philosophical background should be provided. The two most esteemed moral philosophers of the day, though one was dead, were Dugal Stewart, formerly Professor of Moral Philosophy at Edinburgh University, and Dr Abercrombie, first physician to Her Majesty in Scotland. Both wrote in the analytic and introspective manner which produced its final flower in this century with Stout's Manual. There is much of interest in their observations, but very little that could be made the basis of Educational theory; so that the 'Manual' that Dunning produced for his students at the Borough Road after reading them cannot have been very helpful.

Some ten years after Dunn's book, a rather larger and more self-confident work, in the same tradition, was published by A. R. Craig.[8] It is exceedingly well written and is full of good sense. Much of it—the insistence on the importance of love in early training, and the damage that can be done to infants by a failure to show intelligent affection—has been rediscovered nearly a century later. He repeats Dunn's emphasis on the importance of good *habits* in moral training, and in the same spirit claims that only through love and affection can such habits be formed. They can never be produced by unnatural demands or harshness. 'Love not fear must be the basis of action.'

'What can be more intolerable to healthy children than to compel them, under pain of a beating, to sit still in one position for an indefinite period? And when to this may be added the dreariness and stupidity of committing some unintelligible memory lesson, the temptation to exchange a joke with a joyous companion, the physical depression of an ill ventilated room, or wet day'; if he then yields to the temptation to play he does not *feel* that he has done wrong; and will sin again if he be not cowed by fear. Crime and punishment then become a competition, and there is no moral effect. Instead of punishment the child should be shown the advantage of what he is asked to do.

Under these circumstances the use of corporal punishment degrades the child, but it degrades the teacher more. No wonder that school-masters are excluded from good society when they rule by the rod. 'The school flagellator directs his cowardly punishments against mere helpless infancy; so that as long as society prefers courage to cowardice, cool temper to irritability, and talent to incompetency, either the individual or profession that gives proofs of such disqualifications must be kept in the background.'

The passages in both books on intellectual training are rather less enlightened. Dunn gives a sample lesson in what he thinks the best manner. It is for class III in the Borough Road schools on words of three letters.

'Monitor. Spell BEE. B e e. What is a bee? A little insect. What is it fond of? One boy: Sugar. Another: Flowers. What sort of flowers? Roses, tulips, buttercups. What else is a bee fond of, what does it like to do? Work . . .'

Craig does not sink so low. He has some very just condemnation of the common teaching of spelling which he calls 'a labour without the slightest possible benefit as an auxiliary in learning to read or to spell'. He feels that all the grammar necessary for one's own language is learned in learning to talk, but he believes in etymology, which can be studied by anyone even without much knowledge.

'It is a mistake to imagine it necessary to study Latin and Greek, formally, in order to attain a knowledge of the etymology of English. For all practical purposes a vocabulary of Greek and Latin roots and pre-positions is quite enough.'

When he comes to discuss anything further in the way of general knowledge he can only suggest the gallery lessons on objects as given in Glasgow.

In their emphasis on kindness and regard for children these books are closely in accord with the views expressed by the inspectors, and, could they have been listened to, the schools would have been very different. Unfortunately conditions put an intolerable strain, even on the best men; and far too many teachers were incapable of ruling by love and example. On the intellectual side the customs of the day were too firmly fixed to be disregarded, and the teachers could not see their way to the wider world that the more idealistic inspectors imagined.

If we consider the students in training colleges themselves it is impossible to believe that they were even passably happy. As one man put it, 'Whilst I was there I thought we were "hardly done by";—the amount of study, the excessive strictness of the discipline, the extreme exactness with which everything must be done. I and others frequently complained of it among ourselves.'

Undoubtedly, with the very brief time at their disposal, dealing with students who had had no training in books or methods of intellectual work, some strictness of compulsion must have been necessary. The incessant occupation considered necessary could easily lead the authorities to neglect any place for recreation or relaxation. In his 'Orphan House' Kay-Shuttleworth provided a common-room for his pupil teachers but says that they will never have time to use it. In some colleges the men were allowed to go to their rooms for private study; in others they clearly had to sit in the class-rooms under supervision. Being but human they must have found some spot for a few minutes idle conversation and laughter. A Saltley student suggested the kind of gathering place that must have been discovered:

There were no recreation rooms for the students. The only place where they could in the least let off steam was a small outbuilding known as the blacking shop across the yard. It was, in fact, a blacking shop, i.e. where the men cleaned their shoes. It had whitewashed walls, and a stand containing boot brushes and dabs of blacking in greasy paper. It was there that the students joked, quarrelled and grumbled. It was the only place where they might smoke.

The girls were even more carefully guarded. Of the Female Establishment at Monksgate, York, it was recorded:

No pupil to go out without leave, nor write letters without permission. The envelopes of all letters to be signed by the Superintendent or Miss C. Cruse.

A different idea of what one of these training colleges felt like, and could mean to a man, comes from the *Life and Opinions of Robert Roberts*. He was a student at Caernarvon. It was a poor, small place, and the reporting inspector dismissed it with scorn:

In the year 1846 a Normal department was formed in the National school at Caernarvon, with a view of training masters for Church Schools.

It is sufficient to state that the master was himself trained for three weeks only, more than ten years ago; and that in addition to his important duties, he gives private instruction to adult pupils, and has charge of the largest National school in North Wales.[9]

Yet after a brief development, it brought to some men the promise of a new life. The author, aged about 16, was in Liverpool with his cousin:[10]

There was a young man who used to visit cousin Roberts pretty frequently of late, and with whom I had formed some acquaintance. He was a shoemaker by trade, an intelligent sociable fellow who had travelled a good deal, and was a great reader. His health was delicate, and like most shoemakers he hated his trade. He had a fancy for being a schoolmaster as a situation more suited to his weak health, and more intellectual than shoemaking. Some friends had advised him to go to the new training college at Caernarvon, informing him that if he succeeded in passing a good entrance examination he might obtain an exhibition which would help to support him for a year at college, till he was ready to undertake a school. . . .

The young man applied, was examined and wrote in delight at his success:

Glorious news! I've passed with flying colours. The examination is as easy as drinking beer. I have an exhibition of 7s. 6d. a week, which will about keep me, for Caernarvon is a cheap place. I was nearly floored in the Catechism, but they excused me, and I promised to learn it more perfectly. . . .

Robert Roberts followed. His cousin made him a pair of boots. Some clothes were got together in other ways. He went from Liverpool and spent a night at his parents' home in the Conway valley, and next day set off to walk over the Llanberis pass to Caernarvon. When he was beyond Capel Curig, on the long stretch of high exposed road towards Snowdon the snow came on with a bitter wind. He would have collapsed but for the brandy that the kind hostess of Capel Curig had given him. As it was, he staggered into a house in Llanberis, frost-bitten.

He went on next day and underwent his examination. In it he did so well that they decided to give him an exhibition of 4s. a week out of the bishop's fund, besides the usual exhibition of half a crown. He was delighted: 6s. 6d. would keep him in comfort; but when it was cut to 4s. he was hard put to it. 'A shilling loaf of bread, half a pound of butter, and half a pound of bacon were my weekly allowance. This with 1s. 6d.

for lodgings absorbed all the four shillings except a few pence, which went to buy a few eggs (they were three a penny then) and now and then a postage stamp for a letter.'

The students at the time numbered twenty.

We were a miscellaneous lot. Two or three were tolerably well educated. could write grammatical English and knew some Latin and Greek; but the greater number were much less advanced. There was but one teacher, the Principal, and in consequence we were taught in one class for most subjects. It is true that Mr Foster, the master of the model school, used to give us lessons in the evening, but he was too ignorant for his lessons to be of any use. We also had a Music Master, whose weekly lessons were equally void of beneficial result. . . . However I did work, to some extent, and made considerable progress, especially in mathematics, for which the Principal, being a Dublin man, had a liking.

One week out of six was spent at the Model School for the purpose of obtaining a practical knowledge of the art of teaching. As a rule we greatly objected to this as a waste of time. The Caernarvon boys were so thoroughly savage in their manners, and behaved so rudely to the 'Trainers' as they called us, that our attempts at teaching them were on the whole a grievous failure, and the week at the school was a weariness of spirit. If we attempted to chastise any of these promising pupils, we were sure to have a crowd about us on our way home; enraged women volleying Billingsgate, and their precious offspring volleying stones at us. When I went to Caernarvon first, this street war was almost an everyday occurrence; one or two timid students were frightened away.

Robert Roberts was a man of great intellectual ability, and, had fortune been kind, would have made a name for himself as a scholar and linguist. When after four months at college he completed his course honourably, his friends gave him some books: a Septuagint, a Greek Testament, a Homer, Adams' Antiquities, Robinson's Lexicon and a few theological works. He could read all of them with understanding.

Notes

1. Minutes, 1841, p. 3; Correspondence with the Glasgow Educational Society; p. 34, Correspondence with the Educational Committee of the General Assembly of the Church of Scotland.
2. *The Training System at the Glasgow Normal Seminary* (new ed. 1840); it has illustrations; *Teaching and Training* (1847); *Bible Emblems* (1855).
3. Minutes, 1840, pp. 412 ff.
4. The Reports on which this account is based are: Battersea, Minutes, 1842–3, pp. 60, 189; St Mark's, Chelsea, Minutes, 1842–3, p. 283; 1844, II, p. 582; 1845, I, p. 324; Home and Colonial Infant School Society, Minutes, 1842–3, p. 573; Borough Road, 1846, II, pp. 294, 334; 1851–2, p. 397; Cheltenham, Minutes, 1850–1, p. 140; Caernarvon, Minutes, 1852, p. 245; Chester, Minutes, 1844, II, p. 626; 1845, I, p. 366; 1847–8, II, p. 476; Whitelands, Minutes, 1847–8, II, p. 497; 1848–9–50, II, p. 668; Salisbury, Minutes, 1847–1848, p. 506; 1848–9–50, II, p. 717; York, Minutes, 1847–8, II, pp. 525, 542.
5. Kay-Shuttleworth, *Public Education* (1853), pp. 62 ff.; *Four Periods of Public Education* (1862), p. 480.
6. Minutes, 1847–8, I, p. cxi.
7. 2nd ed., 1837.
8. *The Philosophy of Training* (2nd ed., 1847).
9. Minutes, 1852, p. 245.
10. Robert Roberts, *Life and Opinions*, p. 239.

Chapter Eight

The progress of the schools

Kay-Shuttleworth had hardly got his inspectors organized and more or less accepted in the schools when another storm broke, and almost wrecked the policy that he was attempting to establish. The reports on social conditions which were published from 1841 to 1844 produced the most violent feelings in the nation. From them the governing class first really learnt the conditions of children's work in mines and factories; of women's and children's work in agriculture; and the sanitary condition of large towns and populous districts. They were horrified. The physical and mental gap which existed between the rich and the poor had kept the majority of the well-to-do genuinely ignorant of the conditions under which the mass of the people lived. Among the more immediate results was a Factory Act which attempted seriously to limit the hours of work for children, and, as a necessary consequence, to provide part-time education. There were to be Factory schools, supported out of the Poor Rate. The Church immediately demanded control of these schools. The Master was always to be a member of the Church of England, and the clergyman and churchwardens were to be ex-officio members of the governing body.[1] With certain slight concessions to conscience, the children were to be compelled to attend church. The whole non-conformist body united in opposition to this attempt to use public money for the support of sectarian schools; and, in the face of this unanimity, the proposal was dropped.

Kay-Shuttleworth, though he deplored the attitude of the Church, would have accepted their control of schools in the hope that once the rudiments of a state system of education had come into being it might develop into toleration. As it was, he rightly foresaw that the hope of a state system must be postponed for a generation and the field left to the voluntary societies.

The Factory Bill, in the form in which it left the Commons, demanded that children should be compelled to produce a certificate of part-time attendance at school. The school attended must be efficient; and if, in the opinion of the inspector, no suitable school existed, he was empowered to establish one, financed by a levy of 1d. a week from the children's wages, the remaining expense being met by the employers. When the Bill went to the Upper House, the Lords, with their resolute opposition to any form of education, cut out the financial clause, leaving the inspector powerless. With no control over the schools they ceased to struggle. Some children were fortunate and found a decent school. Many more went to some private venture school which had no merit. Inspectors shrugged their shoulders and accepted certificates from teachers who could barely write their names.[2]

Even had the original intentions of the Bill been carried out, half-time education could not be expected to do much good—the children were not in a fit condition. They came

straight from the mill weary from work, and in some circumstances dejected by its circumstances.

In the clothing districts, their faces, necks and hands are deeply stained with the blue of the dye used for the cloth. From the spinning mills they come covered with the 'flock' of the yarn—their hair thickly powdered with it, the black velveteen dress of the lads and the thick brown dresses of the girls bearing on them plentiful memorials of the scene which they have just left—the mill with its fluff-laden atmosphere and its continual whirl of machinery; they seem to take their places in the school as if they did not belong to it, and had no business there. . . .

They were regularly put by themselves, where they would not contaminate cleaner children, and where they would not interrupt the business of the school—to which their short period of attendance made them almost strangers. Yet, undoubtedly, some children learnt something, and the shorter hours of work, even if the time saved was spent in a parody of education, was so much gain.

This failure left the schools to develop without further assistance, and the inspectors to continue their work of education and persuasion.

Throughout this period the number of schools continued to grow. The disturbance of 1843 had been a great stimulus to the voluntary societies. As a cynic remarked, 'the next best thing to the government doing something about education is for it to threaten to do so'; but, even apart from any unusual activity, the list of capital grants for new schools runs every year to some twenty foolscap pages. A time was approaching when most children, except in two classes of districts, had some chance of an education. The exceptions were the very poor small rural parish, and the equally poor, crowded district in the industrial town. The difficulty sprang from the nature of the system. The *Quarterly Review* said in 1861:

> The expenses of popular education in this country are mainly defrayed by private charity, the most gigantic effort ever made by private charity to perform a public duty. . . . This is the only scheme that could have been introduced into our free, tolerant, dissentient, and jealous country. It has grown up gradually, the creation of circumstances, and has adapted itself to them; like some tree, self sown on a rock, whose misshapen but healthy roots bear the impress of the fissures from whence they spring.

In the poor parishes there was no source of charity. A survey of country districts could produce such entries as:

> Llanfanfawr, Brecon: no school. The parish though extensive is one of the poorest in the principality. There is no resident landlord in it, and the inhabitants cannot afford to pay for the education of their children. Every attempt to establish a school has met with no success.

And another, of the towns, revealed that in Oldham and Ashton with a population of 105,000 there was not a single public day school for poor children; and nobody, except perhaps the clergyman, who thought there ought to be one.

The schools were financed by subscriptions, collections, endowments (where these existed) and fees. The fees varied between 2*d.* and 6*d.* a week with a few of the richer children paying 5*s.* or so quarterly. These sources of income were usually insufficient to meet the expenses of the schools. Of a list of 150 schools in the North of England of about this date 77 were in deficit, and some 57 had a surplus. Some were not returned a second time and had presumably died of want.[3] A few examples will show the pattern.

	Subscriptions	*Collections*	*Endowments*	*Fees*
Knottingly	£9. 4. 0	—	£11. 12. 0	£58
Receipts £79	Expenses £87—Master's Salary £85			
Oldfield	£15	—	—	£18
Receipts £33	Expenses £32. 17. 0—Teacher £28			

	Subscriptions	Collections	Endowments	Fees
Harrogate	£22	£90	—	£9

Receipts £121 Expenses £108—Master £90

Salford

| St Mathias | £47 | £100 | — | £138 |

Receipts £285 Expenses £190—Master £160

Such a thriving school as St Mathias in so generous a district can be contrasted with the school at Clayton-le-Moors where the only income was from fees of £25. The cost of the school was £109 and the teacher received £90.

This last example emphasizes the fact that behind nearly all these schools stood someone who was prepared to make up the chronic deficit. Usually it was the clergyman. Again and again the inspectors mention the extent to which education was subsidized by the individual clergyman.[4] He, more than anyone else, saw the value of the school; and, even when he was badly paid, he was still prepared to accept the ultimate financial responsibility, and might easily contribute a tenth of his income.

The inspectors dreamed of a time when the schools could be self-supporting from fees. There is one school mentioned several times as being so. It was at King's Somborne, Stockbridge[5]—a retired spot, which has still not lost its rural character. There, under an unusually able master and an understanding clergyman, the school flourished, unassisted. 'The education of the children meets with no encouragement from the farmers and we have no resident gentry to make it a matter of charity.' The children attended in ever-increasing numbers, and many stayed till they were fifteen or so. The secret was that the children were so well taught that they were pleased to stay, and the parents saw clearly the benefit of their attendance. Unfortunately the school was unique.

The children, with whom most of these schools had to deal, made education difficult. In the country, the boy had often been scaring birds or herding cattle for some years before he came to school, and the nature of the work had already produced premature stupidity. The child from an industrial town, whether he was a recent immigrant, or an established inhabitant, was often rendered almost ineducable by his employment. Perhaps Kay-Shuttleworth is painting too dark a picture, but it must have been true of many children.[6]

The manufacturing districts of Lancashire and Yorkshire have been fed by a constant immigration from the wolds of North Yorkshire and the Border. A family enters a manufacturing village; the children are at various school ages, from seven to eleven. They probably have never lived but in a hovel; have never been in the street of a village or town; are unacquainted with common usages of social life; perhaps never saw a book; are bewildered by the rapid motion of crowds; confused in the assemblage of scholars. They have to be taught to stand upright—to walk without a slouching gait—to sit without crouching like a sheep dog. They have to learn some decency in their hair, skin and dress. They are commonly either cowed or sullen, or wild, fierce and obstinate. In the street they are often in a tumult of rude agitation. Their parents are almost equally brutish. They have lived solitary lives in some wild region, where the husband has been a shepherd, or hind, or quarryman or miner, or turf cutter or poacher. . . . Such children as these form a large portion of the scholars that the schools of the cotton and woollen districts have to civilize and Christianize. . . .

What has to be done in the case of the children who have hitherto worked without protection and without instruction in mines? From eight years of age they have sat daily in black darkness, with their feet in the mud or running water, and the dripping roof of the mine overhead —opening and shutting the ventilating doors—or as they grew older dragging the corves or waggons.

Or take the life of a potter's child. At eighteen months or two years old he is sent to one of the dames who gain a livelihood by taking care of young children whose mothers are at the factory. There from seven in the morning till eight or nine at night he is stowed away in a small room without exercise or change of air, predisposing his constitution to consumption, which is a common malady in the pottery towns. This continues on an average for four years. He is then at five and a half or six years old sent perhaps to the National School, where he stays one, two or at the most three years; but during the latter part of the time he is sure to be kept away very much, to act as an occasional substitute for some boy who is at work. At eight or nine (earlier if his parents are drunken or improvident, often at six or seven) he begins to work regularly for a journeyman potter, turning his jigger (the potter's wheel to which steam never seems to have been applied) and earning from 1s. to 2s. a week. In a year or two the quick boy will begin 'handling' (making handles for cups) or 'figuring' and earn from 2s. to 4s. By this time a great change has come over him—he has been kept at work twelve to thirteen hours each day, and so, even if disposed to continue his studies, has little time to do so; consequently he now reads badly, and writes worse; and in short nearly all he learned in school is forgotten.

Had even these children attended regularly for several years something might have been done. But they did not. They were always changing schools, when there were schools to change to; and they ceased all education very young. One-third of the children were normally under seven and two-thirds under ten.

In the specimen districts, 42·3 per cent of the scholars had been in the same public day school less than one year, and 22·7 per cent had been one year, but less than two. The proportions for England and Wales are 41·65 per cent of the scholars who had attended the same school for less than one year, and 22·58 per cent who had been one year and less than two.

Some town children had been at as many as six schools during their short period of instruction.

Even during this year or two, attendance was most irregular. In the towns, when the child was unemployed, the parents had little strength to use compulsion; and, as almost all the schools were unpleasant, the child had more than the instability of youth to make him change. In the country there was always something to interrupt attendance: haysel and harvest, cherry, pear, plum and apple picking, scaring the birds from the newly sown wheat. Storms blew and the ways were impassable with mud. As John Gibson, the inspector for Scotland, gravely summed up.

It is therefore upon those children only who are not old enough and strong enough to suffer exposure to the inclemency of winter, and too young for employment in the fields throughout the summer, that the master has an opportunity of bringing his skill and efficiency continuously to bear.[7]

As the gap between these two conditions was very small, hardly anyone received even a short period of continuous education.

The teacher's position was a peculiarly weak one. He was largely dependent on fees, and had no power to compel either parents or children, and no prestige to give his words weight. Shiftless parents failed to send their children to school or supported them in rebellion. In Lancashire there was often a difficulty of another sort.

It is not an unusual thing for a child to present himself alone before the master of a school, make enquiries as to terms and smartly make his own bargain, urging perhaps the lower terms of some neighbouring school, or settling for himself whether he will pay for some accomplishment for which an extra charge is made.

Over such a lad, setting out bare-foot and in rags on the conquest of society, the harassed teacher could have little hold. In almost all the

schools the irregularity of the attendance was partly justified by the inefficiency and unpleasantness of the instruction. The teachers were frequently brutal, and the children were left with nothing to do. One
inspector combines these vices in his description of the typically 'bad'
school.

A bad school, the buildings ill ventilated while yet many of the younger
children are compelled to sit still therein without any provision being
made for their employment or amusement, the teacher occasionally
threading his way through the crowd and repressing with blows the more
obvious ebullitions of disquiet—a school wherein what little is communicated of mechanical skill in reading is so communicated as that the intelligence of the children should be left as far as may be wholly quiescent. . . .
Lessons are required that seem to have been designed for no other end
than to occupy the scholars' time with as small a demand as possible on
the pains and attention of the teacher: the frequent recurrence and duration of writing lessons and the solution of useless problems in arithmetic,
are in part to be accounted for on this principle.

At the beginning of this period, when the teacher was left to struggle,
aided only by some childish monitors, with 150 to 200 children, there
was considerable excuse for the confusion and inactivity. Conditions
were impossibly difficult, and in self defence the teacher gave up trying.
'If a teacher has to struggle with this many headed, many minded mass
. . . If he will not quit his post he must either die, or see it taken by the
enemy.'

If we follow the inspectors into the schools, which they were now
inspecting in more detail, it is possible to get an idea of the teaching and
conditions. As the name of each new inspector appears in the reports
there is, at first, a most depressed account of conditions; in later reports
he is more inclined to find some merit in the schools. He has grown
hardened to their characteristics. And, of course, schools varied. But
allowing for these differences, this is something of the general impression. The school was hot and stuffy, and the clothes and bodies of the
children stank. The inspectors seldom mention the odour directly, but
their obsession with ventilation springs from more than a regard for
health. The windows would almost certainly be shut, and the ingenious
ventilators stuffed with rags.

Some of the schools were filthy. An inspector in Northumberland
could write of 'furrows of dirt on the floor, where the bare feet of the
children delighted to burrow'.[8] The school was also noisy, appallingly

so; it was often impossible for a visitor to hear or be heard speaking. All over the place, in lines of desks, or in semicircles on the floor, would be groups of children ostensibly 'working' with a monitor. The monitor was usually under eleven and he was carrying out his tasks unwillingly and with the disapproval of his parents, who naturally thought that he was sent to school to learn. Sometimes to prevent the parents removing a child who was used too much, the monitors were changed daily, the top class taking the work in rotation. Often, because of this, a single monitor would be in charge of as many as thirty children.

All schools had a full age range, but it was to be hoped that the youngest would be in an infant school. If no infant school were provided, children as young as two might be present. One inspector notes that this produces an utterly impossible situation; but that a teacher should be able to manage if only all the children can read three-letter words when they come.

In general the teaching was by rote, and no attempt was made to make the material interesting or even comprehensible. The inspectors were always urging methods which involved the 'exercise of the intelligence' —and failing to find them. Unfortunately much of the material was of a nature that made it very difficult for a child to be intelligent about it. The universal reading book, too often the only book in the school, was the Bible; and both in language and in thought it was incomprehensible. There was also the catechism. This was normally taught by repetition, with no attempt to explain it. 'A monitor, frequently a child of 8 or 9, seldom, in the lower classes, as old as 11, is told to say the answers and make the class repeat them after him simultaneously or in turn. This is done a dozen times consecutively.' The resulting jargon goes unnoticed and uncorrected in the universal uproar.

The earlier reading was from cards, and proceeded by spelling and repetition. In the 'reading books'[9] of the day we find lists of words taking up the major part of the books, and the actual matter to be read compressed into a few paragraphs, which have little reference to the words learned. After the alphabet, which is generally connected with objects (A stands for Arm; B stands for Barn), come the syllables ba, be, bi, bo, bu, by, ca, ce, ci, co, cy, or reversed ab, ac, ad, and so on. They then proceed to two-letter words, and there are a page or so of sentences like, *I am in*, or *Is he up?* or, most dramatically and mysteriously, *Go on ox, or I am in.* The child is then ready for a list of three-letter words, which he must have learned to spell in a dreary chant. The lists of four-, five- and six-letter words follow. In the search for completeness both the child's natural vocabulary and sense are abandoned. The lists contain such words as trull, whelm, whelp, feud, clew, glew, skrew, as well as shew and jew.

The more persevering books go on to dissyllables and even longer words such as 'pur-ga-to-ry'.

The reading provided begins with an 'easy lesson'. 'He that is a good boy and will mind his book, all will love him', and goes on to harder matters: 'The words of the preacher the son of David. . . .'

A few books offer a little information—but it is very little.

'It did not seem', says an inspector, 'that a process naturally irksome to a child's mind was much facilitated by this method.'

The method of reading itself, when there was anything to read, was no more intelligent. 'The selected harder words are spelt by each child in rotation, the monitor spelling them after each', so that he may correct mistakes. 'Next, each boy in succession reads a word of the text, which is read correctly after him by the monitor. A whole clause is then read by each in like manner, and under the like correction, the stops being named as well as observed. Finally each reads a sentence completely, and when he stumbles, appeal is made to the other boys in succession.' This naming of stops is clearly a general custom and is mentioned several times. 'A reader proceeds to a comma, then stops while the whole class repeat the sentence after him; or the reader goes on to a comma when he pauses and says, "comma one", and is then relieved by the boy next to him.' 'If this plan', the inspector comments, 'makes the children "mind their stops", it certainly leads them to neglect the meaning of the lesson.'[10]

Writing was taught in most schools now, sometimes on payment of a special fee. But only about 50 per cent had the opportunity to write on paper—the rest used slates. Steel pens were taking the place of quills, but the quality of paper used was so poor that it was impossible to write well. Moreover economy demanded that the paper be used to the utmost, and as soon as the page was full it was turned round and crossed. In the majority of schools the writing-desks were arranged round the room and the boys sat facing the wall. It was dark here, the teacher could see the writing only with difficulty, and any general instruction was impossible. How much better, they say, to have the writing-desks in the centre of the room all facing the same way. Moreover the tops of the desks were too narrow, and being against the wall the paper could not be pushed up. The last three lines of every page were hopelessly shaky because the

167

child had nowhere to rest his hand. If the master did not write the copies, the children were given books of specimen letters to copy which were often laughable in their inappropriateness. There were passionate addresses beginning 'My dear Charmer . . .' or 'My lovely Emma . . .' There were notes of invitation to dinner or the theatre, or there were hymns and verses whose sentiments and expression the inspector 'could not approve'.

The arithmetic was normally taught by working a sum on the board with all the children, or as many as thought they knew, shouting out the answers to each step. The work might then be 'corrected' in the same way. This is Gibson's comment on arithmetic at Glasgow, where it was much better taught than elsewhere.

A class, consisting of 17, were doing sums in compound division. On presenting their slates the exercises of 7 were right, and 10 wrong. The sum was written down upon the black-board by the teacher, and the boys were requested to direct him how to work it; they were permitted to do this *simultaneously*, the consequence was that those boys whose exercise had at first been correctly performed, and who, it was evident, knew the rule well, again went through the process, and those for whom this second performance of the exercise was necessary sat apparently almost uninterested auditors.

When the sums had been worked in this way, others, exactly similar, were given; so that the process could be repeated with the minimum of thought. The children had no understanding of the process, and no confidence in their power to do any sum. 'In examining arithmetic,' says one man, 'it is painful to witness the deceit and falsehood practised by the children in their attempts to copy from each other.' Very few of them got far with their sums. One inspector estimated that 80 per cent left without reaching compound rules, and only another 7 per cent got to the rule of three and practice.

Dictation was a slow and laborious business:

In writing from dictation 10 minutes are taken to write down 60 words (of which much time is lost in unnecessary repetitions, and still more because of the unequal progress of the children) and then at least 20 minutes are required to correct the errors upon the slates, during which time the children are sometimes entirely without employment.

Very few children went beyond this. A few children in the top class were drilled in mental arithmetic and etymology, which formed very good display subjects for the annual fund-raising entertainment. For the rest there was a little history and geography, sacred or profane, which was learned by heart. Grammar was hardly ever taught. It was felt to be the prerogative of the upper classes. 'It cannot be denied that a prejudice exists in the higher quarters against the introduction of Grammar as an essential or common part of parochial education.' This same prejudice is laughed at in Shakespeare.

The educational improvement which was slowly spreading into the schools, partly upwards from the infant schools, partly from Scotland with the trained teachers, was the simultaneous or gallery lesson. Stow had advocated it as a means of directing and training the moral feelings of the group, as well as of imparting information. In its translation South of the Border, the moral element was largely lost, and the 'lessons' soon became the main means of conveying information. As there were practically no books to which children could refer, they were dependent on the teacher's words, and the assembling and organizing of material for such lessons became one of the major tasks of the pupil teacher or the student in training.

In its fully developed form the teacher gave two of these lessons every day to the whole school (or later to a section). One was secular, one religious. Such topics as silk, flax, cotton, paper, skins, hemp, corn, glass appear in the earliest lists of secular topics; and kindness to animals, speaking the truth, love of brothers and sisters, obedience to parents, the Goodness of God among the moral. There were also lessons on Bible stories, homilies on texts and explanations of the truth typified by such things as Noah's Flood. By no means all could do it successfully. 'The chief variety of method was the occasional employment of Mr Stow's form of simultaneous teaching by teachers trained in Scotland. . . . Certainly in most of the schools where it was adopted the results were unsatisfactory. Only a small part of the scholars had been kept in an active state; and the knowledge of that portion was vague and loose.'

Yet, with the advent of the better monitors and the pupil teachers, this simultaneous lesson could become the basis of a new type of organization. It was felt that instruction in school could be divided into three types. Intellectual teaching, as questioning, moral, or general knowledge lessons, which should be taken by the master; writing or slate arithmetic which merely requires overlooking; reading and spelling which can be done by monitors. If the classes change round, and the master takes each in turn, and the writers are left largely alone, all the monitors can be concentrated on the reading, and there can be groups of only ten to a monitor.

169

Mr Moseley, whose name became associated with this conception of school organization, offered a suggestion for a time-table.[11]

	Senior Class	2nd Class	Junior Class
9	Prayers Singing etc.		
9.15	Learn by heart Faith and Duty & other passages of scripture	Read to MASTER. Exercise in spelling. Play 5 minutes.	Learn by heart by oral repetition by monitor words to be spelled. Learn to read and spell with monitor. MASTER hears later.
10	Play 5 minutes. Say repetition to & read to MASTER —being questioned as well.	Learn catechism or scripture.	Write on slate for 25 minutes. Play 5 minutes. Go over reading lesson with monitor.
11	Write on slate. Abstract of lesson read to monitor— or composition.	Write on slate the lesson learnt by heart.	Play 5 minutes. Go over lesson and reading with MASTER —being questioned.

11.45 Copy books collected—Grace said.

In the afternoon there would be arithmetic and special lessons in religious knowledge, English grammar and geography.

This tripartite division of teaching came quite soon to be reflected in the recommended building plans, and we get the first real indication of a school divided into class-rooms. (See diagram opposite.)

This system, by which the master would be incessantly occupied in the more exacting teaching, while at the same time keeping a general supervision of the school, was not very eagerly adopted. The inspectors comment that, if trained, the teachers have learned a system which they are unable to discard—the more so that they learnt it without understanding the principles behind it. Others are so afraid of adverse criticism that they dare not initiate any new methods, and prefer to continue with practices which, at any rate, have passed without too much disapproval.

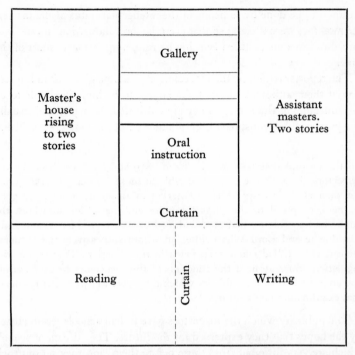

Apart from establishing some order in the schools, the greatest need was for books.

The compilation and publication of a complete set of good school books, which from their cheapness, independently altogether of their excellence, which the great majority of the people are still incapable of appreciating, would find their way into the hands of every schoolboy. It would be difficult to mention anything the accomplishment of which would have a more extensive and beneficial influence upon elementary education.[12]

They were not written in 1842, when this passage was published.

Another matter to which the inspectors continually refer is the questioning of the children. The teaching by rote, which was so universally used, rarely conveyed any true information to the children. Where the book used was in the form of question and answer, the results were almost worse; and the smallest variation, even in the order of the questions, produced answers which were nonsense. If the children could be questioned and made to think about what they read or learned some value might be given to the form of words. But intelligent questioning required to be done by someone of the intellectual status of the master, the monitors were useless; so that even the most industrious master was forced to leave his children learning by rote, unquestioned, most of the time.

The reports written by the inspectors at this time give a vivid impression of their authors. Most of them appear to be highly suitable to be the educators of the nation. They are cultivated, humane, and usually imaginative. They must have gone about their duties with great skill and tact.

All the ground that was won between 1839 and 1846 was won by the inspectors. A result the more creditable to those gentlemen, as they had not then at their disposal augmentation of salary as reward for good teachers, or pupil teacherships for good children. Men in whom the public had confidence had been induced to seek these offices, and Lord Lansdowne and Lord Wharncliffe, on whom successively the appointment devolved, had taken great pains in the selection. That was a wise regulation which limited the function of the inspectors to examination and enquiry, and to the publicity which they were to give to the results of that examination and enquiry.[13]

The publicity which the inspectors gave to bad schools was matched by the hopes that they expressed for the future. They dream of schools which are very different from those before them, and they set out their dreams in their reports so that the world at large can have an ideal of education. Kay-Shuttleworth had given them their cue. In the instructions to inspectors in 1840 he asks questions about the condition of the schools to which few could have given a satisfactory answer.[14]

Enumerate the books used in the several classes under the heads of Reading, Arithmetic, Geography, History of England, Grammar, Etymology, Vocal Music, Linear Drawing and Surveying.

And he explained:

If the mental and moral condition of the rising generation is to be usefully affected through the medium of schools, wider views must be taken of what it is requisite to teach, and of the instrumentality by which it is to be communicated. It is still necessary to repeat that what is commonly called education, namely, the teaching of the mechanical art of reading and writing, with a little arithmetic, and the dogmatical inculcation of scripture formularies, very imperfectly understood, if at all, is not in fact education, or anything more than its unformed, undeveloped germ, possibly containing within it that which may give some additional power to the mind, but very probably in no way reaching and impressing the heart. It is necessary also to repeat, that, if the legitimate educator does no more than this, there are those who will do more—the Chartist and Socialist educator, the publisher of exciting, obscene and irreligious works, he who can boldly assert and readily declaim upon false and pernicious dogmas and principles. . . . To inculcate the leading doctrines of our faith, and to present the main incidents of the holy scriptures in such a manner as shall interest the affections of the young and not alone burden the memory, and to impart some real knowledge applicable to the state of society in which they live and to the world around them, is the work in hand. This the ordinary master or mistress at from 6s. to 10s. a week cannot do.

Following this lead, the inspectors sketched out in various ways their hopes for schools in which vigorous intellectual activity would be assisted by physical exercise, and children acquire knowledge, morals and industry.

Some took complete leave of the possible. Here is Baptist Noel day-dreaming of the perfect school for the children of the poor; and these are the things it should do:[15]

1. The children should be taught to read with fluency and precision, to write in a fair running hand without lines, and to work with rapidity and ease any sum in the first and most necessary rules of arithmetic.
2. Should be made in some degree acquainted with their own language, with the pronunciation, composition and meaning of words, with the elements of grammar, with the simplest rules of composition; and they should be accustomed to express themselves well, by reciting the substance of the lessons they have read.
3. They should learn something of the objects which surround them, beginning with the nearest and most familiar. They may be taught to notice the different flowers, seeds, trees, woods, birds, fishes and quadrupeds of their neighbourhood or county. A thousand objects round them may induce them to examine the principal manufactures of their neighbourhood. (Along with the geography of the British Isles and Europe.)
4. Another subject to which their attention may be turned is cottage economy; especially how they may economize.
5. Children should be taught to take care of their health.
6. Children of the manufacturing districts should know something of the history of their country.
7. To these different branches of knowledge some schools have added drawing, singing, and music; all which studies, besides other advantages,

tend to make children love the school and pursue their studies with greater alacrity.

8. In addition, girls should especially be taught to knit and sew well, to cut out their own clothes and make them; and when any number of children are likely to become domestic servants, they should be taught the duties of that employment in detail.

9. While thus instructed in secular knowledge the children should have such direct religious instruction as they can comprehend.

The inspectors were not of course blind to the real conditions—but they thought the difficulties could be overcome:

I have not been so much struck with a deficiency of the children whom I have examined in that knowledge which is generally the subject of school education as in the want of *general* intelligence and everyday knowledge—a lack of aptitude and vivacity of thought—a paucity of ideas and a corresponding poverty of diction. It is in respect of these matters that so vast a chasm is interposed between the minds of the educated and uneducated man, and it is a distinctive character, I conceive of elementary education, that, to the ordinary subjects of education, it should add these.

The methods of teaching also were to be revolutionized. No longer were the children to sit passively unemployed or engaged in senseless repetition:[16]

A well-trained and skilful teacher will find means to accustom his scholars to put forth and bring into action the faculties of their minds. Quickness of perception, the capacity for accurate observation, a facility in passing from the symbol to the thing signified, are powers educed by exercise and dependent in a great measure for their efficiency upon the habits one forms.

This was to be done 'by a continued and well-sustained effort to give life and vigour to all the processes of instruction', and it was fatal to teach by rote:

For a child to commit to memory that which it cannot understand is a difficult and by no means a salutary exercise of the intelligence; but to conduct the instruction of a child not only without any attempt to cultivate its understanding but to require it to charge its memory with facts which, because contradictory, must be repulsive to its reasoning powers, is worse than useless. The moral sense can only be successfully cultivated by inspiring the child in every process of education with a love of truth. The first step to this result is to satisfy the intelligence on every point which can be rendered clear. By the opposite method schools are rendered repulsive to children.

And, whatever the standard aimed at, all the reports stress that any development of the faculties could only take place in an environment of kindliness. Moreover poor children needed kindness more than the rich.

It seems to me that gentleness is a peculiarly valuable quality in a schoolmaster for the poor. With children of the upper classes, if they get rough treatment at school, they have their kindly sympathies brought out by the education of their home, but with the poor their offspring grow up untoward and stubborn from its never having been realized to them that those with whom they come in contact had any serious care for their welfare.[17]

Worst of all, and destructive of any hope of education, was brutality. The general view of the inspectors was contained in this comment:

I never saw the discipline of a school enforced in so over-bearing and tyrannical a manner, and I never examined children more deplorably and grossly ignorant.

Notes

1. Kay-Shuttleworth, *The School in relation to the State, the Church and the Congregation* (1847), Appendix B.
2. Minutes, 1846, I, p. 439; Newcastle Report, pp. 203 ff.
3. Minutes, 1844, II, p. 300; 1846, I, p. 416.
4. Minutes, 1848–9–50, pp. 195, 309.
5. Minutes, 1847, I, p. 7; 1851–2, I, p. 76.
6. Kay-Shuttleworth, *Four Periods of Public Education*, pp. 582 ff. Minutes, 1846, I, pp. 437, 440.
7. Minutes, 1844, II, p. 286; Newcastle Report, pp. 170 ff.
8. Minutes, 1844, II, p. 249.
9. There is a collection of these books in Liverpool University Library.
10. Minutes, 1840, p. 33; 1844, p. 143.
11. Minutes, 1845, I, pp. 249 ff.
12. Minutes, 1840–1, p. 177.
13. Minutes, 1840–1, p. 177.
14. Minutes, 1840, II, p. 4.
15. Minutes, 1840–1, pp. 169 ff.
16. Minutes, 1844, I, p. 143, Minute on Methods of Teaching.
17. Minutes, 1840–1, p. 318.

Chapter Nine

The Minutes of 1846

The opportunity of development for which Kay-Shuttleworth was waiting seemed to have come in 1846. Lord John Russell was once more Prime Minister, and the repeal of the Corn Laws had checked the rise in the cost of living, and thrown open the ports to the cheap corn which railways and steamships would soon be bringing from the bounteous prairies of North America. The Ten Hours Bill had not yet been passed, but in their hearts the nation had accepted it; and recognized that even the working man had a right to live as a human being. The attitude to education had changed.

The clergy have, God be praised, preached down effectively that heresy of which I remember the prevalence, according to which even good men were induced to suppose that the all-wise God had given to men immortal minds, capable of great things, without the intention, with respect to a large portion of the human race, that it should be exercised. That ungodly selfishness is now exploded by which the upper classes of society were induced to suppose that mental pleasures were a luxury reserved for their exclusive enjoyment.[1]

Under these circumstances there was a trial of opinion in the Commons on 17 July. Lord John Russell promised to everybody's satisfaction to 'give special attention to the Subject of Education'. There was no voice raised against instruction. The 'special attention' was in the form of Minutes of the Committee of Council which were published in August and December.

In draughting them Kay-Shuttleworth had been chiefly concerned with the position and supply of teachers. He rightly felt that on these depended the whole success of education; but that, as things were at present, there was no hope of achieving a satisfactory standard:[2]

There is little or nothing in the profession of an elementary schoolmaster in this country, to tempt a man having a respectable acquaintance with the elements of even humble learning to exchange the certainty of a respectable livelihood in a subordinate condition in trade or commerce for the mean drudgery of instructing the rude children of the poor in an elementary school as it is now conducted.

For what is the condition of the master of such a school? He has often an income very little greater than that of an agricultural labourer, and very rarely equal to that of a moderately skilful mechanic. Even the income is to a great degree contingent on the weekly pittances paid from the earnings of his poor neighbours, and liable to be reduced by bad harvests, want of employment, strikes, sickness among the children, or, worst of all, by the calamity of his own ill health.

Of late years he may more frequently have a small cottage rent free, but seldom a garden or fuel.

Some portion of his income may be derived from the voluntary subscriptions of the promoters of the school—a precarious source, liable to be dried up by the removal or death of patrons, and the fickleness of friends.

Amid these uncertainties, with the increase of his family his struggles are greater. He tries to eke out his subsistence by keeping accounts and writing letters for his neighbours. He strives to be elected parish clerk, or registrar, or clerk to some benefit club. These additions to his income, if he is successful, barely keep him out of debt, and in old age he has no prospect but hopeless indigence and dependence.

To entrust the education of the labouring classes to men involved in such straits, is to condemn the poor to ignorance and its fatal train of evils.

While the condition of the master is one of such privation and uncertainty, he has, by the existing system of school instruction, been placed in a situation the difficulties of which are insuperable, even by the highest valour and skill. Men have been placed without other assistants than monitors in charge of schools containing from 150–300 scholars and upwards. The monitors usually employed are under 12 years of age, some of them being as young as 8 or 9, and they are in general very ignorant, rude and unskilful. The system of monitorial instruction has practically failed in the country under these circumstances. Is it a legitimate subject of surprise that a very large proportion of the children attending elementary schools should not even acquire the art of reading accurately, and that all the higher aims of education should appear to be unattainable?

The essential problem, as he saw it, was to improve the quality and elevate the position of the teachers, and to supply them with assistants who would make their work possible. It was to this end that his scheme was directed.

By no means all the proposals were new. Many of them followed models that he had admired in Holland, and some of them, such as the institution of pupil teachers, had been partially attempted in this country for some years. But now, grouped as they were into an orderly scheme, the proposals represented an entirely new attitude to education.

Kay-Shuttleworth published an explanation of the proposals.[3]

Your Lordships desired to render the profession of schoolmaster honourable, by raising its character by giving the public recognition of impartially awarded certificates or diplomas, and by securing to well trained and otherwise efficient masters a position of comfort during the period of their arduous labours, and the means of retirement on a pension awarded by the Government. They were also anxious to lighten their ill-requited toil in the school by providing them with the aid of assistant teachers trained under their own eyes, and adequate in number to the efficient management of the school.

The arrangements for rearing a body of skilful and highly instructed masters are to commence in the school itself, by the selection of the most deserving of the scholars who are to be apprenticed from the age of 13 to that of 18. By the regulations determining the character of this apprenticeship, the school is to be in a condition fitting to become a sphere for the training of a candidate for the office of schoolmaster. A great stimulus is thus offered to the scholars to qualify themselves by good conduct and by their attainments for appointment as pupil teachers; to the promoters of the school to render its condition complete as respects fittings, apparatus and the supply of books; and to the schoolmaster so to order the discipline and instruction of the school as to raise it to the proper standard of efficiency.

The Regulations then sketch out the course by which a child of thirteen starts on his apprenticeship as a pupil teacher, moves on to a training college and a certificate, and takes charge of a school at a salary of £90 or over. In one of his writings Kay-Shuttleworth gives the salaries of the masters in the school at The Hague. He states that the cost of living was similar, so that the salaries are directly comparable. The headmaster received £75 with a house and garden. His assistants £33–£10. The pupil teachers received from £5 to £2 10s. according to their year of apprenticeship. By this standard the scales for the English teachers and pupil teachers were good.

They were also good when compared with clerkships in the Civil Service. When these were opened to public competition in 1855 men, who were asked in the examination to state the chief merits and defects, as philosophers, of Plato and Aristotle respectively, might be offered a place worth £90 a year and no house. What opportunities of further profit the clerk in the Home Civil Service possessed is not clear. In India his scope was notorious.

On the other hand the salaries offered to teachers compared badly with those of the most highly paid workmen. In the iron works, rollers, the best paid, might make up to £5 a week on occasions. In the cotton mills 30s. was a common wage. A craftsman working independently could earn £2 a week, and feel himself—like Brown the Oxford shoemaker—the 'most independent man in the world'. That was a boast that no teacher was likely to aspire to, even if he earned a comparable wage.

This is how Kay-Shuttleworth describes the imagined progress of his new-style teachers:

> The scholars selected for apprenticeship will for the most part belong to families supported by manual labour; there will thus open to the children of such families a career which could otherwise be rarely commenced.
>
> In each year of the apprenticeship the pupil teacher is to be examined by Her Majesty's Inspector in a course of instruction the subjects of which are enumerated in the regulations. Great care is to be taken that he lives in a household where he will be under the constant influence of a good example.

To prepare them for these examinations, the apprentices were to be taught by the master of the school for 1½ hours a day, and the master was to be paid for teaching them. He also had the benefit of their help in school.

At the end of his course as a pupil teacher the boy would be entitled to a certificate declaring that he had successfully completed his apprenticeship.

Every pupil teacher provided with a certificate at the close of his apprenticeship might become a candidate for one of two employments under the patronage of the Government. In each Inspector's district an annual examination will be held to which all apprentices who have obtained the certificate will be admitted to compete for the distinction of an exhibition

180

entitling them to be sent as Queen's scholars to a Normal School under their Lordship's inspection.

A poor man's child may thus at the age of 13 enter a profession at every step in which his mind will expand, and his intellect be stored, and, with the blessing of God, his moral and religious character developed.

In pecuniary rewards, as a pupil teacher, he will earn from £10 the first year to £20 the fifth year; and as a teacher, if he leave college with a certificate of the third class, the best, he will have an augmentation grant of £25 to £30 per annum, on condition that the managers of the school provide him with a house rent free and with a further salary equal to twice the amount of the grant. He may thus have a house and salary of £90 a year, and even if he has only got one of the inferior certificates he still has his house and £60 a year. In addition he also has an income from school pence and some other subsidiary work as clerk to some benefit club.

Further, the master was to be paid for training the apprentices. If the numbers in the school amounted to 150 he might have six apprentices, one to every 25 children, and he would get £21 a year for the teaching he gave them.

On the other hand, if an apprentice did not get a Queen's scholarship, or did not wish to teach, 'the Government have opened appointments in departments of the public service which have hitherto been the objects of purely political patronage'.[4]

It cannot be expected that members of the middle class of society will to any great extent choose the vocation of teachers of the poor. . . . To make every elementary school a scene of exertion from which the highest ranks of teachers may be entered by the humblest scholar, is to render the profession of schoolmaster popular among the poor, and to offer to their children the most powerful incentives to learning.

The course of learning laid down for the pupil teachers advanced year by year. At the end of the fifth year of apprenticeship the regulations stated:

Pupil teachers will be examined by the Inspector:—

1. In the composition of an essay on some subject connected with the art of teaching.
2. In the rudiments of algebra*, or the practice of land surveying* and leveling*.
3. In syntax, etymology and prosody.
4. In the use* of the globe or in the geography of the British Empire* and Europe*, as connected with the outline of English history. In this year girls may be examined in the historical geography of Great Britain.

5. More completely in the Holy Scriptures, Liturgy and Catechism, *in Church Schools* the parochial clergyman assisting at the examination.
6. In their ability to give a gallery lesson, and to conduct the instruction of the first class in any subject selected by the Inspector.

In the subjects marked with an asterisk girls need not be examined, but in each year they will be expected to show increased skill as seamstresses and teachers of sewing, knitting, etc.

In the examination the Inspectors will observe the degree of attention paid by the pupil teachers to a perfect articulation in reading, and the right modulation of the voice in teaching a class. A knowledge of vocal music and of drawing (especially from models) though not absolutely required, because the means of teaching it may not exist in every school, will be much encouraged. Every pupil teacher will be required to be clean in person and dress.

The training college course was imagined as lasting one, two or three years, and at the end of each year there was to be an examination. This examination was to be conducted by the inspectors acting for the Committee of Council, which thus, through the examination, had the means of controlling the whole course had it so wished. On the results of the examination certificates were awarded, and, as they conferred status, and carried considerable pecuniary rewards, they were eagerly desired.

Within this framework, there were many points which Kay-Shuttleworth felt were important and valuable. One was the device by which the master's salary was made up of different parts. This arrangement gave both protection and incentives for effort. The government grant was given on condition the managers contributed twice as much, and that the school was in a fit condition. That stimulated the managers and protected the teacher. Meanness and caprice, though it might load him with work, or bring treatment that lacked honour, could not depress his condition below a certain level. If the master was to have pupil teachers the school must be adequate and well managed. This supplied a further measure of control. If the return from school pence was to be high the teaching must be acceptable. At the same time the teacher was not left defenceless before the parents, and local charity was provided with a fruitful field in which to do good.

There were other advantages which the Government did not so publicly stress. Now that pupil reachers were paid, they were under the control of the teacher and managers to a far greater extent. As the position of pupil teacher became desirable, the power of the teacher grew; and if a boy or girl behaved very badly he could be dismissed. Towards the end of this phase of development, when the advantages of the education that pupil teaching and training college gave were appreciated, there were abundant candidates of good quality for the posts.

There was something even more important: the Committee had now a firm grip on the early training of those who would become teachers. No longer would the training colleges have to struggle with students who could scarcely write; the Queen's Scholars would enter possessed of a well-defined body of knowledge, which would be fairly constant wherever they came from. They would also be all of about the same age. At the end of the course the Certificate examination sent them out with another hall mark of efficiency.

The financial arrangements made with the training colleges were generous. It was reckoned that each man student cost about £50 a year to train (the women were rather cheaper at £30) and the plan imagined that an efficient college would receive well over half its costs from public funds. Each student, Queen's Scholar or not, who passed the annual examination earned for the college at least £25. The Queen's Scholars received in addition £25 which they would pay to the college. Those who were not Queen's Scholars would have to find the £25 themselves or from their patrons. At first the colleges were only allowed to receive Queen's Scholars up to a quarter of their whole number, but this rule was relaxed after a few years. From the point of view of the colleges, the chief difficulty was that, not knowing how well the students would do in the examination, they could not forecast their next year's income.

There was yet another most important advance made by these regulations. There had been firm opposition to the principle of annual maintenance grants to schools; just as there was, in spite of the Scottish precedent, to annual grants to training colleges. At the same time, one inspector after another pointed out the need for continued support of the schools.

We think that such assistance would be most beneficially given were the Government to contribute towards the salary of good school-masters. The different congregations could more easily raise funds by subscriptions to build schools than to pay the salaries afterwards requisite for really good and competent masters. . . . There is a great chance that schools built by government grants, if not afterwards supported by further aid, would drop, the people being generally too poor to maintain them.[5]

The augmentation grants did just this. They aided the schools where there were trained teachers working under tolerable conditions, and did much to stabilize schools that were satisfactory. The augmentation grant was not dependent on the mere passing of an examination. The teacher must work satisfactorily to continue to receive it. Part of the inspector's duties when he visited the school was to report on the efficiency of the teacher, and to recommend or deny the continuation of the grant.

These Minutes did not become operative without a certain amount of struggle; but the course of the debate is most interestingly different from the fierce battle of seven years earlier.

The winter was quiet. In February Lord Lansdowne made a statement in the Lords and was congratulated and thanked by the Archbishop of Canterbury.[6] The thoughts of the nation were occupied with much more important matters. The Irish potato famine, which also affected Scotland, became acute. Through the latter part of February and throughout March *The Times* had almost daily articles stating the facts, commenting on relief measures, attacking the selfishness of the Irish landlords and the supineness of the peasants. Restraints on shipping were removed, and a struggle started to get a proper Poor Law framed for Ireland. In addition to this the Ten Hours Bill continued its nagging way, being debated interminably and inconclusively every Wednesday night. There was civil war in Portugal, the free city of Cracow had been extinguished—in defiance of treaties; and there was a very interesting scandal about the King of Bavaria and an indifferent dancer called Lola Montez.

It is not surprising that an extension of the existing government aid to education should not seem important.

'The Ministerial plans,' said *The Times* when it did notice them, 'if they can be called plans, for the advancement of Education are remarkable for their fairness and simplicity. We verily believe that, but for the understanding that every sixpence the nation can spare is to be spent on feeding the Irish, there would have been a decided cry for more education, and for something worthy of being called a system.' The present arrangements only continued and developed those already in use. 'All is open as the day, and even if the character of Lord Lansdowne and the Committee were not security enough, the plan left no opening whatever for what are called sectarian predilections.' And the article ended: 'There has been no great manifestations either for or against it. Neither Churchmen nor Dissenters have rejoiced or complained.'

This uninterested acquiescence was broken on 10 March by two meetings in Leeds. Dr Hook, the vicar, who had already published an important pamphlet advocating greater state control of education, pronounced 'with almost redundant emphasis' in favour of the Minutes and the general extension of education; and Edward Baines, editor and proprietor of the *Leeds Mercury* and leader of the Voluntaryists, proposed that 'in the opinion of this meeting the government measures for Education are unconstitutional, calculated to produce a dangerous extension of the influence of the Executive, destructive of the freedom of Education and prejudicial to the independence of the National Character'.

In fact, as compared with 1839, unreason had changed its side; and the Church, with a clear understanding of the problems and an appreciation of what the Government had done and was prepared to do, welcomed the Minutes, while the extreme non-conformists, particularly the Wesleyans, were filled with suspicion. They even went so far as to say that it was undesirable to improve the position of the schoolmaster because he would then have gone up in the world sufficiently to consort with the clergyman. *The Times* has nothing but scorn for Baines, and in its leaders, which become frequent when the controversy is well under way, had such remarks as 'If there ever was an agitation which had all the signs of emanating from some very small and narrow-minded clique, this is it.' The Wesleyans proved that they were sincere in objecting to state aid by refusing it; but their attempts to deprive others of it were, so *The Times* felt, inspired by a most sectarian jealousy.

In the debate on the estimates for education, which lasted for some six nights, there was never the slightest fear of a government defeat;[7] the main points made were that it was now accepted that it was the *duty* of the Government to educate the people, and that it was time some regulations were framed which would allow Roman Catholic schools to apply for a grant. At present they were excluded by the implied regulation that the Scriptures must be read daily in the Authorized Version.

Perhaps the most remarkable statement made in the course of the proceedings came from the Bishop of London who magnanimously denied his past by saying that he thought 'the course pursued by the Government exceedingly wise and prudent, as it involved no unnecessary interference with the present system of education, while they proposed to expand and improve it'. As for the inspectors, 'they were judicious friends and well wishers, who had discharged their duty most judiciously, most zealously and most unobjectionably'.

Quite as significant as the discussions in Parliament were the views expressed in the Reviews. The *Quarterly* and the *Edinburgh* were practically unanimous in urging that education was a civil duty that belonged to the state. 'The State has the *right*', said the *Edinburgh*, 'to see that children are so brought up that they are able to fulfil their social obligations towards their fellow citizens, and are not a plague and a nuisance to the rest of the community.' 'Sooner or later', said the *Quarterly*,[8] writing as an 'avowed member of the Church of England',

popular education must be an affair of the State—of the State not merely making grants to the different Societies and demanding the right of inspection over schools which receive such grants; but as establishing some system administered by an efficient and responsible board for providing masters to work on some well-matured plans, with books under a proper supervision, and paid, at least in part, by the State, or by compulsory and equal local assessments. The schoolmaster must become a public functionary, duly qualified for his office and under due control.

Sectarian squabbles are completely out of date. The matter is far too large to be dealt with by private agencies. The growth of the great towns and the shifts of population make continual and changing demands. Besides, many of the people for whom the schools are intended have no definite religious adhesion; they go to no church, or to several. They are only interested in the quality of the education their children receive, not the particular catechism taught with it.

That a man should be a Christian, and, if so, Episcopalian, Presbyterian and so forth, is not essential to the community—equally blameless citizens can be found among all religionists: but that he should be capable of using his faculties and his fingers, of understanding his social duties and obligations, possessed of habits of honesty, industry and fidelity—these are essential to his character as a good citizen.

The school will offer to the clergyman, for his further teaching, children with the first principles at least of morals firmly taught, with some respect for things sacred, with dispositions which have learned the blessedness of kindliness. They will have none of that ineradicable taint of profaneness, of that ingrained aversion to control, which is the growth of absolute neglect.

Almost for the first time, in a paper for general reading, the state school, detached from any religious denomination, is mentioned with approval as having a real though limited part to play in the education of the country.

The State School will, at first, be as a stranger in the land. Let it not come between the kindly intercourse and the mutual good understanding of rich and poor. Let all the good parish schools of the clergy, all the well-supported schools of the dissenters be alike undisturbed. Attempt least of all to interfere with such schools as are conducted by some of the great master manufacturers. Attempt not to do the duty of those who are disposed to do their own.

Whenever existing schools are below the proper standard, the best way of elevating them will be to establish, not in rivalry in the same district, but in some vacant place in the neighbourhood, some better school. Natural emulation will work improvement more effectually than any compulsory interference or opposition.

The Reviews expressed and formed the views of the well-to-do middle classes; the Parliamentary debates expressed the views of the rulers of the country; education clearly had escaped for the moment from the tyranny of party politics and sectarian religion, and become one of the great social services. Kay-Shuttleworth had won his battle.

Notes

1. *Quarterly Review*, September 1846, p. 327.
2. Kay-Shuttleworth, *The School in relation to the State, the Church and the Congregation*, ch. III; *Four Periods of Public Education* (1862), pp. 287 ff.
3. Kay-Shuttleworth, *The School*, chs. III, IV, V.
4. This privilege was soon found to be 'absurd' and abolished; Minutes, 1852–3, p. 9.
5. P.P., 1847, XXVII, pt. II, 25.
6. Hansard, 1847, LXXXIX, 858.
7. Hansard, 1847, XCII, 952.
8. *Quarterly Review*, September 1846, pp. 377, 416.

Chapter Ten

Results of the Minutes of 1846

The profound change in education, which the Minutes of 1846 made possible, could only take place by degrees. The first year's crop of apprentices was only eight, five boys and three girls, and these would not be ready for several years to take up their work. To speed up the process of providing certificated teachers for the schools, the Committee of Council admitted three classes to their examinations: students in college who had completed a course of at least one year; teachers who had been trained in the past; and those in charge of schools who had never been trained.

This first examination in 1847 was held by the inspectors in different colleges up and down the country; and students, ex-students and teachers were gathered together. The papers were set on the syllabus of the college in which the examination was held; and, where the college could offer no syllabus, as happened in at least one case, the inspector had to do the best he could. In this way the Department continued the principle of interfering as little as possible with the arrangements of the institutions they inspected.

The whole proceeding produced a great furore, it was so entirely new and beyond the experience of most of the candidates.[1] At a women's college teachers and students were much agitated: 'They were not only alarmed on account of the great importance which they attached to success, but they were, unfortunately, not prepared for an examination in writing.' At Battersea the men were equally alarmed but prompt action was taken to fortify them. In the accounts is the item for 13 December 1847, 'Supplementary Account (Housekeeper) £2. 10. 0. for wines and brandy given to students who were low and nervous at the time of the Inspection.' The college committee, rather shocked by this indulgence, recommended that 'for the future the Supplementary Account be discontinued'.

Mr Watkins presided over the examination of serving teachers at Wakefield. He was very thorough. For ten days there were papers from 7.45 in the morning till 8.15 at night. The day began with prayer, and closed, most appropriately, with the singing of the 'Nunc dimittis'. 'They all behaved very well. There were no captious complaints of the difficulties of the examination, though in several instances the papers were returned without answers.'

Of those who sat their first examination many failed. At Chelsea 38 schoolmasters sat the examination, 26 passed, 2 in the first class. Of 13 students who had resided one year, only 5 were recommended as having successfully completed the year's work to qualify for grant. At Battersea, of 54 serving schoolmasters 42 obtained certificates, and 13 students out of 31 qualified for grant; at Chester 15 out of 28 teachers got the certificate, and 7 out of 28 students qualified for grant.

Some of the women candidates who were already teaching shocked the examiner very much.

'You would not expect as candidates for a certificate', he writes, 'those who were deficient in orthography, or who were in the habit of making vulgar and trivial errors in Grammar. Some of the school-mistresses' papers were full of such defects. It will be very difficult for them to acquire a competent knowledge of the English language.' He refused them the certificate, but said that it was hardly their fault.

'Considering that the school library contains no standard work in English History, and that few of the mistresses are likely to have purchased or read books upon secular matters since they left Salisbury . . .' you might expect their knowledge to be poor, but really some knew nothing.

There was, of course, every hope that things would improve before long. The pupil teachers going into the schools now would be ready for the training colleges in 1850 or 1851, and would provide them with pupils infinitely superior in knowledge to those they had to take at present. Watkins, examining Whitelands, found two girls, Susan Kyberd and M. Ould, who excited his admiration, and he states, as a happy augury for the future, that they had both been pupil teachers.

In the inspectors' reports of the next few years the selection and training of the pupil teachers provided the major topic. So great a change naturally provoked much uneasiness, and considerable trouble is taken to prove that all anxiety is unfounded. The young people are chosen with the greatest care, and there is not the least danger that they will escape from the oversight of the church. In church schools the selection of the children started with the clergyman and the managers. Of the numbers which they put forward the inspector chose the best qualified.[2]

The responsibility for selection must rest upon those, who, having full opportunities of knowing the religious principles of the candidates, select them for examination—it rests virtually, in most cases exclusively, with the parochial clergy. I can assert that the great majority of boys and girls now apprenticed in my district are selected in the first instance by the clergy, and are afterwards approved by the local committee.

Nor was the grip relaxed as the apprenticeship proceeded:

The signature of the clergyman is also required and is always attached to the certificate of the candidate's religious knowledge. Before the pupil teachers are examined at the close of each year, a formal certificate is given by the clergyman that he is satisfied by their attention to their religious duties. The great power which this condition insures to the clergy may be easily understood. Each clergyman is thus most properly appealed to in his own parish as the sole and ultimate judge of what constitutes due attention to religious duties in those whose influence tells at present so directly upon the character of the school children, and who will be, in all probability, the educators of the next generation.

These jubilant reports are from clerical inspectors. As there were six or seven times as many church schools that took pupil teachers as those of other denominations it is understandable that after a few years, when these apprenticeships became much desired, this massive patronage in church hands was resented. Besides a lad's churchmanship there were other considerations that a prudent inspector had to bear in mind. The regulations stated that he must be between the ages of thirteen and sixteen; there were his scholastic attainments; the home from which he came; his probable suitability as a teacher.

Many of them—and among these some of the most promising—are the children of labourers; these cannot be free from the temptations which surround poverty. I am accustomed, before I recommend the appointment of a pupil teacher, to assure myself that the abode of his parents is not wanting in that which belongs to the proprieties and decencies of life. From what I know of the deplorable state of the cottages of the poor, I am not, however, satisfied that I have in all cases succeeded in securing these for them.

Where other things are the same, I am disposed, therefore, to think that the selection of pupil teachers is best when it is made from the class of tradesmen, small farmers and shopkeepers.

Another inspector considers that

The children of those connected with the higher classes, gentlemen's servants, gardeners, sons of widows and mechanics (especially joiners and carpenters) have been found the best fitted for apprenticeship.

In some cases it was arranged that the apprentices should board with the master of the school, and a considerable number of grants were given at this period for building dormitories on to the houses of masters. This may have been inevitable in districts with a very scattered population, but the inspectors gradually decided against it. They felt that it would be a mistake to 'congregate them in large numbers, leave them but little room for independence of action or moral responsibility, and deprive them at an early age of the charities and amenities of a home'.

On their first survey of the pupil teachers and their effect on the schools, the inspectors were delighted:[3]

Among so great a number of persons passing through that period of their lives which is more than any other one of trial, there are some who will probably disappoint our expectations, but I very much doubt whether there could be found any body of young persons of like age, in any other condition of life, whose conduct during a like period would be found, by enquiries so searching, to the same extent free from blame. Where cases requiring the admonition of an Inspector have occurred—and they have been very few in number—they have usually been cases in which a spirit of insubordination has manifested itself, and that claim to independence has been set up, which is perhaps natural to an age when childhood is taking uncertain steps to manhood.

Where they failed for moral reasons it was generally because insufficient care had been taken in their selection. Watkins, in Yorkshire, noted a certain irresponsibility in the managers, who seemed to rely less on clerical advice than elsewhere. 'I have seen in more than one instance the manager of a school take a pen in his hand, make a hasty careless enquiry and then, without any personal knowledge, or further thought, write off rapidly a sufficiently satisfactory character of both parents and child.'

But in general they were very good. The teachers pronounced them 'quiet, humble and obedient'. They did their work in school; and out of doors behaved with 'decorum', in a way becoming to those 'to whom the training of the rising generation is, in a measure, entrusted'.

The number whose apprenticeship was terminated was surprisingly few. Even in careless Yorkshire, Watkins could give a good report. Of the 559 pupil teachers that he had in 1850 in different stages of their apprenticeship all except 23 were doing well. Of these 5 died, and 5 left for ill health; 6 were dismissed for 'immorality', and 7 had been lost through the removal of parents, the incompetence of the master, or the ill conduct of parents.[4]

In Brookfield's district out of 300 pupil teachers only 3 were turned away for misconduct; Fletcher inspecting the Wesleyan schools gives the same proportion of dismissals.

These are surprising figures, and the influence of the young people on the schools was felt to be equally good. They were infinitely better than the monitors who had preceeded them—older, better instructed, doing the work from choice, paid and under discipline. 'The most objectionable features', says one inspector, 'of the National system have almost disappeared. If we could judge them by comparing them with previous systems they might be fairly represented as triumphant.' And Morell says boldly, 'A new era has dawned upon our country as regards the education of the people.'

They made possible the first approximation to reasonable teaching.

'Instead', said Fletcher, 'of the lower half of each school being mainly employed, as heretofore, either in listening to collective instruction of the whole school which it cannot understand, or in learning the first lessons in reading in ill-disciplined drafts, alternated with the worse disciplined indolence called writing on slates, it is now possible—with the aid of a pupil teacher—to do better.'

The numbers increased from year to year, as more and more people realized the advantage it offered to their children. In 1850 the following numbers of boys and girls were in the different years of their apprenticeship.[5]

1st Year Apprenticed in 1850:		2nd 49		3rd 48		4th 47		5th 46	
B	G	B	G	B	G	B	G	B	G
1107	551	970	429	303	159	39	14	5	3
1658		1399		462		53		8	

The number continued to rise for the next ten years.

Almost as these paeans were being written, inspectors discerned a difficulty. Many of the best pupil teachers seemed pale and thin at the end
of the first year's work. The inspector made enquiries and found that
they worked too hard, and went to bed too late. He had a talk with the
managers and explained that children must be healthy when they are
selected; and with the parents and said that they must watch their
child's bedtime, and he stressed the importance of cleanliness. 'I have
not hesitated to call their attention particularly to the advantages, in a
sanitary point of view, of frequent ablution and friction of the body.'
But the evil was far too fundamental to be dealt with by early bedtimes
or cold baths. The more they observed the life of the pupil teachers the
more conscious they became of the strain, both mental and physical, to
which they were exposed. A boy of fourteen might live at a distance
from his work. He walks three miles to the school and gets there in time
to have it all arranged for 9 a.m. He remains in the 'large, noisy, crowded
classroom' till 1 o'clock having stayed for the monitors' lesson. He eats a
hasty and uncomfortable lunch in the same room, and teaches there till
school ends. He tidies up and gets away at 5. He then walks home. How,
they ask, can he do any preparation or increase his knowledge'.[6]

The girls fared much worse. This is the evidence given on the point:

She is the daughter of a handicraftsman or labourer. Her parents may
earn from 30/- to 12/- a week. She is not infrequently one of several
children, often the only girl. It is a wrong to her family if she be prevented
from bearing her share of the usual work in the house, and a greater injury
to herself if she is excused from this. These home duties claim on an
average an hour a day of her time.

Next she may have charge of a section of 40 children. She must engage
in teaching daily for not less than $5\frac{1}{2}$ hours and in preparing the school for
her class and putting things away about another $\frac{1}{2}$ hour daily.

These school duties claim at least 6 hours a day for 5 days a week.

She is also sometimes required, with the elder girls, to do all the household work of the school premises, even including scrubbing the larger
and rougher floors.

She is also required to visit to enquire after absent children. These
duties claim another hour a day.

We have already taken up 8 hours a day 5 days a week. There is yet a
claim on their time for another $1\frac{1}{2}$ hours 5 days a week in class with the
mistress, when she is to revise and correct the exercises they have written
at home, to hear the lessons they have prepared at home, to practise them
in arithmetic and English grammar, to instruct them in the art of teaching,

and with their assistance make up the voluminous school register and school accounts.

So 9½ hours a day for 5 days or 8 for 6 days. A 48-hour week. Even allowing for the chance that visiting absentees and scrubbing floors provided 'healthy bodily exercise' the opinion was soon established that 'the young persons labour under the disadvantage of having to grapple with an amount of work unsuitable to their age, and too extensive for the time they can profitably devote to study'. It was no wonder that they were too often found lacking in 'animation and energy'.

If a girl escaped housework she was still liable to overstrain.

It is a system of the highest pressure. A girl of 13, in many cases of the humblest birth, is apprenticed for 5 years to a certificated mistress. At the end of each year she is examined by the Inspector, and if she passes, receives a payment rising from £10 to £20—a larger sum than she or her parents ever saw before, equal, perhaps, to all her father's wages for six months. To enable her to devote her whole time to working for it, she is spared every domestic service. In her father's family she is a little goddess, raised as far above them as an Irish cottier's son when he quits the cabin for the seminary. At 18 she competes for a Queen's Scholarship, and if she obtains one, receives tuition, board, lodging, washing and medical attention from the college, and a small sum for personal expenses, clothes and pocket money, subject, however, like the pupil teacher's pay, to the result of annual examinations. This may last one, two or three years, at the end of which she obtains one of eleven different kinds of certificates, all depending on success at the examinations, which according to its class, entitles her, on her appointment to a school, to a salary, partly supplied by the government and partly from the school, amounting when lowest to £20 a year, and when highest, exceeding £60 a year and a house. For seven years, therefore, her mind is in a state of constant tension: she goes through struggle after struggle, in each of which defeat is ruinous.[7]

It took some time for the condition of the pupil teachers to be fully understood. But there was another difficulty which was noticed almost at once; the problem of how to get them satisfactorily instructed. The supposition underlying the whole scheme was that there would be masters, in large numbers of schools, able and willing to carry the pupil teachers through a serious course of elementary learning. It was hoped that these masters would have certificates of merit, but at first that was impossible to achieve; it was enough if the inspector found the school in good order and well instructed, and formed the opinion that the master knew enough for the work, and was able to be 'a guide and example in the formation of the character of the apprentices'. It was not always easy to find even this. Some teachers were clearly too ignorant. Of a school in Portsmouth it was recorded:

68 girls taught by a mistress with a pupil teacher. The mistress having declined to be examined, I cannot recommend the payment of her allowance for this teacher. The children are very quiet, read very ill, and answer ill in religious knowledge, cipher ill, know nothing of geography, or history or English grammar. The only thing they do well is writing from memory.

Others could just cover the syllabus, but could go no farther. Yet others, as soon as they had got an apprentice, ceased to do any work themselves, and either sat at their desk all day, or walked up and down 'superintending'. But the greatest difficulty was to find the proper time in which to give the pupil teacher the daily $1\frac{1}{2}$ hours' instruction to which he was entitled. Some masters taught before breakfast, others immediately after school, in the lunch hour or crammed it all into 8 hours on Saturday. Each arrangement had ill effects. 'But,' said Watkins, 'hard as it is to find a suitable time, *it must be found and stuck to*. If pupil teachers fail in their examinations it is nearly always due to bad teaching.'[8]

There was a further failing that masters had: they were always changing schools, and thus interrupting the apprenticeship; and the youth might be unable to complete the training to which he had committed himself. Still, for all these difficulties, the hope for English education lay in the pupil teachers, and their numbers continued to increase.

The distribution of the schools which had pupil teachers followed the educational enthusiasm of the different districts. The managers of a school had to be in earnest and eager for improvement. They had to put their school in order, often carrying out quite serious structural changes; they had to apply to the inspector, and select apprentices. They might have to change their master, and get one of a higher standard if they could not attract one with a certificate. A small place could do it as well as a large town, but there must be effort and enthusiasm. In 1850 Oxfordshire had 8 pupil teachers in 7 schools, while Cambridgshire, where earlier there had been a notable indifference to education, now had 52 apprentices in 17 schools. Yorkshire headed the table with 669 apprentices in 221 schools, Lancashire next with 527 in 160 schools, while Middlesex had only 404 in 90 schools. Anglesey had 16 in 7 schools.[9]

By 1850 the first of the pupil teachers were getting ready to pass to the training colleges. They had certificates that they had successfully completed their apprenticeship, and they had been examined by the inspector in the thirteen or so subjects that made up the curriculum. They then applied to the training college of their choice. At first Queen's Scholars were limited to a quarter of the number of students in the college, and, while pupil teachers were so few, that was satisfactory enough. But before five years had passed, such a limitation became absurd, and the colleges were filled with grant-earning students, and could be organized on a much more satisfactory basis and become almost self-supporting.

Year by year after the first examinations the number of certificated teachers increased; in 1849 there were 681 at work in the schools, ten years later there were 6878. They rapidly formed a social class of some importance. Their status and the obligations that their employment imposed on the managers forced upon the public a new idea of education. At first some managers resisted the implications of the new idea. They liked to think that the augmentation grant that the certificate brought to the teacher was a public subscription to the *school*. As one inspector phrased it:

There is in some places a tendency in the Managers of schools to look upon the master as a means of raising money for its support, rather than as a teacher and trainer of the intelligent beings in it. They use him as a lever to lift up the pecuniary burden of the institution, and do not consider that the one chief object of the Minutes is to lift up the master himself, to put him in his proper place in society, and by a severe though necessary ordeal, to cause him to be respected by others, as well as give him cause for proper self-respect.[10]

On the whole, however, the certificated teachers began to establish their position. They were much in demand, and, if the managers of one school did not treat them well, they had no difficulty in finding a more appreciative committee; in fact they moved too often, and My Lords were always trying to devise means of binding them to their schools. They felt a professional unity, and formed societies for mutual improvement and for life insurance. They began to have journals devoted to their interests.

At different times during the decade 1850–60 there were thirteen periodicals dealing with education and the teacher. There had been four during the preceding ten years, and in the following ten, after the blow to their position of 1861, there were seven.[11]

For the most part these certificated teachers taught in schools where there were pupil teachers; and these apprentices made their work considerably more satisfying, because, with their help, they had a possibility of doing it efficiently. In addition they were visited annually. Their certificates needed endorsing, sometimes they resat the examination to obtain a better class; they were exposed to regular criticism, which was in the main friendly, and they had a possible ally in their disputes with the managers. Of teachers in this class it was said:

One striking characteristic is greater self-possession, self-respect and a stronger feeling of security than is common with those whose worldly position is more isolated and precarious. They feel themselves members of a body, parts of a great system, recognized by the authorities of the State; and, if the Inspector is worthy of his office, his visits are rather an encouragement and a protection than a troublesome and threatening interference.[12]

With this sense of unity the teachers became militant. They were in a peculiar position. Their learning, little though it might be, was as great as that of many members of the middle and upper classes. On the other hand they had none of the ease and social confidence of even the most ill-informed country gentleman. They had, in most cases, been taken right out of their home and early environment. They were unwilling to associate with the parents of their pupils, who anyhow regarded them as employees, and the gentry would not accept them. They were quite unable to see what it was that caused their exclusion. *The School and the Teacher*, which was one of the more belligerent papers, put it thus.

It is no strange thing that men who in education, tastes and habits have all the qualifications of 'gentlemen' should regard themselves as worthy of something very much higher than the treatment of a servant and the wages of a mechanic.

What in short the teacher desires is that his 'calling' shall rank as a 'profession'; that the name of 'schoolmaster' shall ring as grandly on the ear as that of 'clergyman' or 'solicitor'; that he shall feel no more that awful chill and 'stony British stare' which follows the explanation that 'that interesting young man is only the schoolmaster'.

More moderate journals might doubt the truth of most of the statements in the paragraph, and suggest that 'earnest industry and effectual services would earn a just claim on public gratitude', but it did not assuage the feelings of the young man who found himself isolated in a rural community, and decided, sadly, that it was vain to day-dream of marrying the squire's daughter. John Snell of East Coker summed up the feeling in his evidence to the Newcastle Commission:

Trained teachers do not dislike their work; there is no reason why they should; it is honourable, intellectual and benevolent; but society has not yet learned how to value them. This they feel with all the sensitiveness that belongs to educated and professional men.[13]

Besides the unsatisfactoriness of their social position the teachers also complained that their work was unhealthy and excessively laborious. When this was seen against the hours and condition of factory or clerical work of the day, it is clear that teachers were applying somewhat unrealistic standards. On the other hand, as inspectors were inclined to point out, the teachers too often made their own Hell.

The obstinacy of teachers in defeating every expedient by which the architect has provided for due ventilation of their schoolrooms, is sometimes very remarkable. It has frequently occurred to me to find the windows and doors of schoolrooms closed at seasons when ventilation is especially required; and I have with my own hands broken open the aperture for ventilation in the ceiling of one, which the schoolmaster had nailed down to prevent the cold air, as he said, 'from entering by it'.

Moreover the hours were short, and the opportunities which this gave were too often wasted. When the inspector saw his teachers looking ill and miserable, too often with the marks of consumption, and when he reflected that they only worked six hours a day, he was moved to a certain indignation.

I have sometimes thought that if I could but have compelled him to a walk, such as I am myself in the daily habit of taking, I should have taught him the secret of a far healthier and happier condition of mind.

Not unnaturally these openly expressed feelings of the teachers brought on them very considerable unpopularity. Education was still somewhat suspect; and nobody, least of all the inspectors, who knew them best, thought very highly of teachers as a body.

Our ordinary teachers [wrote Mr Allen] have very little sense of how much is entrusted to them, and therefore, if a school is to be of real value, there must constantly be at hand the unbought services of someone, either clergyman, esquire or members of their families who will be capable, both by education and intelligence, to give that counsel and infuse that spirit which cannot be looked for from our present race of teachers.

The difficulty, as someone else pointed out, was their segregated education, which prevented comparisons with abler or more cultured students, and gave them quite unjustifiable ideas of their social importance. In the training colleges the 'office of schoolmaster is spoken of as one of the highest in the land in importance, mentally, morally and religiously'. After one or two years of this, the reality could only prove shocking.

Throughout the decade, as the organization of the teachers improved, as their education and their pretensions increased, so did the hostility with which they were regarded. 'Old prejudices' were revived. 'True to the call, class jealousies, which had retired into corners, had come out to bask themselves once more in popular favour. A tongue has been given to an army of little opponents who, in their secret heart, hate and fear the education of the lower classes.' And the elevation of the teacher was seen as the first dangerous step towards the better education of the people.

They were accused of being 'too highly educated'; of being conceited and treating managers with less than the deference due to them. They thought what their education had made them, and not what their original condition was! Worst of all, many were determined to pass from their present twilight social position to the clear light of the professional classes; and they abandoned teaching to read for the Church. Others were even suspected of revolutionary tendencies and of looking forward to the day when Labour would rule and 'set the teachers free from the encumbrances which thwart their efforts and cripple their resources'.

The teachers undoubtedly had many grievances. In Church schools in the country they were often expected to be men-of-all-work in a parish which was largely illiterate.

The Rector was a thin, lanky man, not past middle age, but looking old. His head was nearly bald, fringed by a thin border of sandy hair; his forehead was low and retreating, his teeth large and prominent, and a grin quite satanic completed his very unprepossessing physiognomy. He received me with a touch—I cannot call it a shake—of two fingers of a gloved hand, and entered at once into an explanation of my duties. These were multifarious enough. Besides the school work, which was all I was previously aware of, I was to act as parish clerk, vestry clerk and secretary to a benefit society of which he was the patron. As if this was not enough to occupy my spare hours, I was also expected to keep the books of the poor-rate collector—some protégé of the Rector who was not quite equal to so much literary labour.[14]

Not infrequently the managers dismissed a teacher unreasonably. If it was a Church school, an inspector ominously remarks, an appeal would then lie to the bishop. In other cases the managers were merely rude: 'The clergyman enters the school without removing his hat or salutation of any kind; he interrupts the lesson; he takes the pupils as it were out of the master's hands; he gives pupils, visitors and all the impression that the school is his and not the master's.'[15]

Moreover, as had been said earlier, teaching was a calling that had no prizes. The more forceful teachers resented the lack of effective promotion. They might rise from a small school at £80 a year to a large one at £120, but there was nothing beyond, no haven from the daily drudgery. They began to ask for promotion to the Inspectorate, and they did not always ask politely. During this decade the number of inspectors greatly increased, and it became usual to appoint young men, straight, or almost straight from the universities, like Matthew Arnold, who became an inspector in 1851 aged twenty-nine. The experienced teachers, who had been ready to accept the judgments of men who had grown up with the education system, bitterly resented these young men who had never been in an elementary school before; and had to learn it all from the teachers they were paid to control. They came in, so the teachers felt, by favour, and were just another manifestation of the injustice of the service.

'Of all the Inspectors,' said John Snell incautiously, 'I do not know one who has obtained his appointment because of his experience, his love of the work, or his peculiar fitness for it.'

Nassau Senior said the same thing in different words:[16]

There is no appointment more likely to be jobbed than an inspectorship. It requires no special education. It may be given to any protégé who has decent knowledge and character. The demand for such situations on the part of the innumerable educated men who have failed in other pursuits, or have delayed their choice of a profession till they are too old to enter those which require early training, or who are tired of idleness and old-bachelorship and wish to have something to do and something to marry on, must be enormous.

He adds that the necessity of writing an annual report which will be published in full is a security against the worst applicants.

When such appointments were made, it was galling to the teachers to find that the Inspectorate was held firmly closed to them—for reasons that their pride refused to allow them to comprehend; there was really no avenue of advancement, unless they left the profession.

'The occupation of an elementary schoolmaster', said the Newcastle Commission very wisely, 'is not suited to a young man of an adventurous, stirring or ambitious character. It is a life which requires a quiet, even temper, patience, sympathy, fondness for children and habitual cheerfulness.'

Since at this time, and for long after, the only way that a poor boy could get an education was to train as a teacher, there were many who by ambition or an active nature were unfitted, on this analysis, for teaching, and complained loudly of its conditions.

This jealousy was made all the more acute because, already, the inspector's judgment affected the teacher's salary. The augmentation grants given for the possession of a Certificate of Merit depended also on the state of the school that the teacher conducted. In one year, 1850, Brookfield refused 9 out of 80 applications for grants: in 2 cases good teachers had been refused the necessary facilities by the managers, and the masters suffered through no fault of their own; in 5 cases the teachers were inefficient, and in 2 immoral.[17] These refusals were not always submitted to with meekness. Watkins records: 'Certificated teachers think the gratuity *conditionally* due on a Certificate of Merit *absolutely* due, irrespectively of the state of their schools. In one case where the children were in a very poor state of discipline, the certificated master was both passionate and impertinent when I pointed out to him the necessity for improvement in this respect.'

The inspectors thus began to lose their character of councillors and to become taskmasters. The teachers, at least the mediocre majority, replied by studying their habits, stereotyping methods, and rejecting any innovation on the plea that 'the inspector would not like it'.

Notes

1. Minutes, 1847–8, I, pp. cviii, 210 ff.
2. Minutes, 1848–9, II, pp. 64 ff.
3. Kay-Shuttleworth, *Public Education* (1853), Inspectors' reports on Pupil Teachers, Appendix A, p. 417.
4. Minutes, 1848–50, I, p. 137.
5. Minutes, 1852, I, p. 81.
6. P.P., 1861, XXI; *Report of the Newcastle Commission*, pp. 104 ff.
7. Nassau Senior, *Suggestions on Popular Education* (1861), p. 322.
8. Minutes, 1848–50, I, p. 138.
9. Minutes, 1848–50, I, pp. clviii, clxi.
10. Minutes, 1848–50, I, pp. 142 ff.
11. They also began to form associations, which the inspectors at first encouraged; Minutes, 1855–6, p. 434.
12. *Newcastle Report*, chapter on Trained Teachers, pp. 157 ff.
13. *Newcastle Report*, p. 159.
14. Robert Roberts, *Life and Opinions*.
16. *Newcastle Report*, p. 158.
16. *Suggestions*, p. 350.
17. Minutes, 1850–1, II, p. 376.

Chapter Eleven

Schools and training colleges in the 1850s

One very important effect of all these changes was a vast increase in official work. When Kay-Shuttleworth retired in 1849, after a physical collapse, the Education Department was still almost a family affair. During his tenure of office, the staff had increased from 1 to 40. He had chosen them all, and trained them; and they had imbibed his views and his general philosophy. R. R. W. Lingen who succeeded, fresh from his report on Welsh Education, was faced with a great task of organization and expansion. He was not hampered in this by his predecessor's medical knowledge and human sympathy.

Within a few years Lingen had made himself hated by all the partners in the business of education. His 'snubbing replies had imprinted on half the rural parishes of the country a deep conviction that the Education Department was their natural enemy'. The teachers felt that he was conducting their affairs 'without a spark of sympathy, and no further care than that connected with supply and demand'. His fellow-officials detested him. One clerical inspector wrote: 'The general treatment of the public, and the almost uniform treatment of the Inspectors by the office has been insolent, tyrannical and unwise in the highest degree', and he goes on to say that he scruples to take the Eucharist or say the Lord's Prayer, so ungovernable is his hate of the Secretary. 'When I know what the Education Department and the Education Question *might* be, and when I know what they *are*, I am afraid my indignation is stronger than Christian anger. At times I burn to expose and punish.' For twenty years the image of this personality was cast large on the education of the country.

His influence was the more dangerous because of the peculiar constitution of the Education Department. The Committee of Council never met as a body. At most, in a matter of unusual importance, the Chancellor of the Exchequer and the Home Secretary might attend; but, if they did, they would need to have all the business explained to them, and would have no knowledge of their own. In Kay-Shuttleworth's time the Secretary dealt with everything. The Lord President of the Council came down to the office 'most afternoons', and did a little Educational business along with anything else that turned up. The Secretary decided, absolutely, what matters should be referred to his superior, and if the two men were not in sympathy they would be few.[1]

Undoubtedly Lingen succeeded to many problems which Kay-Shuttleworth's reforms had produced, and which his meticulous mind would not allow him to solve in any simple way. One of Lingen's first acts was to attempt a reorganization of the work of the Inspectorate. The regulations of 1846 had inaugurated a process which continually increased the inspector's work. This is how Watkins describes his duties:

Now, a regular tour of inspection is impracticable to a District Inspector. There are Normal schools to be inspected, examination papers to be prepared and revised when answered, collective examinations of pupil teachers to be held, their papers to be looked over and their teaching criticized. There are teachers' certificates to be settled and revised from time to time. Large schools, professing many subjects, to be examined thoroughly and in detail, and a correspondence to be sustained which often not only occupies a great deal of time, but requires considerable thought and care.

This is the summary that he sent to the office of his activities in the leap year 1848:[2]

Examining Pupil teachers and other candidates	108 days
Visiting schools for other purposes, completion of certificates, reports, inspection	23
Preparing papers for examinations and holding them	153
Vacations and Sundays	82
	366

Only 2 days were spent in simple inspection.

Through the years other inspectors gave similar accounts of their time; though usually they had to include a period of at least 14 days for writing their annual report.

On taking office Lingen at once attempted to bring some order into this confusion. One difficulty was that, owing to denominational inspection, some inspectors had very large districts, geographically, and necessarily spent much of their time travelling. Matthew Arnold, as inspector of British schools, covered 13 Midland counties and most of Wales; and in all this area had only 104 schools. That would have been bad enough if an inspector could have arranged a tour on rational principles, but he could not. He was required to inspect the pupil teachers at the end of each year of their indentures, and they all ran from different dates. Lingen dealt with the matter sensibly and simply. Inspectors were instructed to divide their districts into 6 regions and to give 2 months to the inspections in each; the pupil teachers' indentures were revised so as to make the years of apprenticeship all end at the same time in the same district. Additional appointments were made to the inspectorate. But even so it was difficult to keep pace with the development of schools and the ever-growing number of pupil teachers.[3]

Some of the other problems could not be disposed of so simply.

The increasing number of certificated masters and pupil teachers brought another administrative difficulty. Kay-Shuttleworth wished the augmentation grants and the payments to and for pupil teachers to be personal to them, and not part of the school funds administered by the managers. All these sums were therefore sent direct by postal order. In 1849 when Shuttleworth retired there were at least 4261 of these payments to be made, in 1859 there were over 22,000. As government offices had not even started to be efficient, the payments were often months in arrears; and great hardship was caused to people as poor as the pupil teachers or the impecunious clergymen who had to make payments on account. In addition there was an ever-growing number of special grants, for capitation, books, equipment and so on, and all these sums were calculated separately and paid separately to the persons who were considered most suitable to receive them.

Besides being cumbersome, the system had to be absolutely rigid. It was impossible to give discretion to anyone to deal with this multitude of separate items. Every individual decision must either be made by the man at the top, or all must proceed exactly to rule. Any variation, favourable either to teachers or managers, was sure to be made the occasion for an outcry and a demonstration of political or sectarian feeling. Thus pupil teachers in Caernarvon, where employment was scarce and living cheap, must be paid the same as those in Lancashire where they could be earning far more in the mills, or in London where everything was expensive.

With every new school that was founded, and every new grant to encourage some new and valuable school activity the congestion at Whitehall became worse, and it is easy to see that, as years went on, the conduct of the central office became more and more impossible. It is no wonder that before the end of the decade some change was felt to be absolutely necessary.

The finance of schools is one of the major topics of the inspectors' reports in the first years of the decade. Although schools were multiplying and the best becoming solvent, there were still far too many which only existed through the sacrifices of the clergyman.[4] The farmers still distrusted education, and the non-resident landlords refused to contribute. 'There are four colleges in Cambridge which hold most of the land in this parish, and none of them subscribes to the National Schools.' Again and again they ask in their reports for some form of compulsion; some arrangement which will take the control of education from the hands of a small body of volunteers and place it as a general charge, the common concern of the whole community.

Funds must be available adequate to the creating of good schools, such schools must be provided adequate in number to the wants of the people, and they must be maintained *permanently*. It is contrary to nature that any result universal and permanent in its operation should be effected on the voluntary principle.[5]

By 1853 it was felt that another attempt might be made to extend and improve primary education. There were two methods which might be used, legislation and Departmental Minutes; both were to be employed.

On 4 April 1853 Lord John Russell made a speech in Parliament asking leave to bring in an Education Bill. As outlined, it was to be a comprehensive measure. In corporate towns there was to be a school rate distributed impartially to all schools under the Committee of Council. The educational endowments were to be investigated, reformed and applied to their proper purpose. The Universities of Oxford and Cambridge were to be compelled to start on the path of reform pointed out by the recent Commissions.[6]

The speech was delivered to empty and apathetic benches; but *The Times* next day reported it fully and devoted a leader to reasoned approval of the proposals. It was, in many ways, a remarkable speech; one of the more noteworthy since Roebuck's in 1833. He had said then that 'the infant schools will never be properly conducted while the university is imperfect', and at that time the remark could have had little meaning. Now for the first time a statesman was really proposing that education should be looked at as one continuous process.

The *Edinburgh Review*, commenting on the speech, drew out the implications; and imagined an 'educational ladder' stretching upward for every talented boy.[7]

In England there is no sharp line of separation cutting off class from class. The Charity Commissioners will, we trust, soon find means for insisting that there shall be a good classical grammar school in every town. These higher Grammar schools must be periodically inspected and examined and their funds must, if possible, be made available for assisting the deserving to finish their studies at the University. There will soon be no deserving boy in the kingdom in the lowest rank who may not, if his talents fit him for such promotion, win the highest University education by his industry.

In each grammar school there should be instituted an English or commercial department, which shall give a thoroughly good and useful instruction to the middle classes. These schools will be continually recruited by means of small exhibitions given to promising boys who will rise from the schools for the poor below, and they would hold out as a reward to its own promising scholars the prospect of rising, if they are fit for it, to the Grammar school and the University.

Even though the *Edinburgh* had the experience at home of such a progression, it was for England that it proposed its hopes.

In spite of this approval, there was no strong body of support behind the Bill, and the Government dropped it.

The administrative action was more successful. The Bill, had it been accepted, would have made provision for rate aid for education in corporate towns. It would not have affected the country. Those districts were provided for by a Minute which was published two days before the matter was raised in Parliament. It provided that schools in rural districts and unincorporated towns should receive capitation grants on average attendance of 5s. for boys and 4s. for girls. This was to be conditional on an attendance of at least 4 days a week for 48 weeks in the year, a total of 192 days a year. The teachers were to keep registers in such form as the inspectors might demand, and the inspectors were charged with the duty of individually examining the children and certifying that three-quarters in each of the age groups 7–9, 9–11, and 11–13 'had passed such examination before him as might be set forth in a separate minute of details'.

This Minute established the principle of annual grants to schools, which had been so long resisted. It also forced some organization on the teachers, and it imposed an individual examination of the children on the inspectors. These were all changes of the greatest importance, but at first the new regulations seemed to attract the attention of no one except the Bishop of Salisbury, who, next month, in the Lords, thanked the Government for giving this help, and suggested that it might be a little more liberal. The Bishop objected to the length of the school year. He thought that attendance of at least 4 days a week for 48 weeks in the year seemed not to take into consideration the harvest period, or other times when the children's work would be really needed. The Government accepted his view and the number of days of attendance was cut down to 176.

The schools were delighted with this new help. 'No kind of grant', records Kennedy, 'is more popular, or perhaps more useful.' It was so useful and so popular, that on the failure of the Bill it was extended. There were areas of all the large towns far more in need even than the country. The vicar of a slum parish had thousands of children on his hands, and no parishioner of substance or education. It was unreasonable to exclude him; and if he were included his neighbour must be included also. In 1855 all restrictions of locality were withdrawn and the grant became general. The cost naturally rose. In 1854 the cost of the capitation grant was £5957, in 1859 if was £61,183; a considerable matter when education estimates were jealously regarded.

Moreover, it was now the *duty* of the inspectors to examine children individually as a condition of the capitation grant. It is clear that this duty was not adequately carried out—with the staffing it was impossible that it should be—but 'the practice of inspection gave the direction to the daily teaching in the schools', said one teacher. 'My credit depends on the Inspector's report. If he makes most account of mental arithmetic and etymological derivations, what am I to do?'[8] And in general few masters and mistresses ventured to adopt any system of their own, however much required, for 'fear of the Inspectors'.

But if it had some disadvantages the grip that the inspectors acquired through the annual grants was mainly beneficial.

As one of H.M. Inspectors of schools, I must also be allowed to consider the constant increase of schools under our inspection as a hopeful sign for the future.

In my report to My Lords last year I pointed out the great difference

209

between the schools receiving annual grants, i.e. partaking of all the advantages which are offered to them by the Committee of Council on Education, and those which are, as we term it, under 'simple inspection', i.e. which have received grants for buildings or books or apparatus, but have neither certified teachers nor apprentices at work in them. This difference is very striking, extending to all parts of school life and action. The superiority of the schools representing what may be called the National System is very great. But I believe that the church schools which are not under inspection at all are as much inferior to schools under simple inspection as these are to the annual grant schools.[9]

But, though it now had power, the Government still had to fight every inch of the way. Sometimes the rector was 'in an angry fit and jibbed at all the rules', sometimes there was the old hostility to education.

A large number of the schools are in localities where there exists either a general apathy on behalf of the education of the poor, or where the notions respecting it are mistaken and narrow, or some local proprietor establishes a school and, having done this, resolves upon some arbitrary limit beyond which the studies of the children shall not proceed. With this in view he looks out for some respectable person, who, in addition to a good moral character, can read and write decently and can teach, in what is called a simple way, the first rules of arithmetic. In some instances his prejudices may be strong against the Committee of Council, in others against training colleges, certificates, pupil teachers, etc. In others against geography, grammar, English, history, decimals and the rule of three, with some or all of which he connects irreligion, disaffection, improper assumption in manners or dress; and consequently declines to raise his school to that state of efficiency which your Lordships have determined to be the standard for this country and the condition of Parliamentary aid.

At other times the resistance was to physical improvement.

Existing rooms are often such as to be completely unsuitable for occupation by schools. Yet there is hardly an objection which can be named in excuse of which strong representations (oral and written) are not made to the Committee of Council daily, and while, perhaps, annual grants may be refused altogether in a few extreme cases until improvement has actually been effected, the utmost that, in the majority of instances, can be practically accomplished is to obtain some promise, which in time comes to be more or less redeemed, of amelioration.

The inspectors worked on. They were adamant that floors must be boarded, that brick or stone would not do. They tried to secure underfloor ventilation for the stoves, good windows, high and able to be opened. They asked for playgrounds. There was a delicate problem that modern progress might help managers to solve. 'The confined sites of schools in towns often render it impossible to place the offices at a proper distance from the main buildings. Cheap means of obviating some of the more glaring inconveniences arising from this cause may be seen at almost every railway station, and should be adopted by the Managers of schools so circumstanced.'

Where schools were resolutely opposed to modern improvements they generally pleaded poverty, but the inspectors were convinced that in most cases a very little effort and good will would be sufficient to get the school to the required standard, especially as the Committee would give half the cost of boarding the floor, and two-thirds of the total cost of floor and parallel desks.[10]

Lord John Russell would not have made his speech if the position of the schools and the attitude to education had not been changing. People were beginning to realize that education pays; both nationally and individually. The Great Exhibition of 1851 had given a great impulse to the demand for technical education. The Board of Trade had been forced to establish navigation schools for merchant seamen's apprentices, and the juries of the Exhibition were complaining 'of the great disadvantage under which we labour from the lack of a better education of the operative classes'. This was followed by the perennial complaint that they did things better abroad. German technical education was far ahead of ours. Whilst there were no such means of education in England it was not to be wondered at that 'our glass makers, porcelain manufacturers, our calico printers and others have been obliged to receive from abroad that intellectual element of manufacture which they could not obtain at home'.[11]

In the personal sphere there were new opportunities which demanded education. The attempt to recruit to certain Government posts by examination opened up new vistas to the lower middle classes. More important was the great change in the position of the working classes. The repeal of the Corn Laws, the passing of the Ten Hours Act and the Public Health Act had brought in a new period. The price of food was no longer rising, hours of work were decreasing and wages going up. There was a greater possibility of a healthy life. The Income Tax had been called in to redress the balance of payments; and many of the more vexatious imposts had been removed. There was a spirit of enterprise which the Government now did nothing to repress. In 1844 there was the beginning of the retail Co-operative Movement; in 1851 the Amalgamated Society of Engineers was founded. Mechanics began to band together to seek some of the knowledge that they needed to rise in the world. It was the period of Samuel Smiles and *Self Help*. When the *Quarterly* wished to illustrate the fact that the way was now open to talent, it could quote the life of George Stephenson, who built up his fortune from the happy day when his wages were raised to 12s. a week. Authority smiled on these efforts, and the Bishop of Wells did not scorn to teach in an evening school, and help on navvies whose ambition in life was to become engine drivers. The great cry was for evening schools; and Mechanics' Institutes were founded hopefully.

In a humbler sphere, one inspector points out that in Lancashire there is such a demand for book-keepers that boys in a school were buying their own copy books, so eager were they to acquire the skill of writing.

The teacher's position was also improving. He was more valued for his function and his financial position was also better. The augmentation grants of 1846 were by 1852 costing the country £16,975 a year, a sum which continually increased as more and more teachers were trained. The salaries of pupil teachers and the grants to teachers for instructing them cost, in that year, £79,587, which was half the money spent on schools and colleges. The beneficiaries of these large sums could not but rise in the social scale.

Unfortunately, in spite of these improvements, the manner and matter of education were both unsatisfactory. The teachers had been trained on books of a type which will be described later, and the age believed in 'facts'. 'Now what I want is Facts', said Mr Gradgrind in *Hard Times*; and 'facts' the examiners demanded whether the candidates were children, students or candidates for the Civil Service. To these facts even the inspectors, who ought to have known better, attached an almost mystical significance.

This was especially true in scripture. 'If I found the children acquainted with the minutiæ,' said one inspector, 'I inferred a general knowledge of Scriptural truth.' The result of such examining was soon apparent. 'I find nothing commoner', said Jellinger Symons, 'than a knowledge of such facts as the weight of Goliath's spear, the length of Noah's ark, the dimensions of Solomon's temple, what God said to David or what Samuel did to Agag by children who can neither explain the commandments, the sacraments or the parables with moderate intelligence, or tell you the practical teaching of Christ's life.'[12]

The inspectors were torn in two ways. While on the one hand they talked about the importance of stimulating the children's intelligence and thought, they were on the other so far captive to their age that they believed that a knowledge of the word implied a knowledge of the thing. They were in a hurry; few teachers, especially after the training they had received, could teach in an intelligent way. H.M.I. must either examine unintelligent teaching or not examine at all.

The books that were available were in exactly the same style. *A Short System of Polite Learning* begins:

Q. What is Astronomy?
A. A mixed mathematical science; teaching the knowledge of the celestial bodies, their magnitudes, motions, distances, periods, eclipses and order.

Or the section on geography:

Q. What is this earth on which we dwell?
A. A sphere.
Q. Is it a perfect sphere?
A. No, an ablate spheroid.

Then followed questions about continents, islands, oceans, seas, isthmuses, straits, peninsulas, with parallels of latitude and degrees of longitude and tropics and zones and imaginary lines. At the end of such a course says the inspector, the children knew nothing, not even the name of their own country.

In one compendium the reading matter includes an *Outline of Geography* (in which Africa is dismissed in half a page, with a list of countries and capitals); Chronology; Survey of the Universe; Arithmetic Tables, and three catechisms, presumably to meet all tastes—The Church Catechism; one by Dr Watts; and one for free thinkers, a Social or Briton's Catechism which begins:

Q. What are your social duties?
A. As a subject of the King of England I am bound to obey the laws of my country.

The normal custom was for a class to have a book which it used throughout the year, and which contained all it needed in the various subjects. The most popular series was that published by the Irish Board of Education. They were far from perfect.

The books abound with words needlessly introduced, which are quite incomprehensible to the child. The poetry is taken from inferior sources; dry outlines of grammar and geography (subjects which should be taught in a separate form) are unsuitably introduced; the history is epitome destitute of picturesqueness and incapable of striking the imagination or awakening the sentiments of the child. The 5th book is greatly taken up with science in a form too technical for the purpose. . . .[13]

It might well have been of these books that Matthew Arnold wrote complaining that they contained such sentences as 'The crocodile is viviparous' or poetry like

> She is a rich and rare land,
> Oh, she is a fresh and fair land,
> She is a dear and rare land,
> This native land of mine. . . .

If there were a separate grammar book it would have been of the type of Lindley Murray's *English Grammar* which in various abridgments flourished through a large part of the century. It treated of Orthography, which, it said, 'teaches the nature and power of letters, and the just method of spelling words'. Under this head it deals with phonetics, and tries to give such rules for English spelling as can be extracted from the chaos of forms. 'The second part of grammar is Etymology, which treats of the different sorts of words, their various modifications and their derivations.' The derivations play little part in the book. Instead the section is occupied with the distinctions of the different parts of speech; irregular verbs, paradigms of the tenses; lists of masculine and feminine forms, and examples of the different cases in English. There are also considerations of syntax and style. In the shorter forms there are 'Promiscuous Exercises in Syntactical parsing'. These are so ill-explained and so confused as to defeat an adult intelligence.

Political economy, a subject which the inspectors were always advocating and on which Lady Ellesmere prepared a school text-book extracted from Archbishop Whately's writings, cannot have made much impression on most children. Poor Sissy Jupe when asked, after eight weeks' instruction, 'What is the first principle of the Science?' gave the 'absurd' answer, 'To do unto others as I would that they should do unto me.'

In fact the progress of the 'examination' in Mr Gradgrind's school must have been very near the truth. 'Give me your definition of a horse', demands Mr Gradgrind, and Sissy Jupe, who had spent all her life in a circus, is silent.

Girl number twenty unable to define a horse. Some boy's definition of a horse. Bitzer, yours.

Quadruped. Graminivorous. Forty teeth, namely twenty-four grinders, four eye teeth, and twelve incisive. Sheds coat in the spring; in marshy countries sheds hoofs too. Hoofs hard but requiring to be shod with iron. Age known by marks in the mouth. . . .

Had Dickens cared to follow the text-book of the day further, Bitzer would have described the enamel of the teeth and discussed the uses of the tail as a fly whisk. He would also have given the derivation of the words 'quadruped' and 'graminivorous'.

The curiosities of this type of knowledge were many. One inspector remarks that in a school that prided itself on its history teaching, the chief attainment of the boys was to repeat the names and dates of the kings of England very fast and correctly *backward* from Queen Victoria.

Brookfield, making the point that the unreality of this teaching is sometimes broken up by true knowledge, and that with knowledge the expression also improves, quotes this essay, written by the son of a groom:[14]

THE RACEHORSE

The racehorse is a very noble animal used very cruel by gentlemen. Races are very bad places. None but wicked people know anything about races. The last Derby was won by Mr D'anson's Blinkbonny, a beautiful filly by Melbourne rising 4. The odds were 20/1 against her. Thirty started and she won only by a neck.

There was a further, purely scholastic, feature of the schools which drove the teachers to practise at least some of the children in this type of knowledge—the annual examination conducted by some distinguished local person before an audience of gentry and parents. Such an occasion might be dismissed by Kay-Shuttleworth as 'the annual field day of a paraded exhibition, when the children are initiated in a public imposture, and the promotors of the school are the willing and conscious dupes of a pious fraud'. But it was fun. The school was decorated. As these examinations seem usually to have been just before or just after Christmas, there was doubtless holly and ivy and a well-stoked fire. On the morning of the day there was a rehearsal at which the children sang their songs and were taught the answers to the questions that would be asked. At 6 o'clock the company gathered, the Rector took the chair, the members of the Committee supporting him. In a town like Caernarvon the Mayor might preside, and visitors might come from Bangor, ten miles away. The children were 'examined' in such subjects as scripture history, geography, grammar, English, history, mental arithmetic and reading, there were recitations and songs. Sometimes Conduct Cards were distributed, sometimes prizes, 'the gift of a well-wisher in London'. Then there was an address, and the singing of the National Anthem. The whole performance, as one headmaster records, 'left a good impression in the town'. More important by far to the master and managers, a collection was taken. On one occasion it was as high as £24 in the boys' school and £10 in the girls'—nearly a quarter's salary for the teachers.

It was a common complaint based on these displays that children in school were taught too much, so Frederick Watkins carried out a survey in his northern district.

He found that 1 in 200 children learnt algebra (0·5 per cent); 2 in 200 mensuration (1 per cent); 1 in 300 geometry (0·35 per cent); history of Europe 15 per cent; geography 25 per cent; grammar 25 per cent and 3 per cent can do fractions. 'Surely', he adds, 'these returns will satisfy even the strongest advocates of no-progress.'[15]

Yet such was the curious lack of co-ordinated thought among the inspectors, that Watkins complains in another Report of just this excessive teaching.

We want the few elementary subjects more fully and practically taught, little more, indeed, than the old trio of attainments, if the terms be rightly interpreted,—reading, as the power of readily interpreting the written thoughts of man, and enunciating them clearly and pleasantly by voice to others; writing, as the means of expressing our thoughts legibly and correctly to other men, and arithmetic as the method of handling rapidly and with precision all that work of life which deals with, and depends on figures. With this understanding of 'reading, writing and arithmetic' I confess myself satisfied if children, when they leave school, can read, write and count. If they can do this, they can do all that is needful for the life work of 99 out of every 100 among them,—and they can do *that* which will best fit the hundredth, who rises out of the ranks, and obtains a higher worldly station, for the work he will do there.

Unfortunately it was just this simple knowledge that the schools seemed unable to impart to three-quarters of their pupils. Sometimes almost half the school were reading monosyllables or learning addition. And this is not surprising. It took a child, on the methods then in use, at least two years to learn to read, and many never achieved two years'

216

continuous attendance. A child might even have got a considerable distance on the laborious road when a protracted period of bird-scaring or baby-watching would put him back almost where he started.

The inspectors knew this perfectly well, and the older ones, at least, knew that it was not always the teacher's fault. The less experienced, however, had begun as early as 1853 to suggest that grants 'should be given, not in reference to the number of children or the mere amount of attendance, but in reference to attainment, that it should be the result of something like an enquiry by the inspectors into what was actually taught'.

The real difficulty, as always, lay with the teachers. The staffing of schools was gradually improving. A group of adult assistant teachers was coming into the schools. Ten years earlier it had been asserted that there was 'no recognized sphere of duty or legitimate place' for assistant teachers. In 1854 there were 172 of them, and their numbers were increasing. With their advent it was possible to divide the school into real classes and secure some proper grading. The pupil teachers were now felt to be very inferior. The reports are full of complaints of the inefficient methods that they used.

A child reads a sentence, he commits gross faults. 'Read it again', says the teacher. He reads it again, and, as may be expected, he reads it pretty much as at first. 'Read it again', and so on. It does not seem to enter into the teacher's conception that his own labour and the child's too would be immensely lightened if he would but tell the child what his faults are, and *why* he has to read it again.

Or again:

Reading taken round the class, all having books. Class of 20, 45 minutes lesson. $2\frac{1}{4}$ minutes each. All in the noise of the general room, and sitting behind one another in parallel desks. (If there is a small room, it is not used.) At least the reading class should be in a semicircle.

Worst of all was the fact that for almost all children reading was meaningless.

The mass of children get little more than a trick of mechanically pronouncing the letters, and the words which they read convey hardly any idea to the mind.

One inspector describes an episode to illustrate his point:

A smart little boy read the first verse of the ninth chapter of St Matthew's Gospel, 'And he entered into a ship, and passed over, and came into his

217

own city.' I asked. 'What did he enter into?' 'Don't know, thank you, Sir,' replied the boy politely. 'Read it again.' 'Now what did he come into?' 'Don't know, thank you, Sir.'

He continues,

The truth which has been forced upon me in a way it never was before is, that the language of books is an unknown tongue to the children of the illiterate, especially in remote situations.

The result was that the children could not understand what they were taught, especially when the text-book was the Bible; and wisely gave up all attempt to do so.[16]

The arithmetic teaching was little better. The children could be taught to perform certain calculations when the whole was put up on the board in the exact manner to which they were accustomed; but the question 'What is the cost of 5 doz. eggs at five for 2*d*.?' was only answered by about a tenth of the children in the top classes of 53 schools.

Kay-Shuttleworth did not remain in office long enough to see his first pupil teachers complete their apprenticeship and pass to the training colleges. It was from 1850 that their ever-increasing numbers made it possible to organize and develop the colleges. Numerically, they multiplied, and by 1859 there were 34 of them with over 2000 students. They also, during this period, acquired common characteristics which gradually absorbed their more awkward idiosyncrasies. This, also, was the period in which the first text-books were written. These books remained in use for twenty or thirty years at least, and their nature is a most important factor in the history of the course. In these years books were being written for the schools as well as the colleges, and educational publishing was starting on its great career.

From the point of view of the colleges, the most important thing was the change in the students. They were becoming more homogeneous. The numbers of older or very young students decreased, and the great majority were between eighteen and twenty. They also had a much more uniform body of knowledge. They differed, obviously, in natural ability and in the conditions of their apprenticeship. Some had had good teaching, others suffered because they had experienced nothing better than 'their daily intercourse with an unintelligent, superficial and sometimes worldly teacher'. Yet they had much common knowledge, based on the syllabus that they had all followed; and they had all had experience of school life and school needs and problems.

The colleges were no longer filled almost exclusively with unemployed milliners or discontented artisans who had passed their formative years without learning to study or to use words to express thought. The students were still very ignorant and lacking in any general culture; their knowledge was barren and circumscribed. Yet they had had the rudiments of training in attention and had some knowledge of books and the way to use them. They also were fully used to school life.

It also became possible for the colleges to make some selection among the candidates who presented themselves. So long as all students must find at least half their fees, there were never enough desirable people offering; the college must take any students it could get. In the years just before 1860 Queen's scholars were so numerous that the pessimists feared that the colleges would not be able to accommodate them all; and the need to accept the feeble recipients of some patron's bounty had gone.

With the Queen's scholars came also the possibility of organizing the colleges on a stable basis financially. The student came with a grant which covered half his fees; if he completed his year's work successfully the college received the other half of his costs. There was thus a motive for efficiency, and the various denominational bodies which founded colleges could invest their money in buildings with every hope that the institution would be permanent.

Under these circumstances the colleges began to lose their most undesirable peculiarities, and even the women's colleges acquired tolerable buildings. But there was one thing that kept them from becoming uniform, the lack of suitable staff specially equipped for the work. The teachers' fell into two classes, the principal and vice-principal, who were graduates of Oxford or Cambridge, and usually in Holy Orders, and the inferior staff who had been teachers, and, later, nearly always students of the college.

This method of staffing presented considerable difficulties. The principal and vice-principal spent much of their time teaching religious knowledge, and for the rest taught what they knew, whether it was particularly suitable to the students or not.

Unfortunately with gentlemen in Orders from Oxford and Cambridge, and tutors not specially educated [says one inspector], the training schools were compelled to use as a means of the student's education such subjects as there were found teachers of. So in one training college classical studies must continue to be employed, and in another mathematical, according as officers of these institutions may happen to have been educated in the one or other university, or may prefer the one to the other department of study.[17]

The lives of these superior officials were, to judge by the evidence of architecture alone, dignified and pleasant. The inferior teachers fared very differently. They taught the elementary subjects such as arithmetic and geography, and presided over the periods of preparation or exercised the class in question and answer. 'The services which they are intended to render consist in perfecting the students by examination and by the careful revision of exercises in the matter of their oral instruction.' The chief of this class of teachers was the master of method, who had charge of the practising school, and who tried to give the students some idea of the philosophy of education, as well as supervising their teaching.

It is clear from the inspector's comments, that, materially, these teachers had a hard time. They were overworked, were not provided with 'such apartments as they are fairly entitled to', and under paid. This latter matter, being within the inspectors' power to remedy, received their first attention. In their earliest reports they urged that the teachers should be eligible for the augmentation grant as if they had charge of a school. They would thus not be at a disadvantage compared with other certificated teachers. This reform was accepted almost at once; and the teacher could expect a salary of about £120–£150 a year, and a dog-hole at the end of the students' dormitory in which to sleep; for, from about 1850, the colleges had started building long dormitories instead of providing each student with a separate room.

The women's colleges were worse off. Cook describes the general pattern.[18] 'The instruction of the students is carried out by governesses for the most part, and under the general superintendence of the Principal.' Several had clerical principals living on, or near the premises. In others 'the institutions are under the control or superintendence of clergymen acting as secretaries or chaplains having charge of religious instruction. They are men of good, and some very high University position.' Where there was not a clerical principal, there was a first governess. Also a Lady Superintendent who 'had complete authority in all domestic matters, which includes whatever arrangements may be made for the practical training of the students in domestic economy'.

In the inspectors' view the effect of the highly qualified clerical principals on the conduct of the students was good: 'I may here call attention to the fact that the institutions under the charge of clergymen of high attainments are especially remarkable for the practical character of the institution; for the absence of ostentation and bad taste in teaching, and generally also for the plainness of dress, simplicity of manners and industrious habits of the students.'

Some of these principals did not teach, or taught only religious knowledge, so that their intellectual effect was limited. Without them there was no member of the staff with a degree or reasonable academic development. The worthy widows who assumed direction of the institutions cannot have had much knowledge. As the girls were still expected to spend much time on plain sewing or scrubbing the floors, they might hardly have been able to benefit from more expert teaching, even had it been available.

There thus grew up a very considerable variation in the curricula of the different colleges; and this, in turn, brought about one of the greatest defects in the teaching.[19]

The inspectors were expressly forbidden to interfere with 'the management, organization and educational systems' of the different colleges; and they behaved 'with an anxious care not to interfere, however indirectly, with the existing course of instruction in any training college'. As the inspectors examined the colleges and awarded the certificates, they had a most potent engine of control if they had cared to use it. But they scrupulously observed their instructions. 'In setting their questions your Inspectors have been guided simply by the consideration what *is* the course of the institution to be examined, and not by any judgment as to what it *ought* to be.' In consequence, when they held a common examination, as they soon did, they had to set papers on any subject that was taught anywhere. In their eagerness to succeed, the colleges imagined that the more subjects the students took the more chance they had of a good pass; and the tendency was for the students to offer all subjects, even though there was no hope of their doing them except in the most superficial way. The numbers of failures in different subjects in some of the colleges in 1851 shows how unsuccessful this policy could be.

At Cheltenham, 87 per cent failed in French, 71 per cent in bookkeeping, 40 per cent in vocal music, 21 per cent in natural history, 28 per cent in penmanship. At Warrington 95 per cent failed in drawing from models; at Salisbury 80 per cent in biographical memoirs (women took these instead of the coarser forms of history); at Whitelands 97 per cent failed in Welsh and 72 per cent in history of language and etymology. At Chelsea, a year or so earlier, 86 per cent failed in popular astronomy, and about 90 per cent in Latin.[20]

At York Watkins reported that, in physics, 'none of the students appeared to have any knowledge of the subject', and of the paper in English language and literature he says, 'The penmanship and spelling of these papers is defective, and the deplorable inferiority of all the answers is accountable only on the supposition that the subject has never entered into the professed routine of study.'

This proliferation of subjects, taught at the lowest level, or not taught at all, was the basis of most of the criticism and ridicule to which training college students were subjected in the following years; especially when it was combined with a poor knowledge of English and a low level of culture and taste. 'Their knowledge of the laws of the English language,' says one inspector, 'and still more their practical ability to speak and write correctly is generally unsatisfactory.' Matthew Arnold was struck with 'the utter disproportion between the great amount of positive information and the low degree of mental culture and intelligence which they exhibit'. Dickens describes with fierce derision the accomplishments of Mr M'Choakumchild who ran Mr Gradgrind's school in *Hard Times*.

Orthography, etymology, syntax and prosody, biography, geography, astronomy and general cosmography, the sciences of compound proportion, algebra, land surveying and levelling, vocal music and drawing from models were all at the ends of his ten chilled fingers. He had worked his stony way into Her Majesty's Most Honourable Privy Council's Schedule B. and had taken the bloom off the higher branches of mathematics and physical science, French, German, Latin and Greek.

Others, whose views on education were really the exact opposite of Dickens's, made just the same charges against the training colleges and their products.

It did not take long for the Education Department to discover what was wrong in the training college course, it was much more difficult to decide what to do about it. They could not quite make up their minds to prohibit all the more recondite fields of study; they hoped, vainly, that they might be abandoned. 'My Lords could not but be happy to find that the candidate was able to answer in a greater number of subjects well; but the extent of the subjects attempted will not be accepted in lieu of mastery over those which are indispensable.' It was quite in vain for them to say 'a first class certificate may be attained by a candidate, who being perfect in the elementary subjects, takes up none of the higher in the second year'.[21] The training colleges did not believe that simplicity would pay. They may not have trusted My Lords in the prevailing temper of the age, or their honour may have been involved. In any case they maintained, for a time, the right to teach as many subjects as they had a mind to.

The attempt to devise a logical course for the colleges was made by Moseley. In his memorandum he set out perfectly clearly the defects of the present system.[22]

Efforts continually repeated for the attainment of many things, of which none is ever attained, cannot but tend to dissipate and emasculate the mind.

The sense of a perpetual failure, of an inferiority spread over a large surface—of much attempted but little success in any—is an ill preparation of the struggle of life in any condition of it.

It is more difficult to carry out the principle of attempting no more than can be done well in the training of the elementary teacher because so many subjects present themselves to different minds as adapted to the instruction of the poor.

Another difficulty lies in the fact that it is much easier to attain a smattering of knowledge in many subjects—to gather up many fragments of knowledge over a large surface—than to obtain any depth of knowledge in a few.

As an improvement he suggested that the work to be done should be divided into two sections—one for cultivation of the students themselves, the other to teach them the things that they would need to know for their work in schools. For their own improvement they would take:

I year.
> First four books of Euclid, algebra to quadratic equations.

or
> Latin grammar, nouns and adjectives, and to perfect tenses and supines of verbs.

II year.
> One subject only from this list. Physical science, including inorganic chemistry, elementary physics, electricity and simple instruments.
> Mechanics. Machines in common use.
> Mathematics. Euclid 6th book, algebra, trigonometry, levelling and surveying.

English lit. Chaucer to Milton. Books to be read in short portions and discussed as Latin and Greek are in public schools.
Latin. Grammar and prose and verse set books.

Lest the students should think their own cultivation too important, only about a fifth of the total marks obtainable was allotted for these subjects. 'It would be unjust to say that this part of the syllabus is too ambitious, or that it prescribes subjects unfit for the purpose of training teachers for elementary schools.'

The really heavy part of the work lay in the subjects that they were supposed to need for teaching in school. These were religious knowledge, reading, writing, arithmetic, geography, history, drawing, vocal music, and school management. It was on the teaching and examining of these that criticism mainly fell. The knowledge asked for was too extensive, too minute, and bore little relation to the probable interests or needs of their prospective pupils.

Matters are taught [said Nassau Senior], far too minute and far too extensive to be used as the means of exciting, and directing, and spurring the studies of a girl whose destiny is to teach children, from eight to eleven years, reading, writing and arithmetic. What will her scholars have to do with the minority of Richard II, or with the rise and fall of Cromwell, Earl of Essex, or with the Queens of James II, William III and George II or with the treaty of Aix-la-Chapelle or with the deserts of the eastern hemisphere or with the table lands of Asia?

'Etymology', said Moseley, 'is a method of directing their attention to the derivation of one language, with which they are comparatively unacquainted, from another, of which they are profoundly ignorant.'

'To what generation of labourers' children', said another, 'will it ever be expedient to discourse on the Schism of the Papacy, the Council of Basle, the Pragmatic Sanction, or the Wars of the Hussites?'

Instead of this type of knowledge, Moseley imagined what might be called 'the philosophy of the subjects taught in the elementary schools'. 'Cannot elementary learning, e.g. arithmetic, be elevated to its "philosophy"? Arithmetic may be presented to the minds of children under the form of a demonstrative science so simple as to replace in the discipline of their faculties the geometry of higher education.' But he admits that reading, arithmetic, English grammar, history or geography to be taught in this way require books that had not yet been written, and a man 'with a really sound and deep knowledge' as teacher. There were neither books nor men; and the papers, which were set to test the course, forced the colleges to adopt the worst type of teaching. The questions were generally concerned either with matters of trivial detail, which would only be known if they had been laboriously learnt by heart, or they covered so wide a field that, again, they could only be answered in the words of the text-book. Here are examples of both types from the papers of 1857:[23] in religious knowledge:

What events are associated with these places: Hobah, Beerlahai Roi, Mizpeh, Peniel, Shalem, Shechem, Luz? State clearly the practical lessons or spiritual truths illustrated by one of these transactions.

Enumerate the prophecies relating to Our Lord in these books— Numbers, Psalms, Zechariah. Write out the exact words of three of these prophecies.

In history:

State any facts which show the progress of commerce and civilization in the reigns of James I and Charles I.

Name the chief historical and theological writers of the same period, and give some account of their most important works.

So long as questions of this type were set it was vain to complain of the nature of the teaching. As Senior bluntly said, 'As for the defects ascribed to the teaching and examinations in the training colleges, and to the questions asked by the inspectors, the remedy is altogether in the hands of the Committee of Council, and may be applied immediately.'

Dr Temple estimated that about one-tenth of the students did well on the course, but none showed a real power of organizing his knowledge.

In addition to acquiring all this information the students had to study the principles of education and submit to a most exhausting course of school practice.

In the women's colleges the dreary routine was at its worst. The student

is made to observe an entire course of lessons in every elementary subject. She takes notes of all she observes. She has to state how far the method of teaching agrees with that which she has learned as a pupil teacher, or in what respects it may differ from it. . . . This course occupies a considerable time, not less than three months, and indeed, ordinarily six months, when it is thoroughly done. The entire value of the course depends upon the care, the thoughtful earnestness of the student and her instructor. If her mind has another object little impression is made.

Every student having thus learned the system to be pursued conducts a series of classes through an entire course of instruction in each elementary subject,

and she does it with the full apparatus of lesson notes, a junior student as aid and critic, and formal criticism by the tutor.

The men, in theory at least, suffered almost as much. Perhaps a lack of conscientiousness mitigated the infliction. The system was worse because almost all the students had already spent five years in school doing just this. As one report says, going through the routine of teaching every subject at every stage in the practising school is hardly necessary. 'The students are now almost universally youths who have been engaged in teaching for five years or more; they are perfectly familiar with the ordinary management of a class; mere practice is of no farther use to them; on the contrary, if they have formed any bad habits before coming to the training college, these habits are likely to be confirmed.' They find it useless and dislike it. It is most improbable that 'thoughtful earnestness' characterized their work.

The lectures on the theory of teaching were not much more successful. 'The art of teaching was little understood in England', and when Dr Temple listened to the Master of Method doing his best he was not impressed. 'The lectures were usually too ambitious, and the lecturers were too much in the habit of attempting to deduce practical rules of teaching from metaphysical theories about the nature of knowledge and the constitution of mind.' 'Teaching', says one inspector, 'has not yet risen to the dignity of a science among us.' The teachers in the colleges had not yet reached a standard of knowledge and experience which would fit them for the difficult and original task of rethinking the traditional matter of instruction.

To undertake the careful study of such a subject as religious knowledge with a special reference to elementary instruction, and of arithmetic, geography and history and the art of teaching is another thing. Besides great enterprise, industry and originality of mind, it supposes an actual experience of elementary teaching.

The energies of fresh minds must be brought to bear on distinct subjects. The superficial character, of which we have so much reason to complain, I believe to be mainly due to a neglect of this precaution.

Men were needed in the training colleges who, through their personal cultivation and their knowledge of the schools, could present the subjects of instruction in this new way.[24]

As part of the 1853 reforms a serious attempt was made to improve the training colleges. They were allowed to take Queen's scholars up to their full numbers, the standard course was raised from one to two years, and a two-years' probation period after training in the same school was insisted on. The certificate was not granted till this had been duly performed.

The Minute also tried to improve the staffing, and to provide the type of men needed. The method was to institute a class of Lecturers who were to be experts in some subject and to hold a place intermediate between the ordinary teachers and the graduate Principals or Chaplains. They were to be teachers of approved merit and experience, and might offer themselves for examination. The examination was conducted in London in Easter week before an inspector, a senior official of the Education Department and some eminent authority in the subject offered. The candidate was allowed to offer set books of his own choice. He was allowed to offer one, or at most two subjects from among history, English literature, geography, physical science and applied mathematics. If he passed successfully his reward was 'a sum of £100 annually to augment the salary of £150 already due'. The numbers of these lecturers to be appointed to any college was limited. They spread slowly. Ten years later there were only about fifteen of them, all men. Such a high salary and such exalted attainments hardly seemed suitable for females.

These lecturers did not, however, at once produce the books or the novel methods that had been hoped for. The real trouble was that the training colleges were attempting to provide a new type of education for a new type of student; and they had no reliable guide.

'We are accustomed', said Moseley, 'to look upon every other kind of knowledge as an inferior form, a fragment, of that which in our Universities attains its perfection. It was easy to break off such a fragment from a university education and give it to an elementary teacher, and that was considered to be enough.'

But it was not enough. The presupposition of a university, even in the mid-19th century, was that the students were fully literate, with a background of early acquired knowledge. The training college student too often knew nothing but the arid scraps that he had crammed for his annual examination. His real knowledge of farm or workshop he considered irrelevant or almost disgraceful, and put aside. Too often he really could not learn from books. Some of the colleges relied almost exclusively on the 'oral' method, and taught by question and answer.

227

Cheltenham and Battersea who worked this way were considered to do better on the whole than the others, and the inspectors approved, though they hoped that in time the students would arrive at the use of books.

Furthermore, the training colleges, unlike the universities, had a practical aim. The purpose was not to provide general culture but to train teachers; and, though a teacher could not know too much for his work, he must know it in a special way.

Experience has convinced us that studies pursued by the school master ambitiously and in forgetfulness of the wants of the school, are commonly in themselves vapid and fruitless; and, in taking the place of others of humbler pretentions but more useful application, they leave him at once without resources for an efficient discharge of his duties, and give him an ambition beyond them.

If teachers were to be both educated and humble it was hard to know what to do.

It was easier to formulate the problem than to devise means of solving it. All that the inspectors could suggest as a means of overcoming the fundamental illiteracy of the students was that they should 'read more books written in a good style, and requiring written and oral accounts of the subject-matter of these books, and insisting upon committing large portions of good prose and verse to memory'. Unfortunately for this remedy, the world never seems to hold quite the books required; and true literacy is a characteristic that is hard to begin to acquire after the age of eighteen. Shakespeare and Milton were the favourite authors for learning by heart; they hardly formed models for ordinary speech or writing.

As a book for the test in reading aloud the colleges by common consent settled on one as little suitable for the purpose as possible: *Select Extracts from Blackstone's Commentaries, For the use of schools and young persons*, by Samuel Warren, F.R.S., of the Inner Temple. The 419 pages of close type on bad paper must have been very discouraging. The material and language must have been beyond the students' range of knowledge and interest. A sentence from the chapter on the clergy, shows the style:

'These appropriating corporations of religious houses were wont to depute one of their body to perform divine service and administer the sacraments in those parishes in which the society was thus the parson.'

The alternative prescribed book was Sir John Herschel's *Discourse on*

228

Natural Philosophy. The nature of the book and the uses to which it was put can be seen from this examination question set in 1862.

English Grammar. Males 1st year.

Punctuate this passage, and then paraphase it. Parse the words in italics.

In the course of *this* decent to particulars we *must* of necessity encounter all those facts *on* which the arts and works *that* tend to the accommodation of human life depend and acquire *thereby* the command of an unlimited practice and disposal of the powers of nature co-extensive with those powers *themselves* a noble promise *indeed* and one which ought *surely* to animate us to the highest exertion of our faculties especially since we have already *such* convincing proof *that* it is *neither* vain nor rash but on the contrary has been and continues to be fulfilled with a promptness and liberality which *even* its illustrious author in *his* most sanguine mood would have hardly ventured to anticipate.

It is no wonder that an inspector, who was enterprising enough to substitute a more amusing book in the reading test, found a considerable improvement.

In other fields the books were just as ill-adapted to the capacities of the students. Grammar was a subject that dominated the minds of inspectors, and, through them, of teachers. It was, at the moment, enjoying the additional prestige springing from German philology, and Englishmen, in emulation, were trying to scale the 'transcendental heights of philosophical grammar'. Professor Latham, Fellow of King's College, Cambridge, and Professor of English Language and Literature, University College, London, had published a substantial book on the English language in 1841. In it he discussed Anglo-Saxon, Icelandic, varieties of Celtic and layers of Latin influence. It was perhaps from Chapter XXIII of this book that the lecture on the ending '-ing' was taken.

A few years later he produced a shorter form—of 214 pp.—called an *Elementary English Grammar for use in Schools,* and it became a best seller. It is hard to imagine a school for which it would have been suitable, but training colleges used it.

The author took his work very seriously, and provided an Introduction giving hints as to how it should be used. Part I, Historical Introduction, was to be studied with a 'map of Germany and Northern Europe'. All Anglo-Saxon words should be written down and the 'parts wherein they differ from the English carefully underlined'. In the second part—sounds, accents and letters—'the assistance of a teacher will be most wanted to exhibit the nature of our elementary sounds orally'. The third part was Etymology, and 'the first 14 sections should be studied slowly and repeatedly. Before starting upon the syntax, Part IV, the etymology should be gone through twice, and the sections explanatory of the structure of propositions more than twice.'

The section on propositions, which required at least three readings, was as follows:

We have now seen that there are at least three sorts or classes of words: (1) those that can, by themselves, form either subjects or predicates; (2) those that can, by themselves, form predicates only; (3) those that can, by themselves, form copulas. To these must be added a fourth class, consisting of words like NOT that can convert an affirmative copula into a negative one. . . . The copula, subject and predicate may respectively be expressed by a single word. In this latter case a proposition would consist of three parts, but only a single word. In the English language, however, this variety of the form of the proposition is comparatively unimportant. At any rate the knowledge of it may be deferred.

One more sentence, to show the kind of material with which students struggled, concerns a point of syntax:

In the two sentences, *I have ridden a horse*, and *I have ridden a mare*, the word *ridden* is in the same *gender*, although *horse* is masculine and *mare* is feminine. Moreover the word *ridden* is in the *neuter* gender, and, as such, equally different in gender from the two substantives 'horse' and 'mare'. This is the case not only with the sentence in question, but with all the others like it. Whatever may be the gender of the substantives, the participle that follows the word *have* is always neuter.

Professor Latham probably knew little of schools or training colleges, but James Cornwell was connected with the Borough Road for twenty years, and ended his career as Principal. He tried hard to carry out the inspectors' recommendation that subjects, especially arithmetic, should be presented in scientific or even 'philosophical' form. This, from the *Science of Arithmetic*, is an example of his exposition, mathematically valid, but liable to cause the greatest confusion in an ill-prepared student.

§443. Example I. Find the square root of 25.
We first choose a number, 3, whose square is certainly contained in 25; on taking this away we observe 16 to remain. Now if we were to take the square root of this number, which is 4, and add it to the 3, we should be

clearly wrong, for the square root of (9 + 16) is not (3 + 4) any more than the square root of $(a^2 + b^2)$ is $(a + b)$. But since a number, if it contains the square of the sum of two others, must contain the sum of their squares and *twice their product*, we must be able to take from the 16 not only the square of the new part, but also twice the product of it and the other part. Now if we choose the number 2 we observe that its square, 4, and twice the product of itself and the first found number, 3, will make up 16, 2 + 2(2 × 3) = 16. Hence the number 25 has had taken from it in succession, the square of 3, twice the product of 3 and 2, and the square of 2.

∴ 25 contains the square of (3 + 2) for

$$(3 + 2)^2 = 3^2 + 2 \times 3 \times 2 + 2^2 *$$

Of a rather different nature was his book on geography which went on being reprinted, in one edition after another, for forty or fifty years. It was written with the most admirable intentions: 'This book will have failed in its purpose if it does not call into exercise the reasoning faculties of those who use it, and thus render Geography a philosophical study, instead of a mere list of hard names and numbers.' So good an intention was sadly unfulfilled. The book is a fat and revolting volume of 338 pages. It covers the world and is a mass of verbal facts, every one of which is to be committed to memory. It had cost him, he said, much labour to compile it; it would cost any student an incredible amount to master it. 'Definite information is furnished in its proper place. The large type should be committed to memory (that is at least half the book), the notes and smaller type should be read and the information elicited by questions. The exercises are usually long. A question is put respecting every fact stated.' The pupil can thus test himself to see if he really knows it.

The following is a sample of the information given in big type:

BELGIUM

Extent.	195 miles long, 110 broad, 11,400 sq. miles.
Coast.	Only 40 miles; dangerous sandbanks.
Mountains.	None. Hilly in S.E.
Rivers.	Remarkably well watered by the Maas and the Scheldt and their tributaries. Tributaries of the Maas:—Sambre, Ourthe and Lesse.
Climate.	Humid and foggy, except in S.E.

---

* When this was complicated by a misprint, as in the Bodleian copy, the student would have been doubly confused.

Of the ordinary run of questions this may serve as an example: 'Describe England as compared with the rest of Great Britain.' The answer, as given in the text, was, 'England is the largest, wealthiest and in every way the most important part of Great Britain.'

No scrap of information is spared: 'State some particulars concerning Spithead.' The answer, contained in a footnote of type so small as to be hardly legible, is 'So named from a sandbank called the Spit.'

The history books were rather better. Gleig's *School History of England*, which was used at Eton as well as some training colleges, was a substantial work in the tradition of historical writing. If the style is laborious and the morality continuous and Victorian, it does give a connected account in which it is possible to take some interest. Yet even with a book as good as this, the fundamental nature of the teaching remains unchanged. An inspector prescribes how the subject should be taught:

The lecture should always begin by close examination on the subject of the preceding lecture; then on the portion prepared; and then should follow the illustrations and amplifications of the text which the lecturer thinks needful. Notebooks are a doubtful advantage.

Inevitably with such books and such a curriculum the students worked very long hours, and the out-of-door work in garden or farm had been almost entirely given up. There was no provision for games, and very little for recreation. One college might have a boat or do a weekly period of drill; another might allow ball games in the yard and put netting over the windows to avoid damage; but the life of most of the students was extremely confined and sedentary. At Stockwell they tried to rationalize the domestic employment of the girls by saying that training in domestic science and laundry was valuable, especially as 'affording a healthful change and comparative recreation amid their ordinary studies'. But it was not till 1865 that 'at the insistence of the Ladies' Sanatory Association, a lady attends weekly to give instruction in gymnastic exercises which are persued with much interest and spirit'. In other colleges they made no excuses. It was stated: as a general rule the girls 'clean and dust, not scrub their own dormitories; keep clean the lecture and class-rooms; gain some insight into cooking; wait upon each other at meals; prepare the tables; wash up breakfast, tea and supper things; iron and sometimes wash their fine linen'. At Ripon they washed 'each week for $1\frac{1}{2}$ hours in relays, and iron for 1 hour a week'.

At the same time, the attempt to make the period at college a training in the humbler virtues was admitted to have failed.

'It is important to remember', said a report, 'that Sir J. Kay-Shuttleworth's hopes that the teachers might be taught to look upon Popular Education in a missionary spirit, and be trained for a life of humility and self-denial, have been disappointed.' Even Westminster College's device of establishing itself in a slum proved unavailing.

Yet attempts were made to continue the tradition. The minutes of one college in 1858 read: 'It appearing to the Committee that the dietary contains too great a variety and is too luxurious, that the Principal be requested to give instruction to the Matron to prepare the meals of the students with more simplicity and greater frugality.'

A report on the domestic arrangements of Chester Training College in 1857 gives some idea of the conditions:[25]

Each student on entering the college, must provide himself with a plain cap and gown for both of which he himself pays a guinea. This, it is supposed, besides giving a status to the young men themselves, has a tendency to raise the college in their estimation, and to raise them in the estimation of those who are out of college, without any additional expense to the institution.

The crockery is altogether of the common Willow Pattern, that being considered cheaper than any other, and so easily replaced.

All the bread is baked in college, there being a large brick oven within the building. They bake every day. The Principal recommends buying the best flour.

Each bed has four blankets, which are considered ample, a white Maseilles quilt and three calico sheets: the latter article being considered cheaper than linen. Also a bolster with pillow ends. All washable articles and materials are preferred to coloured ones, and such as will contract dirt.

Each student has to furnish himself with a clothes bag.

Some of the washstands are moveable, others are fixtures, being small shelves of wood in the corner of the room.

The chamber ware is white consisting only of a urinal, a basin, tooth brush and soap stands. There are no jugs, as they would be knocked about and might be broken. The water is supplied daily by the servants to the basins. There are other lavatories to be used during the day.

Each student has to find his own looking glass. Some of the dormitories are furnished with small chests of drawers, some without. They are not considered needful.

The students are allowed to take their trunks into their rooms, and most of them do.

There should be one windsor chair and one hanging peg in each apartment.

Six or eight footpans will do for 50 students. There are appointed evenings in the college for feet washings. One of the students supervising and taking the whole responsibility upon himself.

Each student has two shirts a week, and one nightshirt a fortnight.

None of the students are allowed to go to their rooms during the day. Each makes his own bed and brushes his clothes.

Rooms washed monthly, sheets changed once in about three weeks.

The cost of each student, including coal, wages, candles, household washing, vacation expenses, all but gas, amounts to about £18. 18. 0 per annum. Deducting household and vacation expenses it would be less than 9/- a week.

There is a splendid laboratory in the college, and workshops on a large scale, with all sorts of mechanical apparatus for work in carving and handwork, where the students are employed to advantage during their leisure hours.

There is no mention of baths, and this point is underlined in a report on a women's college. In connection with the health of the students, the inspector wishes to make two points: the necessity for regular and sufficient hours of recreation, and the far more frequent use of the bath. 'The latter has been reserved in many instances for the sick, and is therefore practically unused.'

Yet unsatisfactory as the training colleges might be in some respects, they did a great work. 'So far as I have been able to observe', says Maurice, 'the training colleges are the greatest blessings that have been conferred on this land in the last quarter of a century.' To a large extent responsible persons shared this view.

Throughout this period the colleges were organizing their material life with the aid of public money. They received large capital grants for building, and annual grants which covered the larger part of their running expenses. During the seven years from 1844 the Government gave £137,623 in building grants, and in 1852 the Government gave £15,996 for capital building grants and £17,545 for annual support. Over the whole number the Government supplied 64 per cent of the running costs, and that included Congregational Homerton which refused all Government money. The Church colleges on an average received about 74 per cent; at Cheltenham the Government contribution was 94 per cent, at York 89 per cent and at Durham 80 per cent.[26] The colleges ranged in size from the Home and Colonial's Institution with 172 students to Peterborough with 15 men.

One curious and isolated episode of this period was the life and death of Kneller Hall as a training college. A year or so before his retirement, Kay-Shuttleworth returned to his original plan of a government training college to prepare teachers for workhouse and other Government schools. When the scheme had been abandoned ten years before it had been stated that the Government, 'owing to the difficulties which they experienced in reconciling conflicting views', were reserving their original design for further consideration, and postponing taking further steps 'until greater concurrence of opinion is found to prevail'.

If people did not 'concur' at least they no longer cared—and the project could be proceeded with.

A suitably 'Elizabethan' house with large grounds, a mile from Twickenham station, was bought and adapted for the purpose. The Rev. Frederick Temple was appointed principal, and Francis Turner Palgrave Vice-principal. Religion and letters having been thus admirably provided for, the other lecturers were as good as could be obtained.

Unfortunately the life of a Poor-Law schoolmaster had no attractions. Often he was paid only £20 a year and expected to live in the workhouse under the control of the Master or Matron, who, all too often, lacked both education and charity, and made his work impossible. It was futile for an inspector to hope that Poor-Law teaching might become 'one of the best prizes open to Merit'. There was no sign of it, and any youth, even of the most modest pretensions, knew that he could do better elsewhere. The Government offered Queen's scholarships, and exhibitions in addition of as much as £30. They were prepared to continue the grants for a second year. In 1850 apparently five students took the examination, after an average stay of 10½ months. At one time there seem to have been fifteen men in residence. Of the seven who went out during one year, one went to Australia and got a post in a convict school at £120 a year and house, another went to the Royal Naval schools at Greenwich at the same salary. The other five were recorded as 'not settled'. With students so few it was far more expensive than any other college. A Parliamentary reply stated that it had cost the country £70,000, and that each student trained had cost £1200 to train. Naturally its life was short. In 1855 it was closed down.[27] In due course the buildings housed the School of Military Music.

The importance of the episode was that those who wished to restrict

state action, particularly in the training of teachers, vocally attributed
the failure of the college to the part the Government had played in its
foundation, and not to the narrowness of its aim and the repulsiveness
of the work for which alone it claimed to train students. Moreover, its
very purpose departed, for, before it was closed, the workhouse children
were already being sent to the ordinary schools, and thus there was no
need for masters to teach them in isolation.

Notes

1. P.P., 1865, VI: Report of Select Committee to enquire into the constitution of Committee of Council on Education. Lingen's evidence, pp. 1 ff.
2. Minutes, 1848–50, I, p. 133.
3. Minutes, 1848–50, I, p. xxxiii.
4. *Newcastle Report*, pp. 321 ff.
5. *Edinburgh Review*, April 1853, p. 504.
6. Hansard, 1853, CXXV, 522.
7. January 1854, p. 158.
8. *Newcastle Report*, p. 232.
9. Minutes, 1859–60, p. 44; P.P., 1860, LIV, 85.
10. Minutes, 1855–6, pp. 325 ff.
11. *Edinburgh Review*, April 1853, p. 465.
12. *Newcastle Report*, p. 260.
13. *Newcastle Report*, p. 351.
14. Minutes, 1857–8, p. 395.
15. Minutes, 1851–2, II, p. 116; see also Kay-Shuttleworth, *Public Education*, Appendix B.
16. *Newcastle Report*, p. 257.
17. *Newcastle Report*, p. 118.
18. Minutes, 1855–6, pp. 732 ff.
19. Minutes, 1850–1, I, pp. 84 ff; 1851–2, pp. 326.
20. Minutes, 1851–2, I, 326, 348.
21. Kay-Shuttleworth, *Public Education*, Appendix C, p. 434.
22. Minutes, 1854–5, pp. 14–21; for the Training Colleges in general, *Newcastle Report*, pp. 113 ff.
23. Quoted Nassau Senior, *Suggestions*, p. 323.
24. On the 'philosophy of subjects', see Minutes, p. 1848–50, I, p. 27; 1854–5, p. 305; 1850–1, I, p. 39.
25. Preserved in the Log Books of Caernarvon Training College at St Mary's College, Bangor. Also on food, see Minutes, 1851–2, I, p. 348.
26. *Newcastle Commission*, p. 115.
27. Minute of Committee of Council, 25 November, 1854.

Chapter Twelve

The Newcastle Commission

1856 saw a definite change in the position of the Committee of Council on Education. Up till now Parliament had had very little influence on its workings. When the estimates came up they could be debated; but they generally only covered sums which had already been promised or spent, and it was very difficult to refuse them. As the Chancellor of the Exchequer was a member of the Committee, he had, in theory at least, the opportunity to comment on the estimates before they came to the Commons; but there is nothing to say how often he, in fact, considered them. It was felt that the position was not satisfactory. Education was getting out of hand. It was proposed that now there should be a Vice-President of the Council who was to be a member of the Government, and to be answerable to Parliament for the affairs of the Committee. The Bill creating this office originated in the Lords,[1] and was passed with great speed and unanimity by a Parliament which was distracted by the Crimea War.

It is quite clear that it was intended, not to assist the spread of education, but to enable Parliament to restrain the growing cost of the service, and to keep the Committee of Council from having too many ideas for the public good. As the vote for education was now about £500,000 and rising at the rate of almost £100,000 a year, it was felt that this sum was too large to be at the disposal of 'an irresponsible body'. A political head to the department, particularly if he cared nothing for education, would keep things in order.

The character of the men appointed shows that this was the intention. During the first few months the office was passed back and forth between Adderley and Cowper who held it concurrently with, or in suc-

238

cession to the Presidency of the Board of Health. Adderley had shown some interest in education in the past, but he cared more for getting vagrant children off the streets than for any development of literary education. In 1856 he declared:

There should be an extension of surface, so as to reach the 400,000–1,000,000 children who were now left wholly unprovided with education. Besides extension of surface, however, they should also see that there was a restriction of object. The object of the present system appeared to be, not to make ploughboys or mechanics, but to make scholars. Parents did not want that. . . . If they were to pass a law to compel poor parents to send their children to school to be made scholars of, they might just as well pass another law to compel the noble lord to send his children to a school where they would be educated for becoming ploughboys or artisans. The one law would be no more absurd or tyrannical than the other.[2]

Cowper had not spoken on education for more than a year before accepting office—even though there had been considerable debates on the subject.

Under Lingen's management the affairs of the Department were already in disorder. The inspectors' annual conferences had become contentious. In this temper it was natural for authority to discontinue the meetings, and to declare that the inspectors' loyalty lay, not with truth and progress, but with the head of the Department. In July 1858 Cowper asked Adderley, who was then Vice-President of the Council, to make a statement on inspectors' reports. The reply said that they would no longer be published individually in full, but that they would be digested into a single report with 'the excision of such matters as the Committee conceived to be unnecessary and not of the nature of a bona fide report'. In fact, he felt the inspectors' reports 'instead of being collections of facts were essays propounding new theories and startling systems of their own, and in these respects he thought there ought to be an alteration'. He meant to impose this alteration, and put an end to the process by which the inspectors led the nation in matters of educational thought. The inspectors reacted sharply, and, for the moment, retained their right to say what they thought of the broader aspects of education. Yet we can perhaps take this as the point at which the inspectors cease to be missionaries, and from which the inspectorate gradually became the haven for idle and incompetent gentlemen—as Senior foresaw—and the special field for the petty tyrant under the regulations of the next forty years.

At the same time, as there were now sixty inspectors, a full report from each made a large and expensive volume for annual publication—and economy had become the watchword of the day.

In 1859 the worst appointment of all was made to the Vice-Presidency—Robert Lowe. Lowe came to the office from being Paymaster to the Forces and Vice-President of the Board of Trade. He had never spoken on education for at least three years, and his character and policies would ensure that he would be unsympathetic.

He was an albino, and this afflicting singularity weakened his eyesight and sharpened his temper. He had gone to Australia, made a fortune, and served his apprenticeship in politics. He came back with ambition, and a pathological loathing of democracy. His famous attack on the electoral reforms of 1867 contained the sentence: 'If you want venality, if you want ignorance, if you want drunkenness and facility for being intimidated: or if, on the other hand, you want impulsive, unreflecting and violent people, where do you look for them in the constituencies? Do you go to the top or to the bottom?'

He was no more popular with his social equals. A premature epitaph reads:

> Here lies the body of Robert Lowe,
> Where he has gone to I don't know.
> If he has gone to the realms above,
> That's an end of peace and love.
> If he has sought a lower level,
> God have mercy on the Devil.

His position as leader writer for *The Times* gave him a power to influence public opinion possessed by few politicians—and he could do it anonymously.

The damage that he did came largely from his association with Lingen. The two men fitted perfectly together. With the same classical background, the same keen intelligence, the same dislike of democracy and the same harshness of nature they could co-operate harmoniously in destroying much of Kay-Shuttleworth's work. As Lingen's published letters become more insulting after Lowe's appointment, so Lowe's early speeches, which are intelligent and reasonable, contrast with the regulations of which he and Lingen were the joint authors. The circumstances of the day gave them their opportunity.

In 1856 Lord John Russell had made trial of the feeling of the House by introducing a number of resolutions on education. The first said: 'It is expedient to extend, revise and consolidate the Minutes of the Committee of Council on Education.' The others proposed a survey of the country to discover what deficiencies existed, and a scheme by which deficient districts might raise a rate for education and appoint a committee to administer it.[3]

These resolutions produced considerable debate, but all except the first were decisively rejected. It was clear that opinion was not ready for any forward step in education.

That being so, Sir John Pakington asked for a Commission to survey the state of education; and he suggested that the report, when it came, might be followed by radical legislation as the Commission on the Poor Law of 1833 had been. The terms of reference that he proposed were 'to enquire into the present state of popular education in England, and to consider and report what measures, if any, are required for the extension of sound and cheap elementary education to all classes of the people'.

Undoubtedly he had in mind the notorious inadequacy of the educational provision in certain districts and the poverty of many of the people for whom education was most necessary. Unfortunately, in the event, the 'all' was ignored and the 'cheapness' transferred from the individual to the state.✗

Lowe, in a rather unwilling speech on the estimates of 1859, sets out very well the problems before the Commission.[4] The present system had done well in so far as it had brought about a great increase in the number of schools, and, through the inspectors, a great improvement in teaching and accommodation. The system had grown up in conformity with the general wishes of the nation, and nothing else that had been proposed had had even a chance of acceptance. On the other hand voluntary effort would never cover the whole field, the central machinery was impossibly clumsy and rigid and there was need for local partnership with the central office. Moreover the denominational system, especially in regard to inspectors, was very wasteful. Out of the present sixty inspectors, twenty could be dispensed with if denominational inspection were given up, and if each had a compact district for which he was responsible. In the civilized world, we stood alone 'in having no element of compulsion in our entire educational system', and if the work was to be adequately done we needed to add something that would to a certain extent take its place.

The Commission was appointed with the Duke of Newcastle at its head. He had had the misfortune to be in charge of the War Office during the Crimea War, and was now Secretary of State for the Colonies. The members of the Commission were carefully chosen. Sir John Coleridge was a Member of the Privy Council and a friend of Keble. He brought knowledge, intellect and the favour of the high church party. Edward Miall balanced him as a dissenter and an opponent of state intervention in Education. There was Nassau Senior, the economist, who had served on the Poor Law Commission and on the Hand-loom Weavers' Commission. There was the Rev. William Rogers who had played a leading and successful part in developing London education; and from the Universities came the Rev. William Charles Lake and Professor Goldwin Smith. They had at their disposal the reports of the inspectors, but they preferred to send out their own Assistant Commissioners who would look at things freshly, and also provide more general information than was contained in the Reports. They arranged to sample different types of district, choosing those where the farms were big and those where they were small; where industry was on a large scale or where it was mainly domestic. They took evidence from Kay-Shuttleworth and from one of the inspectors; but on the whole they tried, at least in their public sittings, to approach the matter without being too closely engaged by the past.

Thus informed, they surveyed the schools and training colleges as they have been described, and gave them modified approval. The Commission found that the schools and certificated teachers were satisfactory, except in one particular.

It is clear that the character of the teachers is greatly raised by their training. It is equally clear that they fail to a considerable extent in some of the most important duties of elementary teachers, and that a large proportion of the children are not satisfactorily taught that which they come to learn. [In fact] the junior classes in the schools, comprehending the great majority of the children, do not learn, or learn imperfectly, the most necessary part of what they come to learn—reading, writing and arithmetic.[5]

As to the training colleges it said:

We have expressed our fears that the hours of work are too many; that the time given to out-door exercise is too short; and that the attendance of the students in the practising schools tends to confirm any bad habits which they may have acquired as pupil teachers.

It definitely disapproved of the type of examination paper set. 'As to the examination papers prepared by the Committee of Council we have stated our opinion that in the character of the questions there is too much minuteness, too much which appeals to mere verbal recollection, and too little attention to the real importance of the subject-matters enquired into.' But they did 'not propose to disturb the existing arrangements as to the examination of students in the Training Colleges'.[6]

The chief problem they felt was to devise a means of securing that the elementary subjects were taught in school in a satisfactory manner. The Commission was convinced of the difficulty and laboriousness of teaching little children to read, and it sought to find means of forcing the teachers to undertake the work with determination. At present the grants depend on the 'general character and management of the school', not on the success of individual children in elementary subjects. There must be a reform.

There is only one way of securing this result, which is to institute a searching examination by competent authority of every child in every school to which grants are paid, with a view of ascertaining whether these indispensable elements of knowledge are thoroughly acquired, and to make the prospects and position of the teacher dependent, to a considerable extent, on the results of this examination.

There can be no sort of doubt that if one teacher finds that his income depends on the condition that his scholars do learn to read, whilst another is paid equally well whether they do so or not, the first will teach more children to read than the second.

The object is to find some constant and stringent motive to induce them to do that part of their duty which is at once most unpleasant and most important.[7]

There was needed, then, a method of paying the grants which would give this stimulus without crippling the schools. There was also needed some way of redistributing the cost of the schools so that part of it was borne locally and fell upon the landowners, who had, too often, scandalously evaded their social duties. Furthermore, some means must also be devised of relieving the Central Office of some of its work. The scheme they proposed was directed to all these ends.[8]

They suggested that all assistance given for the annual maintenance of schools should be simplified and reduced to grants of two kinds.

The first should be paid out of the general taxation of the country, the second out of the county rates.

The Government grant would be given on the average attendance of

243

the children: 4s. 6d. for each child, plus a further 2s. 6d. for each child who has 'been under the instruction of pupil teachers or assistant teachers, allowing 30 children for each pupil teacher and 60 for each assistant teacher'.

The local grant was to be given on examination.

The managers of schools shall be entitled to be paid out of the county rate a sum varying from 22/6 to 21/- for every child who has attended the school during 140 days in the year preceding the day of examination, and who passes an examination before the county examiner in reading, writing, arithmetic and who, if a girl, also passes an examination in plain work.

Scholars under 7 years of age need not be examined, but the amount of grant shall be determined by the average number of children in daily attendance, 20/0 being paid on account of each child.

The Government grant continued the established capitation grant, and carried the same conditions that the schools should be 'healthy, ventilated, supplied with offices' and should allow eight square feet per child in the principal room. The local grant was to be administered by

a County Board of Education appointed in the following manner: The Court of Quarter Sessions shall elect any number of members, not exceeding six, being in the Commission of the Peace, or being chairmen or vice-chairmen of Boards of Guardians; and the members so elected shall elect any other persons not exceeding six. The number of ministers of religion on any County Board of Education shall not exceed one-third of the whole number.

In corporate towns with a population of 40,000 or over the town council appointed the Borough Board of Education.

Payment of grant to the schools should be made, as to the government grant, to the county treasurer for all the schools in his area on the report of the inspector; and the treasurer should pay it out to the managers of the individual schools plus the amount which might be due to them on the local grant.

By this arrangement the work of the central office would be greatly simplified; and the fact emphasized that the teachers were the direct employees of the managers.

'The council office has always, and in our opinion properly, avoided any direct recognition of either principal or pupil teachers, and has confined all its relations to the managers of the individual schools.'

The sums that were due under the two heads had been adjusted so that 'All schools should have a reasonable prospect of earning from

9   Robert Lowe, Viscount Sherbrooke. Portrait by G. F. Watts

10 School or Gaol—A Sketch from Life

public sources ⅓ of the total expense of educating all children as well as they are educated in the present annual grant schools; the best schools, however, should be able to earn a higher sum, with the limitation that this shall in no case exceed half the amount of their expenditure.'

As it was reckoned that it cost about 30s. a year to educate a child, 15s. per child on the average attendance was fixed as the highest grant that could be earned.

The chief subtlety in these proposals was the device for appointing the County Boards of Education. The objection to financing the schools from the rates and giving local control had always been partly the fear of religious intolerance, but, still more, the dreadful example of the Poor Law, and the dread of the lowest parochial jealousy and petty tyranny. County or Borough Boards would deal with larger areas, and, if their members were J.P.s or Chairmen of Boards of Guardians, their social status and, presumably, their education would be to some extent guaranteed. Ministers of religion would always be in a minority, so there was some hope of avoiding the worst interdenominational quarrels.

The areas, and the bodies from which these Boards are to be appointed, appear to us the only ones likely to secure a class of local administrators to whom so delicate a subject as education could be safely entrusted. In arranging the constitution of the County Boards we have attempted to secure the presence of persons whose standing, experience, and local knowledge would give weight to their proceedings and ensure their interest in their functions. We think, also, that in most counties persons will be found who, without holding any official position, have much experience of popular education, and take great interest in it. We propose, therefore, that the other members of the County Board should have the power of associating with themselves any number of such persons not exceeding six. And we propose that, in addition, an Inspector selected by the Committee of Council shall have a seat upon this and the Borough Board.

These Education Boards would not *control* education; that would be the work of the managers, whose position was strengthened. They would hand out the money that the school became entitled to, and thus would be *associated* with the work.

The Commission also considered the manner of examining the children. They felt that it was not reasonable to ask an inspector to spend his time on such simple and unrewarding business; and they proposed a class of examiners, drawn from the teachers themselves. The examiners would be paid £150 a year, and it would offer a sense of promotion to the aspiring, or a haven to those who were no longer able to bear the hurly-burly of school life.

The other real point was the generosity and balance of the financial proposals. The capitation grant would have given every reputable school 7s. a head on average attendance for the older children, and 20s. a head for the younger. On the statistics which the Commission had, 43 per cent of the children attended 150 days and upwards, and this figure might be expected to increase as the schools improved. Half the children, at least, would be eligible for examination, and an ever-increasing proportion of these should be successful. The schools had thus a reasonable security in the capitation grant, and a handsome reward for success. Particular encouragement was given to the younger children, since it was felt most important to get them to school early, especially as they would leave at 11 on the average. In the past the Government grant had normally met about a third of the cost of the schools, and to give the schools the opportunity of earning half was generous.

This very reasonable and forward-looking scheme was not new in its main outlines. The individual examination of children had been proposed several times. There had been five attempts since 1850 to transfer some of the cost of education to the rates. In fact, the *Quarterly*, wishing to damn the proposals, declared that they had all been anticipated in an article in the *Encyclopaedia Britannica*.[9] The local control of education by school committees had been proposed twenty-five years earlier, and had recurred as part of many subsequent bills; the contribution of the Commission was to suggest a larger area for the districts, and to try to ensure that the persons charged with the administration of education were of good social standing. The other main recommendation, that the grant should in part depend on the individual examination of children, was an idea well established since 1853.

This regulation, however, had proved to be a dead letter.[10] Cook might hanker after such an examination; he might even assert that he conducted one, but the facts were against him. When he told the Commissioners that he could examine the *staple* work of a school of 150 in 1½ hours, and that in this time he 'could hear every boy read, see the writing of every boy and try the arithmetic, and in fact go through all', they made a sceptical calculation and found that he needed only 30 seconds for each scholar.

Senior said quite plainly that 'the individual examination of each child which was originally imposed as a duty on the inspectors' was now abandoned. Thus the Commission was only going back to the former regulation, with added guarantees for the performance of the task.

In the debate on the *Newcastle Report* on 11 July 1861 Lowe spoke mainly in favour of the existing system.[11] Any system administered centrally must necessarily be expensive. The officials charged with spending money did not have to provide it, and the peculiar circumstances of the Department of Education made it almost impossible to budget accurately in advance. He had little doubt that the clever children at the top of the school received more attention than those at the bottom, but then that happened everywhere. He did not think the teachers were too highly educated. Critics must remember that they had to train the pupil teachers as well as the children. In any case the Government did not run the training colleges, and could not control their curricula. The organization of the central office was certainly complicated. 'There are 7000 certificated teachers, and 15,000 pupil teachers. We pay everyone of them by Post Office order sent direct to his address. We keep a registry and biographical notice of them all, so as to be aware of their character.' This method of direct payment ensured that the money they paid reached the person for whom it was intended. 'It was not', he declared, 'the intention of the government to infringe on the organic principles of the present system', but he did feel that in one matter they had failed. 'Looking back to the system we think it quite possible that we have erred in not devising some machinery for testing more particularly the results of the schools.'

In view of all this there would be no fresh legislation, instead there would be regulations, and he was going to suggest (1) economies in inessentials, (2) that all moneys should be paid to the managers of schools and not direct to the teachers, and (3) that a single capitation grant would take the place of the augmentation grants and the salaries of pupil teachers. This capitation grant would be payable on three conditions: (*a*) attendance by the children, (*b*) that the school was under the superintendence of a certificated master, (*c*) that the children passed an examination in reading, writing and arithmetic.

Public reaction to the *Report* was even less favourable, and the Commission's suggestions for reform were largely ignored. Instead the Reviews concentrated on the defects of the schools. The sentence stating that the children did not learn 'the most necessary part of what they came to learn' was quoted on every hand with glee. The statistics of

247

irregular attendance were rehearsed, and the early leaving age approved. Neither the finance proposals nor the Boards of Education drew favourable comment. There was no demand for a real advance in education.

The task of preparing the new regulations went on in secret. The code was 'concocted' says Matthew Arnold in *Fraser's Magazine* 'in the recesses of the Privy Council office, with no advice asked from those practically conversant with schools, no notice given to those who largely support schools, and the new scheme of the Council office has taken alike their friends and enemies by surprise'.[12]

If the educationalists were excluded from the discussions of the Code, it was generally accepted that Gladstone as Chancellor of the Exchequer had exercised his right to be present, and his influence was most important. His only interest was in economy, and there is no doubt that he demanded some reorganization of education which would halt the increase in cost, or perhaps reduce it. How the reduction was to be brought about was immaterial. The framers of the actual Code were Lowe and Lingen. Lord Granville, the nominal head of the Committee was mainly neutral, Lowe had to answer in Parliament and accept the responsibility for the Code. He certainly rejoiced in it and his speeches show the motives with which it was conceived. He did not do it alone, As the *Saturday Review* said, 'Mr Lingen is quite as powerful as Lowe, and a good deal more offensive.' They both shared the 'spirit of hostility to the system which they administered', and which made even their later concessions of small value.[13]

The result of their work was a document of startling simplicity.[14] After repeating from earlier versions certain regulations about sites. those concerning grant are given. 'The managers of schools may claim 1*d.* per scholar for every attendance after the first 100, at the morning or afternoon meetings. One third part of the sum thus claimable is forfeited if the scholar fails to satisfy the inspector in reading, one third if in writing, and one third if in arithmetic respectively.' The children were to be examined in groups by age: three to seven years, seven to nine, nine to eleven, and eleven and upwards.

There were to be no other grants for schools. The calculation offered to justify these figures was of an equal simplicity. The Commission had found that more than half the children attend school for 140 days in the year. Divide these days into morning and afternoon sessions and you have 280. Deduct 100 and you have 180. That in pence is 15*s*. Therefore to pay 1*d.* for every attendance over 100 would give the schools

15*s*. for each child *if he were properly taught* (and this was to be ascertained by examination); 15*s*. a head had been suggested by the Commission as the maximum grant—so that was exactly right.

What Lowe failed to mention was that the Commission had suggested a maximum of 15*s*. a head on the *average attendance* and had provided a capitation grant to give the schools stability.

Lowe announced these regulations as a small and unimportant variation in the method of paying the education grant; and laid them on the table in February 1862, as inconspicuously as possible, just before a recess. They could thus have lain there the statutory thirty days and come into operation before the House had an opportunity to debate them. Viewed in the context of the times, perhaps, they were unimportant. Men's minds were largely preoccupied with events abroad. Italy was in process of unification, we were almost at war with France. Maximilian was drawing to the end of his unhappy adventure in Mexico. There was a struggle as to whether the navy should have ships all of iron or of wood plated. The Great International Exhibition opened in May. Civil Service Examinations were being introduced and India reorganized. Most important of all the American Civil war was beginning, and the cotton famine had brought destitution to Lancashire. It is against this background that the fight for the soul of education took place.

When the Revised Code was examined by those interested in education it brought consternation, for two reasons. It was realized at once that it would bring an enormous drop in the income of schools, if only because the conditions attached to the grant would be impossible to fulfil. And, secondly, it showed a complete change in the conception of the relation between the schools and the state. Whereas previously the state had attempted to guide and develop education by an ingenious, perhaps too ingenious, system of rewards and incentives, now there was a stark threat: achieve what we ask—or perish. The negative import of the Code was emphasized by the *Quarterly*:[15]

Simplification is the key-note of the Revised Code. This is carried out with regard to book grants, by abolishing them; with regard to scientific apparatus grants, by abolishing them; with regard to grants for drawing, by abolishing them; with regard to grants for industrial work, by abolishing them; with regard to grants for infant schools, by abolishing them; with regard to grants for ragged schools, by abolishing them; with regard to special grants for evening schools, by abolishing them; with

249

regard to retirement pensions, by abolishing them; with regard to grants to school societies, by abolishing them; with regard to small building and furnishing grants, by abolishing them. We have no fault to find with these simplifications. It is time for these grants, or most of them to cease; but it is a more serious matter when it appears that the same sort of simplification is employed with regard to the augmentation grant to the salaries of masters and with regard to the grant for pupil teachers, which have been hitherto considered the bone and sinews of the whole system.

Matthew Arnold saw it from the other side; his article continues: 'This system withdraws from popular education, so far as it can, all serious guidance, all initiatory direction by the state: it makes the action of the state upon this as mechanical, as little dynamical as possible.' Under this system it is assumed that 'the duty of a state in public education is to obtain the greatest possible quantity of reading, writing and arithmetic for the greatest number' and this is, so far as the state is concerned 'the education of the people'. To these subjects, therefore, it confines its grants. Under the previous system it has done much more. 'It has paid for a machinery of instruction extending itself to many other things besides these. It has been paying for discipline, for civilization, for religious and moral training, for a superior instruction for forward and clever children . . .' and he ends with the lament 'Now is your hour and the power of darkness.'

It follows from this changed conception of the duties of the schools that the character of the teacher becomes of far less consequence than before. If examinable results are the only criterion of success, it matters little by whom or by what methods this success is achieved. The demand, which was almost immediately made (on the excuse of helping poor schools), that the employment of a certificated teacher should cease to be a condition of receiving grant, was the logical application of the principle. The resistance of this demand is the one good deed of the rulers of education at this period. For all the motives that we can discern in the framing of these regulations were bad.

There was meanness and hate. Gladstone must be held responsible for insisting on a reduction in the money spent on education; and behind him were those payers of income tax who were beginning to shoulder the burdens that had been taken from the poor.

Some of the hate was directed against the Church. Undoubtedly the present organization of education suited the Church perfectly, as both friends and foes of the Establishment understood. The nonconformists were jealous of the extent of Church patronage, and were opposed to any state help in education. But there was an enemy nearer the heart of things. Lingen was commonly supposed to have been the main author of the regulations, and his views were known. 'How far is your friend Lingen at the bottom of all this?' wrote Dean Close. 'He is a secularist and he said "the present system worked too well".'

The greater part of the hate was directed against the teachers; and in this hostility churchmen and anti-clericals joined. The social jealousy which had sprung up between the teachers and their mainly clerical employers had been mentioned during the hearings of the Commission, and it was felt by both parties. Wilkinson, one of the assistant Commissioners reported that the teachers 'felt that their position in society is lower than it ought to be, which is the fault of the clergy, who either spoil their work by foolish interfering or, if it succeeds, take all the credit'. The *Quarterly*, speaking for the employers, is equally bitter. Snell of East Coker in his evidence had revealed the heights of presumption. 'We think', says the article on the Revised Code, 'that some of the certificated teachers have shown symptoms of turbulence and discontent, which not only require to be summarily checked and put down, but which, if universal, would be sufficient to justify the extinction of the whole class. Mr Snell did not know into what a pit of destruction he was being gently led.'[16]

This was a serious enough matter, but the teachers had committed an offence which damned them with both Whigs and Tories; they had threatened to organize for political action and form the sinews of a new Radical Party. Lowe plays on this jealousy and fear, suggesting that those who oppose the new regulations do it to maintain the privileges which cause such social damage.

The great danger is that the grant for Education may become a grant to maintain the so called vested interest of those engaged in education. If parliament does not set a limit to this evil, such a state of things will arise that the conduct of the Educational system will pass out of the hands of the Privy Council and of the House of Commons into the hands of the persons working that educational system, and then no demand they choose to make on the public purse would any Ministry dare to refuse.

And from there he goes on to quote, with horror, the words of one of the more militant educational journals.

If teachers remain quiescent now, they deserve all, and more than all of the indignities heaped upon them. If they do not now rise, they deserve

251

to be for ever fallen. A goodly proportion of the 9000 certificated teachers are possessed of the elective franchise. It is not likely that the friends of the 3000 students and 15,000 pupil teachers will stand tamely by and see the prospects for life of those in whom they are interested so materially damaged. We must make it unmistakably understood that our votes and our influence are for the men who aid us in this conjuncture.[17]

Such an attitude was clearly intolerable, and Lowe, looking back on these years from 1865 when he had ceased to be vice-president, boasts of how effectively he had scotched it.

The Revised Code [he said], swept away the vested interests of some 10,000 teachers, who had begun to consider themselves as government employees, having a claim on augmentation grants for the rest of their lives; it altered the relations between the government and some 7000 or 8000 managers who from that time received in a simple grant payments which had before been made to them in a complicated form. We got rid of the enormous incubus of some 15,000 pupil teachers who were receiving grants; we reformed the training colleges, putting them on a footing by which the burdens of the state are limited, and arranged so that the money is only paid for work actually performed.

We took from the schoolmasters considerable payments which they had been receiving from the Government, and thus many clever men, over-educated men scattered pretty equally all over the country, were provided with a grievance against the Department.[18]

Such spite could have found the majority acquiescent only in special circumstances; and 1860 and the following years were such a time. On the one hand, the Government had no real domestic policy; it retained office merely because the nation approved its foreign policy, particularly in regard to Italy. On the other, the spectacle of America on the brink of civil war produced a general distrust of democracy.

The troubles through which America is passing undoubtedly prompt the popular mind to steer a point or two clearer from democracy than it usually cares to do.

At the moment the disturbances in America make England conservative:—it would be a mistake to reckon on this as a durable influence. In some way or another America will settle itself before long, and when we have got accustomed to the settlement we shall take up reform as a purely domestic question.[19]

This prophecy was certainly fulfilled; but at the moment democracy was suspect, and teachers as the nurses of democracy were made the objects of attack. The consequence was that the true foes of popular education had the acquiescence if not the support of a large part of the nation. To quote Matthew Arnold again:

That tide of reactionary sentiment against everything supposed to be in the least akin to democracy which, in presence of the spectacle afforded by America, is now sweeping over Europe, it is useless at the monent to try to stem. The friends of the Revised Code are numerous, resolute and powerful. There is Mr Lowe . . . there is *The Times*, which naturally supports Mr Lowe. There is the *Daily News* unable to shake off a super-stitious reverence for the old watchwords of the extreme dissenters. There are the friends of economy-at-any-price. There are the selfish and vulgar of the upper classes . . . there are the clever and fastidious . . . All these will be gratified by the triumph of the Revised Code, and they are many. And there will be only one sufferer:—the education of the people.[20]

If the circumstances of the time did not allow the educationalists to defeat the spirit of the Revised Code, they could attack the more out-rageous provisions. The piece of political chicanery, by which the regu-lations would have come into force before Parliament had had the chance of discussing them, displeased the House and moved Mr Disraeli to particular wrath. He demanded a debate. After many evasions and postponements, it was fixed for 25 March.

The interval was filled with controversy. Kay-Shuttleworth wrote a long pamphlet, which sold 10,000 copies, setting out all the disadvan-tages of the proposals. Leaders appeared in *The Times*, written probably by Lowe himself, defending the Code. In the House of Lords the Bishop of Oxford, who seems to have accepted the task of spokesman for the Church, presented petitions against the regulations. In the debate, the tone of the House was violently hostile.[21]

The attack was directed not so much against the central provision of the code—the individual examination of children—as against its details. In particular the abolition of the capitation grant, the examination of infants, and the grouping of children by age, irrespective of the time they had spent in school or their level of attainment. So strongly were these points urged that on the third day of debate Lowe gave way, and announced that the Code would be held over for reconsideration.

When it emerged in its new form it was far nearer that proposed by the Commission. The essential provisions were as follows:

The Managers of the school may claim at the end of the year:
  a. The sum of 4/- per scholar according to the average number in

253

attendance throughout the year at the morning and afternoon meetings of their school.

b. For every scholar who has attended more than 200 morning or afternoon meetings of their school:—

1. If more than 6 years of age 8/-, subject to examination.

2. If under six years of age, 6/6 subject to a report by the inspector that such children are instructed suitably to their age, and in a manner not to interfere with the instruction of the older children.

Every scholar attending more than 200 times in the morning or afternoon, for whom 8/- is claimed, forfeits 2/8 for failure to satisfy the inspector in reading, 2/8 in writing and 2/8 in arithmetic.

Every scholar for whom the grants dependent upon examination are claimed must be examined according to one of the following standards and must not be presented for examination a second time according to the same or a lower standard.

The standards go from I to VI. In Standard I the demands were slight. 'Reading, Narrative in monosyllables. Writing, form on blackboard or slate from dictation letters capital and small manuscript. Arithmetic, form on blackboard or slate from dictation, figures up to 20; name at sight figures up to 20. Add and subtract figures up to 10, orally from examples on blackboard.'

In Standard III they were required 'to read a short paragraph from an elementary reading book used in the school, to write a sentence from the same paragraph, slowly read once, and then dictated in single words, and to work a sum in any simple rule as far as short division (inclusive)'.

Although it is not stated in the regulations inspectors made a break between Standards III and IV. In Standard IV the children gave up using slates, and higher education was felt to have begun. The crown of their time at school was reached in Standard VI when they were required to read 'a short ordinary paragraph in a newspaper or other modern narrative'. Write 'another short ordinary paragraph slowly dictated once by a few words at a time'; and work a 'sum in practice or bills of parcels'.

These appeared to the Committee of Council, in the person of Robert Lowe, very modest requirements: and they were quite unable to understand that any teacher of reasonable diligence should fail to enable his children to reach them. They were also felt to be sufficient accomplishments for poor children who started to earn their living at eleven; and they were such a foundation as would enable the child of exceptional brilliance to go farther and achieve his destiny.

'This system of education', said Lowe later, 'is not intended to apply to the upper or middle classes, but to those who are too poor to educate themselves', and therefore a knowledge of the 3 Rs was quite sufficient.

On these regulations, children over six could, if they fulfilled all the demands of attendance and examination, earn a maximum of 12s. a year, and children under six, 10s. 6d. This compares with the 15s. thought reasonable by the Newcastle Commission. Moreover the balance of the parts of the grant was changed. The Commission had thought that the capitation grant should be nearly a half of the total amount available. Lowe cut it to a third. On the Commission's calculations infants, unexamined up to the age of seven, could earn 27s., Lowe would examine them at six and give only 10s. 6d. Moreover, under the Commission's scheme, an able child could earn for the school 29s. 6d. while Lowe's maximum was 12s. If the Commission's figures were reasonable the Revised Code would deprive education of the means to develop; and the drop in education grants over the next few years must have brought satisfaction to Gladstone.

This individual examination of children was the central point of the system, and, looking back, we deplore it. Yet at the time it was generally accepted. In 1869, after six years' experience, when he knew all the disadvantages perfectly well, Matthew Arnold could still write:

No one questions the advantage of an individual grant-rewarded examination, or that the Newcastle Commission did well in suggesting it, or that the Education Department did well in giving effect to their suggestion. . . . These changes gratify respectively one or other of several great forces of public opinion which are potent in this country, and a legislation which gratifies these ought, perhaps, to be pronounced successful.

The first of these 'gratifications' was that the Code put an end to some aspects of the tight bureaucratic control by the central office. By denying help it gave an illusion of liberty. Matthew Arnold had said, 'We must avoid following the Continent into complete, rigid central control' and he pointed out that it was the English genius to manage as much as possible of the national affairs locally. Nearly everybody thought that he was right. 'It is the essence of English administration', said the *Edinburgh Review*, 'to leave details in great part to local agents and authorities.' Secondly the ideas of the age favoured a system which appeared to give value for money. To those with little knowledge of education it seemed indisputably better to pay for what you got; and if children did not learn, what right had the schools to large sums of public money? The famous remark, 'If the schools are expensive they will be efficient, and if they are not efficient they will be cheap' seemed to be supported by justice and common sense.[22] Moreover teachers, like everybody else, ought to have their rewards geared to their exertions; and there was no way to ensure their diligence but by financial sanctions. 'We must appeal to the passions of the human mind,' said Lowe, with more popular support than usual, 'we must enlist hope and fear to work for us.'

From its introduction, the Revised Code was hated by all concerned in or for education. Its authors were even more unpopular. Much of their doings were hidden from sight behind the walls of the office, but their dealings with the inspectors, and with Parliament were public. Lingen could act, and let Lowe take the blame; and Lowe did not make a good impression. 'It is his absolute want of intellectual sympathy with his fellow men that disqualifies him from dealing with a popular assembly', said the *Saturday Review*. His attempted sharp practice over the first introduction of the Code had infuriated Parliament; but there was nothing in that to form the basis of a serious charge.

However there was another matter on which those who believed in education could assail the Vice-President with some hope of success. This was the matter of the inspectors' reports. The great majority of the inspectors were completely opposed to the Revised Code, and were prepared to find its results in the schools bad. Lowe and Lingen were determined that there should be no criticism. The inspectors had successfully resisted Adderley's attempt to make them send in their reports 'digested under heads', and they continued to offer 'general discussions and comments' in spite of prohibitions. They continued now to refuse to give up their right of free speech, in spite of renewed pressure. They believed that the office was censoring the reports, removing all passages criticizing the Code, and retaining those in its favour. As the inspectors continued to stir up public opposition to this office censorship, Lowe devised the scheme, so he told the House with every sign of self satisfaction, of 'making the Inspectors their own censors'. An unsatisfactory report was sent back to its author with a direction 'To make it conform to the Minute, intimating, at the same time, that if he failed to do so, the report would not be published or laid before Parliament.' This was explained to Sir John Pakington on 27 March 1863 when he asked about the suppression of Watkins' report.[23] Apparently for the last two years Watkins had been among the three inspectors who had refused to make the excisions demanded. With simple logic Lowe explained his further refusal to make the MS copy of the report available to Members: 'If he were to consent to lay these reports on the table, and give them the notoriety and publicity of being specially distributed among Hon. Members, he would really be offering a premium to Inspectors to disregard the rules of the Department, and be therefore striking at the foundations of discipline.'

The character of the discipline which Lowe and Lingen wished to establish in the Department is well illustrated by the treatment of J. R. Morell, a junior inspector, and the cousin of J. D. Morell. J. R. Morell had been very unco-operative over the censoring of his reports; and the case of St Mary's School, Coventry, had received national publicity. It is clear that Lowe and Lingen determined to get rid of him as a warning to the others. A certain drunken and discredited schoolmaster sent in a complaint about Morell's conduct in school. This was taken up by the office, and not dropped till it became perfectly clear that none of the charges could be substantiated. In the course of the discussion Morell explained that he had had to leave Cardiff rather early on a certain day, so that he could start the long and awkward journey to Plymouth that evening. In his diary, owing to the arrangement of the printed form, he had put the journey down as being entirely performed on the following day. This was seized on, he was accused of entering a falsehood in his diary, ordered to resign, and, when he refused, dismissed. The correspondence was carried out by Lingen and it was generally agreed that the secretary had complete control 'of all matters relating to the appointment or removal of Inspectors'.[24] Lowe undoubtedly agreed, and accepted the comments in the House on his 'ferocity'. No one had the slightest doubt as to the reasons for the attack; and when Parliament discussed the matter of the inspectors' reports this was one of the cases which sharpened hostility to the Vice-President.

In June, Forster raised the question again; and next year, when the time for reports came round, Sir John Pakington returned to the matter. In March 1864 he asked if the 'Reports of Inspectors would be published in their usual manner without omission or mutilation'. Lowe's reply was that they would be published as received, provided that it was understood that only those which had already been purged of all offensive matter would be deemed to have been received.

This was really too much. On 12 April 1864 Lord Robert Cecil introduced the motion of which he had already given notice—

That, in the opinion of this House, the mutilation of the Reports of H.M.

Inspectors of schools, and the exclusion from them of statements and opinions adverse to the educational views entertained by the Committee of Council while matters favourable to them are admitted, are violations of the understanding under which the appointment of the Inspectors was originally sanctioned by Parliament and tends entirely to destroy the value of their reports.[25]

His argument was simply that Parliament was asked to authorize the 'enormous amount' of £800,000 to be spent on education, and the only means that Parliament had of knowing if it was spent to the best advantage was from the inspectors' reports. He was supported by Walter who agreed that this was not just a matter of departmental discipline, but of serious public interest. 'The Inspectors', he said, 'are gentlemen of very superior education; they get high salaries; and I think I may say that it is believed by this House, that of all others they are eminently competent to guide the House on this subject; under the present system the House is deprived of their guidance.'

Lowe's defence was weak, and the only person who spoke in his favour was Sir George Grey who said that they censored reports in the Home Office. All the same, the motion was only carried by eight votes. Lowe thereupon resigned and his resignation was accepted. Lord Granville, the Lord President, also offered his resignation in support of his subordinate, but this was refused. He was not what the critics were after, and, since Lingen, as a permanent civil servant, was beyond their power, Lowe was the victim.

Lowe and primary education were thus parted; but a committee appointed to enquire into the matter later exonerated him, and the House, in July, rescinded its motion of censure. Four years later he became Chancellor of the Exchequer. In 1880 when he retired from active political life, almost blind, he went to the Lords as Viscount Sherbrooke. As soon as Lowe became Chancellor he took Lingen from the Education Department to the Treasury, so that the two men continued to work together.

Notes

1. Hansard, CXL, 449.
2. Hansard, CXLI, 804.
3. Hansard, CXL, 1955.
4. Hansard, CLV, 313.
5. *Newcastle Report*, p. 154.
6. *Newcastle Report*, p. 136.
7. *Newcastle Report*, p. 157. ⅃
8. *Newcastle Report*, pp. 328 ff.
9. *Quarterly Review*, January 1862, p. 83.
10. *Newcastle Report*, p. 241.
11. Hansard, CLXIV, 719 ff.
12. 'The Twice Revised Code', *Fraser's Magazine*, March 1862.
13. *Saturday Review*, 16 April 1864.
14. P.P., 1861, XLVIII, 372; letter by Kay-Shuttleworth, ibid., p. 295, and paper by Tremenheere, ibid., p. 307.
15. *Quarterly Review*, January 1862, p. 97.
16. *Quarterly Review*, January 1862, p. 98; see also Ascher Tropp, *The School Teachers* (1957), ch. III.
17. Hansard, CLXV, 191.
18. Hansard, CLXXVII, 869.
19. *Fraser's Magazine*, March 1862.
20. *Fraser's Magazine*, March 1862.
21. Hansard, CLXVI, 21, 137, 240, 1204; also Kay-Shuttleworth, *Memorandum on Popular Education* (1868).
22. Hansard, CLXV, 229.
23. Hansard, CLXX, 22.
24. P.P., 1864, XLIV, 529.
25. Hansard, CLXXIV, 897.

Chapter Thirteen

The effects of the Revised Code[1]

The next few years of the history of the schools are filled with the consequences of the Revised Code. Some were clear, others matters of debate.
The financial saving was considerable. In 1862 the Education Grant
was £840,000, by 1864 it had fallen by £135,000 to £705,000. Kay-
Shuttleworth had forecast a drop of almost exactly that amount. This
saving to the Exchequer brought hardship to the schools. Managers
found themselves compelled to make economies; and, as by far the
largest expense was for salaries, it was the teachers and pupil teachers
who suffered, now that the protection of the augmentation grant and
salary scales had been withdrawn.

The payment of the whole grant direct to the managers, a grant
which was 'earned' as to two-thirds by the success of the children in
the examination, took from the teachers any status. They must bargain,
and be told that their low pay was the result of their inefficiency. The
law of supply and demand, which Lowe invoked with such enthusiasm,
was to take its way, untempered by any considerations of social justice.
The teachers faced with a vast, organized employing-corporation were
to fare as other workmen, and they were encouraged to make up their
inadequate salaries by evening or other work.

Some of the other results were less desired and not so clearly foreseen. They sprang in large measure from the fundamental conception of
the Code. If the main grants to the schools were to depend on the
children passing an examination, the subjects and standards of that
examination must be exactly regulated. The schools must know what to
teach, and the minimum level of attainment that would be accepted.
There thus began the competition, which bedevilled education almost to

260

11 A Meeting of the London School Board in the Council
Chamber, Guildhall

12   A School Board capture

the end of the century, between the teachers and the Department, the one side trying to teach as little as possible, the other trying, by ever more complicated regulations, to raise the level of attainment. Possibly the Education Department won in the end; but certainly, to begin with, the honours in this unholy competition went to the teachers. As Matthew Arnold sadly remarks, 'The school examinations in view of payment by results are a game of mechanical contrivance in which the teachers will, and must more and more, learn how to beat us.'

From now on the regulations embodied in each annual Code became the ruling power in the schools; and the smallest variation in wording had great effect on the education given. In the codes we can follow the struggles of the official mind, just as we can follow the struggles of the teachers in the early log-books. The one source of information complements the other.

The Department was determined that every attempt at evading the rigours of the system should be checked. Two instances may be given now. The first form of the regulations merely said that infants who had attended 200 half-days earned 10s. 6d. without examination. In 1863 the phrase 'if present on the day of the examination' was added—with results that will be described later. Next year it was realized that some schools had endowments. It was at once ordered that these should be deducted from the government grant. This brought dismay to certain schools. One inspector remarks sourly, 'I am prevented by the terms of my instructions from saying whether I consider endowments to be a hindrance to the cause of education, but . . .' and he then gives a list of schools in his district which had been closed since the regulation.

The Department was also determined that grants should not play too large a part in the finance of the schools. The total grant payable to a school was not to exceed (*a*) the amount of school fees and subscriptions, or (*b*) a rate of 15s. per child. It thus asserted the principle that the cost of education should be divided roughly half and half between central and local funds. At the time the regulation brought additional hardship to certain types of school.

In 1864 £1389 was lost to schools under (*a*), and only £7 1s. 6d. under (*b*). The small well-taught school in a poor district would clearly be the chief sufferer.

If the individual examination of children was to be the centre of the whole system, the actual manner in which this examination was conducted was of importance. The inspectors had failed to do it before;

arrangements must now be made to ensure that it was carried out. The Secretary in Whitehall, apparently knowing nothing of the normal behaviour of children or the weakness of adult attention, produced a memorandum which laid down exact rules of procedure. In a circular to H.M.I.s he said:[2]

It is assumed that you have before you the examination schedule filled up by the managers as far as column VIII inclusive and that the school is placed before you in the order of its usual classes. . . . It is also assumed that you have a paper before you containing the dictation which you mean to give for writing and arithmetic under each standard.

All the children will remain in their places throughout the examination.

You will begin with writing and arithmetic, and you will direct the teachers to see that all who are to be examined under Standard I have before them a slate and pencil, under Standard II and III a slate, a pencil and a reading book; all under Standards IV–VI a half sheet of folio paper, a pen, ink and the appropriate reading book.

You will then call 'Standard I stand up throughout the school.' The children answering to this description will stand up in their places without quitting them. . . . When this has been correctly effected by the assistance of the teachers, you will call 'Standard I sit down and write on your slates as I dictate.'

You will then dictate the letters and figures which they are to write down.

You will persue the same course with the other standards.

The whole school having thus had their dictation given to them, and being at work on their arithmetic, you will allow time enough to elapse for the completion of their exercises, say three-quarters of an hour.

You will then call them by name from the examination schedule to read, which you will hear each do, and, immediately afterwards, mark each in Column IX of the schedule for writing and arithmetic also, as far as time will admit. Otherwise you will mark the reading and slate work and bring away the paper work to mark later.

My Lords are informed by Mr Cook that from four to six hours will suffice for examining and marking 150 children.

But, of course, in the actual conditions of the class-room everything was different. The children would not sit still, the inspector could not see, or, if he could, was unable to endure the boredom and bother.

In addition to this new exactness, the Department hope that the inspectors would maintain all that was best in the old system. The Instructions said:

The grant to be made to each school depends, as it has ever done, upon the school's whole character and work. . . . You will judge every school by the same standard that you have hitherto used, as regards the religious, moral and intellectual merits. The examination under Article 48 does not supersede this judgment but presupposes it. That article does not prescribe that *if thus much is done, a grant shall be paid,* but *unless this much is done, no grant shall be paid.* It does not exclude the inspection of each school by a highly educated public officer, but it fortifies the general test by individual examination.

This hope by My Lords could not be fulfilled. The nature of the inspection changed at once, and Matthew Arnold sets out the alteration at some length:[3]

Inspection under the old system meant something like the following. The inspector took a school class by class. He seldom heard each child in a class read, but he called out a certain number to read, picked at random as specimens of the rest; and when this was done he questioned the class with freedom, and in his own way on the subjects of their instruction. As you got near the top of a good school these subjects became more numerous; they embraced English grammar, geography and history, for each of which the inspector's report contained a special entry; and the examination then often acquired much variety and interest. The whole life and power of the class, the fitness of its composition, its handling by the teacher were well tested. The inspector became well acquainted with them, and was enabled to make his remarks on them to the head teacher; and a powerful means of correcting, improving and stimulating them was thus given. In the hands of an able inspector—an inspector like Dr Temple, for instance—this was an instrument of great force and value.

On the other hand,

The new examination groups the children by its standards, not by their classes; and however much we may strive to make the standards correspond with the classes, we cannot make them correspond at all exactly. The examiner, therefore, does not take the children in their own classes. The life and power of each class as a whole, the fitness of its composition, its handling by the teacher he does not test. He hears every child in the group before him read, and so far his examination is more complete than the old inspection, but he does not question them; he does not, as an examiner under the rule of the six standards, go beyond the three matters, reading, writing and arithmetic, and the amount of these matters which the standards themselves prescribe; and, indeed, the entries for grammar, geography and history have now altogether disappeared from the forms of report furnished to the inspector. The nearer, therefore, he gets to the top of the school the more does his examination, in itself, become an inadequate means of testing the real attainments and intellectual life of the scholars before him. Boys who have mastered vulgar fractions and decimals, who know something of physical science and geometry, a good deal of English grammar, of geography and history, he hears read a paragraph, he sees write a paragraph, and work a couple of easy sums in the compound rules or practice. As a stimulus to the intellectual life of the school this is derisory.

The new examination is in itself a less exhausting business than the old inspection to the person conducting it; but it takes up much more time, it throws upon him a mass of minute detail, and severely tasks hand and eye to avoid mistakes. Few can know, till they have tried what a business it is to enter in a close ruled schedule, as an examination goes on, three marks for three different things against the names of 200 children whom one does not know one from the other, without putting the wrong child's mark in the wrong place. Few can know how much delay and fatigue is unavoidably caused before one can get one's 600 communications fairly accomplished by difficulty of access to children's places, difficulty of seeing clearly in the obscurer parts of the schoolroom, difficulty in getting children to speak out—sometimes of getting them to speak at all—difficulty of resisting, without feeling oneself inhuman, the appealing looks of master or scholars for a more prolonged trial of a doubtful scholar. Then there are enquiries and returns to be made by the inspector about log-book, portfolio, accounts, pupil teacher's engagement and stipends which had not to be made formerly. An enquiry has just been added respecting the means and position in life of school children's parents, to discover whether they are proper objects of state aid. All this makes the new examination a business of so much time and labour, as to deprive the inspector of the needful freshness and spirit for joining with it, on the same occasion, the old inspection.

In fact, the highly educated gentlemen of the inspectorate could not bear the monotony and uselessness of their task. Various of them record in their reports for these years their devices for dealing with the matter. One man had all his sums ready written out on cards and distributed them, another boasts that by the method of standing children back to back with slates 'I can examine the writing of *any number* of children in Stage I in 10 minutes easily.' From the various experiments a soulless technique was rapidly developed. Sneyd-Kynnersley describes it, but prefaces his description by an admission that he knew that what was boredom to him was life to the schoolmaster:

Our plan of campaign was delightfully simple. Most of the children were in the two lowest standards. These were supplied with slates, pencils and a reading book, and were drawn up in two long lines down the middle of the room. They stood back-to-back to prevent copying, and did dictation and arithmetic, sometimes dropping their slates, sometimes their pencils, sometimes their books, not infrequently all three with a crash on the floor. When we had marked the results on the Examination Schedule, all these children were sent home, and the atmosphere was immensely improved. Then we proceeded to examine the rest, the aristocracy, who worked their sums on paper. As a rule, if we began about 10 we finished about 11.45. If the master was a good fellow, and trustworthy, we looked over the few papers in dictation and arithmetic, marked the Examination Schedule, and showed him the whole result before we left. Then he calculated his 'percentage of passes', his grant and his resulting income; and went to dinner with what appetite he might. . . . Half an hour in the evening sufficed for making up the Annual Report, and the incident was closed. Think of the simplicity of it.

To fill up the time, if he were an inspector of Church schools, he 'went to the Rectory, and inspected the garden, or played croquet with the Rector's daughter, and had a noble lunch'. At night he dined with the Squire and the local clergy, and exchanged Oxford stories over the port.[4]

In addition to the actual examination of the children the inspector was expected to check the registers and all other documents, inspect the material condition of the school and look over the accounts. If this work had been done properly it would have occupied many hours, but 'the great aim of inspector, teacher and children was to finish by 12.30 at the latest'. In the log-books it is not uncommon to find that the inspector arrives at 11.30 and leaves at 1. There was a tradition in County Durham of one of these inspectors, a hunting man, who used to arrive at school in his pink coat, tie his horse to the railings, slap his boot with his whip, examine the school, and be off in time for the meet. From the inspectors' side these annual examinations became more and more routine, and, as men's weariness grew, their tempers deteriorated. Idealism and humanity were alike discouraged by the system and punished by the Department.

From 1863 we have a new and intimate source of information about the schools, the individual log-books. The Department, with the lack of realism characteristic of bureaucrats, decreed,

The Diary or Log book must contain the matter specified in Articles 61–3 and in other respects be a record of school keeping.

The progress of the classes, the value of the methods, fluctuations of attendance, cooperation of parents, rates of taking school fees, the visits made and the examinations made by the Managers are matters the like of which passing under the notice of an observant teacher, and relating to which he may, without writing essays, record many valuable facts. He should keep his diary as if he were taking notes for a report of his school at the end of each year.

No reflections or opinions of a general character are to be entered in the log-book.[5]

The early log-books, as produced, did not live up to these expectations. They are far less records of 'valuable facts', in the official sense, than jottings that reveal the personal worries and hopes of the teachers. In consequence it is possible to get a feeling of the different teachers as human beings. It is not of great historical significance that one master took three days' holiday for his wedding tour, or that another 'felt in no humour to teach as his dear mother was dangerously ill'; but it does establish them as individuals.[6]

The Revised Code made a twofold demand: that children should attend school for a certain number of days in the year, and that they should pass the examination. In reason the two demands were linked, but in practice they presented themselves separately to the teachers. Attendance was a daily recurring worry. As a man glanced round his benches in the morning his heart rose or sank as he considered the numbers. Academic preparations for the examination did, indeed, last the year; but there were days of intermission, or the hope of last-minute cramming. In the log-books the first concern that shows itself is with attendance. This was still deplorably irregular. The teachers had done what they could to improve it because of the capitation grants, but now the necessity is sharpened. The log-book of the school at Llanfairfechan, a seaside resort in Caernarvonshire, plunges into the heart of the problem.

July 6. Got the Log Book. Attendance small. Hay harvest commanding attention. July 7. Field labour making wide gaps today. 8th. Bilberry-gathering season sets in sweeping many away. 9th. Donkey riding getting very fashionable. Boys leave school to attend to the ladies. Learning English so.

In Bangor, the girls are kept at home to help their mothers with the summer visitors. At Nayland, in Suffolk, there is the continual succession of agricultural work. At Caernarvon itself the children seem to

266

do no work, but a calendar of entertainment keeps them from school: the launching of boats; the assizes; on 1 May the Militia starts to train; on 15th there is a fair; the annual regatta follows and the rural sports. In all districts there is frequent illness, measles, fevers, even the cholera. Wet days cut the schools to half, and some poor children stay at home for lack of shoes. The parents do not co-operate with the teachers, and will keep a child at home for the most trivial services.

The teachers lament that they have no power of compulsion, and their thoughts fly to other incentives. In the second entry in his book the master at Llanfairfechan realizes that 'a tea party or something must be promised to counteract this desertion of duty', and by the 14th the party is promised. The school has 'a larger gathering in consequence'. Mr Platt, the local rich man (he had made his money in Oldham) gives the party, and the day is fine: 'The hopes of many little hearts realized by witnessing a cloudy morning gradually clearing into a glorious day for the celebration of the Annual School Treat.' The party sent up the attendance for a day or two, but almost immediately the good is lost; and potato picking, a bad day or some religious festival disturbs everything.

A comparatively empty school this morning set me to my wits end searching for a cause, and on enquiry found that the Calvanistic Methodists had sounded the horn calling the sires and dams together, and nature had prompted the lambs to follow. These meetings may well be set on the list of uncontrollable difficulties the teachers will have to sucumb to in striving to gain an honest high average, good attendance and sound attainments.

The most common way of trying to keep attendance steady was by sending out notes to parents whose children were absent. The pupil teachers took them round, and, presumably, the teachers wrote them. Entries regarding these notes recur continually; some teachers sent them out daily, some once a week with the reports of home lessons. Another method was to have a clothing club, with a bonus depending on attendance. When everything else fails, they try beating the children for truancy. These entries dealing with attendance are by far the most numerous in the books. It was a perpetual anxiety, and when for a day or so things go well there is a jubilation of relief: 'Very large school today. I feel I could work three times as well having so many present.'

The log-books give a good idea of the daily fluctuations of attendance. 'There have been 54 boys present this week thus leaving 24 absent,

267

13 through sickness and the remainder for work.' In another school, a good day would bring an attendance of 167 and a bad day only 87; while a local funeral might leave the teacher with 'practically no school at all'.

When annual figures are given the difference between the average attendance and the number qualified by individual attendance to take the examination is considerable. In one year, at Llanfairfechan, it was 127 to 74, in another 142 to 84; and these are normal figures. In such a district as Norfolk they would be far worse. One school in the county had 121 on the books, but only 36 had made the requisite number of attendances, and, of these, 11 were kept away on the day of the examination by a snow storm.

The parents were fully conscious of the teachers' anxiety and of the power which their control of attendance gave them. They used it with varying degrees of reasonableness. 'Heard that one parent complained that his children did not learn and that he had withdrawn them. I enquired into the matter and found that the real cause of complaint was that I did not send so many books to be bound by him as my predecessor had done.'

Jane Parry of Bangor met these attacks with more spirit: 'A person made a complaint this morning that her girl did not learn; having been admitted last six weeks and home more than half the time. I gave her a good lecture, and if the girl does not attend better in the future have threatened to dismiss her.'

On the other hand the complaints of brutality and the subsequent withdrawal of the child were often justified.

The daily struggle to maintain attendance was only the preliminary labour to earning the grant; the children must be prepared for the examination. It is in this work that the under-staffing of the schools becomes most apparent. The staffing was poor at the beginning of the period, it became steadily worse between 1863-8.

Teachers deserted the profession. Stewart reporting from Cambridge in 1864 said that 22 teachers had left his district. Two had gone to India, one to France, two to private schools and the rest were unknown. Boys were less inclined to take up apprenticeships now that their salary was only what the managers cared to give—which was almost always less than the government salary had been. Teachers made less effort to attract apprentices now that they received no payment for teaching them. At Luton, a boys' school at the beginning of the period had two masters and seven pupil teachers and the girls four pupil teachers under

268

a mistress. Now, in 1866, the boys' school had one certificated master, and one untrained assistant, and two very unwilling pupil teachers. The master and the youngest pupil teacher shared the teaching of 80 boys in four classes and the assistant and older pupil teacher had 120 boys between them. 150 girls had one trained teacher and one pupil teacher, who always failed her examination.[7] Moreover the down-grading of the staff was often policy, and the first thing that managers thought of when short of money. Assistant teachers were replaced by pupil teachers, and pupil teachers by monitors; it was only the firm stand of the Department which kept any certificated teachers in the schools at all. The Department also attempted to check the understaffing of schools by making deductions from the grant when the establishment fell below a certain level. But it was useless. The cost of the teachers would have been greater than the deductions. The down-grading of the teaching staff was followed by a drop in the achievement of the children and a decrease in grant—so that the school had less money than ever. The figures given for one school show the effects. In 1864 92 per cent passed. An apprentice resigned and next year only 59 per cent passed. There was another resignation and the figure in 1866 fell to 49 per cent. The inspector's comment is: 'The losses of grant . . . are in some instances entirely due to the deliberate appointment of inferior teachers who will serve for lower salaries than those who are well trained will accept.'

With his teaching power continually shrinking, the master's task became almost that of a juggler hastening from group to group and trying to keep all working. These struggles were not seen by the inspector, but the log-books are full of them. In a school of about 150 children there might well be one teacher and two pupil teachers. The school would thus have three classes. As the government examination was by VI standards, the classes and standards could never coincide—unless all work was to be kept at the lowest level—and the most intricate system of group work was necessary if anything was to be accomplished.

The contrivance needed to accomplish this supervision with the teaching power available is suggested by many entries. This about a school of 120 girls. 'The two higher divisions were put under the superintendence of my elder pupil teacher. The last, being small, it may be done with the help of a monitor, and I can superintend the lower four classes which appear to me the most backward this year.'

Had the population of the schools been constant, even this difficult organization might have been stabilized, and there might have grown up a body of children who understood the routine and moved up from stage to stage in an orderly way. Presumably this was what was expected —but it did not happen like that. Apparently the master was almost surprised to find 'familiar faces' greeting him at the beginning of a new term. In a few cases the examination schedules are given in the log-books for two or three consecutive years. Studying them, it is difficult to pick out more than a few children who occur more than once. A very few can be found in, e.g., Standard I the first year and Standard II the second. Others appear in Standard I two years running, having, presumably, failed the first year. In just one or two cases a child can be followed into the top standard and then into an apprenticeship, but this is very rare. The number of admissions recorded week by week is large, and the departures, except for potential examinees, go unrecorded. When children are admitted from another school the master invariably finds them ignorant or careless.

The difficulties were particularly great in an industrial town. Every time a child changed employment he changed his school—if he continued in school at all. Children were still being recruited into the mines under the age of twelve and at Brierley Hill in the Black Country, with a population of 11,000, there were, in 1866, only two or three boys over twelve years old in National Schools. 'The vast majority of the children leave school to be absorbed in exhausting and often unhealthy labour, where there is no restriction in their employment as there is in the textile or pottery districts.'

The impression gained from looking at the log-books is confirmed by the official calculations. In 1869, in one area 25,000 children were in school for the examination, but only 13,000 were qualified to be examined. Of all the children in school only a quarter stayed more than two years.

The village schoolmaster who had been ambling on in reasonable usefulness; the harassed town master trying to snatch utterly untrained infants from the gutter were alike brought up short by the new regulations, and looked at them in often uncomprehending horror. 'Reorganized the school to commence the Routine of the Revised Code', writes one man, and he posted up the results of his thoughts, prominently, on the wall so that they should be ever before the eyes of staff and children alike.

To many masters the restricting nature of the Government examinations came as something of a surprise, and is commented on before they had grown hardened to it. One man, who was fully alive to the value of variety in reading books, and who even tried the bold experiment of taking 'The Expedition of the Argonauts' with a class, now finds himself confined by the necessities of the Code. 'The reading of the whole school seems to me to be getting more dull and drawling, arising, no doubt, from the want of occasional change in the Reading books, which is hardly practicable under the silly restrictions of the New Code.' Such complaints are soon forgotten. The realities are accepted.

It needed only a year or two for the competition between teachers and inspectors to be in full swing. The Code prescribed that a child should read from the book 'used in his class', and this regulation provided a ready opportunity for ingenuity. After two years the publishers had seized their opportunity:

> The minimum is brought still lower by the issue of new reading books, each series shorter and easier, and, as some persons think, sillier than the last; so that the reading book formerly used by the 3rd class of good schools surpasses in difficulty of language and extent of information the highest book now employed; and the 'poetry' of the 5th standard sometimes comprises little more than a few simple ballads.[8]

Other subjects suffered too, and the teachers and inspectors both mention the change. One inspector notes:

> Higher subjects, as history, grammar, and geography are very generally neglected except in some large and flourishing town schools. For my own part, I have been unable to find time to examine in the higher subjects even when they are taught.

Some schools tried to preserve something of their old standards. A village schoolmaster clung to geography as a prestige subject. 'Felt convinced today in the Geography lesson that to ignore this subject altogether for the sake of the 3 Rs would prove most injurious to the local reputation of the school.' But he discarded grammar without regret. 'The time devoted to Grammar, from this to the Government examination, given to revise all dictation exercises.' Even scripture suffered, although this was a Church school: 'Modified the Time Table a little to give more time to secular instruction from this to the examination.'

The old-style lessons of information in geography or general knowledge became in fact survivals in the training college course, without hope of their actual use in schools. Brodie, reporting on the lessons he heard at the Borough Road, says: 'So good were these lessons that I can only regret how much such lessons seem to have fallen off of late years in our elementary schools, teachers being, I presume, now so absorbed in grinding for the 3 Rs as to find no time for them.'

The infants, though immune from examination, also suffered. Mitchell, in the Eastern district, found a total abandonment of the Infant system of instruction: 'The grand object now is to make the children read, write and cypher. There is no time left for songs, lectures or handclapping or Kinder Garten.'

This impoverishment of the teaching brought nothing but boredom and increasing restlessness; followed by more numerous punishments and greater reluctance. To counteract this, the master tried to be in a state of continual activity, teaching or examining. 'Examined school, found a stronger desire in the two higher classes to obtain good marks, which must be fostered as much as possible. The *Dictation* lessons must obtain stricter attention with the *Third Class*, and *Arithmetic* with the *Fourth*. The Fifth defective in all subjects. Found it hard to rivet their attention.' Having detected weakness the master then attempted to improve the backward groups: 'I spent my time as usual stimulating the backward ones.' Too often he reflects how much more he could accomplish if he had the time: 'Examined the lower classes today and found myself wishing that I could be in 2 or 3 places at one time. The pupil teachers are too young to work the girls up.' 'I find I can produce greater effect in one week than the subordinates in six.'

Unfortunately while the master was teaching one subject another might be neglected. 'The writing, for some reason, is not what I wish. I fear that the attention of the master is not sufficiently exclusive to this lesson. His anxiety to know the progress of some other class in some other subject is too often too strong and leaves this lesson to substitutes.'

In addition, he tried to build up a state of anxiety, almost amounting to hysteria. We can follow it through some months in one school.

Jan. 11th 1864.
Must get on faster with the Reading to get through the course of reading prescribed for the next examination.
April 5. (After a week's holiday) Teachers and taught look fresh and active. All are reminded of the coming examination and exhorted to prepare manfully for these hard contests.
April 7. I discovered now, at the close of the year, and on the eve of the examination that one class at least must be examined in the 4th standard

or lose 1/10 of the grant. Being of no use to kick against authority, I informed my first class that they must now move ahead, throw down the slate and pencil and have ink, paper and pens etc. without delay.

April 27. Preparing for the New Code examinations is strange work, I believe it affects my nervous system, for many failures in Dictation or a sum makes me tremble, while a successful trial elates me perhaps beyond measure.

April 28. The classes are now counted out each day to distinguish between those who have succeeded and those who have failed, but more especially to enable the teachers to see the weak points in their respective garrisons and to repair the breach.

May 4. A stricter adherence to the requirements of the New Code demanded from the teachers of the lower classes—we are all apt to falter.

May 10. Insisting upon better results in the 3 Rs from all classes by speaking encouraging words to the industrious timid and openly threatening the careless and indolent; hoping by some means to get them to emulate each other in progress and well doing.

May 25. The importance to them of a coming examination impressed upon the children. To be doomed to stay in the same class for another twelve months as the consequence of failure produces a very good effect.

The next concern was to see that the children duly qualified by attendance appeared on the great day. This was always a matter of great difficulty. If the examination was in the summer there were always agricultural activities, and that too was the time in other communities when the big girls might go out to service.

'The approach of summer, as usual, begins to tell upon the attendance. Today I was grieved to find that the best girl in the school has been withdrawn for service. Every year as the examination draws nigh the elder portion of the school suffers in this way.' And, worse still, 'no amount of persuasion' could influence the parents to send the children back just for the one vital day. In other cases the reasons for absence were more frivolous. 'I found that many of the pupils had, through their parents, made arrangements to visit their friends just before the inspection. I tried to persuade them to postpone their visit, showing them how unfair it would be, but I am afraid it was to little purpose.'

The Department was concerned that a teacher should not show too much anxiety about the children attending for the examination, as it would give the parents a wrong idea of their respective positions. They suggest that attendance certificates, 'tastefully executed' should be distributed on that day—as both a bribe and a cover.

The effects of the Revised Code

But it was vain to hope that the parents would not perceive their advantage; and some people did not hesitate to use it as a form of blackmail. 'A boy withdrew from school who was qualified to pass an examination because I refused to become surety for his father for a large sum of money. We shall lose 8/– because another leaves now, a few days before the examination.'

When the children were assembled, the next task was to assign them to the standards in which they were to be examined. This was by no means automatic, and the teacher regarded it as a matter of major strategy; and each year, when the examination is over, there is a note that he had not done it to the best advantage, and that he would be wiser next time.

The grouping was not by age, except, obviously, that the highest standards would have the older children. In Standard I the age range might be from seven to eleven, with the majority aged eight and nine. A boy of eight might be in Standard III. If eleven were accepted as the general leaving age very few children would rise above Standard III. Just a few, who would be eleven on their next birthday, were in Standard IV; in the standards above that, the few children presented were aged twelve, thirteen or fourteen years.

The more perceptive inspectors fully understood the problem and sympathized with the teachers' difficulty. Rev. G. R. Moncreiff in a report which Lowe tried to suppress wrote:

Suppose for example, that 3 months before an examination, there are 12 boys now rather beyond the work of standard III, who could obviously be brought up to standard IV: Should they be taught accordingly, and passed under that standard, the teacher incurs a twofold risk: 1) They may, by illness or otherwise, be prevented from reaching standard V next year; 2) they may pass V and VI in due course and remain another year without profit to the school. Whereas, if he kept them for three months in one of the subjects (say arithmetic) at the same point where they are, he passes them in standard III without any imputation of 'packing'; has them, as it were, safe for next year at standard IV, and can depend on them as money earners for three years longer instead of two, if they continue so long in the school.[9]

As an additional worry, just before the examination, came the Government forms, which had to be filled up in the greatest detail and signed as correct by the managers. The registers had to be made to tally, the children arranged by classes and standards, with all their ages given—

the accounts prepared. Inspectors complained that this was ill done. There was a general impression that the registers were filled up to suit the abilities of the children, and, as inspectors were not allowed to pay surprise visits, this could not be detected unless the master was unusually clumsy or some enemy informed against him. The accounts tended to be made up from memory. Stokes notes that the books he saw were 'not the genuine records of cash transactions under the date of each occurrence', and that account books were usually destroyed by each outgoing priestly manager.

Even if the master sat up all night doing the returns for the girls' school as well as his own, he had to be alert in his preparations for the great day.

Not quite all the children qualified by attendance were presented, perhaps to avoid too high a proportion of failures, or to reserve a doubtful child to be a certainty next year. When this number of unpresented children grew too large the inspector commented on it unfavourably. Those who were presented were mainly grouped in the lower standards. In one school in 1864, 81 children were presented in Standards I and II, and 28 in III, IV and V. The next year there were 70 in I and II and 29 in III, IV and V. No one attempted Standard VI. In a girls' school 48 were in Standards I and II, and 30 in III and IV. No one went higher. Some schools must have been even more reluctant to justify the regulation that some children at least must be presented in Standard IV. Matthew Arnold found that, in his district, 73 per cent of his children were in Standards I, II, and III. Waddington, reporting on the British Schools in the south-west of England, gave the proportion in the different standards as follows:

Standard I, 35 per cent; II, 24 per cent; III, 20 per cent; IV, 14 per cent; V, 4 per cent.; VI, 2 per cent.

The British Schools were rather more expensive than the National and received more middle-class children. There was also a remarkable school in Plymouth which provided almost all those in the top standards.

The final fixing of the standards took place at the last-minute rehearsal. On the eve of the day the children were all assembled and told what they had to do. They were taken through the questions that might be expected, and given a final cram—unless of course the teachers were too nervous to do it. Then the children went home: to return the next morning under dreadful threats.

At this point again the teachers' results became a matter of chance. It was of great moment at what time of the year the annual examination took place. There would be more or fewer children in school according to the agricultural calendar, but a time of year when field work was slack would also be a time of bad weather, and a downpour might leave the school empty. One master excuses himself, when detected in falsifying the registers, thus: 'In extenuation I can only state that I acted from impulse and vexation owing to the time of year at which the inspection takes place.' His fell in June, when the children were in the fields; but every month seemed to have its inconveniences.

The inspector arrived to a hushed school and proceeded to get on with business. Usually, of course, the children were too awed to be anything but submissive, but there were schools where the discipline was so bad that even the great day did not bring stillness. These are recorded sharply.

It was intended that the examination should be entirely impersonal and rigid, a divine judgment of absolute validity. It was this quality about the examination which made it so hated and feared. There was no latitude, no room for discretion. No allowance could be made for circumstances quite beyond the power of anyone to alter. In many schools in Wales the children did not know English, and the master had to *translate* the day's reading lesson, before leaving them to learn it by heart. Again there could be no consideration for particular difficulties as of staffing. The books are full of crises when the master is left entirely alone to manage the school; or has to entrust it, during a period of illness, to an unreliable deputy. If the mistress of the adjoining girls' school is incompetent or absent that too is added to his cares. If he takes over a school from a previous master he nearly always finds it in a decayed condition: if he is starting a new one there is the problem of a savage district.

The inspectors, who knew so much more than the office, struggled, for a time, to maintain some discretion. On one school an inspector remarked: 'The number of failures has been large and the condition of the school altogether below the mark', but he adds that the present master was not to blame, as he had only been there five months; and 'the results of failure should not be visited upon him'. As the managers never had any spare money, and were dependent on the grant, it is hard to see how he could escape the effects of past mismanagement.

The dissensions which ended in the dismissal of J. R. Morell began with a report on a Roman Catholic school in Coventry.[10] 'The teachers had not long been in charge of the children: they were of the roughest description, and ignorant of the first elements of discipline and instruction, and when they were first brought in many of them were perhaps 12 or 13 years of age.' There were passes in Standards I and II (none higher) and Morell reported that the school had done very well under the circumstances and recommended grant. Lingen refused the grant, and deleted the recommendation for mercy.

When questioned about it by the Select Committee of 1865 he replied uncompromisingly,

the Revised Code expressly paid for the result produced, and an Inspector was not at liberty, in conformity with the Code, to lead the managers to expect that a different examination would be accepted in one school from what was accepted in another; that they ought to feel that they had to surmount all the difficulties, what ever they might be, that stood in the way of a satisfactory examination, and that that satisfactory examination must be of one kind, and one kind only.

Even so, some of the inspectors tried to help the schools. One man explains his methods:[11]

I have allowed the children to pass if any one of the sums were right, but by the late circular from the Council Office it is ordered that *the sum* done right must be at the extreme limit of the standard. If I were to adopt the rule of requiring 3 sums to be done correctly for a pass in the V standard, I am afraid at least 70% would fail. With regard to girls' schools it certainly seems a hardship to expect girls (who are generally supposed to have less aptitude for arithmetic than boys, and who are employed for nearly half the day in sewing) to do the same sums as the boys.

His solution is to set sums for them with fewer figures. As an indication of the standard which he expects he gives examples of the work set for different standards:

Standard II   From 562,306
            Take 275,820
            $7,509 \times 78; 46,812 \div 7$

Standard IV   £   s.   d.
            From 17,608 11 $4\frac{1}{2}$
            Take 9,350 11 $10\frac{3}{4}$
        £   s.   d.   £   s.   d.
        57 17 $5\frac{1}{4} \times 37; 7,408$ 13 $9\frac{1}{2} \div 11$

There are various figures given for the degree of success in the examination. Some are in the log-books, some in inspectors' reports. The log-books do not always give the detailed results of the examination; but some years the master does record them, and we can see what was considered a good or bad proportion of passes. Here is the record of a satisfactory year.

Presented for examination above 6 years 75
Presented under 6 years   45
Passed in Reading   70
    ,,   Writing   74
    ,,   Arithmetic   75
   The financial rewards to such a school were:
Grant on average attendance   £34 – 12 – 0
  ,, ,, examination   £29 – 4 – 0
Infants 45   £14 – 12 – 6
                           £78 – 8 – 6

For comparison, here is a bad school which received a very scathing report, and had its grant reduced:

Number presented for examination   84
Passed in Reading   64
    ,,   Writing   71
    ,,   Arithmetic   56

Over the larger area of his district Matthew Arnold, inspecting British schools, found that, in 1866, 15 per cent of those in Standards IV, V and VI failed, and 11 per cent of those in Standards I, II and III. In a backward agricultural district with much child labour the percentage of passes in one school might be as low as 18, and in another 22·5.

In most cases the passes in reading were the highest, in arithmetic the lowest. This again was perfectly well understood by the inspectors. The children knew the reading book by heart—and were unable to read anything else—even of comparable difficulty. Dictation was taken from the same reading book and was learnt in a similar fashion; only arithmetic required a little genuine knowledge. Yet this was made as simple as possible.

As one man says in 1864, 'Upon an average ¾ of grant obtainable by examination has been secured . . . now that the dictation is limited to a single sentence . . . and the arithmetic has been much simplified by the abandonment of many of the higher rules, as decimals or vulgar fractions . . . which have hitherto been taught in elementary schools.'

It did not take the schools long to discover the one loophole in the

Code. Children under six need not be examined, and they received their
10*s*. 6*d*. provided only that they were 'suitably instructed' and did not
interfere with the older children. The log-book of the school at Llanfairfechan naïvely remarks that by charging infants only 1*d*. a week, it
gets them in early and can increase its numbers. Others did not hesitate
to take them at fifteen months—when they tended to be an 'intolerable
nuisance'. Others came at two 'and early learnt to idle their days away'.
Other schools, particularly those serving the Irish populations, did not
know the children's real age, and gladly classified them as under six.

For the first year all these children drew grant on the school's assertion that they had attended 200 times. But next year, Lingen, perhaps
suspecting something, published the supplementary regulation requiring Infants to be present on the day of examination. The result was
horrifying. Where the school had sufficient influence, the infants came
—whatever their condition. Many inspectors mention the facts in 1864
and 1865. Perhaps the most telling passage is in Stokes's report on the
Roman Catholic schools in the Midlands:

> To hear paroxysms of whooping cough, to observe the pustules of
> small pox, to see infants carefully wrapped up and held in their mothers'
> arms or seated on a stool by the fire because they are too ill to take their
> proper places, are events not so rare in an inspector's experience as they
> ought to be. The risk of the infant's life and the danger of infection to
> others are preferred to the forfeiture of a grant of 6/6.

Others found children with scarlet fever, and one man records:

> I subsequently found the mother of one of these children crying outside
> the door from anxiety respecting her little boy who had been brought out
> of his sick room to be present at the inspection.[12]

It was necessary to take action. Two circulars were published on 7 April
and 19 December 1865 which permitted some allowance to be made in
the case of illness, if it could be classed as 'epidemic sickness' or if there
was 'a cause of a general nature which opposes a physical obstacle to the
presence of the children'. They 'declined absolutely to consider causes
which apply only to individual children'.

Grudging as this concession was, it was apparently successful in abat-
ing the nuisance: or inspectors may have grown hardened and ceased
to mention it.

There was yet another practice which sprang up which the Department attempted to check. Many managers were so irked by all the

Government regulations, that they, in effect, leased out their schools to the masters. For an agreed amount, perhaps 7s. a week, the master hired the schoolroom, took the children's pence, the endowment or contributions and any grant that he could earn. This was not done officially. The managers still signed such returns as the master submitted to them, and were nominally in charge of the school. When this arrangement was detected, it was naturally objected to. It took away from a responsible body of people all control of the education given, and, also, it tended to pervert the schools from their real purpose—the education of the poor. A master who had thus got control of a school tended to limit its numbers to around ninety—a number which he could manage single handed with monitors, and to pick and choose the cleverest children from well-to-do families, while he rejected the needy.

What was the real effect of all this machinery on the schools? The great majority of voices condemn it. The idea of minimum standards, which are rigidly enforced, tends inevitably to make these minima the maximum. The denial of the right to individual thought and experiment enforces the most stupid conformity. The refusal to admit special circumstances breeds despair. On the other hand careless managers were made sharply conscious of the defects of their schools, and teachers were compelled to try to raise the performance of their children.

But after a year or two the general opinion was that there had been 'a general progression on the part of the scholars in elementary attainments, and an equally general retrogression both in the information and intelligence of the first class'. Fussell writes on Middlesex in 1864: 'I cannot call to mind a single instance in which any of the best schools have, as yet, been benefited by the working of the Revised Code in the schools. Not only has there been no improvement, but there has been a falling off of efficiency in many respects.' Even the elementary subjects have become worse because of too steady application to them.

In the Reports there is one passage of praise which it is hard to accept as serious:

The improvement in discipline effected by the Revised Code has as yet scarcely received its due measure of attention. Masters, who used formerly to devote their abundant leisure to amusement, to the cultivation of music or drawing or to private preparation for degrees at the University of London, are now recalled by the stern necessities of our individual examinations to the more homely, but indispensable duties of their office. Pupil teachers no longer while away in chat the tedium of long afternoons. Even the little monitoress instead of idly looking on while her little ones cover their slates with bad imitations of the single letter or figure hastily chalked upon the black board, is now seen quietly moving to and fro among her class, busy with the work of explanation and assistance.[13]

Some of the worst schools did improve. There was a school in Lancashire, which, from its numbers, clearly filled a want.[14] It was raised in a few years, by adverse reports and the refusal of grant, from the condition 'of a Sunday school, with only a few loose benches', to that of an institution with 'a school room with class-rooms, apparatus and appliances superior in size and equal in arrangements to any I inspect'.

Many such improvements had been effected in the past without the terrors of individual examination; but the greater precision of the Revised Code, and the more flexible scale of rewards, or punishments, certainly gave the inspectors a much more efficient engine of discipline.

From the log-books we can build up a picture of the master's daily life under the system. He was clearly continually overworked and worried. Quite frequently he started teaching the pupil teachers at 6.30 or 7 a.m. He superintended, though he did not always teach, an evening school at night. The big boys or young men who came there were very ignorant, some only learning the alphabet, and they were often rowdy, and the master might be 'compelled to use unusual severity with several of the scholars'. In the lunch hour he either taught the pupil teachers again, pushed in some private coaching or prepared apparatus. During school hours, if he was not actually teaching, he managed to get in a little clerical work on school registers or returns, in which case the school discipline rapidly deteriorated. He frequently had a group of boys whom he taught separately, apart from the others, either for a fee, or as a personal favour to their parents. It was no wonder one woman could say, 'My time is very limited—occupied all day in actual teaching and with teaching pupil teachers and making preparations as writing bills etc. Have no time for recreation.' Or a man more simply 'I find teaching a very hard occupation', and 'My health is not good through overwork.' Everything was made more fatiguing by the uncertainties of the examination results and the difficult relations with managers and parents.

In some cases we can trace in the log-books the gradual deterioration of a man's character under strain. In a curious passage in one of the reports, an inspector explains that a woman teacher's life is a satisfactory one, and that she is always treated with courtesy and frequently with great kindness; the man teacher did not usually enjoy these advantages. Unless he was of unusual moral stature he found the life too hard. Indiscipline increases in the school and is met with punishment, and this in turn by fresh insubordination. Then there is a bad report from the inspector, and, a few pages on, there is a new master who finds the school in a 'very poor condition'. Much of the day-to-day punishment went unrecorded, but sometimes when it was on a major scale it is reported. 'This day I had to enforce the lesson of obedience. A rough boy from the Quarry was told to hold his hand out; he would not. I took pains to inform him that I insisted on prompt and unreserved obedience from all in my school and unless it was given I invariably enforced it. He took no heed. I then punished him until he gladly gave in, in the presence of the whole school.' Or on another occasion: 'Had to punish a boy rather severely because it was useless to reason with him as to his offence, in as much as he repeated it in going to his place every time.'

A Lancashire school had a master whose manner, according to the inspector, was 'loud but ineffective'. His records are full of the unpunctuality of staff and students, and equally full of notes of punishment: 'Chastised several children for unusual late-coming.' or 'Compelled to take very severe measures with the children for late-coming.' He was dismissed by the managers for a variety of failings.

The parents added another element of anxiety, social and financial. They complained if their children were punished, and they would not pay their bills. It was the custom for the teachers to collect the fees, and this added considerably to the work. The sums charged frequently varied with the status of the parents. At Nayland, in Suffolk, the fees were collected on Monday. Tradesmen paid 6*d*. a week for their children, mechanics 3*d*., labourers 2*d*. There were a considerable number who paid 5*s*. a quarter. The master generally entered the weekly takings in the log-book. It varied between 8*s*. 3*d*. and 35*s*.: the higher sums in the weeks when the quarterly payments were made. All this involved much book-keeping, made all the more difficult by the fact that most of the fees were always in arrears. 'Gave out 6 weekly bills', says one man, 'that I had written in the evening. It takes a long time to write these bills on account of the arrears on the books. I have never seen such difficulty to get in school fees as here.' 'Adam Jones', says another, 'is troublesome. Getting school money from him is like drawing his teeth.' Some

282

parents were so averse to paying that, when the master became too importunate, they withdrew their children.

Troublesome as collecting school fees was, the master preferred to do it himself. He did not trust the managers to show sufficient energy.

A circumstance occurred today which confirms me in the opinion that it is more to the interest and happiness of the Managers and Teacher for the latter to receive the school pence as part of his salary; and this applies with peculiar force to the present regime, for so much financial responsibility is now thrown upon the Managers that to prevent ever-recurring bickering it is of great importance to hand over as much as possible of the pecuniary care to those most interested, viz. the teacher.

In another matter the teachers were always in uncomfortable relations with the parents. Parents liked the children to be given home work: it somehow contributed to their dignity, just as the sight of 'a road full of merry school children wending their way homeward with their satchels round their necks' supported the ego of the master. At the same time the parents did nothing to see that the work was done. Lessons went unprepared, and books were lost. The inferior teachers neglected to enforce it. 'The absence of one of the pupil teachers on leave, brought me to closer and long continued connection with the 3rd class. Had trusted too much to the teacher in looking over the home lessons. They were all, without exception, incorrectly and negligently done. I shall for the future inspect them all personally.' But even when he did inspect them, what could he do? Sometimes he records that he kept the children in, sometimes that he inflicted 'some other punishment'. There is no evidence that the work was ever satisfactory.

With masters living and working in this way it is no wonder if the pupil teachers decreased in number and attainments. The log-books are full of complaints about the difficulty of obtaining them, and the poor quality when obtained. It is probable that these boys and girls were never quite such paragons as they were represented in the 1850s, but there was no shortage of them then, and schools and inspectors had a considerable choice. Now that they no longer received a nationally guaranteed salary, and had a much less attractive prospect of ultimate employment, they were much harder to come by.

Besides taking from the pupil teacher his guaranteed salary and from the master his payment for teaching him, the Revised Code decreased the amount of teaching the lad must receive. It cut down the hours to five a week and it allowed those five hours of teaching to be given in an evening school, when there were other pupils of a very inferior quality present. The indentures of apprenticeship, which previously had been considered binding on both sides for five years (though Lowe asserted that, as they were not stamped, they had no legal effect), were now declared to need only a short notice to end them. All this together produced a state of mind very unfavourable to good work. 'Ten years ago,' said Matthew Arnold, 'a pupil teacher had a master who was rewarded for teaching him, was proud of his own profession, was hopeful and tried to communicate his pride and hope to his apprentice.' Now the 'work of teaching in school is less interesting and more purely mechanical than it used to be'. The teacher is discouraged and communicates his discouragement to his pupil. Is it any wonder that 'under these influences the pupil teacher's heart should be no longer in the work, that his mind should be always ready to turn to the hope of bettering himself in some more thriving line, and his acquirements meanwhile weak and scanty?'

Under these circumstances there was a drop in numbers as well as in quality. In the schools the rate of pupil teachers to scholars had been, in 1861, one pupil teacher for every thirty-six scholars. In 1866 it had fallen to one to every fifty-four scholars.

If the numbers of pupil teachers diminished, so apparently did their knowledge and aptitude. The inspectors thought poorly of their scholastic attainments, and the picture that we have of them in schools suggests that, as in the case of monitors, it was not long before the difficulties inherent in the use of such young teachers became apparent. In the log-books we find mainly their misdemeanours mentioned. The majority were probably good children, and, like Maria Gott in a Durham school, went through all the usual stages of object lessons and poetry learning. Others caused a lot of trouble. A Lancashire school was plagued with a pupil teacher, John Jones, who was permanently 'insolent' and 'inattentive'. He always arrived late and never did his home work; offering, with school-boy simplicity, the excuse that he had forgotten his book. Yet, unaccountably, whenever his class was examined it did well. He held his place in the school for four years; and then, when a new master was appointed, was dismissed. Others besides John Jones were late, and the consequences were serious—as the pupil teachers did all the schoolroom jobs, like preparing pens, filling ink-wells, dusting and drawing the lines on the floor for the different groups to 'toe'.

They were unreliable teachers, 'young and inexperienced', as one man said, and he 'often caught them playing when the children were for a moment engaged'. Perhaps worse was when they actually joined in the horseplay of the boys. From the examination lists we can see that the oldest boys in the school might be fourteen or fifteen, and the pupil teacher might be as young as thirteen; so it is no wonder if their conduct approximated. 'Complaints of S. Owen's conduct. That he played with his class when out of my sight, kicking their caps, calling them thieves, and so I have made up my mind that he is not fit to be trusted with a class for some time again.' Owen had other vices: 'Heard complaints from parents that S. Owen was receiving bribes from the pupils in his class, giving the most merits to those who could bring the most apples and sweets. Gave him a severe reprimand.'

Many of them were brutal and struck or beat children. One master, returning from dinner, found K. Warner, his girl pupil teacher, chasing a boy round the playground with a stick, while a Caernarvon mother, arriving to fetch her child home, saw S. Owen punching his head in the playground. There is no proof that these children had really behaved any better before 1862, but the schools are very ready to assert that they find a marked deterioration. Of course the violence was not always committed by the pupil teacher. A boy beginning his apprenticeship might well find himself put to teach boys as big as he was, whose school life had been made hateful by their failure to learn their letters. They would attack him, and he must defend himself. Not only knowledge, but an indomitable fighting spirit was a necessary qualification for the work.

The school buildings themselves seemed to suffer from the general gloom. In addition to the small, leaded panes that had been in use since the first plans, there was now a tendency to put in larger windows of semi-transparent glass. The children hated these, and in the rougher districts regularly broke them.[15]

The lawless character of some of the neighbourhoods in which the schools are situated will be best evinced by my report on the state of the windows. In one school visited there were 137 panes broke in the boys' school, and 37 in the girls' at the time of my visit. These panes were large thick diaphane, semi-transparent, and the stones ordinarily made small round holes as a pistol shot would have done, starring out on the inside.... Many of the rooms are so sombre from lofty broad dark painted roofs, from very small low down windows, thick mullioned and leaded, filled with very inferior glass, that in winter days it is impossible to see in them, and even in full summer light the effect is cheerless and melancholy. The schools lighted solely by diaphane are equally objectionable, and are the cause of intense headaches and depression.

Some schools were even worse.

St George's in the East, Christchurch—Is held under three railway arches, and the trains rumble overhead every 2 minutes with a noise reminding much of an incessant Alpine thunderstorm.

Yet there were good schools, even in the slums.

St Paul's, Stepney. (Bow Common)
Excellent rooms, large play ground, a good swimming bath, much frequented by the boys who pay 1*d.* the week. A neighbouring water company supplies water at 5/- a week. Also a fife and drum band, well drilled, and intellectually as good as the rest.

The equipment and furnishing of these schools was very inadequate. In 1872 when the Bangor School Board took over Garth School, which provided education for some 240 boys and girls, they bought the existing furniture at a valuation:

> In the Boys' school.
> 12 parallel desks with forms in large room.
> 4   ,,   ,,   class room.
> 1 large cupboard and platform.
> 5 small cupboards.
> 1 large bell.
> In the Girls' school.
> 12 parallel desks with forms and stationery.
> Platform filled with cupboards and drawers.
> 1 moveable desk and forms.
> Value in all £21. 9. 6.

When Chester in the 1870s opened a new school for 166 children, the school furnishings and fittings cost £26 18*s.* 7*d.*, that is 3*s.* to 4*s.* a head.

Books were equally scanty. Inspectors are always complaining that a whole class has only one reading book and passes it from hand to hand. If they were more numerous they were sure to be tattered and dirty. Ever so often they threatened to make deductions from the grant unless the supply of books improved. There is little evidence that it did; and the suggestion that there should be books of information of some 200 pages went unregarded.

How did these schools appear to the children in them? The fathers of men alive now were pupils in these schools of the 1860s. Here are the infant memories of Charles Dodd, himself to become a notable school-

master and the father of distinguished sons, at the British school at
Wrexham:

I was put by Mr Fyfe in the 'Penny Books'. We had no such things as
standards. We were simply in the 'penny' or the 'fo'penny' books as the
case may be. Then I was put to 'toe the line', and toeing the line occupied
a very considerable part of each day; there was very little sitting. The
space allotted to the two lower classes was so small, too, that the backs of
the 'penny book' boys touched the backs of the 'fo'penny book' boys, and
there was not even a curtain to divide them. . . . The school curriculum
was meagre in those days. It went little farther than the three Rs. . . .
Geography must have been taught, but to what extent I am unable to
say; and as to whether grammar appeared on the Time Table I am equally
uncertain.

But once a week on Friday afternoon, there was a singing lesson which
I always enjoyed when I could get it. We little ones were not admitted
unless we paid a half penny for the privilege; and it was one of the events
of the week (whenever I could muster the necessary coin, which did not
occur every week) to don my Sunday best and take my place among the
singers.

The walls were unadorned with plaster, and the one dividing the two
rooms was built of bricks which seemed to be freaks of the brickyard; and
one of my favourite occupations was to count the knobs on the bricks and
to discover certain resemblances in the fantastic excrescences to human
faces, hunchbacked men and animals of mythological construction. The
desks were made to accommodate the largest number on a given floor
space. The walls were as destitute of pictures as the reading books. There
was one coloured diagram called 'Johnson's Natural Philosophy' that had
great attractions for me. There was a man splitting a log of timber by the
application of wedges; a horse striving with all his might to draw a cart
up an incline, a well showing one bucket in the act of ascending and the
other descending; two children on a see-saw.

For ablutions, a galvanized iron bucket was filled every morning and
mid-day by one of the monitors with water from the stream. Soap was
apparently considered a superfluous luxury, so we got none, and I am no
quite certain about a towel, but I believe it was an innovation of later
years.

The playground was neither flagged nor tarred, and got fearfully
muddy. No gravel was ever put upon it in those early days. I remember at
one time some black ashes were put upon the play ground,—imagination
must complete the picture. The schools were brushed daily, but it was
only at holiday times that they received a wash. The windows, too, were
left pretty much to themselves. A heavy shower of rain and (for a short

287

time) the play of the hose-pipe of the 'Prince of Wales' fire brigade supplied to the outside what was lacking in manual labour.[16]

A less happy account of a village school of the same date reads:

I am sorry to say that I cannot speak well of the school, or at least of the village schoolmaster. He was very cruel and very ignorant. The cane was in his hand from the opening of the school in the morning to its close at 4 o'clock in the afternoon: faults, errors, slips, a constant succession of petty nothingnesses led to its use either on the hand or on the back, or on both hands and back. Some child whispers; he cannot find out which. He thrashes the class all round. The answer to the sum is wrong, the boot is not exactly on the chalk line, a child has turned his head round, there are more than a certain number of errors, say three, in the dictation,—any of these might be a reason for a whacking; and there was lamentation in the school all day long. The master had one merit. He was thoroughly energetic. But it would have been better, I believe, had he been lazy and careless, and left the children a lighter burden of care and fear.

But probably what the boys disliked most in him were his obvious favouritisms. These were shown invariably to the well-dressed children of the well-to-do who attended, not the Methodist or Baptist chapel, but the village church. They were hardly ever caned, even lightly. But the chapel going children, and especially those who were poor or slow, suffered many a blow, and were stung by many a vulgar sarcasm levelled at their 'religion'.[17]

In 1860 the training colleges were in a generally thriving condition. They had been given moderate approval by the Newcastle Commission, and were looking forward to a period of further expansion. Some were still abuilding in the grandiose tradition. The new college at Peterborough, designed by Scott, might seem to some critics 'hideous' and ill-designed, but when finished it could be favourably reported on:

The new building, which is 240 ft. long, stands upon 2 acres of ground adjacent to the cathedral. It contains 40 students' bed rooms, a dining room, two class rooms, a general sitting room, washing rooms etc. The rooms are large and well fitted for their purposes. The living rooms have a South frontage looking across the College lawns and the Deanery garden. There is a recreation ground with a fives court, gymnastic apparatus and bowling green: and the students have the use of an excellent cricket field adjoining the College grounds. The diet and general arrangements of the College are liberal, and are carefully adapted to the promotion of health and comfort. The students are allowed to leave the ground at certain hours daily. On Wednesday afternoon they are free from dinner time till 6 p.m. and on one or two other days they have 2 hours outdoor liberty. Three afternoons of two hours each are given to garden work. The musical training of the students is especially cared for.[18]

The staffs too were improving. The more progressive colleges had lecturers, and even the women's colleges had competent instructors. Cook reported on the women's colleges in 1864:

Two great points have been secured, in the first place all the governesses now employed have 1st class certificates and have been thoroughly trained, with very few exceptions, in the institutions where they are employed. In the next place, a sufficient number of governesses are now employed to do the work thoroughly and without any undue pressure upon their physical and mental powers. . . . The best governesses are most willing to overwork themselves. I have cases before my mind in which the work has been done admirably,—while the constitution of the governess was undergoing a process of excitement which, but for timely interference, would have issued in speedy and irreparable exhaustion. In some cases, it has only been by dint of most careful inquiry into the amount of work actually done by the governesses that I have been able to convince the Managers of the importance of increasing the staff.

The proper staff for 40 students is two governesses when the Principal, as at Lincoln, takes an active part in the teaching; or three if he confines himself to general superintendence or religious instruction.[19]

In the men's colleges the use of the teaching staff was far more variable. A survey of the hours of work of the staff of different colleges shows what might happen. At Battersea, with 79 students, the Principal lectured for 11 hours and also had the general management of the college and the correspondence to take charge of. The vice-principal lectured 13 hours, and the assistant master 12. There were visiting masters for music and drawing, as was the usual practice. At Chelsea, the Principal, the Rev. J. G. Cromwell took religious knowledge in the 2nd year, which seemed to come to 4 hours a week. At Cheltenham the Principal taught 6 hours, the vice-principal 13, the superintending master 5 and the assistant master 11. Of the newly opened Normal College at Bangor it is recorded:

Principal Rev. J. Phillips.
Teaches religious knowledge, and has general control. He is also much occupied in preaching in the chapels of the Calvanistic Methodists throughout Wales, in lecturing and in otherwise advocating the cause of the Normal School in country places.
Vice-principal. Mr John Price. Teaches grammar, composition, Latin, history, geography, school management, reading, repetition, and criticism lessons. 35 3/4 hours a week.

This official account is supported by the memories of Sir Henry Jones, one of the institution's most distinguished alumni: 'The Principal gave us Bible lessons once a week, otherwise we did not see him.' He also records that the Principal, before his elevation, had been a tailor, and was ashamed of it; whereas he himself had been a shoemaker, and was proud of it.

The students in the colleges, though they still caused the inspectors grief by their fundamental ignorance, were improving; and at Derby, at least, their general progress was 'quite equal to the expectations and wishes of the supporters of the institution'.

The colleges were also practically full, and of the 2655 students who passed the entrance examination in 1860, 2604 were Queen's Scholars.

Naturally all this could not be achieved without considerable expense, and the annual cost of the colleges, quite apart from the large capital expenditure, was always rising. Between 1858 and 1859 the grant rose by £15,855 and stood at £89,587. In the general search for economy, training colleges were a matter of obvious interest. At the same time it was the training colleges which produced the certificated teachers, and it was not unnatural to include the colleges in the general attack on the class.

The first blow was struck in 1860. In twenty years the nation's investment in training college buildings had been £121,522, and this was felt to be enough. On 21 January an inconspicuous Minute stated: 'Their Lordships will not entertain any new applications for grants towards the expenses of building, enlarging, improving or fitting up training colleges.'

This was recognized at once as putting an end to all expansion. Cook, reporting on Cheltenham Women's College a few months later, says: 'It is much to be regretted that larger premises were not secured, or a new building commenced before all present hopes of extension were extinguished by the Minutes of 21 January 1860.'

With capital expenditure at an end, the next task was to limit the annual grants. The Code of 1861, which offered the schools 1*d*. for each child's attendance, treated the colleges less harshly. It continued the exhibitions to Queen's Scholars, the allowance for examinations passed, and gave the practising schools the same terms as other schools. In the amended form of the Code in 1862 it, in addition, restored to certificated teachers in the colleges the augmentation grants that they had received under the old regulations, and it continued the payments to lecturers.

The annual grants were thus back on the old footing. This was not to last. In 1863 Queen's Scholarships were abolished and the colleges were told that they would 'hence forward settle their own scale of charges and exemptions'. In 1864 the principle of payment by results was brought fully into operation. Colleges existed to produce teachers, and therefore it was reasonable, as Lingen's acute mind told him, to base the grant on those students who actually made teaching their career. 'To the colleges annual grants are made of £100 in five successive payments of £20 p.a. for every master, who having been trained in them during two years, has during the past five years completed the prescribed period of probation and become qualified to receive a certificate.'

Even this was felt to leave loopholes for evasion, and in 1867 the regulations were made more precise; the number of students in a college was not allowed to exceed the number for whom accommodation was provided in 1862. That took care of expansion. The other half of the regulation guarded against shrinkage, and said that the grants must not exceed £50 per head of those in residence, or 75 per cent of last year's expenditure. This latter regulation involved the college in an unaccustomed amount of book-keeping, and the reports of the official auditor are full of complaints about the ignorance he found of even the most elementary systems.[20]

In consequence of these regulations the colleges had to charge some fees. In most cases they were low, in a few non-existent. Battersea, the most expensive, demanded £20 on entrance, and that covered tuition and board and lodging for two years. A common charge was £6 for the two years. Others took the students free. Caernarvon, the most generous, perhaps of necessity, charged 10s. a quarter, which was returned with an additional £6 when the certificate was obtained. It also paid travelling expenses four times a year from the student's home to college at the rate of 1d. a mile. In the women's colleges it was common to charge a girl with a class I entrance examination £3, and with a class II £5. Other colleges, e.g. Lincoln and Norwich, took them free.

The result of these financial changes was to impede the colleges rather than damage them mortally. The status of the staff fell slightly. Cook puts it delicately when reporting on the women's colleges: 'The teachers' salaries, though they may upon the whole fall somewhat short of the amount upon which they might formerly calculate, are quite enough to maintain them with comfort and respectability in their station.'

At the same time he sees dangers in the tendency of managers to economize still further.

I have already observed a desire to lessen rather than strengthen the present teaching power. I do not believe that the salaries of governesses can or ought to be reduced. The best students cannot be had, or permanently retained, without liberal treatment. . . . My successors will, ever and anon, have to contest the point, if not with committees of management, yet with persons upon whose influence the prosperity or popularity of the system is somewhat dependent.

These comments are made about the women's colleges particularly, because there was always a tendency to under-pay the governesses, and also because these colleges maintained their numbers, while the men's suffered a serious drop. This was the result of the Revised Code which attracted most attention, and which in the end caused the Government most concern. It was not only that the numbers and quality of the pupil teachers declined; large numbers of boys who had, or were just completing their apprenticeship gave up the thought of becoming teachers, and used their education in more promising fields. 'It cannot be concealed', said one inspector, 'that the operation of the Revised Code is prejudicial to the Training Colleges, especially for young men.' He goes on to give figures. 1863 was the last year in which the annual rise, which had been going on for some 18 years, continued. In 1863 there were 1167 men and 1177 girls in training colleges; in 1865 there were 860 men and 1156 girls. Cowie, reporting on the Church of England colleges for men, says that in 1864 there were only 300 applicants for 500 places, and that one college, Highbury, had been closed and its money transferred to Cheltenham. As he saw it, the drop was due to the conviction that teaching was no longer a good calling, and also to the fees that were now demanded.

From the point of view of the economists, these first results must have been satisfactory. The threat of an ever-expanding teaching body was halted, and the new regulations had produced a considerable drop in grant. The Church of England men's colleges alone had £3550 less in 1864 than in 1862. However, as the years went on and the numbers continued to fall, the Government became alarmed, and by 1867 they were once more attempting, with some success, to stimulate recruiting to the colleges.

In one way the colleges improved during this period of austerity: the Department succeeded, at last, in forcing a reduction in the width of the curriculum. The number of subjects which a student might offer was reduced, and the scope of the compulsory subjects decreased. For example, in religious knowledge the work was confined to certain carefully selected portions of the Bible and Prayer Book; church history was abandoned. No student could now take more than one 'alternative subject', which was to be taken from the list: physical science, mechanics, mathematics, English literature and Latin. Welsh or Gaelic could be taken by those students who wished; and, if they did really well, and then taught in an appropriate school, it would bring them an extra £5 a year.

The inspectors were not, of course, happy. Even Lingen felt that something better could be done, and he sent out a circular to the women's colleges on a more enlightened teaching of history. He was prepared to maintain the regulation that 'no questions will be set except such as can be answered from text-books in common use'—(these are named as Hume, Lingard, Pictorial), but he felt it to be

desirable to introduce some improvement in the manner of teaching it with reference to particular biographies, and to the progress of the country in arts, wealth and civilization.

If the lives of representative persons, and the national changes in food, clothes, dwellings, locomotion, police and knowledge could be taught incidentally to the political outline by governesses or lecturers who had studied one or other of the larger histories for the purpose, the students, without being called upon to extend their own reading, might perhaps acquire a more vivid idea of their country's history than they do at present, and might be more likely to make use of it in their schools. . . .

He hoped that the colleges would consider this, but he promised that no change would be made in the character of the examination papers in 1867. In fact no change took place in either the teaching or examination for a long time.

At this time, the inspector's contempt was focused most particularly on the criticism lessons which they were required to hear as part of the examination of each student. The schools were becoming more and more mechanical and less and less time could be spared for imparting general knowledge, yet the colleges had elaborated a scheme of formal lessons, given, out of any context, to children who were drilled to the unnatural exercise. Matthew Arnold, commenting on the performance at the Borough Road in 1864, wrote:

To a class of some 30 children, with whom they have little acquaintance, they have to give a set public lesson on some subject or other for 20 minutes. A sketch of this lesson is prepared beforehand and given to the Inspector. I have several such sketches now before me: a sketch of a lesson on the *Hand*; a sketch of a lesson on the *Isle of Wight*; a sketch of a lesson on the *Crocodile*; on the *Honey Bee*; on the cause of *Day and Night*. Inevitably the lesson becomes a means of showing the student's own knowledge of the subject and power of arranging it, rather than his faculty of teaching. Of this, with a class of children before him who do not profess to have learnt the lesson beforehand, who cannot therefore be examined on it, who cannot certainly be taught it in 20 minutes, and who are wearied and bewildered by being made the apparent object of a number of these performances one after another, it is really scarcely any test at all. The Inspector would learn far more by seeing him give to a single pupil a reading lesson of five minutes.[21]

Tinling in 1866 found that some women's colleges added deceit to futility:

In 1865 I stated that in some of the training schools the lessons given were not the real work of the students themselves, and that the notes upon which they relied were the completed work of the teacher of method. I have since ascertained that before our official visit in some instances the lessons have been actually rehearsed in the presence of the teacher of method.

Without undervaluing the power to give a conversational lecture on a pump or the manufacture of bread, it must be evident that the usefulness of a teacher depends still more on his mode of handling a class at its everyday work.

Notes

1. For the whole of this chapter, see Kay-Shuttleworth, *Four Periods of Popular Education*, Period Four; *Memorandum on Popular Education* (1868); Matthew Arnold, General Reports for 1863, 1867.
2. Minutes, 1862–3, p. xxi, *Instructions to Inspectors*.
3. General Report, Minutes, 1863–4, p. 186.
4. Sneyd Kinnersley, *H.M.I.* (1908), pp. 57 ff.
5. Minutes, 1861–2, p. xxv, Revised Code, Arts. 55–9.
6. The quotations from the log-books which follow are drawn mainly from those of the Garth School, Bangor and British School, Caernarvon, Caernarvon C.R.O.; Llanfairfechan, Caernarvon, in possession of the Vicar; British School, Nayland, Suffolk, in possession of Headmaster; New Jerusalem British School, Kearsley, in possession of Headmaster; and Commonhall Street School, Chester, Chester C.R.O.
7. Minutes, 1864–5, pp. 144, 214; 1865–6, pp. 149 ff.
8. Minutes, 1867–8, p. 196.
9. P.P., XLV, 183.
10. St Mary's, Coventry, P.P., 1864, IX, 529.
11. P.P., 1867, XXII, 322.
12. P.P., 1866, XXVII, 407; Minutes, 1866–7, p. 292.
13. Minutes, 1866–7, p. 33.
14. New Jerusalem British School, Kearsley.
15. Minutes, 1866–7, p. 127.
16. Quoted by permission of Prof. A. H. Dodd.
17. Sir Henry Jones, *Old Memories*.
18. P.P., 1865, XLII, 442.
19. Minutes, 1864–5, p. 361.
20. Accountant's Report on Training Colleges, P.P., 1865, XLII, p. xxvi.
21. Minutes, 1864–5, p. 387.

Chapter Fourteen

The Act of 1870

The greater precision which the requirements of the Revised Code gave to every aspect of school keeping enabled the inspectors and others interested to see just how far short the schools fell from an acceptable standard. The ignorance of the children and their irregular attendance were well known; but the numbers of children who did not go to school at all gradually assumed greater prominence in men's thoughts. The inspectors' reports for 1866 and 1867 are full of comments on the position. This was worse in the towns than in the country. Capel, reporting in 1866 on Birmingham and Warwickshire, said:

> In Birmingham there is a class of children which does not exist in rural parishes, who do not profess to go to any school, and who pass the day idling about the streets, learning nothing but evil, and acquiring habits which, in a few years, utterly unfit them for honest labour.[1]

His enquiries showed: 1 in 25 of the population was in Church schools in Birmingham; 1 in 9 in rural Warwickshire. A canvas in Birmingham showed: 8044 children aged 3–12; 887 at work; 3972 at school; 3185 neither at school nor at work.

In Birmingham the majority of the local trades were, at that time, heavy, and children had little place in them. The schools of the city had, indeed, grown in numbers, but then so had the population, and the ratio of school places to children had not increased in the last ten years.

In Liverpool a survey taken in certain sample streets showed that 5890 children attended school and 4761 did not.

In London things were worse. The Metropolis swarmed with children, abandoned, wretched, struggling to live in any way they could. Dickens

in the *Uncommercial Traveller* has a terrible description of a horde of
starving children fighting over a halfpenny, till put to flight by the
threat of a passing policeman.[2] The pages of Mayhew are full of the
children watercress-sellers or the mudlarks searching for scraps along
the Thames foreshore, lost in misery and ignorance.

These town children, uneducated, unemployed and usually also un-
cared for and uncontrolled, were commonly referred to as street arabs,
and were much on the conscience of reformers. Lord Shaftesbury and
others did what they could; and they may have helped many children
to some extent. They put their faith in ragged schools; but these institutions, where the waifs submitted in return for shelter and a meal
to a few hours of confinement and instruction, could never achieve any
real reform.

In other towns the conditions were different but as unfavourable to
education. Sandford reported on the Black Country:

I doubt whether there is in the whole of Europe, except perhaps in
Spain or S. Italy, a population of the same extent with so small a number
of children of any considerable age in the public schools as this of Brierley
Hill, where there are about 11,000 inhabitants, and only 2 or 3 boys over
12 years old in National Schools.[3]

In Luton all the children were employed, and from a very early age,
in straw plaiting; and if their places of work were called 'schools' that
did not mean that any education was given in them: it only served to
lend a tinge of respectability to merciless exploitation.

In the country, some districts were fortunate. In contrast to Birmingham, Capel found that in Warwickshire 'In rural parishes very few
children are growing up without any schooling. All between 5 and 15
would be at school or work.'

In other districts the provision was far less.

There are more than 11,000 parishes in which no school gets Government help for education. Something must be done, either by combining
parishes, or in some other way to spread to these the help they contribute
towards.

There were, in fact, not enough schools, or, if there were school
places, the children did not attend. The inspectors ask continually for
some means of increasing the number of schools and for some power of
compelling attendance. The conclusion that could be drawn was that
the present system had reached the limit of its development. The

aphorism that 'a system cannot at the same time be voluntary, efficient and universal' was becoming generally accepted. It could even be asserted that 'never before was the voluntary plan in Education more fairly, more liberally yet more thoroughly put on trial: and that never was its inadequacy more signally proved'. Even the convinced voluntarists, like Edward Baines, who had fought against every extension of government aid to education, were beginning to accept defeat and preparing to abandon their schools as soon as some public authority would accept them.

Throughout the more responsible part of the nation, moreover, a belief was spreading that the religious squabbles over education were out of date. The evidence given before the Newcastle Commission emphasized the fact that parents were indifferent to the religious adherence of the schools so long as they gave a decent education. The evidence from different districts was all in the same sense. Of Hull and district it was reported:

'Everywhere I have found Jews in Christian and Roman Catholics in Protestant schools; Nonconformists in National schools, and Church children in British and positively Dissenting schools.' Of the Potteries: 'The genuine, unstimulated opinion of the poorer classes of parents who desire education for their children appears to me to be universally a simple desire for a good useful plain education, with little care about religious distinctions of doctrine or discipline.'

Or Durham and Cumberland: 'Parents will send their children to which ever they deem the best school, quite irrespective of religious peculiarities.'

In general: 'On the subject of religious instruction I do not find among teachers, parents or pupils that any practical difficulty exists.'[4]

It was the managers and priests who made all the trouble.

The *Economist* (7 January 1860), speaking for a different section of the population, 'rebukes those who have brought their feuds and quarrels to be fought out on neutral territory', to the confusion of questions of political and social concern; and advises men of good will 'while avoiding all irritating treatment, all unnecessary offence to those whose feelings are already in a state of extravagant soreness, to indicate unshrinkingly a determination to act without them, and if need be against them'.

The *Edinburgh Review*, in 1861, put the matter more bluntly, and spoke of the 'intolerable cant of the religionists and the equally extravagant pretensions of the lay school managers'.

So eminent a churchman as Dr Hook, Dean of Chichester, could say: 'The truth is, I have always regarded the "religious question" as merely a political squabble.'

If the Nonconformists were preparing to abandon their schools, the Church of England was modifying its attitude of exclusion. Since 1863, when the Education Department received an application for a building grant for a Church school in a parish too small to support two schools, it had insisted on a conscience clause which prevented any discrimination against children who were not members of the Church. At first this clause had been resisted; but by 1867 'the agitation against it was assuming its proper proportions', and the Archbishop of Canterbury said that he approved of it.

Even the more stiff-necked were yielding to the pressure of facts. One man replied from Christchurch, Bridlington Quay, to the Visitation enquiry in Yorkshire in 1867: 'We do not *require* day school children to attend Sunday school. The feeling of the parish would not allow it.' There were in the parish Methodist, Primitive Methodist and Reformed Methodist chapels.

When the opponents of Church schools unearthed some example of bigotry—as the village clergyman who refused to take any pupils in his school who had not been baptized in church—the more responsible *Quarterly* hastened to express its disapproval, and to assure readers that such things hardly ever happened. It even went so far as to agree that undenominational religious teaching was possible; though it resurrects that hoary bugbear the 'latitudinarian schoolmaster', whose mere presence could be guaranteed to wreck the life of any village.

Politically, too, things were changing. The time foreseen by *Fraser's Magazine*, when peace in America would liberate democratic feeling in England, had come; and it had come in a manner particularly favourable to education. War in Europe had reinforced the lesson. Lord Morley said: 'The triumphant North in America was the land of the common school. The victory of the Prussians over Austrians at Sadowa in 1866 was called the victory of the elementary school teacher.' The English were beginning to see that education could be considered a munition of war.

But events at home were even more important. The Representation of the People Act of 1867 enfranchised a whole new section of the population: the lower middle classes and the working men of the towns. It also convinced such men as Lowe that ignorance was no longer a safeguard for his class. The new electorate, when it went to the polls, returned a Liberal Government. Gladstone took office in a religious fervour of reforming zeal. Church rates were abolished, preparations made for disestablishing the Irish Church, an Irish land bill promised, the beginnings of army reform undertaken, and competitive Civil Service examinations commenced. In the Queen's speech of 1868 education was mentioned as one of the topics due to receive attention: 'The general question of the education of the people requires your most serious attention, and I have no doubt you will approach the subject with a full appreciation both of its vital importance, and of its acknowledged difficulty.'

This was well received, and it was stated in Parliament that 'the present time was favourable for the passing of a wise, a large and a well considered measure for the education of the people'.

It was not, however, done at once. W. E. Forster was Vice-President, the first holder of that office to feel himself responsible for the expansion of education. He came of a passionately Quaker family, and his early life had been divided between his parents' modest home at Bradpole near Bridport and Northrepps Hall, the seat of his mother's family, who were connected by marriage with the Gurneys. He thus knew two worlds. He had worked twelve hours a day as a wool sorter, and he had been introduced to the higher and powerful ranks of philanthropy. Political ambition came early; and when he had made a comfortable fortune in business he became member for Bradford. He had ceased to be a Quaker, expelled from the Society, hardly against his will, when he married Matthew Arnold's sister. With a genuine reforming zeal, based on sympathy and knowledge, he had friends of all denominations among those who cared for education.

His first task was to see the Endowed Schools Bill through the House. This, the result of the Taunton Commission on Endowed Schools, gave to the Charity Commissioners power to make schemes for the administration of educational endowments. It was hoped that a proper use of these would provide, for the middle classes (admittedly out of endowments originally meant for the poor)[5] a reasonable education and a means of advancement to higher, even university education. The progress of the reorganization was slow.

Meanwhile the nation-wide debate on elementary education continued. Forster had been president of a conference to discuss the 'complete provision for the primary instruction of the children of the poorer classes, by means of local rates, under local administration, with legal powers, in cases of neglect, to enforce attendance at school'. His companions in educational thought had been men of such diverse views as Canon Jackson of Leeds, and Wickstead the Unitarian minister.

Before Forster embarked on the preparation of his bill for primary education he wished to be sure of his facts. He therefore sent out some of his experienced inspectors to report on Birmingham, Leeds, Liverpool and Manchester. The figures collected showed that of some 4,000,000 children of the poorer classes 1,569,000 were on the registers of schools and of these only just over one-third were offered for examination. 173,662 were presented in Standards IV–VI. Of this last group 26,162 were under ten and 147,500 over. Of all the children over ten in school, 118,809 were in Standards I–III. These figures naturally suggested that some administrative action should be taken to increase the proportion of children offered for examination, and to ensure that all were doing work suited to their age.[6] The reports from the great towns showed that in every case, less than a tenth of the population was in school; that the distribution of the schools was haphazard, determined by plain chance, or, too often, by sectarian rivalry; so that in some cases the National and the British schools stood back to back, both drawing grants and competing for the same children. Thus, while the schools provided reasonably well for one district, they left another almost destitute. In most places the Workshops Act of 1867, which provided for part-time employment of children, was either not observed at all, or, where an attempt was made to enforce to, the employers dismissed the children, and left them to roam the streets, unemployed and untaught. The development of machinery had decreased the need for children's labour, and in Leeds the number of half-timers fell in ten years by 50 per cent, so that these children increased the population of the streets. The 'private schools' were as bad as ever; and many schools belonging to the voluntary bodies still refused inspection, and were in a deplorable condition.

Forster had no seat in the Cabinet, and in October 1869 he was asked to prepare a memorandum on the different proposals of the various bodies interested in education. He did this, giving the various difficulties that he saw in each plan.[7] There were four main types.

1. The plan just propounded at Birmingham, which provided that local authorities should establish free schools when want of schools was proved, such schools to teach no religious dogma; to be built and

301

maintained by rates and taxes, the rates paying a third of the cost, the taxes the remainder; to be managed by the rate-payers, but to be inspected and kept up to a certain standard by the central Government.

This he thought too expensive, and it would deprive the central Government of all real power. Moreover, as the schools were to be free, it would almost certainly result (as the authors of the scheme hoped) in the gradual closing of the existing denominational schools.

2. The Bill brought forward by Bruce in 1868, which was the first proposal to make compulsory provision for English schools, and which, while allowing districts to rate themselves for existing schools and the erection of new schools, enabled the Government to compel them to levy such a rate upon educational destitution being proved.

This broke down on the old difficulty of rate aid for denominational schools.

3. The plan sketched out by Robert Lowe, which proposed that the Government should make a survey of the educational provision and need in each parish, should inform the public of such need, and, after giving time for its supply by voluntary effort, should compel the district to provide such supply, upon proof of the continued existence of the need.

This, he thought, was the best, as it provided for compulsion only where necessary.

4. The plan proposed by the National Educational Union, of inducing and tempting the volunteers to cover the whole country, by so increasing the aid given by Government to such volunteers as to make any compulsory provisions unnecessary.

This last, which was but a more expensive version of the present system, could be dismissed as totally inefficient.

The Cabinet considered this, and instructed him to prepare the draft of a bill. The aim, quite simply, must be to (1) cover the country with good schools and (2) get the parents to send their children to them. It must be a bill that was acceptable to the majority, and it should make the best of what already existed. The Bill which Forster drafted disappeared to the Cabinet, and he was in the uncomfortable position of being excluded from the discussion and only knowing the fate of each clause when told the result. The Bill, when it reappeared, had undergone changes; and it was his duty to recommend the various provisions in the House whether he approved of them or not. Although the Bill itself was sure to pass, it was always being squeezed out by more urgent matters. At one point it was held up for three months while, urged on by murder and incipient rebellion, Gladstone carried his Irish Land Bill. Moreover as the duties of Vice-President combined the care of the education of children with an oversight of the health of cattle, Forster had on occasion to break off his parliamentary duties to deal with animal disease and stamp out cattle plague. But he was a man of great patience and resolution, and he struggled through.

The Bill was an exceedingly moderate and skilful one. It preserved the diversity of English education, and asserted the principle of local as opposed to central control. It took nothing from the Church, and it opened a field of local government which enabled people of all walks of life to co-operate for the public good. This was of great importance in the towns; in the country, with insufficient parliamentary representation and a long history of pauperism and dependence, it was invaluable. Women were eligible for election, and they could begin to play their part in official public life.

In its main provisions, even in its title, the Bill offered a new point of view. The principle that some education was the *right* of every child was asserted, and, following from that, it was the *duty* of the community to provide facilities for it. It did not universally compel parents to take advantage of these facilities: partly because to make education compulsory before adequate schools had been provided would bring the law into contempt; and partly because a period when compulsion was local and optional gave a valuable opportunity for experiment.

Furthermore public education was to be dissociated from the concept of the Poor, and from the stranglehold of dogma. The abortive Bill of 1867 had been entitled Education of the Poor Bill; Forster's was 'to provide Public Elementary Education in England and Wales'. The Department of Education had, for some years, referred to 'elementary education' in its reports; it is only after this Bill that Hansard adopts the same terminology. In addition, the Bill introduced the concept of the '*public elementary school*'.

The term 'elementary school' means a school at which elementary education is the principal part of the education there given, and does not include any school at which the ordinary payments in respect of each scholar exceed 9*d.* a week.

A 'public elementary school' shall be conducted in accordance with the following regulations.

1. It shall not be required, as a condition of any child being admitted into or continuing in the school, that he shall attend or abstain from attending

any Sunday school or any place of religious worship, or that he shall attend any religious observance or any instruction in religious subjects in the school; [. . . He may be withdrawn by his parent].

2. The time at which any religious observation is practised. . . shall be at the beginning or the end of . . . the school meeting.

3. The school shall be open at all times to the inspection of Her Majesty's Inspectors and they shall not enquire into the religious instruction or examine in it.

4. The school shall be conducted in accordance with the conditions required for grant.

Only public elementary schools, as here defined, could receive grant. The Bill thus effectively prevented public money from being used for proselytizing.

If the Bill did not, as the more extreme opponents of the Church hoped, do anything to destroy denominational schools, it did set a limit to their multiplication at the public expense. No more capital grants for building were to be made to schools after 31 December 1870. The period from August, when the Act was passed, to December was full of frantic activity in the National Society. In 1869 there had been 226 applications for building grants; in the last five months of 1870 there were 3003. Once again the threat of Government action had stimulated voluntary effort.

The main provision of the Bill was the division of the country into school districts, each of which would, in time, assume responsibility for its own area. These districts were, in the country, the civil parishes —that is the districts in which a rate was levied. In the towns, the boroughs; and in London, the Metropolis. The honour of inventing this unit goes to W. M. Torrens, M.P., who proposed it on 4 July 1870. Forster, who had previously considered the problem of London most anxiously, was delighted with the solution.

In each of these districts a survey was to be carried out of the numbers of children and schools so as to ascertain if any educational deficiency existed. Then, if the deficiency was not supplied by other agencies, 'a School Board shall be formed for such a district and shall supply such deficiency'. School Boards might also be formed at the wish of a district, even if no deficiency existed.

The Boards were to be elected by the ratepayers or burgesses and to number from five to fifteen, except in London where the Board was to be larger to provide adequate representation of all the different boroughs.

The method of election was unusual. In order to ensure minority representation, each voter had as many votes as there were candidates, and he could give them all for one or distribute them as he thought fit. This enabled well-organized minorities, as the Roman Catholics, to return at least one candidate, often at the top of the poll. There was another innovation, and an important one. In London, outside the City, voters were not required to write their names and property qualifications on the ballot paper. Thus a first experiment was made with the secret ballot, which was at the moment the subject of heated controversy. The Ballot Act, which Forster passed two years later, could be recommended with more confidence after this trial. The Boards, when elected, held office for three years.

The purpose of the School Boards was primarily to see that there were adequate schools for the children of the district. If sufficient voluntary schools existed, or could be provided, and the district did not wish to have a Board, there was no need to elect one. If a Board were formed, and so wished, it could make by-laws on compulsory attendance, and be granted powers to enforce them; but there was no regulation requiring a Board to make these by-laws, and many, in fact, did not.

Forster's belief was that 'if there ever was a question which was not a party question it was the question of education', and in that spirit he was prepared to accept support from any party in the House.

The extremists on both sides naturally found the Bill distasteful. Some churchmen felt doubts about the religious teaching in the new schools, and feared their competition; anti-clericals, encouraged by the recent abolition of Church Rates, the disestablishment of the Irish Church, and the talk of disestablishment of the Welsh, were furious that the Church was left with its schools intact and the prospect of continuing support.[8]

They demanded that the new schools should be secular and *free*, with the intent that the voluntary ones should wither away with their fees and their religion.

The sober periodicals, the *Edinburgh* and *Quarterly Reviews*, show significant differences. The *Edinburgh* ignored the whole matter of primary education. For the three or four years when the matter was under discussion, before and after the Act, there is no article on the question; though the Universities and technical education are discussed. The *Quarterly*, on the other hand, is cautiously welcoming. In April 1870, when the Bill was first under discussion, it published an article

305

which, though it suggests certain problems for the consideration of churchmen, contains such phrases as: a bill 'conceived in a generous and manly spirit, and intended to give effect to the public will . . .', 'The wisdom and moderation of the Bill . . .' or '. . . such are the provisions of this remarkable Bill'. It pointed out that it was only twenty-five to thirty years since 'voluntary effort for the education of the people and the action of the state have been brought into the presence of one another' . . . and that the nation was now on the verge of a most beneficial advance.

The great body of sensible and well-intentioned men carried the Bill through Parliament, and made the Act a success. If in the early stages of its application neither party scorned a little sharp practice, after only a year or two confidence and reasonable amity were established.

The first task under the new Act was to carry out a survey of the educational needs of the country. A number of inspectors of returns were to do the work. In the towns the difficulty of finding out the numbers and dwellings of the children was so great that special local arrangements had to be made. It was in the country that most of the work for these inspectors lay.

It appeared that Returns were answers to questions sent by the Department to every parish in the country; What was the population? What schools had they in the parish? What schools outside the parish did they use? and so on. When we had verified the answers, we were to recommend the recognition of such schools as we found to be efficient, and to state what further provision was required, with detailed suggestions. . . .

This seemed simple. But the word parish gave us infinite trouble. When we speak of a parish we think of an ecclesiastical district; and we picture a cluster of houses, a long street and an old church. But parliament meant or defined a *civil* parish; that is, a finite area in which a separate rate can be collected. In most parts of England the difference is immaterial, but . . . in others the movements of population had produced towns which had far outstripped the old centres after which they were named. There was thus much difficulty. Also in the more rural parts of the country the level of education was too low to allow the parish to have reliable representatives. If a school were ordered it would probably be built and managed by a School Board; and in Anglesey the members of the Board would be five men whose opinion on a pig might be accepted, if the pig belonged to a perfect stranger, but on school matters the pig's opinion would be equally valuable.

Further, the parishes were often so small that for efficiency they would have to be united, and they resisted union.[9]

The inspectors of returns worked hard, and returns poured in; to such an extent, indeed, that the London office was overwhelmed and could hardly keep pace with them and send its orders out in return.

The returns received, there were three ways in which a School Board could be established. The district could ask for one, whether it was deficient in schools or not. A district with enough schools could become deficient through the threatened closure of one of them. This was quite a common state of things, as the Nonconformist bodies were anxious to surrender their schools. In this case a School Board was formed, with the good will of the district, to take over the threatened schools and to continue them under new management. In the third case a district could be really deficient in schools, and, having failed, after due notice, to supply the deficiency voluntarily, could be forced to set up a Board. Districts with sufficient schools would not be forced to do anything.

To take examples of each kind of procedure,[10] a large number of towns did not hesitate at all. London, Bootle, Manchester, Leeds, Birmingham, Coventry and others all had their Boards in office before the end of the year. Barnsley, Durham, Exeter, Oxford and Sheffield were among those that followed the next year. They did not wait for the result of the survey of schools and children: the need was too obvious. Birmingham, for example, was authorized to start building schools for 5000 immediately, as the smallest number which would be needed. London started to provide for 100,000 children, though everybody really knew that 250,000 was the proper figure. Sheffield had a deficiency of about 12,000, and set to work immediately on two schools. Some country parishes were equally prompt.

As an example of the second type of School Board formation Bangor, Caenarvonshire, will serve. It was well supplied with schools, as it always had been, but on the passing of the Act the managers of the British and of the Wesleyan schools announced that they proposed to abandon their schools, and a Board was demanded to take them over. There was no reluctance.[11]

On the whole, apart from the big towns, the nonconformist districts were the most eager to form School Boards. Cornwall was early covered with them. In 1878 there were 90 of them covering a population of 236,832. At least three-quarters had been formed voluntarily. There were 25 in Caernarvonshire with three-quarters voluntary formations. On the other hand in Berkshire there were only seven covering a population of 40,227 and three had been formed by compulsion; and in rural

Buckinghamshire of 23 boards covering 36,000, only eight were voluntary formations.

In the Visitation Returns of the Diocese of York the existence of a Board School in a parish at Northallerton is explained as due to the fact that two-thirds of the population were dissenters, and 'the leading family and the only one of influence are strong dissenters and active propagandists'.

A passage in the log-book from Llanfairfechan suggests how social and sectarian rivalry sped the movement: 'One of the three reasons why the dissenters wish to form a School Board in this parish is that the teacher said the Dissenters' children were treated as Black Sheep in the school.' We can see from the returns that the dissenters were unsuccessful. Llanfairfechan had a rich landlord who took an interest in the National School.

On the other hand we can see the struggles of those districts that resisted School Boards. The *School Board Chronicle* for 1871 gives news of the movement in different places. Of Durham it records: 'The town council has passed a resolution favouring the formation of a School Board, and the citizens are resisting the action of the Council with so much feeling that the Education Department is likely to have considerable trouble with the northern city.' Here the Town Council triumphed.

In Cambridgeshire, 'during the closing months of the past year strenuous efforts were made by the clergy, headed by the Bishop of Ely, and the influential laity, headed by the Earl of Hardwicke, to raise funds whereby the educational requirements of every parish in the county might be provided for. . . .' The result was a collection of about £1,500, and in most parishes the formation of Boards was postponed.

The struggles of the city of Chester to avoid the hated innovation can be followed in the Minute Book of the Accommodation Committee, a body set up to deal with the problem:[12]

1873, 11 Feb. The schedule received from Education Department stating the deficiency in school accommodation that had been ascertained, and what was needed to remedy it.

The district was about 1000 places short. It was decided that £2000 would be needed to provide what the managers of existing schools said that they could not afford, and a committee was formed to try to raise the money. On 27 February the committee met. It was mainly clerical. The Dean was in the chair. There were eleven Ministers of

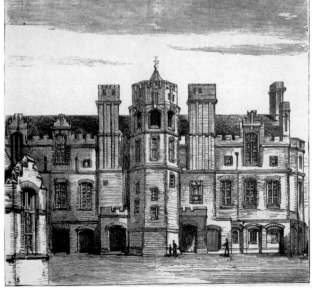

13   Architecture of the London School Board—I
a   Above   Nightingale Street School, Marylebone. Note the roof playground
b   Below   Winstanley Road School, Clapham Junction

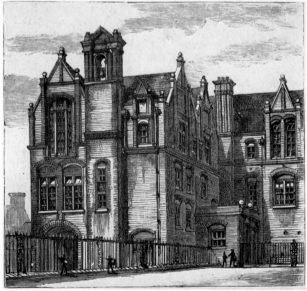

14 Architecture of the London School Board—II
a Hanover Street School, Islington. This is the most typical
example
b Gideon Road School, Battersea

religion (two or three Nonconformist, the rest Anglican, with two canons of the cathedral) and three laymen. The lay representation was increased later, and five solicitors, a bank manager, a hosier, a cabinet maker and some other tradesmen joined. It was decided to set up an undenominational school for 200 infants in a disused chapel in Common-hall Street and suggested that the Ragged School Committee should take charge of it. By June the Ragged School Committee had refused to manage the school, and the cost of founding this, and enlarging and improving other existing schools had risen to £2620. The committee had in hand, or was promised £910, thus leaving them with a deficiency of £1710. At the next meeting it was decided to hold a large public meeting in the Town Hall to try to raise the money. The meeting was carefully planned, and the way prepared by sending out a circular which said:

Apart from the question of the desirability of a School Board for Chester [which they would not discuss], the necessary school accommodation may be provided more economically by voluntary effort than by the machinery of a school board, and the Committee would respectfully remind the public that the City has no option but to obey the orders of the Education Department, and that if the funds be not at once raised by voluntary effort, a school board will be appointed which will collect the necessary funds by a compulsory rate.

If a compulsory rate is levied it will cost £5000, instead of the £1500 now estimated, because of the loss of subscriptions.

They therefore asked the citizens to agree to a voluntary rate of 6d. in the £. '. . . it being understood that 1) those who have already contributed might deduct the amount of that contribution, 2) if a compulsory rate become necessary, sums paid voluntarily to be set off against it.' Mr Shone, Corporation Rate Collector, was given the job of collecting it. He was not very successful. By January 1874 he had actually received £430.

In May, the Educational Department wrote asking what had been done, and threatening:

I am to point out that if, at the expiration of the time to be limited by the final notice, the whole of the accommodation required . . . has not been supplied, a School Board would have to be formed, not only of the contributory district of Saltney but also for the school districts of Chester, Great Boughton, Blacon cum Crabhall and Bache.

The rate collector is urged to greater efforts; but by October he reports that out of £2499 due he has only got £586. In November some progress has been made: The lease of the Commonhall Street chapel is nearly ready, and the British School Association has agreed to manage it. In February 1875 the committee, having done what it could and collected in all £894 3s. 7½d., ceased to exist, leaving the new school to its fate.

Its life, as can be learnt from its log-book, was brief and inglorious. In fact the poorer inhabitants of Chester were as unwilling to receive education as the richer sort were to provide it. The school was opened in April 1875 and closed in May 1876. 'The school closed today in accordance with the resolution of the managers.' 151 children had been admitted; 83 had left; 69 still on the books. Only 10 had made 250 attendances. Of these, 3 were under three years of age, and 1 over seven. The finance was hopeless:

School pence	£11. 9. 0
One donation	£5. 18. 0
Total	£17. 7. 0
Expenses for a year and a month	£107. 7. 6

There was a Government grant of about £10 due but not yet received. 'No help . . . There being no prospect of it being anything like self supporting in the absence of any power of gathering in the children and enforcing their regular attendance.' We learn from the *School Board Chronicle* that even in 1877 Chester was still some 900 school places short.

Chester was not the only city which successfully resisted having a School Board forced upon it. In 1878 the School Board year book shows that York, Cambridge, Folkestone, Winchester, Ely, Windsor and Birkenhead, among others, had escaped. The smaller towns and the country districts, where there was no really energetic anti-board leadership, gave way and formed a board; the more readily, perhaps, if it were remote. For example, the first School Board in Cambridgeshire was at Soham on the very edge of the fens.

Bellairs reporting on Oxfordshire in 1872 remarked, 'The Act of last session, so far as the rural parts of this district are concerned, will be, for many years at least, almost wholly inoperative.' 'There are places', said the Rev. C. Du Port, 'where clergyman, squire and very anti-education farmers are the only people to be on the Board.' The farmers, as yet another inspector reports, 'are anxious to avoid a rate for the furtherance of an object to which they have as yet contributed little besides hostility.'

310

When in time Boards were forced, compulsorily, on these districts, the Boards themselves did their best to defeat the Act. Typically, they consisted of the vicar, the churchwardens and three farmers. The vicar had a conscientious objection to School Boards, and the farmers thought that the younger a child started on agricultural work the better for everybody. They gave exemptions to all who asked, and employed, illegally, those who did not bother to do so. They also, generally, made the teacher's life very difficult.

Something of this sort had been foreseen, and Section 63 of the 1870 Act dealt with Boards in 'default'. The defaulting members could be removed, and the Department would proceed to appoint new members to supply their places. When this had been done the old members would 'be deemed to have vacated their offices as if they were dead'. In a few cases the Department took this action, dissolved the offending Board and appointed a new one on the advice of the local inspector. On one occasion they thought it wise to include a large and athletic policeman among the new appointees—just in case the former members were not quite 'dead'.

Notes

1. Minutes, 1866–7, p. 47; also Minutes, 1856–7, p. 266.
2. Ch. XXXIV.
3. Minutes, 1866–7, pp. 194, 199.
4. *Newcastle Report*, pp. 34 ff.
5. Cf. Brian Simon, *Studies in the History of Education* (1960), pp. 328–36.
6. & 7. T. Wemyss Reid, *Life of Rt. Hon. W. E. Forster* (1888), pp. 457 ff.
8. John Morley, *Struggle for National Education* (2nd ed.)
9. Sneyd Kinnersley, *H.M.I.* (1908), pp. 7 ff.
10. For dates of formation of School Boards and their composition and other details see School Board Directory, 1878, library of the Ministry of Education.
11. Many of the following details are from the Minute Books of the Bangor and Caernarvon School Boards in the Caernarvon C.R.O.
12. Chester C.R.O.

Chapter Fifteen

The work of the School Boards

The formation of the School Boards was the beginning of a social revolution in England. It brought to the well-intentioned a regular and defined field of work whose utility was obvious, and which was maintained by official regulation and not by the fluctuating force of personal enthusiasm. It opened to the eyes of the world the facts of life in the cities, and allowed numbers of people to have daily experience of conditions which, before, it had required a Royal Commission to reveal. In the country it brought the first opportunity that many districts had ever had of democratic organization. The School Board was the assertion of independence against the dominance of squire and clergyman. Moreover as there was no property qualification for membership of the Boards, as there was for membership of the Town Councils or the Boards of Guardians, working-men could be elected, and after a few years were; Birmingham, for example, having a regular working-class representative on the Board. Also, as women were eligible to serve, it was their introduction to official public life. Something of this was felt at the time, both by those who supported and by those who opposed the creation of Boards.

The London School Board was both the earliest and the greatest, and on it and its elections public interest was first centred. *The Times* writing about the election on 29 November took a high and serious tone:

No equally powerful body will exist in England, outside Parliament, if power be measured by influence for good or evil over masses of human beings.

There is such a thing as being more anxious to elect thoroughly

313

efficient members of the School Board than to secure the triumph of a particular dogma, religious or political; there is such a thing as desiring to see an equally satisfactory representation of all parties, creeds and classes, including those which are not our own.

The Board, when elected, adopted the same attitude. Said Baron Lawrence, the Chairman, when the new body was assembled for the first time in the Guildhall:

> I trust that by God's help we shall be able to do the work in such a way as to afford an example to the whole kingdom, and to establish a sound and excellent system of education for the great masses of the people.

The quality of the men and women who secured election was worthy of these aims. In London there was a galaxy of talent. The Board started its work under the Chairmanship of Baron Lawrence, recently returned from being Viceroy of India. Professor Huxley was a member, Elizabeth Garrett Anderson, Emily Davies, Viscount Sandon, several M.P.s, including Mr Torrens and W. H. Smith, and many others who had been associated with education for a long time. When the other big towns came to elect their Boards there was the same willingness of the leading citizens to serve, and the same sense of responsibility in the electors.

Among the members of the first School Board for Birmingham were the industrialists Sampson Lloyd and A. J. Elkington, the politicians Joseph Chamberlain and George Dixon, M.P., Rev. F. S. Dale, the popular preacher, Rev. R. W. Dale associated with the civic university, and others.[1]

At Sheffield there were such wealthy and philanthropic manufacturers as Henry Wilson, Mark Firth, Charles Doncaster, Sir John Brown and there was Skelton Cole the draper.

At Liverpool there was at least one shipping magnate. In the Oxford list there are doctors and solicitors with one woman; in Bangor, in North Wales, there was the owner of the flour mills, the auctioneer, the Honorary Secretary of the British Schools, presumably a nonconformist minister, with the local landowner as benevolent, though frequently absentee, chairman.[2]

In some districts the Boards were elected after a lively contest, largely on the religious issue. At Sheffield the religious adhesion of each member of the first Board is given as if it determined his policy. The distribution of seats between the sects seems very equitable and probably well represents the views of the city. They were: one Roman Catholic, four Churchmen, seven Nonconformists, two Unitarians and one Quaker.

At Liverpool, which had many years' experience of the public running of a school, the various parties agreed in advance on the representation of each, and there was no contested election. The smaller places varied in the same way. Caernarvon avoided an election, Bangor had one; but in every district there seems to have been the same standard of responsibility and reasonableness. As the *Quarterly* said, 'Nothing is more remarkable than the deep interest shown in the School Board elections, and the high class of men who have become candidates and been elected. The rate-payers have elected men who put education first and economy second.'

Nor did the members, when elected, fail in their trust. They showed 'the intellectual zeal for the discovery and the spread of truth—the warm spirit of sympathy which shrinks from seeing the misery of ignorance in others, as it would from the misery of poverty and starvation . . .' This zeal was due, in large part, to the 'education' which they were receiving.

'It appears', said the *School Board Chronicle* (22 April 1871), 'that the persons who will henceforth undergo the strictest process of education are the members of the School Boards themselves . . . Already there are several hundreds of gentlemen and a few ladies whose minds are now devoted to the subject of education as a reality. They are brought face to face with all sorts of ideas to which they have been hitherto strangers, or which they have previously shirked . . .'

They have had to meet, work with and treat with respect all sorts of people whom they have previously shunned.

They also, very soon, went to places that they would never before have visited. Ladies and gentlemen now actually went into the schools, and saw them at their ordinary work. They looked at the lavatories and tried to open the windows. All the things that had, at most, been a sentence in a report, became facts to them. But something more happened; they came face to face with the real ignorance of the children and their parents; and they formed some idea of the way thousands of families lived. Where there was an attempt to make school attendance compulsory they had to try to understand the economics of the poor home, or the state of mind of a parent who genuinely preferred ignorance. Their sympathy was actively engaged. They were committed to a new way of

315

thought—and the most remarkable results followed in the course of a few years.

There was a further result after a short time: the Boards, up and down the country, formed an unofficial alliance, and the *School Board Chronicle* became the organ of their communication—the 'Hansard', as it claimed, 'to the great educational parliament of the United Kingdom which circulates from the Vice-President of the Education Department to the higher class of elementary teachers'. The Boards were even allowed to take it officially, and an over-officious auditor, who disallowed the expenditure, was snubbed. The *Chronicle* took to the smallest Boards the achievements of their greater brethren, and it listed, impartially, the members for Lanfor, Merioneth and Sunderland. The Boards, too, corresponded with each other: Bangor would write to Liverpool asking for copies of their by-laws and advice on administering them; Leeds would write to Sheffield suggesting a joint deputation to the Department protesting about some proposed change in the law. If a School Board excluded the public from its meetings, the *Chronicle* makes harsh comments. There was power and direction behind the movement. The unco-ordinated, uninformed struggles of the past were over.

The history of education for the next thirty years is the account of how the national conscience, as opposed to bureaucracy, dealt with a great social problem. Each year of experience uncovered new needs and new problems. For twenty of these years the Boards fought the Education Department. The legacy of Lowe and Lingen could not be cast off at once; and each beneficial innovation was blocked by appeals to regulations which could have been altered, had the rulers so wished, by a stroke of the pen. A clause, so small as to escape detection by any but the most passionate enemy of progress, could have been inserted in the Code, and the thing was done. But no. The old regulations, framed by Kay-Shuttleworth in liberality to deal with a totally different situation, were given the status of immutable Laws. For these years, while forces inside and outside the schools were gathering strength, the old structure remained. In 1890 George Kekewich became Secretary, and, with the power that the office still possessed, took up the task of liberal development. In his ten years of control he carried matters so far that some new and wider organization was inevitable; and the School Boards, having done one of the great works of the century, ceased to exist.

In all the events of these years it is important to remember the diversity of the Boards to which much of the control of education passed.

They ranged from the burningly progressive Boards of the big towns, through the well-intentioned but less powerful, to the frankly obstructionist. The London School Board might have 'jurisdiction over a population of some 4 million', the Board of Thorngumbald, Yorkshire, over 536. Instead of meeting in the Guildhall with a Clerk at £800 a year to record their doings, some made suit to the Mayor for a cupboard to put their books and papers in, and suggested that some well-intentioned solicitor should be asked to give them advice gratis. How simple some of the arrangements were is shown by the Minute Books of the Bangor board. There, on election, they acquired a Minute Book, bought a 'strong tin box' (£1. 13. 1), commissioned a seal (£3. 17. 0) and were ready for business. There is the same diversity in the problems with which the Boards were faced, but the system of inter-communication ensured that common solutions to the more general problems were found.

The Boards, newly elected, looked round on their provinces. For most of them the first problem was finance. The Boards had no money and they were plagued with bills. There were always election expenses, even when there was no contest; and these appeared high in a poor district. Bangor, which had an election, had to pay £62. 4. 8; Caernarvon, which did not, found the bill of £13 excessive, and wrote to the Department:

. . . believing that the present system of School Board election to be attended with more expense than what is really necessary, in as much as the returning officers are almost universally solicitors, and have in a great number of cases charged exorbitant fees . . . and believing the present mode of election to be a great obstruction to the formation of school boards in country parishes . . . your petitioners pray that Your Lordships will without delay prescribe a simpler and more effective code of election rules, limiting such charges in all cases to fixed items.[3]

In the cities, with their vastly greater electorate the costs were proportionately higher. These are the figures for the cost of establishing a School Board at Brighton:

	£	s.	d.
Stationery and printing	8	15	0
Rent of Pavilion room	38	10	0
Clerk's salary (which roughly depended on population of town)	215	8	0
Clerk's disbursements		12	0
Cost of collecting statistics	21	0	0
Cost of election	150	0	0
	£434	5	0

The legal duty of the Boards was to take a survey of the children in their districts and the provision of efficient schools, and make the two match. These returns produced great difficulties. The Census was being taken at the time and the Boards hoped that the census figures would be made available. The Registrar General was most unco-operative. He resisted in every way the request for a 'premature disclosure' of the figures, until threats were made that the matter would be raised in Parliament. He then offered to provide some figures at a cost of 7s. per 100 names, which Sheffield, at any rate, felt to be excessive. In the event, each district had to number its children as best it could. In the country it was easy. The smaller towns demanded a little more labour and organization. It was the big industrial towns that set so great a problem. In Sheffield it was done through the police, in other places various types of enumerators were appointed. The task in London was enormous. The children of the courts and alleys, those who slept rough with no established base, those who had been sucked into employment at an early age, and whom their parents would deny to keep their earnings, ran into tens of thousands. The so-called schools, the hovels in which children were crammed for a penny or so a week, were very numerous. The city was divided into districts, and these into streets, and enumerators employed. The Board could not believe the results as they came in.

The survey carried out before the Act gave an indication of the numbers of uneducated children, but the facts as they were gradually revealed to each district were a shock. When an attempt was made to evaluate the schools, to which many of the children professed to go, the usual inefficiency and appalling conditions were found to prevail. In the big towns the outstanding need was to build new schools, but that could not be done at once. The Boards were also authorized to take over existing schools if their managers wished to surrender them. Many did.

The Department had some doubts about the motives which might inspire such wishes and made regulations: 'Managers have power to transfer their school only in order to relieve themselves from the responsibility of maintaining it, and for no other purpose. It was not the purpose of the legislature to enable trustees or managers to obtain money for property held by them in trust.' The consideration for the transfer must be *nominal*. The regulation continued: 'No payment of rent beyond that charged upon the premises by the original lease and no other valuable consideration, except an undertaking to insure and keep the premises in repair will in general be sanctioned.' . . . From the entries in the Sheffield Minute Books it appears that there, at least, these regulations were not always obeyed, but there may have been special circumstances.

Those who surrendered their schools were actuated either by a genuine belief that public ownership was the right thing, or by despair of maintaining them under their present management; and each body of managers acted by its own arbitrament with little regard for government policy. The Nonconformist bodies as a whole surrendered their schools, some enthusiastically, others just as a matter of course. An enthusiast, John Calvert, Minister of Zion Chapel, Attercliffe, wrote that he regarded the School Board system 'as the dawn upon England of a glorious morn . . . and, as a proof of my confidence in the scheme, I secured the entire transfer of a lucrative denominational school at Attercliffe to the management of the Sheffield School Board'.

Others influenced more by prudence:

1875 Fulwood School. Master died, and trustees considering that premises were insufficient and hard to find another master, offer to transfer the premises, *and endowment* to School Board.[4]

From Brighton came despair: the Brighton Board was asked to take over a school.

The children had, it appeared, come from a ragged school in Carlton Hill. Of 200 who thus came only 12 could read and none could write. The school was entirely free, the cost of their management, about £200 a year, being defrayed by subscriptions and donations, but they were in debt to the treasurer. The average attendance was 120 boys and girls (only a few of whom were over 12 years of age) but during the present winter it had been less, some of the children, in consequence of the poverty of their parents, having had to go to the workhouse.

It was represented that, if the Board did not take over, the school could not go on.

The London School Board in its first year accepted the transfer of 10 schools, four of which had been under Church management; but as three were ragged schools, a type which was being generally abandoned, it shows no general willingness in the Church to transfer any but the most unsatisfactory schools. In the course of its life, till 1904, the Board accepted 149 schools, almost all of which were closed as soon as possible.

In spite of the regulations the terms of transfer varied. In 1874 the

Sheffield Board was offered the large and well-organized Wesleyan Day Schools at a rent of £35 for six months (to include warming, lighting and cleaning). 'The school appliances to be taken at a valuation. The Committee will also expect its due proportion of the Government Grant in the event of its being obtained.'

The trustees of the Lancastrian schools were more generous. They offered their property to the Board at a 'moderate valuation', the purchase money to be applied to the foundation of scholarships. The money paid was £6540.

In other cases the suspicions of the Department were justified. The New Jerusalem School, Summer Lane, Birmingham, was offered to the Board at a rent of £40 for five months. The Board must promise not to dismiss the teacher or disperse the school. The buildings were ruinous, and the Board refused to consider the bargain.

In the Bangor accounts there is no indication that the Board paid anything for the school buildings that they took over, only that they bought the 'fittings' at a valuation.

Indeed, in most cases, the buildings accepted were in a very poor state, and the immediate concern of the Board was with their inspection and repair. One or two of the members of the Board were deputed to visit and report. They were not, we may suppose, unduly squeamish, but at one school the immediate needs—repairing the defective W.C.s, mending the pipes to the stoves, and trimming the hedges to produce some reasonable tidiness—cost £50. Then they started cleaning the schools and made bargains with the cleaners to provide brushes, and chips for lighting the fires. The teachers were required to certify that the work was properly done.

The building of new schools took time, but the big Boards started on it as soon as possible. In London the first Board school was opened in 1873, and by 1875 there were 99.

As soon as the Boards were constituted they could turn to finance. The Boards were empowered to issue precepts on the rates, and this they did in due time. It was commonly hoped that the education rate would never exceed 3d. in the £. At first it was round about 1d. But here, as in all else, there were great differences between the Boards. In the bigger towns, before the greater schemes began, this was enough. A penny rate in Birmingham produced £3000; in Brighton £1500. In Liverpool a rate of 0·65d. brought in £7322; at St Blazey, Cornwall, on the other hand, it needed a 6d. rate to produce £166. A town such as

Bangor with two schools under the Board educating some four or five hundred children took from the rates £350 in the first half-year. This included the expenses of the election and of the urgent repairs to the schools. In 1873 the cost was £220, in 1874 £370 and in 1875 £550. There seems to have been no difficulty in raising the money. On the other hand there were some very modest bodies. Golalington, Bedford, received £50, the proceeds of a 2·25d. rate, £6 12s. 8d. in fees, and had no debts. Bodmin in Cornwall, which had rushed into a School Board prompted by political and sectarian motives, probably, as much as by educational, found itself with debts of £83 6s. 8d. and no resources except £3 13s. 7d. in fees.[5] The School Board Directory of 1878 shows that, in that year, Blackburn was managing to educate 6921 children and employ five attendance officers on a ½d. rate, while Llanfihangel-y-Traethau in Merioneth needed 1s. rate for 400 children and had no officers. It is thus impossible to give an account which is true for all the different Boards all over the country, but the big town Boards set the pattern, and it is to their work that the main development of education is due.

The London School Board began its work under the Chairmanship of an ex-Viceroy of India, and ended under the guidance of an ex-Governor of Bombay. In his valedictory address in 1904,[6] Lord Reay made the point that the Act of 1870 had left so many things undefined that it had ·been the honourable task of the London Board, as the greatest and the earliest, to set a pattern to the whole nation, and to bring about in due time the advances in education which the Act had been unable to prescribe, but had been too wise to preclude. The three most important points which were omitted were the definitions of 'child', 'elementary education' and any direction as to the type of religious teaching to be given in Board schools. They were forbidden to give instruction in any formulary distinctive of a particular sect, but there was no positive indication as to what they were to give, and no statutory obligation to give any. In the eyes of the age this question of religious instruction was of supreme importance. *Punch* on 2 July 1870 had a cartoon repeating the hoary jibe that it was the theologians who prevented the spread of education. The picture shows a group of disputing clerics, with a Dean in the middle, obstructing the door of a school, while Mr Punch explains to the policeman that it is no good to attempt to make children go there when they can't get in. The early meetings of the London Board were rent with arguments on this issue.

They were deeply conscious of their responsibility in the matter, particularly as they felt that their example would be followed in most other parts of the country. The final compromise was due to W. H. Smith, 'That sturdy and singularly sweet-tempered axe-man' as a newspaper called him:

That in the schools provided by the Board the Bible shall be read, and there shall be given such explanations and such instruction therefrom in the principles of morality and religion as are suited to the capacities of the children . . . provided that no sectarian teaching is given, and that special arrangements shall be made where necessary [e.g. in Whitechapel where the population was mainly Jewish].

In principle, this was accepted everywhere—with local variations.[7] For example one Board decided, without argument, that 'every day a portion of scripture should be read in the schools, the Lord's Prayer said and Bishop Ken's Morning and Evening hymn Sung'.

There were, of course, exceptions. In Birmingham the first School Board consisted of eight Conservative churchmen who asked for 'the Bible and the explanation of the schoolmaster', six members of the League who maintained 'that the Bible and the Bible only is the religion of protestants', and a Roman Catholic who maintains a most dignified neutrality among his colleagues' heretical squabbles. Under this first Board religious instruction of the normal kind was given; but under its successor, in 1873, when the strength of the parties was reversed, no religious teaching was given in the schools as part of the normal timetable. Instead, the schools were 'let' two days a week, from 11 to 12, to the Religious Education Society which was allowed to send teachers to instruct those children whose parents wished them to be taught. This arrangement was found successful, and was continued for many years. Its advocates maintained that the teaching, being given by enthusiastic experts, was far superior to that normally provided. When the Cross Commission in 1888 collected information about religious teaching in schools, Birmingham was one of the Boards which did not give any religious instruction, along with Padstow, St Neot's and a few others.

On the whole, this permissive system worked to the general satisfaction. No one, in fact, questioned or objected to the arrangement till 1893, when Athelstan Riley found a child in school saying that Joseph was the father of Jesus, and became concerned about the teaching of the doctrine of the Trinity.

But, after nearly two years of furious controversy, the sanity of Hyde

Park Corner prevailed over the fanaticism of Kensington Court; and Riley, for all his fine house and his election posters, was pushed off the Board—largely by the efforts of the teachers themselves.

The omission of a definition of 'elementary education' also had important results. It allowed the Boards to extend the scope of education far beyond that imagined at the time the Act was passed. By law the schools must be conducted in accordance with the Code, and a large part of their money would come from grants earned under it, but there was nothing to prevent the Boards enriching their curriculum, and trying to make the Department modify its regulations to meet the new needs. Professor Huxley, surveying the field of desirable knowledge, and knowing, as yet, nothing of the limitations of schools and children, went back to the dreams of the early inspectors. Morality and religion, he thought, should be taught, reading, writing, arithmetic, English grammar, elementary physical science, geography, English history, elementary social economy, drawing, singing, mensuration (Boys), needlework (Girls), physical exercises. Also discretionary subjects: algebra, geometry, domestic economy and 'any extra subjects recognized by the new code'.

More practical demands were for physical training, swimming, manual training and domestic science. On the whole these were opposed by the Department. Whereas, in the past, the central authority had pressed reforms on the schools, now the energy released by the Boards pushed forward a protesting Department. The first cookery centre was built in 1878; manual training was not recognized in the Code till 1890, swimming lessons were recognized as 'school attendance' in the same year, physical education went in and out of the Code sometimes being fully recognized, and sometimes confined to boys only. As education became more firmly established, and as the standard rose, there was a demand for more advanced instruction, and higher-grade schools were established. New arrangements were made for pupil teachers, again against the opposition of the Department. In fact the blessed indefiniteness of the Act allowed a whole system of education to grow up under the Damoclean sword of the District Auditor.

The third matter on which the Act allowed discretion was the age of children to be educated. It did not state the maximum or minimum ages at which children might be received in school or might qualify for grant. The result was that some schools received children at three, and before the end of the period some authorities were providing education to eighteen—driven to it by the logic of the situation. In the same way, the Act allowed Boards to make by-laws requiring the attendance at school of children aged five to thirteen, but it did not compel the Boards to make these by-laws, and it allowed them to exempt children between the ages of ten and thirteen from whole or part attendance. In the first years of the Boards, the great towns, where the need for by-laws was greatest, were quite unable to supply enough school places; but this did not prevent them from passing the by-laws and getting the apparatus of 'compulsion' organized. In the smaller towns by-laws were generally passed fairly soon, as also in those rural districts which formed Boards of their own volition. A few Boroughs, who resisted School Boards, resisted by-laws also, even when they were forced, in 1876, to form School Attendance Committees. Such were Abingdon or Newbury. Others, like Preston, pleaded that 'compulsion' was too expensive, though their more progressive neighbours assured them that a rate of three-farthings would suffice.

The form of the by-laws was almost uniform throughout the country. This was natural as the Boards corresponded with each other, and the smaller wrote for advice and help to their larger brothers. The main differences lay in the conditions for exemption. The normal arrangement was that any child over ten who had passed Standard V could have total exemption, and if he had passed Standard IV partial. Some towns, such as Bath, put the standards for exemption one higher, others one lower. In some places where there was a shortage of suitable work, e.g. Llanbeblig or South Shields there is no mention of partial exemption. London allowed any child over ten who was 'beneficially and necessarily at work' to be partially exempt, and Roche allowed 'any child between five and twelve years who has reached Standard IV to be totally exempt'. The requirements of the Code for a pass in Standard IV were, at this time, to 'read with intelligence a few lines of prose or poetry, to write eight lines slowly dictated once from a reading book, and work the compound rules [money] and reduction [common weights and measures]'. The amount of instruction that most schools, even at this date, could provide at a higher level was slight, so it is possible that the custom of excusing the cleverer children from continuing their education did not matter much.

The passing and publishing of the by-laws was the first stage, it had to be followed by the organization of the engine of compulsion, and the presentation of the idea to the people.

324

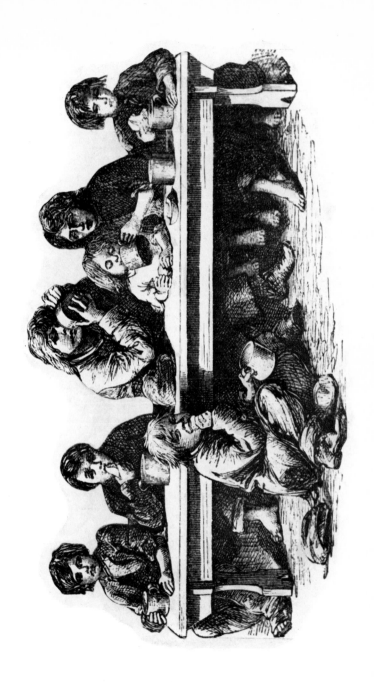

15 Penny dinners

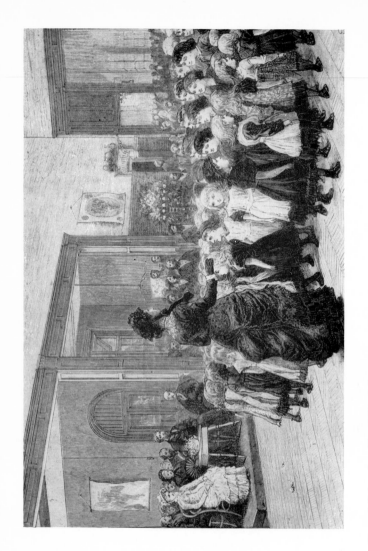

16 Physical training in Board Schools 1881. The Maze

'Compulsion', said a memorandum of the London School Board, 'is new to England, and should therefore be carried out, especially at first, with as much gentleness and consideration for the circumstances and feelings of parents as is consistent with its effective operation.' In this spirit the Boards acted. Their first care was to appoint an official to organize the work of compulsion. In the large cities this was full-time work and the officer was supported by a number of visitors. In London there were 92 visitors at the end of 1872, 25 of them women. Their task was to go from house to house in their districts and enquire for the children reported missing from school. At first they penetrated into the courts and alleys in peril of assault. Things were thrown on them from upstairs windows as they waited at a door; abuse was common; children were hidden. The women mostly found the work too hard; and the 'School Board Man' became a kind of bogy, whom children and parents combined to defeat. In a small town, where all were neighbours, £20 p.a. would buy the services of 'an intelligent, active and sober man' for part of the day, while he continued his ordinary work, perhaps in the Post Office, for the rest of his time.

Personal persuasion was supported by pamphlets. In one Welsh town a circular was sent out reminding parents that 'whatsoever a man soweth that shall he reap' and that playing truant led to 'idleness, ignorance, lying, deceit, poverty, drunkenness and misery'.

'Our object', they explained, 'is to raise your children's life by compelling them to attend school.'

This general exhortation was not very successful. Returns from this town showed that of 1709 children on school books, 909 had made the 250 attendances which qualified them for examination, and 800 had not.

The Board then provided printed forms for the teachers to send out to the parents of absentee children, saying, 'should no reply be made to this notice the officer of the Board . . . will undoubtedly summon you to appear before the Board, which I should much regret'.

As the next stage the officer called and explained what the notice said and meant. If the child was still absent the parent was summoned to appear before the Board and explain.

These informal sessions were conducted with the greatest humanity. The parent was asked to state his difficulties. They might be trivial. The child took his weekly school pence and spent them on sweets on the way to school; and then told his mother that he could not go as he was afraid of the teacher. The Board suggested that an escort might get over the difficulty. Sometimes the parent pleaded poverty. He could not afford the fees, or the child had no clothes or shoes. In some places free schools had been established, and the child went there; in others the Board paid the fees. Charity was organized to provide clothes. It was only the most determined offenders who finally appeared in court.

The regulations allowed a fine of 2*s*. 6*d*. which could rise, with costs, to 5*s*. Some Boards had great difficulty in getting convictions. It is possible that the magistrates disapproved of compulsory education in principle, it is certain that they greatly objected to the extra amount of work that these prosecutions involved in a large town. They would accept the excuse that the child was really attending school, though the place that he occasionally entered was grossly inefficient. They would fail to convict when the evidence was overwhelming. In one district, mentioned in Parliament in 1880, the magistrates refused to have anything to do with School Board prosecutions, and half the children were permanently absent from school in consequence. The London Board protested continually against the behaviour of the magistrates, till, in 1888, they reported the magistrate of the Wandsworth Police Court to the Lord Chancellor for 'rarely inflicting a fine on parents' even in the most flagrant cases. After that things improved slightly: but the enormous volume of the work involved can be judged from the fact that, even in 1902, when the idea of compulsion might have been accepted, there were 20,584 prosecutions in London.

The law did, undoubtedly, bring hardship to many people; though it was not as great as the opponents of compulsory education would have had people believe. Every month there were questions asked in the House, stressing the hard fate of pauper widows who were not allowed to keep their daughters at home to guard sickly infants while their mothers went charring. Viscount Sandon in the Lords replied civilly that he did not think 'the facts were quite as stated'; and he added, expressing the general sentiment of good men, 'I share the feelings of natural pain at the hardships which must, I fear, necessarily arise in dealing with the great evils which the Act of 1870 endeavours to meet.'

The real problem of compulsion was not the idle truant, birds' nesting or tickling trout on a summer's day, or the child of well-intentioned but temporarily destitute parents. It was the homeless and starving street arabs picking up what they could round the markets or railway stations, and the miserable infants condemned by their parents to endless hours of destructive labour. This is from a contemporary account of Bethnal Green:

The children's lives were a constant round of sunless drudgery—they never played as children play, they never seemed to think; they were prematurely old, and the victims of an awful cruelty. They worked at matchbox making many hours, and at other times assisted their parents in disposing of their wares in the streets. The mortality among the young children was appalling.

The parents of these children could not conceive of an attitude towards children which was altruistic. They believed that the teachers employed the children to work just as they did. If they were induced to allow the children to come to school, they were eager to reclaim them at the earliest moment. In the first days of the Boards the school corridor would be thronged with men and women come to demand their children at 12 and 4.30.

'You have had him for $2\frac{1}{2}$ hours,' they would argue, 'now I want him to do a turn for me. He has been putting money into your pocket, now I want him to put some into mine.' And the child would be sent off to carry baskets of fish or oranges, or dragged home to turn the mangle —civilization's dreariest slavery.[8]

The Boards could do very little against these parents. For one thing the fine was too small. It was more profitable to pay 5s. than to forgo the child's earnings, especially as the fine might not be inflicted. Moreover, the Factory Acts allowed children to work half time from the age of eight and the opportunities of evasion were countless. Nor were children protected out of school hours. The Act of 1876 expressly stated, 'No person shall be deemed to have taken any child into his employment contrary to the provisions of this Act if . . . that employment, by reason of being during the school holidays, or during the hours during which the school is not open, does not interfere with the efficient elementary education of that child.' When it occurred to educationalists that a child who had been working from 5 in the morning might still have his education 'interfered with', though he sat at his desk at 9, a survey of children's working hours was carried out. It was found that many children worked 30 to 40 hours out of school, some even 60, and most worked lesser amounts. The boys worked in barbers' shops or as news or errand boys, the girls in domestic work. Many were used in the lowest forms of street trading. The first attempts made by the School Boards to get a regulation passed prohibiting the employment of children before 6 in the morning or after 9 at night were a failure. It was not till 1904 that children received this measure of protection. In the country, exemption from school was regularly granted to meet special agricultural requirements.

A different problem was presented by the street arabs, the children without parental care or control. They lived frequently in gangs, sleeping under arches or old packing cases, picking and stealing for their living, and knowing nothing of regulation or order. No one was responsible for them, or had control of their doings. They slipped through the fingers like quicksilver, and were gone to some new lair in a patter of bare feet and a flutter of rags. Since 1866 there had, in theory, been industrial schools, day or fully resident, to cope with these children who were 'in need of care and protection'; but there was no person empowered to bring these children before the magistrate for committal, and no body to supply the funds for their maintenance. The Act of 1876 gave the Boards the power of building or contributing to an Industrial School, and the compulsory attendance clauses gave them a machinery for collecting the children. The School Board men went out hunting their prey. Markets and railway stations were places where the children congregated; but better still was a Punch and Judy show. Some of the perfidious showmen co-operated with the authorities in apprehending these non-paying customers. The prospect before the children, if they were trapped, was terrifying.[9] Unfortunately for them this was a generation which equated misfortune with wickedness, and on these unfortunate children the full fury of righteousness fell. The comfortable and well-intentioned citizens of the big towns set up Truant and Industrial schools of an unimaginative horror which is hardly credible. They were intended to receive: '*a*) incorrigible truants, *b*) children of a still more hardened class, *c*) neglected children'. There were plenty of them. In three weeks at Sheffield 395 children were caught during school hours. Many probably escaped, and of those that were taken several gave wrong addresses.

This is the scheme which, in all virtue, was set out for their redemption.

On admission to a truant school

A boy is isolated for a few days and set to the tedious occupation of oakum picking, and he only mingles with the rest of the inmates at prayers, at meal times and while under instruction. Afterwards he is put upon his good behaviour and allowed to mix with the rest both at work and at

328

play, on the distinct understanding, however, that any misconduct will be visited with adequate punishment. . . . About three months seems to be required in an ordinary case [and the child is then licensed out].

The 'punishments' envisaged—even after the intervention of the Home Office—were up to 10 days' solitary confinement (by the mercy of Whitehall in a *lighted* cell) and deprivation of 'not more than 2 meals in succession'. The food, even when the child got it, was enough to prevent starvation, but of a type to render him liable to all the deficiency diseases.

What actually happened in these schools can be imagined from this incident. About 1883 two members of the Sheffield Board visited the Liverpool Industrial School where several of their boys were kept. They asked to see the boys alone and speak to them. The request was 'peremptorily refused' by the headmaster, who declared that 'he must be sole master, that he would not allow his own Committee to take any such course, and that, in fact, he would not permit even H.M. Inspector to speak with the boys except in his presence'. The Sheffield Board complained to the Home Office, but the control from London was slight.

It took many years before anyone thought of the real answer to the problem. Only in 1895 was a Day Truant School opened in Goldsmiths Street, Drury Lane as a test of the new policy. The doors were open from 8 a.m. till 6 p.m., and three good meals were provided. The teachers were kind. In no time the average attendance reached 92 per cent–10 per cent above the general level in an ordinary school. As Mary Carpenter of Bristol had been advocating just this type of industrial feeding school since the 1850s, officialdom had been as slow as usual in assimilating a new idea.

The extension of compulsion over the country was not as rapid as the framers of the 1870 Act had, perhaps, hoped, and a number of Acts during the decade were passed to speed the process. Lord Sandon's Act of 1876 declared for the first time that it was the *duty* of a parent to see that his child received education, and, to help him to do so, School Attendance Committees were set up compulsorily where no School Boards existed. It was hoped that these Committees would pass by-laws and carry on compulsion in the same way as the Boards. As long as employment was open to the children, parents would always find an excuse for non-attendance at school, so it was farther enacted that no one should take into his employment any child under the age of ten years, and that he should be liable to a penalty not exceeding 40s. if he did so. The age of full-time employment was fourteen, unless the child had made the statutory pass or was qualified in some other manner.

Two things soon became clear. That the Attendance Committees were, in some cases, still going to refuse to make by-laws; and, secondly, that the by-laws conflicted with various provisions of the Factory Acts, which allowed the part-time employment of children from a much earlier age. When the comparative validity of the by-laws and the Factory Acts was tested in the courts, one judge found for the Acts and one for the by-laws. In consequence another Act was passed in 1880 compelling all Committees to make by-laws, and simplifying the method of doing so, and also declaring that, in cases of conflict, the by-laws should take precedence over the Factory Acts.

By 1880, then, all children were legally obliged to attend school till the age of ten; what happened then depended on the district. At Huddersfield, parents saw to it that all children passed Standard IV by ten and that they went to work at once. In other districts employers disliked half-timers. At Stoke-on-Trent, for example, the children obtained a pass at eleven, and then ran about the streets for the next two years to the horror of the inspectors.

Whilst the great cities were struggling with their unmanageable populations, the smaller towns were doing what they could to improve their transferred schools. They began by re-engaging the teachers, or, in some cases, getting new ones. Each appointment was the subject of a separate bargain, and was, presumably, in line with custom. Normally the salary was composed in varying degrees of a stated sum, and a proportion of the Government grant or of the children's pence. There might or might not be a house. These are some of the bargains that were made with the teachers in Bangor and Caernarvon, and were probably characteristic of those made elsewhere. A mistress received all the school pence, half the Government grant and a fixed salary of £25. There was a guaranteed minimum of £90 a year. A master in the boys' half of the school, perhaps with larger numbers, had all school pence and half the Government grant. At these schools in 1875 the half grant in the boys' school was £47 3s. 6d. plus £7 6s. (the drawing grant, which was given in full). At the girls' school the half grant was £44 10s. At the Free School the master took the whole Government grant and £40 salary, with free house, rates and taxes (gas alone excluded). In another case the master

330

had £80 per annum, half the Government grant and the master's house. The mistress had £50 p.a. and half the grant. In these cases the children's pence went to the Board, and there was frequently difficulty about the way in which the teachers accounted for the money.

In the cities there was the same diversity in payment. In London, after the first year, the Board gave a fixed salary, paid monthly, and a share of the grant paid at the end of the year. The head teacher took half the grant, and the assistant teachers divided the rest, but so that no one got more than a quarter. The fixed salary ranged, for men, from £65 for the lowest rank of assistant to £200 for heads. The 'pence', presumably, went to the Board. It was not till 1883 that the teachers received a full fixed salary, and the uncertainties of the grant ceased. In Sheffield, by 1874, head teachers received £120 fixed salary, £5 for each pupil teacher and one-quarter of the general grant. In 1884 the Board followed London and paid the head teachers a regular, all-inclusive salary. The teachers were not always satisfied with what they got, and in the smaller districts, where their employers were more approachable, did not hesitate to demand more, and resign when it was refused.

Besides the teachers, the Boards also had to pay the pupil teachers. Here again they were often in trouble, and the young people demanded increased wages, and played off one set of schools against another. In districts where suitable young people were few, they managed to get their salaries back to the 1846 level.

Besides attending to the structural condition of the schools which they received, the Boards were forced to spend comparatively large sums on providing books and other scholastic necessaries. There had been a time when the managers could say of a teacher, 'He is very incompetent but we like him, for he gives us no trouble and is very civil—duly touching his cap and never troubling for money for books or maps, etc.'[10] When schools were a private charity that attitude was not surprising; now that education was becoming a public duty the needs of the schools could no longer be ignored. The teachers began to send to the Boards lists of the things they required, and the Minutes record that the teachers were supplied with what they asked for. In the first three years of its life the Bangor Board spent over £75 with the booksellers, and it was resolved that 'the children should have free use of pens, holders, slates and slate pencils'. In London it was decided, as early as 1872, 'that the use of all books, stationery and apparatus be allowed in Board schools without any additional charges'.

These are the materials ordered for the Garth Girls' School, Bangor, 11 February 1875:

                    1 bottle of ink
                    4 boxes slate pencils
                    2 boxes pens
                    3 doz pen holders
                    1 quire blotting paper
                    2 quires examination paper
                    3 doz slates
                    1 doz Standard V Exelcior Readers 8*d.* each
                    1 doz Standard VI   ,,   ,,   9*d.* ,,
                    1 doz Standard III Reading Books
                      Greyson and Kirby   7*d.* ,,
                    2 doz Standard II   ,,   ,,   6*d.* ,,
                    2 doz Standard I   ,,   ,,   5*d.* ,,
                    1 set reading sheets and alphabet
                    8 registers
                    Quarterly register.

From this list we can see not only the increased provision, but also the development of the school; there are a significant number of children in Standards V and VI, whereas, a few years previously, there were none; and there seem to be eight organized classes, in place of the shifting groups which made the teacher's life so distracting.

There was thus now a real market for school books and appliances. The publishers' advertisements offer desks, maps, registers, reading books, courses in Latin or French, geography or nature study. Prize books are provided, and it is cheering to see R. M. Ballantyne introducing youth to the heroics of *Fighting the Whales* or *Black Ivory*; there are illustrated reading books for every standard, the most advanced running to 400 pages; there are books of poetry and elementary science. Moreover the new 'extra subjects' provided for in the New Code of 1871 made the provision of text-books necessary and the publishers rushed in to fill the gap.

All this detailed care of the schools was possible because the Boards made a practice of appointing one or two members to take charge of a certain school, to visit it and make a monthly report. These visits were made in friendship, and established a very valuable personal relationship; they also kept the schools up to the mark and could detect early signs of a deterioration in the teaching. For the British schools this was a new experience. In most cases they had been left alone for years on end, their needs and achievements alike unregarded. It also meant that the Boards could conduct their business with knowledge. In a large district, like London, the personal knowledge of the Board members alone made the work possible.

The transferred schools and the temporary buildings were only the first step to the new schools which the Boards would build. The opening of the first London Board School was a matter of ceremony and importance. The opening took place on Saturday, 12 July 1873, and *The Times* of Monday, 14th, gave nearly a whole column to the event; which put it on an equality, as news, with cholera in Vienna, and rather above the Shah in Paris. The newspaper account gives a vivid impression of conditions:

> About 100 yards off the busy thoroughfare of the Whitechapel Rd. surrounded by a maze of narrow streets and lanes, courts and alleys and in the midst of a dense population, is a street, known by name to only a few of the better informed policemen, called Old Castle St. . . . There are swarms of children everywhere to be seen,—swarms which a gentleman present, well known for his benevolence, is said to have likened to locusts . . .
>
> To get to Old Castle St. when you are in Whitechapel is not a very easy matter. The most direct way from the Whitechapel Rd. is down a long narrow lane which takes you straight to the door of the school. But it requires some courage to plunge down this passage, for you have before you a long perspective of clothes lines, which on Saturady were loaded with a miscellaneous freight of household linen hung out to dry and in some cases reaching to within three or four feet of the ground. . . . Under these flapping shirts the visitors to the Opening had to struggle. . . . The School is a plain brick building, for the most part 3 stories high and enclosing a rather limited space designed for a playground. . . .

In this playground the ceremony was held, as there was no room big enough to hold the assembly. Lord Lawrence said, 'The school seems to me to be capitally well built, well lit, with 5 lofty rooms.' It was to hold 1275 children, which seems to give an average of 250 children to a room. The Board believed that a means of advancement should exist for clever children from their schools, and to emphasize this made the first presentation of the Mortimer Memorial Scholarship. It went to W. E. Barker of the Portman Chapel National School. This was a fortunate choice, for the boy went from the City of London School to Trinity,

Cambridge and a Fellowship. From there he passed to the Board of Trade, but he died young—the only one of the early Board School scholars to rise above mediocrity.

In the schools which followed, the London Board gradually evolved a pattern of school building. The plans which the Committee of Council had offered in 1840 were now hopelessly out of date, and they had no successors. The School Board had no architects, and, indeed, no architect in England had ever designed a school.

The early schools of the London Board were little more than groups of rooms squashed on any site that the Board could acquire. A quarter of an acre was considered to provide space for a school of 300 children. Naturally they built high, and the three-decker, sometimes with a roof playground, was born of necessity. The architects, 'though of considerable reputation' but without experience, managed badly.

'The staircases were long, steep, narrow and ill lighted. Cloakrooms were either insufficient or altogether absent. The class-rooms were of unsuitable sizes; the lighting was bad, being chiefly from the backs of the scholars. Most of the rooms were passages, and, in addition, the sites were so small that the playgrounds were very insufficient.'

Even when the Board got its own architects things were little better. 'The dominant idea was still that of a schoolroom holding several classes, supplemented by a moderate number of class-rooms. Corridors for reaching the end rooms were introduced, but these were made also to serve the purpose of cloakrooms; they were far too narrow, and the hanging of cloaks in them was inconvenient and dangerous.'

When the Board looked abroad for help, it decided that the Prussian system, which divided the school into permanent classes each with its own room and teacher, was the best. But with the staff available, how was it to be done? On the Board's standard of staffing there should be one adult and two pupil teachers, or one teacher and one assistant teacher to every 100 children. In the general way, rooms were built for classes ranging in number from 50 to 90. The bigger rooms were often built with a sliding partition which would allow the class to be divided when it was being taught by the pupil teachers. It was not long before the authorities began to demand that all rooms should be able to be cleared without the children passing through another room. That meant corridors. They also soon began to think that a hall was desirable. The difficulty was expense. The limit for borrowing for capital expenditure was £8 or £10 a school place. Anything beyond that had to be found directly from the rates. The Sheffield Board built its first school, New-hall, in the old tradition. The building was 'of stone, in Gothic style of architecture' and cost, exclusive of furniture and fittings, £3419. The fittings came to another £2000 or £3000. It accommodated 750, so that the cost was about on the level authorized. When halls were felt to be absolutely necessary the cost rose. In Sheffield the cost per place was about £12, in Bradford £20, and in London £18. This was in the early days. Towards the end of the century, when London was building its more palatial three-decker schools, like Peterborough, Chelsea and Fulham Palace Road, the cost was around £25 a head. It was only in 1891 that the Department recognized halls by giving a grant for them.

In their final form these schools consisted of a central hall, lit from one end and with borrowed light from the surrounding class-rooms, which were in units for 60 or 70 at 9 or 10 square feet per child. The infants occupied the ground floor, the girls came next and the boys on top. The façades were impressive. Around the playgrounds were walls topped with high iron railings. It was never explained whether these fortifications were to keep the children in or parents out.

In Birmingham the rate of architectural development was compara-tively rapid. The Bristol Street schools opened in October 1876 show most of the features of the developed plan, with hall, surrounding class-rooms and other refinements.

The new Board Schools in Bristol St. will be opened today for inspection by the public, and on Monday for the reception of scholars. The building has attracted considerable attention. As a school it may be considered a model in every respect, and architecturally it is an ornament to the neigh-bourhood. . . . The general appearance of the building is very striking, and the effect is much assisted by a lofty and very strikingly handsome tower and spire. The materials of which the buildings are composed are mainly brick with stone dressings, the roofs being covered with tiles. The window frames are of wood and so arranged as to open. The general style of the building is Gothic, adapted to modern requirements, and charmingly enriched with constructional ornament. The building will be heated by hot water apparatus. Ventilation is secured by a number of flues, which are carried into the tower, the upper part of which is, in reality, a shaft for ventilating purposes [and not, as the critics of the Board said, a gross piece of ostentatious waste]. When these noble schools were opened, they were crowded during two days by 7,000 persons whose expressions of admiration and delight were unanimous.

The work of the School Boards

The Hospital Street schools, opened next year with a ceremonial breakfast, were also the objects of universal admiration. One suspects that the architect of these and other schools of about the same period had had ecclesiastical experience, for most of the halls end in apses, and the cast-iron girders carry trefoil ornament.

The Sheffield School Board was rather less successful in its plans. An inspector writing a few years later commented:

The Sheffield Board Schools, though handsome buildings, are so draughty that we have constantly to wear hats or other headgear while we are inspecting them; and all are supplied with galleries the steps of which are used as seats, not a platform for benches, which is their only right use. Being quite level and far too low, these steps afford a most uneasy seat, as might be expected by anyone who reflects that a sphere can touch a plane only at one point.

In fact, he thought them so bad that he threatened to withhold the grant next year if there was not some improvement.

These schools, planted deliberately in the most degraded and least educated areas of the city, and filled with children brought in largely by compulsion, made the greatest demands on the teachers. A considerable number of men and women went into these schools with a true missionary spirit. They hoped that they saw the end of ignorance and the beginning of social justice—*Post tenebras lux*, as the motto of the London Board put it. But enthusiasm could hardly cope with the reality. A few teachers survived to lead the educational forces of the nation, but the conditions broke all but the strongest.

'The majority of the children', said an inspector, 'are of lower social grade than those attending voluntary schools. In one school in an extremely low locality several scholars are well known juvenile thieves who have been forced in to the school by the action of the Education Committee. In many other instances a large proportion of the scholars are of the "street Arab" class, who are now for the first time brought under the influence of discipline and good example.' Another description said: 'Some were hardy enough, some were very intelligent in appearance, some were cowed and sly but vicious, and some were dulled into semi-imbecility by hunger, disease and ill usage. Almost all when spoken to, winced in expectation of a blow.' In addition they were totally ignorant. 'Not one knew the alphabet or had any idea of order and discipline or of obeying orders, and none could attend for more than 5 minutes.' When these children were gathered a hundred or more to a

336

room, and that room with no direct exit or sound-proof partitions, conditions were terrible. Violence was useless against so many, and an unpopular teacher might be overwhelmed by a barrage from massed
peashooters. One teacher found that music was the only way of controlling his class.

Some idea of the social manners of the children can be formed from
a lecture which William Jolly, H.M.I., gave in 1876 on *Physical Education in Common Schools*. At one point in his talk he stresses the importance of cleanliness and condemns the following bad habits: wiping the
hands on the dress, spitting on the floor, spitting on the ground without
putting the foot on it, picking the nose, cleaning the boots on the dress,
wiping the pen by sprinkling the ink on the floor, sucking it, drawing it
through the hair, rubbing it on the dress. At about this period, too, the
great improvement was made of attaching a damp sponge to a corner of
the slate, so that it was no longer necessary, as one inspector remarked,
to use expectoration and the coat sleeve.

Everything was made more difficult by the requirements of the Code.
The schools must earn their grants, and the principle, established in the
past decade, that no relaxation of the regulations would be allowed
whatever the difficulties, forced the teachers to drill the children in
the most unpalatable elements. They had, at first, little success.
Of one district the inspector reported that 'Of all children over 7
years of age 53% are below Standard I. In some schools it is as
high as 80%. In another school 2% were in Standards IV, V, VI
together.'

Under these circumstances the regulation of the London Board,
which was imitated elsewhere, forbidding anyone but the headmaster
to use corporal punishment, caused much difficulty. The Board had
reason. The use of the birch rod was still one of the chief activities of
the guardian of youth, and an advertisement in the *Church Guardian*
1871 shows the common idea:

Barrister's daughter (35), healthy, good tempered, cheerful, desires a
matronship. Is experienced in applying the birch rod.

Compulsion to attend school was bad enough, it would be an intolerable thing if the schools were as brutal as they might easily become. On
the other hand the teachers resented this restriction on their actions, and
found it insulting as well as inconvenient.

The parents too often supported their rebellious children. They would lie in wait for a teacher after school with a brickbat, and a knowledge of boxing was almost a necessity for a man in certain districts. Mothers were as bad as fathers, or worse. In one month of these early years four mothers were prosecuted for personally assaulting mistresses.[11] They did not understand hygiene and saw nothing but malignity in the school's attempts to clean the children up. One mother, who preferred words to blows, sent the following note:

I should like to know how much more spite you intend to put upon my child, for it is nothing else. First you send the Sanitary inspector and I have my home taken away; then my husband has to get rid of his few rabbits and chicken, and now you cut the few hairs that my girl was just beginning to get so nice. I think you had better hang her and be done with it.

Some schools however made their own way into the favour of their districts, and began the social work that they carried on through the century. The teachers collected money; they stayed behind after school and made clothes; the headmistress would write letters for any parents in need. The Board too was flexible in its policy. A school in Whitechapel was boycotted till a Jewish headmaster was appointed, and the fears of proselytism laid at rest.

The attendance officers investigating the cases of absentee children uncovered some of the worst cases of destitution. One man reported:

In a family which I visited last week there were 9 children who had been deserted by their father, and some of them were running about at midday amid filth and dirt, without a vestige of clothing, while others wore the merest shreds. . . .

In cases such as this, the school was the agency through which help came.

It did not take the schools long to find that too many children suffered not from stupidity but hunger. The Department would not authorize expenditure on food, so that the schools had to turn to charity and organize as best they could. There was considerable response from individuals; sometimes complicated by the views of the benefactors. One organization could only serve vegetable stews because the chief donor did not approve of meat eating. The quaintly-named Central Council for promoting self-supporting Penny Dinners, with A. J. Mundella as president, worked for years to feed those who could pay; and other bodies brought help to the destitute.[12] In the worst districts the teachers allowed the badly overworked children to sleep at their desks and make up some of the rest they were deprived of at home.

By 1875 the London School Board had provided 99 new schools with places for 88,913 children. Other big towns had made proportionate efforts. The money had not come from revenue. Applications to build a school had to be made to the Department.[13] If a 'need appeared to exist' the Department would 'consent' to the Board borrowing money, and it could do it in the open market on the best terms it could get. If there appeared to be 'a deficiency in the general provision' the Department would 'recommend' the Board to the Public Works Loan Commissioners who would lend at $3\frac{1}{2}$ per cent the money to be paid back in 50 years. This was not always found to be the cheapest source of finance; and the Sheffield Board devised an ingenious method of lending itself the money from the general rate, and paying interest to itself. The amounts recommended were large. In 1871 London was recommended to borrow £250,000; Birmingham £15,000 and Pembroke £400.

If the Department encouraged or compelled the foundation of Board Schools, there was continual opposition locally. Sectarian jealousies still raged, and no field was considered too small for a battle. Athelstan Riley could assert that 'Every Board School was a knife held at the throat of the Voluntary system', and, once the needs of the most notoriously neglected districts were provided for, the Board had only to propose a new school to find opponents. The grounds for this opposition were various: there were voluntary schools which adequately served the area; children flocking to school would bring down the tone and therefore the rateable value of the district; the cost to the rates would be excessive if all these schools kept on being built. In fact 'few new schools were not objected to by the clergy, ratepayers' associations, vestries, Commissioners of Sewers and local residents'. Vestries passively resisted paying their education rate, and wealth and learning did not make them more prompt. In July 1873 St George's, Hanover Square, was £2099 5s. 7d. in arrears and the Inner Temple £30 9s. 10d. Even in Birmingham the Board had difficulties, and on one occasion had to get a mandamus to compel the Overseers to hand over the money to which it was entitled.

One important result of the School Boards was a change in the relation between the teachers and their employers. The individual clerical manager too often felt himself an irresponsible tyrant. One manager, after a disagreement with his teacher, wrote off his annoyance in a letter to the press: 'I, not he (the Master), am vicar of Dudley; I, not he, am chairman of the Managers; and I will not allow him to insult me openly without letting him know that our relative positions are those of master and servant.'

On another occasion at Moxley, not far from Birmingham, the vicar barricaded himself in the schoolroom, from which he claimed he had dismissed the master, and had to be ejected by force before the school could continue.

Such unseemly incidents could not so easily occur with a Board, and the teacher had some protection from personal spite and caprice. A Board, whose meetings were usually public, must proceed with more show of reason. The teachers were still employees, and were dismissed if their work was not satisfactory, but a body of men, five or more in number, were unlikely to act in a completely unjustifiable way. Moreover the bigger Boards, controlling many schools, soon evolved scales of salary and methods of procedure that brought some regularity into a teacher's conditions. There would inevitably be local variations, but the web of intercourse between the Boards did much to keep these variations small. For the first time, since 1862, the teachers could feel themselves to some extent public employees, with the consequent greater dignity.

As well as improving the teacher's status, the Boards made his work more possible. There were now books, maps and pictures. The London standard of staffing was, as has been said, one adult and two pupil teachers to every 100 children. This was 'far above the average', and was sufficient to allow of some reasonable teaching. Moreover the multiplication of schools greatly increased the demand for qualified teachers. In London it was hard to supply the schools. In the country things were even more difficult. Wales has always inclined to teaching as a profession, but frequently in the Minute Books of Bangor and Caernarvon it is noted that a pupil teacher has left and that they are driven to tide over an awkward period by appointing 'two monitors at 1/- a week each'. In the same way, when an adult assistant teacher leaves, the head is left to struggle with no help but a junior pupil teacher, and the work of the school suffers severely in consequence.

The Boards had no direct power to increase the supply of trained teachers. The training colleges were all voluntary, and Boards had no power, and had not yet thought of the possibility of founding ones of their own. All they could do was breed up a supply of pupil teachers; and to this London especially gave its mind. Again it was met with

steady opposition from the Department, and had the discouraging experience of seeing its candidates refused in large numbers by the colleges, simply from lack of places. All this gave the certificated teachers a
position of considerable power.

The general result was a change in the attitude of the teachers.
During the months that the Act was being passed, they were preparing
for their new position by forming a general association. The National
Union of Elementary Teachers held its first conference in September
1870, and started its career as the spokesman of the profession. It was a
forceful body, and had returned to its earlier claim of considerable
political power. The *Schoolmaster* of February 1872 records that
teachers are already lobbying Members of Parliament and adds: 'It is
well that teachers generally should awake to a sense of their power. Few
classes of the community could exert more influence in a contested election than teachers, if they only choose to exert themselves.' They also,
through the Union, began to exert pressure on the Department. Sir
Francis Sandford disagreed with the Union and its policy, but he gave
its communications 'uniform kindness and attention', though nothing
else. Yet this semblance of consultation, if largely useless, was gratify-
ing, and an augury of better things.

A more immediate sphere of influence was in the School Boards themselves. Teachers began to be elected to them in 1874 when T. E. Heller
was elected in London. The Code of the following year not unnaturally
prohibited serving teachers from being members of the Boards which
employed them; but there were ex-teachers, often full-time officials of
the Union, who were eligible for election; and every candidate for a
School Board could be waited on by deputations of teachers to ascertain
his views on matters which concerned them. This power they used
widely.

Notes

1. Lists published in the *School Board Chronicle*.
2. Local oral information.
3. Arrangements were made in 1873 for taxing these costs.
4. J. H. Bingham, *Sheffield School Board* (1949), ch. II.
5. Minutes, 1872–3, p. xlviii.
6. See the Final Report of London School Board (1904).
7. See the detailed returns, P.P., 1888, XXXVI, 719 ff. Especially the London regulations, p. 1080.
8. Thomas Gautrey, *Lux Mihi Laus* (1937), ch. V; also Hugh B. Philpott, *London at School* (1904), ch. III; and P.P., 1899, LXXV, 433.
9. J. H. Bingham, *Sheffield School Board*, ch. IX, pp. 199 ff.
10. Quoted in Asher Tropp, *The School Teachers* (1957).
11. See *Schoolmaster*, 5 October 1872, p. 135; 27 August, 1881, p. 214; Final Report of London School Board (1904), p. 320.
12. In 1910 feeding in schools was first officially sanctioned.
13. Regulations, P.P., 1872, XLVI, 689.

Chapter Sixteen

From the 1870 Act to the Cross Commission

It took nearly twenty years for the reforms of 1870 to be digested and
the difficulties understood; but it was a very different world, educa-
tionally, that the Cross Commission surveyed in 1888 from that which
had existed in 1870.

All through the period the School Boards continued their growth,
their schools multiplied and the number of children they taught increased. More and more children attended more and more regularly
and for a longer time. There were, of course, disadvantages. The fields
of Norfolk, which before had been kept like a garden by gangs of
labouring children, now sprouted with weeds;[1] but on the whole the
process of beneficent social change was approved.

Within the schools themselves there was a very great change. The
scope of education widened, and a beginning was made in teaching
beyond the elements. But the period did not bring happiness to the
teachers. Probably at no time were their relations with the Department,
and the inspectors in particular, so embittered.

The engine of control was, as before, the Code. This document, which
had practically the effect of law, but without the law's safeguards, was
an annual anxiety to the teachers. It was arrived at, in theory, by a
Committee, but, in reality, it was composed by the Secretary and the
Vice-President. By regulation it was laid on the table of the House for
thirty days. As Lowe had demonstrated earlier, this period could be
considerably curtailed; and as Cumin admitted to the Cross Commission, criticism could be made more difficult by a failure to print the
Code till the last minute. The Code was, in fact, a piece of bureaucracy
of the kind most hated by reformers. It depended absolutely on the

343

personal views of an official; it allowed of no appeal; and it was adminis-tered by a body of men who did not command the confidence and respect of those they controlled. In consequence the personality of the Secretary remained the most important factor in the development of education.

When Lingen became Secretary to the Treasury in 1869, he was succeeded at the Department of Education by R. F. Sandford. Sand-ford was a man of pleasant manners, and was invariably polite. The change from Lingen was hailed with delight, and the teachers thanked him for 'his uniform kindness and attention'. In fact, these good manners covered a determination to maintain education in its existing condition, and a conviction that when the teachers asked for changes they were only trying to cover their inefficiency and get more money for less work. His successor in 1884, when he went to take charge of the educational work of the Charity Commission, was Patrick Cumin, a Scottish lawyer, who did not hide his dislike and contempt for the whole teaching body, and his belief that what was good enough for the past would do quite well for the present. The pretence of consultation which had existed under Sandford appeared to him almost indecent; and teachers, in spite of their growing power, were treated as inferior beings. Mundella, the Vice-President during this period, was a big employer of labour in the Midlands, and he also had business interests in Saxony. He thought the English worker appallingly illiterate, and admired the efficiency of the German system. He saw in regulation and control the only hope for his own country.

The Codes from 1870 to 1888 were the creation of these men, and they were all directed to the process called by the teachers 'stringing up'—increasing the demands made on the schools while closing all the loopholes for evasion. When it is considered that this is the period when the School Boards and Compulsion were forcing education upon a new section of the population, the strain on the teachers can be understood.

These Codes abandoned Lowe's dream of an education permanently reduced to its elements, and tried to extend the curriculum. It did this by devising a tripartite division of subjects, and rewarding them with grants of different amounts and under different conditions. By 1878 the scheme was as follows:

Grants based on average attendance	*s.*	*d.*
For each child		4
plus If singing is taught		1
If organization satisfactory		1

344

Grants on individual examination s. d.
  For each pass in Reading, Writing and Arithmetic, if 250 attendances have been made
  3/- each 9

Grants for class subjects
  On average attendance of children over 7, if classes pass a creditable examination in one (or two) of grammar, history, geography, plain needlework 2 for each subject.

Specific subjects
  For every child in Standards IV–VI who passes in not more than two from the list[2] 4 each subject.

It was thus possible, in theory, for a child in the upper part of the school to earn 27s.; but to prevent good teaching reaping too high a reward, the total grant payable was fixed at 17s. 6d. per head on the average attendance, as this was reckoned to be half the cost of a child's education; and the principle was preserved that local sources contributed half.

This scheme had something to recommend it. It distinguished the essential from the desirable, and it allowed an ambitious teacher with a small number of clever children to provide advanced teaching for the few. The class subjects which were for Standards II–VI were intended to provide variety and enlarge the thoughts of the average child. The teachers accommodated themselves to the demands, some hesitantly. One man, after much thought, decided to take geography and allowed the girls to join the boys in this study, but found them backward. Charles Dodd on the other hand rushed forward enthusiastically, and embarked on the more difficult specific subjects, such as Latin and mathematics. He learnt them himself, and within two years had the best results of any school in the district.

The teachers, naturally, found some means of mitigating the demands of the Code. In the inspectors' reports for 1880 there are complaints that too many children are withheld from examination (it might be 10 per cent in Standard I), and that far too many children were working in classes too low for their ages. Walter Bailey made an elaborate calculation of this 'backwardness', based on the supposition that children should pass Standard I at seven and Standard III at nine and should progress a standard a year. Instead of this, one-eighth of Standard I are over ten, and one-third of Standard II, while, on the whole, children are from one to two and a half years retarded. The reason, he

345

explains, is obvious. It is bad policy in a teacher to push his children on too fast; naturally he prefers to make certain of their success.

The Code which came into force in 1883,[3] and was the culmination of the series, was Sir Francis Sandford's legacy of woe to the teachers. It was introduced with ceremony. On 8 August 1881 Mundella made the speech which had been announced some time in advance. He stated that the Code he was about to introduce was the result of much work.[4] He had collected, he said, 'Memorials from School Boards', 'papers from 20 or 30 inspectors', and, with this help, he and Sir Francis Sandford, Mr Sykes and Mr Cumin, along with the inspectors Mr Wharburton, Mr Sharpe and Mr Finch, had produced a scheme. This had been subjected to further criticism, and the teachers had even been allowed to express an opinion. As a result of all this thought, he had decided that the grant on individual examination should be paid on the percentage of passes obtained. That is, if 100 per cent passed, each child would earn 100 pence—8s. 4d.; if only 50 per cent passed then the *per capita* grant would be 4s. 2d. Every child who had been on the register for six months *must* be presented, unless there was a written statement from the managers giving good reason for withholding him. This scheme had two advantages: by paying grant on percentage of passes we 'shall keep the work level', and by demanding that children be on the register for six months instead of having made 250 attendances 'we shall remove from the teachers the temptation to a tremendous fraud'. He elaborated this most scandalous statement with an emotional passage about a poor man who, by just two strokes of the pen, had ruined his life.

He then went on to say that he was adding a new grant, for merit, which would serve to distinguish between the good and the merely competent, and that education had now progressed so far that he was adding a Standard VII to the normal course. He ended by saying that there was a shortage of teachers, so, as a great concession, he would allow graduates, and women over eighteen who had passed recognized examinations, to become certificated teachers after a year's probation. This he thought might be a valued privilege, as teachers were rising in the social scale almost to the level of curates.

The House listened to the speech. No one made any comment on it. The next speaker started quite a lively discussion on the supply of local museums as an aid to industry; and they then went on to consider the case of the infamous Mr Goffin who had been making £400 or more a year (in addition to a salary of £500) by getting little boys through the South Kensington examinations—having discovered some means of seeing the papers in advance. A similar statement on the Code in the Lords was received with equal unconcern.

The three features of the Code, the percentage grant, the merit grant and the regulation that all children who had been on the register for twenty-two weeks must be presented formed a most efficient engine of tyranny. This last requirement avoided certain technical difficulties—it also prevented a teacher from evading the examination of a backward child by omitting to record his presence. It also added a new spur to the teachers to improve attendance. The attitude of Mundella and his Secretary are made shockingly clear in that he should recommend his provision in terms which accused the teachers of widespread and persistent fraud. There is given each year in the Minutes of the Department the names of the teachers whose certificates have been cancelled or suspended and the faults for which this action has been taken. In the two years before the Code, 1881 and 1882, nine teachers lost their certificates for serious offences such as immorality and embezzlement and twenty-two had them suspended for registration offences. In the two years after, 1884 and 1885, ten were punished for serious offences and fourteen for errors of registration. Out of a teaching body of 36,000 this does not give a high rate of crime, and the improvement brought about by the change in regulations is not very great.

The teachers recognized the dangers of the Code.[5] When Mundella had to answer questions on it in Parliament he adopted a tone of reasonableness and compromise; but as applied by inspectors it was inflexible and oppressive—and it was with the inspectors that power lay. There was a divorce between the inspectors and the office which left the inspectors free of any control. The Education Department was unreformed. The Secretary, as has been said, had almost complete power. Below him in the central office were the examiners, young men of brilliant academic attainments who continued the tradition of the great civil servants, such as the Mills and Charles Lamb, and did their daily two hours' work in the intervals of common-room gossip and the pursuit of the arts. They were supposed to calculate the grant due to each school on the report of the inspectors. The clerks corrected their mistakes. They knew nothing of the schools, and took no interest in them. They were incapable, had they been willing, of exercising any discretion.

Parallel, but distinct, was the body of inspectors. Since 1870, when denominational inspection was abolished, no more clergymen had been appointed to the Inspectorate, but a considerable number remained who had been appointed before that date, and had now reached positions of considerable seniority, and often held rich sinecures in addition to their official pay. They and their contemporaries seldom left London, and had developed their idiosyncrasies and their idleness to the full. Those next in rank did reside in their districts, and sometimes appeared in schools; but their visits were short. There were two grades below them: junior inspectors, young men from college, of the same social rank as their superiors who were learning the work from the worst models, and sub-inspectors who were certificated teachers who did all the work of marking papers and checking results and returns, and in all probability acknowledged their promotion by oppressing those whose ranks they had just left.

Moreover the inspectors had almost absolute power.[6] Till 1890 no complaints that the teachers made were ever listened to. All communication was with the managers, and, if the managers could be induced to complain, there was nobody, except the Secretary, to consider the complaint. Till 1890 the whole bias of the Secretary's mind was against the teachers. Naturally the inspectors degenerated. The fussy, the cranky, the cruel all found a perfect field for the exercise of their defects. Too often the only amusement of an otherwise barren day was a tussle with a hysterical teacher who could be baited almost to madness with perfect impunity. Under these circumstances it needed a man of very high moral character to be always courteous and just. Matthew Arnold had that character, and it is perhaps his chief claim to educational eminence. The teachers saw these dangers clearly at once.

When the *Schoolmaster* reviewed the Code the article stated:[7]

> For the teachers the one point more important than any other . . . is the enormously enhanced power of H.M. Inspectors. The power of those men who are thoroughly efficient and reliable will be increased for good. The power of those who are inefficient and unreliable will be increased for ill. . . . It is no use blinking matters. For various causes a considerable number of these gentlemen are not fit for the discharge of their responsible duties.

The writer continued by saying that the teachers could not wait till Mr Mundella had reformed the body of inspectors, but they and the managers must unite against the tyranny of the worst.

In the February number of the same paper James Runciman who, with Macnamara, was the most gifted writer among the teachers of the day, had an article on *Mr Puzzle, H.M.I.*[8] It is a very straightforward article, and sets out the teachers' case against a certain type of inspector. He has been a clever boy, and at twenty-two or twenty-three did very well in a university examination; but he lacks character and generosity. 'The brow is good in its feebly intellectual way. . . . The mouth is feeble, nervous, cynical, cruel, with the cruelty of a weak nature. . . . He has never denied himself the luxury of small tyranny; he has never held back a cruel word or useless sneer.' Such a man bullies teachers, lets out his spleen especially on women teachers, confuses the children with trick questions, demands that the teachers order certain books published by a publisher that he takes an interest in, and marks the school down next year if they have not done so. The writer contrasts him, as a man of straw, with General Gordon, the hero of the hour, or, as a peevish bully, with Matthew Arnold whose courtesy never failed. He ends with the exhortation to join the Union, since only by joint action can the teachers protect themselves from these attacks.

In a jubilant paragraph in another issue, the *Schoolmaster* reports the case of E. H. Brodie, H.M.I., twenty-one years in the service. He had behaved so badly in school that the teacher was in tears, the children terrified and the chairman of the School Board insulted. He was reported to the Department for 'his insolence, bad temper and unbecoming conduct to the Chairman of the School Board'.

There were two points that might have been made in addition; one, that there was no evidence that Brodie suffered from being reported, and, secondly, that it was a School Board which complained —a far stronger and more militant body than mere managers.

The chief administrative provisions which put power into the hands of the inspectors were the merit grant, an absolute judgment made by the inspector; the necessity of presenting every qualified child for examination, and advancing him a standard each year; and the need for the inspector to sign the teacher's parchments after an inspection and record the quality of his work. But it was the payment on the percentage of passes, which really caused the greatest harm to the teachers. As the *Schoolmaster* said, 'Nothing works such incalculable mischief as the striving after percentages.' It was not only that each failure was magnified and the larger the school the greater the damage (for every failure cost 1*d. per child* over the whole school); there was a psychological result of the regulation which was even more disastrous. The percentage grant provided a means by which one teacher could be directly

349

compared with another. Before, the size of the school and difference of courses made any such direct comparison difficult, now the question could be asked and must receive a plain answer. The result was that teachers were obsessed with percentages, and insisted on homework, kept all the children in for long periods, and bullied the incompetent.

Undoubtedly some inspectors behaved badly—and it is in these years that they came to be really hated. Reading the *Schoolmaster* it is possible to piece together the agonizing course of an annual inspection. But, in considering the teacher, one must not overlook the children, who were too often half-starved, sickly, short-sighted or deaf. They had been bullied and coached for this day and were as nervous as the teacher, and all too often, were hopelessly confused by anything outside their normal routine.

The first stage in the ordeal was the schedule of those excused from examination without loss of grant.[9] If the list were long, the inspector always objected to it. Mundella might declare in Parliament that circulars had been sent out to the inspectors authorizing them to excuse from examination children in delicate health or suffering in other ways, but there was no certainty in advance that the inspector would be reasonable, and the children must be prepared just in case.

It is clear that, in fact, the inspectors were not reasonable, and the teachers countered by asking that they should be allowed to withhold 10 per cent of the children of right. In districts where children of eight and nine or even older were still being brought into school for the first time, this would have seemed natural. When the managers supported the teachers and approved the exemptions the inspector could not examine, but he could always damn the teacher by the entry he made in his parchment, and he could certainly refuse the merit grant.

The exceptions settled, the inspector could object to the children being presented in the wrong age groups. The limit of the infant school remained at seven, and after that age a child must be presented in a standard. The regulation of 1872 which prescribed that no child over nine would be examined in Standard II, thus establishing a direct and unbreakable association between age and standard, had been dropped; but there still remained a feeling that the link existed, and Birmingham School Board insisted that 'all children should be presented in their proper standards'.

Moreover each child must be presented in a standard higher than the one in which he had last passed in that school or another. The teachers wished to represent a delicate child or one who had only passed by a fluke; and they wished to be protected against children who had come on from another school insufficiently prepared. It was in relation to all these points that teachers demanded 'liberty of classification'.

The inspector's powers of annoyance did not end with the regulations. His conduct of the examination could make all the difference to the children's success. His manner might be terrifying. He could choose passages for dictation which contained words quite outside the children's vocabulary, or he could deliberately exploit the difficulties of the English language. One man would set a passage from *The Times* for older scholars, and the Rev. D. J. Stewart, the most hated of the inspectors, confused the six-year-old infants of Greenwich with the sentence 'If you twist that stick so long you will make your wrist ache.' Another used a passage which began 'While Hugh was culling yew, his ewes . . .'

The reading books, too, were a constant cause of friction. The regulation said two sets of reading books must be used in Standards I and II, and three sets, one of which must relate to history, in the higher standards. The books were not suitable. One inspector comments on 'the extreme unsuitability of the books at present in use. The words are so long, the sentences so involved, the ideas so abstruse and the information so technical that the books are mere nonsense to children of 13 or 14 years of age.'

The inspector was not content merely to hear the books read. He asked niggling questions, grammatical or otherwise, on all of them. This involved endless work in teaching children how to parse every work or answer questions on every point. In addition, in the top standards poetry was also learned. In Standard VI one hundred lines. The explanatory note said: 'The passages for recitation may be taken from one or more approved authors. . . . Meaning and allusions to be known. . . .' The Rev. J. G. G. Fussell considered Byron's *Siege of Corinth* and the *Prophecy of Dante* suitable for the children of Finsbury. *The Siege of Corinth* begins with the verse:

> Coumourgi—he whose closing scene
> Adorned the triumph of Eugene,
> When on Carlowitz' bloody plain,
> The last and mightiest of the slain,
> He sank, regretting not to die,
> But cursed the Christian victory. . . .

and the *Prophecy of Dante* contains near the beginning the lines:

> And language, eloquently false, evince
> The harlotry of genius, which, like beauty,
> Too oft forgets its own self-reverence,
> And looks on prostitution as a duty. . . .

It can be imagined what a really ingenious inspector could do to a class with such material. Fussell also pressed on the teachers the use of *Richard II* as a poetry book since it was 'simple enough to be pleasing and intelligible to the children'.

It was in vain that Matthew Arnold condemned even the *Deserted Village* and suggested Mrs Hemans' *The Graves of a Household*, or *The Homes of England* or a *Better Land*. It was in vain, too, that 'Professor Seeley rightly defined the true purpose of teaching English Literature: not, that is, to find the material with which to teach English Grammar, but to kindle a living interest in the learner's mind, to make him feel the force and beauty of which the language is capable, to refine and elevate his tastes.'

The Instructions to inspectors in 1884 said:

The general object of lesson in English should be to enlarge the learner's vocabulary and to make him familiar with the meaning, the structure, the grammatical and logical relations, and the right use of words—

and books went on being produced and used in which every trivial story was followed by a page or two of notes and questions along with pieces of unnecessary and often incorrect information. As an example, in the notes following a vapid story of Nelson's boyhood there is: 'De-táils, little things or parts, de, down; talea a cutting.' The Code was as much to blame as the inspectors. It never, in the course of the century, imagined that any book of reputable prose fiction would be read in its entirety.

The inspectors also went in for trick questions. Mr Puzzle asks a class, presumably doing geography, 'If all the land were water, and all the water land, what would England be?' The answer was a 'Lake', but he was very unlikely to receive it. Real-life inspectors were as bad as the fictional ones.

In 1879 Hugo Rice Wiggin, formerly H.M.I., published a book called the *Elementary School Manager*. In it he gives some hints on how to examine in history. He says, 'The 1st chapter of Macaulay's *History of England*, teeming as it does with allusions, may be very useful in examination: i.e. by reading a passage and requiring the children to specify the events, persons, etc. referred to.' He also advises, 'Make sure that they understand the use of the word "century" in History, e.g. that they do not suppose the year 1650 to be in the sixteenth century.'

Arithmetic was a subject which lent itself to questions beyond the children's power. Under the plea that they were encouraging 'intelligent teaching' the inspectors set puzzles to eight- and nine-year olds which demanded an arithmetical sophistication far beyond their years. The following problems were set to Standard III in 1889:

(1) What number, divided by 154, brings the quotient 154 and remainder 54?

(2) What is the nearest number greater than 13,476 which is exactly divisible by 47?

In some cases the inspectors went farther and refused the children the possibility of success. The *Schoolmaster* contains an account of an examination in which among the sums set was: '$5\frac{1}{2}$ yards make one pole. Draw a diagram to show that $30\frac{1}{2}$ sq. yds. make one perch.' When the children asked 'What is a diagram?' the answer was 'Never mind what a diagram is—work the sum.'

The inspectors increased the teachers' suspicions and distress by their habits of secrecy. They refused to allow them to see the sums on the cards which they distributed to the children for examination, and they carried off the worked papers and marked them in private.

The teachers trained the children to report the sums that had been set, but even so they felt that there was no equality between the work asked for from different schools—and they had the gravest doubts as to the way in which the papers were dealt with. Moreover the method deprived the teacher of any opportunity of complaint—even when they were sure an injustice had been done. 'He cannot', said the *Schoolmaster*, 'appeal against a decision when all the evidence is kept from him.'

The results of an injustice, if one occurred, were not confined to one year's grant. The record was entered on the 'parchment', and the disgrace followed the man for the rest of his life.

The actual examination over, the teacher's trials were not at an end. The inspector must endorse his certificate, and in cases of very unsatisfactory work or fraud he could recommend that it be cancelled or suspended. The regulation said 'a certificate may, at any time, be recalled, suspended or reduced . . .; but not until the Department has, through the managers, given the teacher an opportunity of explanation'. By specifying the managers as the medium of communication the regulation denied to the teachers any effective right of appeal.

This matter of cancelling or suspending certificates was all the more difficult because of the legacy of hate which Lingen had left to the Department. George Kekewich has a story of how he went to Lingen to discuss the grant for a school. He suggested that there might be a deduction of two-tenths of the grant. Lingen rebuked him for mildness and wrote across the form: 'My Lords have ordered a deduction to be made from the grant of 5/10 for faults of instruction, and have suspended the certificate of the teacher.' He added: 'There, I think that will do for them.'[10]

The final horror to a long day might come for a woman teacher when the inspector declared—on no particular evidence—that the children had not really worked the needlework samples that she showed, and threatened her with the loss of her certificate.

But even when there was no question of cancelling or suspending a certificate the matter was serious enough. Each year a report was written in, and a bad report clung to a man for life. For instance the London School Board advertising for a headmistress specified:

Applicants for H.Mistress-ships must be 2 year trainees with I or II class and have at least 6 'good reports'—For assistantships they would be content with 2 or 3 'good reports'.

The same system was applied to training college lecturers, who were certificated teachers, with the result that the best ones left to teach in high schools where they would be free of this annoyance.

In this, as in the other matters, the teachers' anger was aroused by the injustice of the inspectors, quite as much as by the system itself. An H.M.I., if he were in a bad temper, or if the candidate belonged to a denomination of which he disapproved, could refuse to sign a parchment, thus delaying or preventing a young teacher from getting a certificate. He could give a bad report on any occasion, no matter how hurried or perfunctory his inspection. If it were a senior man he might only be in school a few minutes and then idly he would scribble the same few words on every certificate. He might even, if he was the Rev. D. J. Stewart, write some trick comment which would make it almost impossible for the man to produce a paper so defaced, and the victim of spite or carelessness was left without any redress.[11]

The immediate reaction to the introduction of this system was an outcry of 'overpressure'. The same arguments were used by two very different sets of people. There were the teachers who were trying to protect themselves and their pupils from a state of affairs which was caused directly or indirectly by the Code; and there were the opponents of more advanced education who saw in the 'class' and 'special' subjects a threat to the simplicity of elementary education, and seized on the agitation as a means of checking this dangerous tendency.

The National Union of Elementary Teachers published a pamphlet in 1884 full of heartrending stories of the teacher who raised the school's percentage from 50 to 97 and 'broke down directly afterwards and returned to his father's house and died in a few weeks', or of children of seven who died of brain fever and muttered with their last breath, 'Father, I cannot do my sums.'

When Mundella was asked in the House if 'the number of children and teachers going to lunatic asylums had increased recently', he answered 'No, sir.' But in the Lords, this statement of Dr Crichton Browne's was quoted with approval:

Of the many conditions tending to the increase of mental disease I would especially direct your attention to Education. . . .

It is a curious fact that, since the recent spread of education, the increase of deaths from hydrocephalous has not been among infants, but among children over 5 years old.

It was claimed, by their opponents, that this 'over-pressure' was particularly bad in the Board Schools, and, in so far as they dealt with a more unfortunate type of child, this may well have been true; on the other hand the teachers in these schools were receiving more protection from the stringencies of the Code, and therefore were less likely to resort to the forms of terrorism used in less fortunate schools. The fact was, as Sidney Buxton and others began to point out, that 'over-pressure' was merely another name for overworked, underfed children, bad premises, and unintelligent teaching.[12]

On the side of the teachers, it was claimed that the death rate was excessive for young men and women who had just been passed as healthy at the end of their training college course. One ingenious statistician calculated that the death rate among teachers was three times that of the armed forces, and six times that of prisoners in gaol. At this point Edwin Chadwick entered the fray pointing out, characteristically, that good ventilation and 'washing from head to foot in tepid water' was the best way to avoid infection and disease.

Once the matter had been raised it was seen that the neglect of the children's physical welfare was extreme, and the reformers began to demand action. In 1855 a commission was discussed to enquire into the Education of Blind, Deaf and Dumb children, and Sheffield School Board, feeling that there were real 'disadvantages suffered in the prosecution of school work by children whose eyesight was defective', decided that 'spectacles be provided in the schools of the Board for *us during school hours* by children who may need them'.[13] There is no record that the children had their eyes tested professionally, so that for many years the teacher opened a box and distributed pairs of spectacles haphazard to the class.

It was even suggested by the reformers, though the scheme was at once declared 'impossible', that there should be systematic medical inspection in schools, and that children should be weighed and measured.

This slight attention to the physical well-being of the children was not the only good thing that came from the Code. The School Boards made a move to protect their servants. The London School Board in 1883, and the other large ones a year or so later, gave their teachers fixed salaries and left the rates to bear the fluctuations of grant that might be experienced. This was almost inevitable in towns where children were still being forced into schools and where some schools were notoriously 'difficult'. Justice would have demanded the same thing in the country, but so many of the country schools were voluntary and had no financial reserves, and the small Boards were in no better position. By 1888 41 per cent of the teachers were on fixed salaries and the movement was spreading into the voluntary schools.

But if the Boards were to protect the teachers from the unreasonable consequences of the Codes they must have some guarantee that the work was done as well as circumstances allowed. In consequence they appointed their own inspectors who partially duplicated the work of H.M.I.s only with more knowledge of local conditions. They also, particularly in London, appointed specialists to teach and encourage the teachers. These specialists were not always welcome. They were enthusiasts who saw education from one angle. One whose influence dominated the teaching of his subject for full fifty years was T. R. Ablet, the adviser for art. Another, who nearly drove her victims frantic, was Miss Lynschiuka who inspected and ran classes on German Kindergarten. On one occasion she demanded that a group of teachers prepare three lessons on a snail—one of them to deal with its teeth.

356

Not all the Boards took the part of their teachers—some saw in the Code an excuse for economies. For instance in 1882 the South Shields Board decided to reduce its teachers' salaries, and hoped that 'by increased exertions' they might in some two years raise their salaries to the former level.

In London the salary scales for men assistants went from £60–£155 and for headmasters £150–£400 and there was extra pay for schools recognized as of special difficulty. On the other hand there were schools with very low rates of pay. In one village school the mistress was offered £16 with house and garden, with constant work for her husband on the farm. In the same issue of the *Hampshire Chronicle* a cook was wanted at £40 a year, and, of course, all found.

But there were even lower depths in private schools. An advertisement in the *Schoolmaster* in 1891 read:

Wanted in a private Boarding and Day School Male ex-P.T. to teach English, Mathematics, Natural Science, Latin, French, Drawing, Freehand, Model, Perspective, Geometry, Book-keeping, Drill. Preference given to one who is musical. Must be good disciplinarian, teetotaler, Non-conformist and non-smoker. Apply stating age, salary required resident with testimonials to: Mr E. R. Smith, Annesley School, St Leonards-on-Sea.

This sort of thing was possible because there was no regulation of teachers. To earn grant a school must be in charge of a certificated teacher, but the training colleges were quite unable to supply sufficient trained teachers, and teachers could obtain certificates by other means. These far outnumbered the trained, and the proportion increased. In 1883, 831 trained teachers were certificated, 39 per cent of those starting that year; and 1317 (61 per cent) were certificated without training. In 1885 the proportions were 32 and 68 per cent. Below these certificated teachers—of whatever grade—were uncertificated, or ex-pupil teachers who just stayed on. The teachers protested and demanded registration, and were snubbed.

By 1880 Board Schools and compulsion, working with the Code, had produced a great change in the education of the country. But it is true that in some districts the standards for exemption from school were still very low. Sir William Hart-Dyke, who became Vice-President in 1887, stated in reply to a parliamentary question, that there were 29 parishes where compulsion extended only from five to ten years of age; 5 parishes gave Standard III as the level for total exemption and 25 Standard I for partial exemption. These he said were survivals that the Department had no power to alter. On the other hand there were far more cases where the problem was to provide advanced instruction for those that needed it. The big School Boards were pushing forward into new territory, and receiving encouragement. For example in 1880 the Sheffield School Board wrote to the Department asking what would be the attitude to more advanced work. The reply stated: 'My Lords entirely concur with your board in the desirability of providing in a single school for the instruction of the more promising scholars in the higher subjects at a higher fee. . . .'

It was maintained that these were 'simply advanced elementary schools' and were not for the middle classes or for secondary education.

There were similar schools in Bradford and Barrow-in-Furness, and a particularly outstanding Standard VII school in Birmingham, and another similar one in Deansgate, Manchester.

The existence of these schools, which carried children beyond the standards of the Code, was possible because a new power had arisen in education which could supply money when the Department of Education could not or would not do so. This was the Department of Science and Art—commonly called, from its local habitation, South Kensington. It had existed feebly since 1837 under the aegis of the Board of Trade, but it was taken up seriously in 1852 as part of the aftermath of the Great Exhibition. It was first established at Marlborough House as a Department of Practical Art. It was to be a school of design, and design of one kind only—ornament. The purpose of the school was 'to teach the art of designing ornament, both in respect to its general principles and its specific application to manufacture'. It held special classes in wood engraving, painting on porcelain, silversmithing, jewellery, textiles and other artistic crafts. In the next year science was added to its concerns.

In 1856 it came under the Committee of Council on Education, and became an equal yoke-mate with the Department of Education in Whitehall; but it kept its own staff, offices, finance and aims. Loosely attached to it were the Royal School of Mines, the Geological Survey, the Normal School of Science, the British Museum, the Zoo, and parallel institutions in Dublin and Edinburgh. The idea behind all this was, perhaps, to emulate the great technical and artistic schools of Paris—but the institutions in London failed to attract more than a handful of students, and the art school was so determined not to train artists but only teachers or designers of ornament that its numbers were small and its work deplorable. Nor did it spread its work far abroad. Its first attempts in 1854 were to arrange classes and examinations for art teachers and to allow pupil teachers to join them. If they passed, it brought them some reward in their certificate; and their teachers, if certificated, got a £3 bonus for each pass. There were very few candidates. The science classes were no more successful. In 1858 the only classes in existence were at Aberdeen, Birmingham, Bristol and Wigan.

It was just at this time that Lyon Playfair, who had been involved in the Department from its beginning, left it for a political life; and Captain John Donnelly, R.E., took charge of the science side and later of the whole Department. He guided it triumphantly through its course, and when he retired in 1898 as Major-General Donnelly, K.C.B., his charge had only one more year of independent life. Before he came, the Department had trained some Royal Engineer officers in photography, so that it had a connection with the Corps. During his tenure of office he continued to make full use of the talents of sappers as examiners and in other ways. In fact, had the Department continued in being, it would have become one of the group of institutions managed by that versatile and accomplished branch of the Army.

Captain Donnelly went to South Kensington just before the Minute of 2 June 1859[14] which really started the Department on its way. By this Minute a certificate granted by South Kensington in some science subject was counted for augmentation of the teacher's salary, and qualified him to receive grants for any successful candidate he might present for examination. The subjects that might be offered were practical and descriptive geometry, physics, chemistry, geology (for mining) and natural history.

In the year after the passing of the Minute, in spite of the fact that it was not advertised, and teachers had had no time to prepare, there were 57 candidates, offering 104 subjects. 'It is rather surprising,' says the contemporary report, 'that candidates came up in every subject, and that some were successful in all except geometry.' The examining Board at the first examination included Professor Bradley, Dr A. W. von Hofmann, Professor Tyndall and Professor Huxley. This policy of employing the most eminent men as examiners or advisers was continued, and hardly anyone appears in the records who was not an F.R.S. at least.

The Whitehall code of 1862, establishing payment by results, and

359

abolishing the augmentation payments on certificates, had no direct authority at South Kensington. But it fitted in well with the policy that had already been started. Henceforth South Kensington worked by making grants to teachers, and rewarding the pupils with small prizes. The Department of Science and Art had no concern for buildings or conditions of work. It was payment by results in its simplest form.

The two sides of the work of the Department, art and science, were to a considerable extent separate, though under one general administration. The art grants were comparatively small and were intended for school children, though the training colleges took the examinations. The science grants, of much larger amounts, were primarily intended for artisans and other older students.

The grants for drawing were welcomed eagerly by the schools. It was a little extra money, not restricted by the conditions of the Whitehall grant. The children cannot have learnt much. The log-books record the assiduous teaching of drawing till the date of the examination—but it disappeares immediately afterwards.

The science grants operated, at first, outside the schools. The grants that could be earned were very considerable and ranged from £1 to £4 according to the grade of the examination and the class the candidate achieved.

This encouragement led to the gradual spread of classes, but the real development began in 1872. The Minute of November 1872 said:

Payments are made to the qualified teacher on account of the instruction of students of the Industrial classes including: . . . g) All scholars in Public Elementary Schools within the meaning of the Elementary Education Act 1870.

This threw open to the schools the more valuable science examinations.

Naturally there must be teachers, and next year training colleges were admitted to the golden field. Training college students who took the examinations of the Department of Science and Art might have credit for it in their certificates and their teachers would be paid. Large numbers responded. In that year 1547 male candidates took a total of 3559 papers, and between a half and two-thirds passed. There were also some women, but not so many.

By the next year the rush to enter children in schools became excessive, and the Whitehall Department felt it should be regulated.

4 July 1874

'No pupil in a school receiving aid from the Dept. of Education, White-hall, may be presented for examination in science unless he has passed St. V of the Code, nor who has been examined in the same subject by H.M.I. in the last six months.

This slightly checked the abuse of the examinations in the schools. But over the country as a whole the movement spread like wildfire.

In 1874 there were nearly 50,000 students taking various science subjects. In order of popularity they were:

Physical Geography	21,000
Electricity	11,605
Pure Maths stages 1, 2, 3,	11,168

The high quality of the examiners was maintained, and some forty R.E. officers were engaged in inspecting and examining—which they could manage as the majority of the classes were evening ones.

By 1878 institutions of all kinds up and down the country were preparing students for examination and sharing in the bounty. To name but a few from the record (which also gives in some cases the amounts received): Luton Engineering works; Litton Grammar School, Newbury; Fenny Stratford National School; Church of England Young Men's Society (£181), Cambridge; Falmouth Polytechnic; Ilfracombe Girls' and Infant School; Plymouth Navigation School; Telegraphists' School, Aldersgate; Nottinghill High School for Girls; Crewe Mechanics' Institute (£191); Plymouth Group of Higher Schools (£200); Village Hall, Main St, Oadby (£1).[15]

The number of subjects, also, was continually increased. The most popular were animal physiology; electricity; sound, light and heat; botany and physiography. There were also geometry, machine drawing, building construction, naval architecture, mathematics, mechanics, chemistry, geology, mineralogy, mining, metallurgy, steam, nautical astronomy. Agriculture and hygiene were added later.

The system suited everybody, and it provided the most wonderful stimulus to social and educational development. For the first time there was opened to the artisan class the possibility of some secondary education; and, to the abler men and women, this must have come as a marvellous pleasure. In addition, the grants earned by the students made possible the organization of social clubs. The Mechanics' Institutes which had languished, now could maintain themselves. The

Co-operative Society now had a basis for its social-educational work. The first taste of knowledge increased the desire for it, and the new university extension movement followed and supported the other teaching. In the schools and training colleges the grants brought much-needed increases in salary. These were often considerable, in 1875 the Borough Road teachers shared £630,[16] £278 going to one man. There were sometimes quarrels about the distribution of the grant. Canon Hector Nelson, head of Lincoln Training College, living up to his name, declared that he would be quite within his rights if he took the whole grant—and would do so if there was any more trouble. The teachers in schools often did well, but not as well as in the colleges—unless, of course, the school was organized in a certain way. The payments for drawing were also considerable, and increased rapidly. Though, as far more schools took drawing, the individual rewards were less. These figures give some idea of the increases in the grants:

Drawing in elementary schools

1871 £9729
1880 £48,935

In training colleges

1871 £514
1880 £1742

In addition, the Department gave a few small scholarships, and had also in its gift the valuable Whitworth Scholarships which went to senior wranglers who also took an interest in engineering.

Not only did South Kensington supply the incentive to learning, the very means to do so were inspired by it. A library of text-books was produced aimed directly at the examinations. Between 1870 and 1880 the whole style of these scientific books changed. In 1872 they belonged to the class of '*The Reason Why*, a careful collection of many hundreds of reasons for things which, though generally believed, are imperfectly understood, by the author of *Enquire Within Upon Everything*.' At much the same date Dr Dionysius Lardner published *Natural Philosophy for Schools*, a

volume compiled to supply the want felt by a large number of teachers in public and private schools of a Class Book for Junior students.

It is now hoped that this volume may be the means of extending instruction in the first notion of Physics into Ladies Schools. Female teachers in general will find even the Handbook easily intelligible.

The frontispiece of the books was a sectionalized drawing of the Britannia Tubular Bridge.

The text covered general properties of bodies, gravity, molecular force, elements of machinery, moving power, hydrostatics, pneumatics, sound, optics, heat, electricity.

These early books are followed, year by year in the 1880s, by textbooks written by men of note. Professor Henry Tanner, M.R.A.C., F.C.S., Professor University College examiner in principles of Agriculture for the Government Department of Science and Art, wrote the *Elementary Lessons on the Science of Agricultural Practice*. The Astronomer Royal wrote on *Astronomy and Mathematics*. G. Croom Robertson, Professor of Mental Philosophy at the University of London, wrote *Elementary Lessons on Psychology*, and Professor Huxley, Roscoe and Balfour Stewart (all F.R.S.) edited a series for Macmillan. Todhunter produced his *Algebra* in this company, Jevons his *Logic* and J. R. Green his *Short History of the English People*.

Some ten years later, less eminent men had taken up the work, and Collins had an Elementary and Advanced Series 'adapted to the requirements of the South Kensington syllabus for students in science and art classes and higher and middle class schools'. The volumes of this series ended with sample papers in the subject and examination questions. Longmans, Green had another similar series. It is clear that the publishers understood the growing market.

It was in this context that the School Boards extended the work of the primary schools. Cunningly taking advantage of the dual system, they obtained grants from Whitehall for all children in the standards, and supplemented this with whatever they could earn from South Kensington. From Standard IV children could be working at class or specific subjects under the Whitehall syllabus, and next year transfer their knowledge to the South Kensington requirements. After Standard VII they could devote all their time to South Kensington. Under Whitehall regulations no child might earn more than £1 2s. 6d. in grants and the total earned by the school might not exceed 17s. 6d. a head. Under South Kensington he might earn £3 14s., and there was no 17s. 6d. limit to keep down the overall sum; so one or two clever children could be very profitable indeed.

It was not only primary schools who made a good thing out of the regulations. Many secondary schools lived almost entirely on South Kensington grants.

In the 1890s a yet more ambitious form of organization came into being. South Kensington encouraged the promotion of Organized Science Schools where there was a planned two- or three-year course. A capitation grant of £1 a head on attendance was made, as well as the usual payments for examination successes. It was conflict over these schools between the London County Council and the London School Board that precipitated the final battle over Secondary Education.

As conditions in the schools improved and the level of teaching rose, the deficiencies of the pupil teachers became more obvious. The age had no good word to say for these poor children. 'Whether we look at these young people as teachers or students they are the most unsatisfactory part of our educational system', said the Cross Commission.[17] Dr Allbutt speaking at Huddersfield was even more direct. 'The pupil teacher is a mischief to his scholars, a mischief to his superiors, and a mischief to himself.'

No one however seriously thought of getting rid of the system. It was cheap; it pleased the head because the pupil teachers were 'more pliable than adult teachers', and early learnt all the tricks of the trade and passed beyond the power of criticism; most important of all, it was the only real source of recruits for the profession. For as yet there was no alternative secondary education available for the great bulk of the population, especially those sections which furnished the teachers.

Rather there was concern over their physical welfare and their education, and attempts were made to improve both.

The Act of 1870 found the pupil teachers bound to their schools, teaching thirty hours a week and being instructed as best they might by the headmaster. It had always been difficult to fit in these hours of instruction, but it was now realized that a head with several pupil teachers in different years of their apprenticeship was in an impossible position, and that the young people were most unlikely to be taught— even if they had the energy to learn.

By 1875 the Rev. John Rodgers of the London School Board was trying to alleviate the hardships of their lot. He proposed that they should not start their apprenticeship till fourteen, should not go to evening schools, should not have charge of a class till the last three years, and that the day's one hour of instruction should be in a separate centre.

The Department of Education refused to sanction this. Basing itself on the regulations, it refused to allow anyone but the head teacher of the school to instruct the pupil teachers and insisted on their doing a full day's teaching.

The School Boards continued to press their demands, and in 1880 the Code was so far altered as to allow pupil teachers to be taught by any certificated teacher—not necessarily the head of his school. Thus it was now possible to gather pupil teachers in centres and provide some adequate teaching.

At first the children were expected to fit in an hour before school from 7.45 to 8.45 and to come back in the evening. But in 1884 the Department so far relented that they were only required to teach three hours a day, and could attend the centre half time. There was then the task of organizing the centres. New buildings were not even thought of, and pupil teacher centres were mostly in abandoned buildings. The Rev. Stewart Headlam called one such a 'rat hole'.

The first pupil teacher centre in London was in Stepney, and in the next ten years twelve more were opened—but, even so, many of the children must have had long journeys between the centre and their schools.

In these inadequate buildings, and in the rush from one place to another, the pupil teachers were in a continual stretch of work. Examinations were continuous. One head of a centre records: that the pupil teachers were examined quarterly in the centre: there were the Science and Art examination in May, and the examination for Queen's scholarships at Christmas. There was special teaching in scripture so that the School Board candidates should not be at a disadvantage at denominational training colleges when compared with those who came from Church schools.

But if their work was incessant, it did not go very deep. An inspector in 1880 commenting on the examination says:

'In $2\frac{1}{2}$ hours the male pupil teacher has to work papers in History, Euclid, Algebra, Mensuration, write an essay and produce samples of copy writing. The female has to do her portion in 1 hour, the other $1\frac{1}{2}$ hours being occupied with Needlework.'

Difficult as all this was, the pupils who attended centres did far better than those who were left to the teaching of the school. In Liverpool, for example, in 1885, the proportion of pupils in centres gaining I classes was 66 per cent as against 26 per cent for the rest of the candidates. In London in 1884 it was 50 per cent against 24 per cent. All this time the proportion of pupil teachers to adult teachers was falling. In 1870 it had been about half but by 1885 it was down to 30 per cent.

Just before 1870 the number of places in training colleges had been sufficient to receive the pupil teachers who were qualified for admittance, and to supply the schools with the certificated teachers they needed. From that period, with the rapid increase in the number of schools and the demand for teachers, the training colleges had become inadequate—something like half the qualified pupil teachers were unable to obtain a college place, and the schools needed at least a thousand more certificated teachers every year than the colleges could supply. This led, as has been said, to the wholesale granting of certificates to untrained teachers.

The regulation of 1862 which cut off the capital grants to training colleges checked their multiplication, and the drop in the position of teachers discouraged recruitment for a time, so that some of the smaller ones actually perished. In 1870 there were forty-three still in existence. A number were founded during the 1870s and 1880s, Swansea, Saffron Walden, Edghill, St Katharine's, Tottenham, West Hill R.C., Darlington, and Oxford—(a strange family affair). Chester reopened. They could not, however, supply the numbers needed and the gap between the demands of the schools and the supply of teachers widened.

Unfortunately the training colleges were as outdated in ideas as they were inadequate in accommodation.[18] The buildings which had seemed grand in 1850 now seemed horrible with thirty years' grime, and the change in the outside standard of living. 'The asceticism of the workhouse', says one inspector of Church training colleges, 'was blended with the solidity and ugliness of a gaol', and he goes on to describe the bare tables and the workhouse bread and 'coffee'. The log-books, or reminiscences of students, give details of some of the arrangements. From the H.M.I.'s reports contained in the log-book of the men's college in Caernarvon come these scraps:

Only one staircase in case of fire. No bathroom, the students wash in each other's presence.

All go to wash at one tap for occasional washing.

The men send out for beer—they are allowed to smoke after dinner—the kitchens are wretchedly unwholesome—very hot—no circulation of air—indecent writings about privies.

The kitchens exceedingly bad—had killed under-housemaid.

Reminiscences of Lincoln, a women's college, show the same conditions:

The room used for bathing was on the ground floor and was known as the boot house. Its window was decorously veiled with a curtain, and it was provided with a portable bath and a chair and a mat that had seen better days. The students worked in twos, one to fill the bath, and one to have it. While the friend was filling the bath with cans of water which she fetched from the kitchen, the bather went upstairs and undressed into her dressing gown. Then she made a secret run to the bath avoiding the principal and governesses alike. . . .

The kitchen could only provide one bath a day, and there were 40 udents.

In 1881 Canon Whatburton, the inspector, demanded:

A cold water tap on the upper floor,
more W.C.s (only 2 for 40 students)
a bathroom with facilities for every student to have a bath every week or ten days.

Two years later, by September 1883, the work was done, and the college connected to the city sewerage.

The staff had not improved either. In fact it was probably on the whole worse, in comparison with the general body of teachers, than it had been earlier. It was more profitable to be a headmaster than to be a lecturer in a training college—unless, of course, South Kensington grants came to a large sum—and the annoyance of Government inspection had to be endured. In Church training colleges the men who aspired to rise were expected to take orders, and some refused; one man in the hope of becoming an inspector—for which post orders were now a disqualification. The ablest undoubtedly left for other work.

With these teachers and the demands of examinations the students' work still consisted of learning the text-book by heart or committing to memory 300 lines of poetry—with parsing and paraphrasing—from Gray's *Odes* and *Elegy* or Dryden's translation of *Aeneid II*. The fact that the entrants to colleges were now better taught, and, under the conditions of extreme competition, cleverer, made no difference to the syllabus or teaching. In 1882 there were no failures, so the best candidates must have been deprived of all mental stimulus.

The only living part of the course—and this only in a few colleges— was the principles of teaching, which became psychology. By 1883 it appeared in the second year syllabus.

The training of the senses and of the memory; the processes of reasoning; the order in which the faculties of children are developed; the formation of habits and of character, all considered in their application to methods of teaching and moral discipline.

367

In 1888 Dr Fitch, reporting on Lincoln Training College, condemned the teaching there and added, 'in other colleges such lectures are given by a person specially appointed, sometimes by one of the female teachers trained at Girton or Newnham, but more usually by a male lecturer'.

Miss Manley of Stockwell told the Cross Commission that she thought 'psychology and mental science one of the most practical parts of our work' and added:

Mr Sully, who has had considerable experience in lecturing on 'Mental Science in its bearing on Education', has kindly allowed me to make use of his condensed syllabus of lectures.[19]

Sully's *Handbook of Psychology* was in its third edition by 1890.

Besides their academic learning the students were still kept at the dreary round of school practice and demonstration lessons. One college had the intelligence to point out that after their years of drudging as pupil teachers this was a sheer waste of time and spirit—but all the rest who were asked for their opinion accepted it without demur.

The life was bad—as the *Schoolmaster* said:

Long hours, little exercise and too much food of a solid, not to say coarse kind. Ten hours per day of reading is far too long, and one hour for exercise is far too little.

James Runciman, a man who loved the sea, published in 1886 a book of sketches called *Schools and Scholars*. In it he gives a bitter account of his life at the Borough Road a few years before. The buildings were revolting.

There was not a picture in any room.... No man could have a moment of privacy until he was in bed. . . . The barren foetid rooms, with their greasy forms and notched desks, were the only places where a letter could be written. . . . If a man had tried to go up to his bedroom for an hour of quiet thought, he would, in all probability, have been dismissed for the offence. . . . If the student went out he was in the slums, and the only college open space was a narrow flagged yard, like the square in which the Millbank prisoners take their exercise.

The teaching was as bad. 'He was expected to learn his country's history from a tiny 5d. book which contained strings of names and dates arranged in horrifying sequence.' The teaching equalled the book. 'The teacher entered. The men squatted in the dingy theatre like a set of charity boys and awaited the first question. "What event happened on the 25th September 1066? Hands up those who know." The men held up their hands in a childish way', and the teacher picked on Mr Jones who did *not* put up his hand.

Geography was the same. 'We will now take the coast of South America from Cape Corrientes southwards.' And the names of capes, bays and rivers are recited in turn.

Grammar was a sixpenny text-book of rules and definitions crammed by heart.

Sundays were the worst affliction of all. 'There was no place of refuge for the future instructors of the people: there was no library: the news room was closed on Sabatarian principles, and the sickly rooms depressed the very soul. There was not a cushioned seat in the establishment, and the men were reduced to lolling on tables or straddling the forms.'

The girls fared worse, as they were expected to take part in the domestic work. At Lincoln 'Work in the college laundry consisted in turning the mangle for about an hour at a time. This was usually done from about mid-day, during what was known as "recreation hour", and some students seem to have carried out this duty three times a week. Writing about this work years afterwards some said that they could still remember their blistered hands and the back-aches.'

Their lives were also more closely controlled. Miss E. Young, senior teacher at Stockwell, wrote these rules on the first page of a student's autograph album in 1874.

Things to remember.
1. Never go out alone.
2. Don't talk at dinner time.
3. Never speak after 10-10 p.m.
4. Always wear a bonnet on Sunday.
5. Never go upstairs without asking.
6. If you go for a walk with a young gentleman always leave at the corner.
7. Never leave a square inch of dinner on your plate.
8. Take a constitutional daily either between 12 and 1 o'clock or 6 and 7. Hoping you will attend to the above.

> I am
> Yours truly,
> E. Young.[20]

There were other more subtle difficulties due to employing clerical

369

principals in women's colleges. Runciman in the same book has a sketch of the attempt of one man to tame an independent-minded girl. It is called the *Ritualist*.

'The Rev. Athanasius Faulkner . . . treated the pupils much as he would have treated the maids in his own house. He ordered the fashion of their dress, he was strict in the mode in which the girls put up their hair, and he rather liked to see a pretty girl disfigured by ridiculous bands, brushed, like a Sussex spaniel's ears, well over the cheeks.'

The girl in the story, though dutifully conforming, refuses to adore the tyrant. She will not go to confession, and when he orders her to assist in robing him for service she turns sick and runs away—back to her healthy and affectionate fiancé.

The result of the discipline, in the men's colleges, was periodic outbreaks of violent insubordination—usually directed against one member of the staff. Some of these outbreaks were so serious that correspondence on them reached the Department. There was one at the Bangor Training College in 1891 and another, at about the same time, at Exeter. Both these outbreaks were followed by a 'reconstruction of the staff'.

There were two institutions which threw into sharp contrast the defects of the majority. One was the training school run by the Roman Catholic Church at Mount Pleasant, Liverpool, the other the reconstructed Chichester College.

The inspectors frequently remark on the great superiority of the girls trained at Mount Pleasant, and give the cause. These small groups of girls were in constant contact with women of birth and education, who possessed a culture very different from that of the ordinary training college lecturer. Born into well-to-do families they had adopted teaching as a profession with their vows, and gave to it a whole-hearted devotion.

Chichester was an experiment of a different kind.[21] As refounded in 1873, Bishop Otter College was to open primary teaching to a different class of woman—'ladies' who had not been pupil teachers, but who, through poverty, were forced to earn their living. The numbers were small, about thirty-three, and while in residence they had to conform to the worship of the Church of England—though their private beliefs were not too closely enquired into. They were the daughters of merchants, officers in the army or navy, doctors, and particularly the lower-paid clergy. Many were orphans, and a large proportion came from the North of England. The Principal, Miss Trevor, said in evidence that most had been educated at home, and many were very ignorant, but they had intelligence, standards of application and honesty, and the results in the examination were well above the average, since 'they had not had the intellect so crushed out of them by working before they were fit to work and by cram teaching'. Some of the young women came as Queen's Scholars and had to take posts in public elementary schools, others as private students and paid £50 a year each, and could teach where they liked—one became head mistress of the Watford Orphan Asylum. After one year's experience in a school they obtained their certificates.

It was agreed that when the girls had posts they did well—the difficulty was that many head teachers were reluctant to have them as assistants, fearing their superior social class—or, as it was unkindly suggested, their stricter honesty. There was a great demand for them in country schools but the pay was so wretched that the college could not advise them to accept. Miss Trevor insisted on £70 a year as the minimum living wage—or £65 if there was also lodging. They went mostly to the Board schools in the large towns—often to the higher grade schools. This college, by dispensing with the period of pupil teaching, showed a completely new way of approaching the problem of training; a way which was not followed for many years.

Notes

1. Earl Fortescue in the House speaking on education.
2. Specific subjects in 1878: English literature, mathematics, Latin, French, German, mechanics, animal physiology, physical geography, botany, domestic economy.
3. P.P., 1884, LXI, 161.
4. Hansard, CCLXIV, 1210; also *Schoolmaster*, 13 August 1881, p. 159.
5. *Schoolmaster*, 20 August 1881, p. 193; also articles in the following months.
6. P.P., 1865, VI, Lingen's evidence, p. 261 onwards.
7. *Schoolmaster*, 18 March 1882, p. 289.
8. *Schoolmaster*, 25 February 1882, p. 195.
9. P.P., 1888, XXV, 65 ff.
10. G. W. Kekewich, *The Education Department and After* (1920), p. 11.
11. *Schoolmaster*, 10 January 1901, p. 65; 17 January 1901, pp. 109, 110; Gautrey, *Lux Mihi Laus*, p. 112.
12. P.P., 1884, LXI, 259 ff; Sidney Buxton, *Overpressure* (1885).
13. J. H. Bingham, *Period of the Sheffield School Board*, p. 227.
14. Report, 1858–9, p. 13.
15. Report, 1878, pp. 264, 535.
16. Report, 1875, pp. 112, 188.
17. P.P., 1888, XXXV, 111 ff.
18. P.P., 1888, XXXV, 117 ff.
19. P.P., 1886, XXV, 495.
20. MS in possession of Prof. A. H. Dodd.
21. P.P., 1886, XXV, 503.

Chapter Seventeen

The Cross Commission

By 1885 it was felt that a survey of the working of the Elementary Education Acts was due, and the next year a Commission under the chairmanship of Sir Richard Assheton Cross was appointed. When it reported in 1888 it once more set educational reform in motion. The recommendations of the Commission fell into two main groups. One concerned the developing work of schools which were feeling towards technical and secondary education, the other modification of the present elementary system. Among these latter it suggested that school premises should be improved—and teachers should have greater freedom of classification; but, on the all-important topic of payment by results, it could not bring itself to give a definite decision. The system was condemned on all hands. No longer were the teachers alone in their protests. The *Nineteenth Century* had published an article saying:

> Children are treated by a public department, by managers and schoolmasters as suitable instruments for earning government money

—and as of little other importance.

The London School Board passed a resolution condemning payment by results without a single speaker supporting it. The difficulty was to invent in its place a system which would not cripple the schools, and yet give some confidence that the national resources were well used. The Board Schools presented no problem. It was the great mass of voluntary schools over which the state had no hold except through the grant. As Sidney Buxton put it:

> Three-quarters of our elementary schools are run by practically irresponsible managers. The Education Department pays out every year

something like £2,000,000 to these irresponsible managers, so that for every £1 these managers provide the State supplies £3.

How far could the state safely go in trusting these managers?

Faced with this problem the Commission suggested that the system should be mitigated by making a much larger part of the grant fixed, and by protecting the teachers by paying them fixed salaries.

These points were taken up in the Code of 1889[1] which very honestly and fairly attempted to carry out the recommendations of the committee. Under it the most offensive features of the old system were abolished.

Individual examination, except as an aid to a judgment of general efficiency, was given up; the merit grant and percentages disappeared; the schools received a fixed grant varying from 12s. to 15s. 6d. on average attendance, plus grants for class and special subjects; the attendance qualification was withdrawn, and all children present were liable to examination. The teachers might classify them as they wished—provided it was reasonable; and children need not be in the same standard for all subjects; the inspectors no longer endorsed certificates, instead they made a general report to the managers which must be published; staffing ratios were made a little more liberal (e.g. the number of children whom an adult assistant was required to teach dropped from eighty to seventy) and, in the hope of alleviating the shortage of trained teachers, it was proposed to open day training colleges.[2]

The Commission had said in its recommendations:

The time has come when the State may be more exacting in requiring for children a proper amount of air, light and space, suitable premises, and a reasonable extent of playground. We approve the rule of the Department that 10 sq ft should be the minimum accommodation provided for each child in average attendance.

This also the Code accepted and stated 'the Department will endeavour to secure 10 sq ft of space per unit of average attendance'.

This Code was received coldly. It was too great a change. Almost all that the teachers had been campaigning for for ten years to obtain was offered to them, but they were suspicious—the more so as the Department refused to publish the 'Instructions to Inspectors' which usually accompanied the Code. Moreover Cumin was still in office. His successor, who professed a high regard for him, yet says: 'He was too fond of concealing his intentions from interviewers, and of a procedure which he called "turning their corner".' The teachers had had six years' experience of his methods, and they feared that what he gave with one hand he would take with the other. The *Schoolmaster* in a paragraph records that a meeting was held to discuss matters between Heller, Pope and Wild representing the teachers and Sir W. Hart-Dyke and Cumin. 'The result was highly satisfactory. . . . There is, we are informed, a determination on the part of the vice-president of the Council to see that matters run smoothly.' Perhaps deliberately, there is no mention of the Secretary's views.

There were other doubters besides the teachers. A few still clung to the old system; others like Lord Norton utterly condemned 'variable state aid for Education instead of a secure provision of its requisite means'.

All these, however, would have accepted the Code. The real opposition came from the Church. The Archbishop of Canterbury[3] and the Bishop of London alike feared that if the voluntary schools were compelled to provide 10 square feet of space for each child they would perish; and argued on the implied principle that children should pay for the spiritual benefits of a sectarian education by a loss of physical amenities. Sydney Buxton even accused the Archbishop of saying at a conference 'that the Code must be destroyed in the interests of the Church'. The Government gave way. On 11 July it withdrew the Code. The *Schoolmaster* commented:[4]

> The Code has been withdrawn. . . . Once more the country is in the full possession of a system which it condemns. . . . The Leader of the House announced on Thursday last that in consequence of the criticism to which they had been subjected, and the diversity of opinion which seemed to be prevalent among the members themselves, the new proposals would be withdrawn for the present.

The teachers settled to spending the coming year in agitation for a still more liberal Code, and the Department to thinking of a way of satisfying all parties.

At this point Patrick Cumin died. His death, as much as the temper of Parliament and the nation, opened the way for a more radical change. His successor was George Kekewich, and his appointment at this time was important.

George Kekewich had refused to accept the family living and vegetate in the country. He wished to go into business, but he found that a good university degree was a disqualification. His father was in Parliament, he had been at Eton. It was not long before his penniless reading for the Bar was interrupted by an invitation to join the examiners in the Education Department. For some twenty years he shared their pleasant life, gradually, as he had a natural talent for organization and no great literary aspirations, collecting more and more duties. In 1890 after acting as unofficial secretary to Cumin he was promoted Secretary over the heads of a good many seniors. His appointment was doubtless due to his ability and power of work and organization; but the choice was also certainly influenced by his attitude to the teachers. Sir William Hart-Dyke was an astute politician, and the Government was not strong enough to scorn any type of support. Teachers are always a potentially dangerous body (as H. A. L. Fisher admitted in 1918) and it had become clear that now was the time to conciliate them.

Already teachers were being elected to the County Councils. Very soon—in 1895[5]—they would be elected to Parliament. They had perfected the arts of lobbying and publicity—they were well organized—they were formidable. Kekewich, the first Secretary since Kay-Shuttleworth who really believed in education, saw in the teachers not instruments to be degraded and harried, but partners in a work to which they would give intelligent and faithful labour if they were trusted and encouraged. He was the man for the time, and his appointment ushers in a completely new period in the relationship between the central office and the teachers.

His first official task was to prepare the Code for 1890. In his not very honest autobiography he claims that the Code of 1890 was his own work.[6] In fact it was essentially the same document as the Code of 1889 that had been withdrawn.[7] There was one important omission, and a few minor, but still important additions—dealing with permissive physical training, manual work, and the liberalization of evening schools. The Government took the matter of the Code seriously:

> The framing of the Code produced a phenomenon—the only meeting of the Committee of Council on Education that I remember. . . . It was an extremely odd, and very perfunctory proceeding. The Code, or part of it, was read out to the Committee by Lord Cranbrook, but apparently few of them understood it or took the smallest interest in it. Lord Salisbury, however, who was present, by way, I suppose, of saying something, criticized an article which provided that a proper supply of lavatories should be provided for the use of the children. He insisted on a reduction

376

of the grant if the lavatories were out of repair. Lord Cranbrook then took alarm. He said that there was nothing more of importance, and, as Lord Salisbury was in a hurry, the meeting ended.

This account ignores what must have been the real purpose of the meeting—how to ensure that the Code was successfully passed. That was not difficult. The only serious opposition to the last one had come from the Church and on one point only. The Code of 1890 abandoned the attempt to improve the material condition of the schools, and left that to a Liberal Government two years later, with Circular 321.

With the Church placated, and the teachers' fears at rest, the Code had a triumphant progress through Parliament. There was no opposition—only a few sighs that it did not go further. It gave in fact 'general satisfaction' and if the debate was 'worthy of a much larger audience' at least those who were there were interested and appreciative.

Moreover, for the first time, the teachers were objects of praise. Sydney Buxton speaking on a resolution condemning payment by results said:

I agree with my Hon. friend that we have reached, and, indeed, I think we have long passed the time when we may place the fullest possible trust in the loyalty, honour and discretion of our teachers. . . . There is no class of men or women in the kingdom more entitled to our thanks and praise for the way in which they have conducted their work.[8]

The Instructions to Inspectors which accompanied the Code were drawn in a way to convince the teachers that their grievances had been understood and attended to. There was to be real freedom of classification and 'It is desirable that no difficulty should be experienced in the honest classification of scholars according to capacity and attainment.'[9]

Teachers had an absolute right to know what sums were set and to see the papers worked; they might themselves read out the dictation if their voice and manner were more familiar; irregular words were to be avoided even if they were short; intelligent reading was enough without a detailed knowledge of the matter of the book. There might even be silent reading. Any system of writing which produced a 'bold and legible' style would do, and 'Officers of the department were not at liberty to prescribe or recommend any particular book', and the familiar exhortation to the inspectors to hard and punctual work was included:

My Lords would again remind you that all hurry and undue haste on

377

the Day of Examination is incompatible with the proper discharge of your main duty.

This document must have been drawn up in consultation with the teachers; and, from the first, Kekewich recognized the N.U.T. as the teachers' official body and its officers as their spokesmen.

But after all the years of oppression and hatred something more was needed. A body of men do not forgo the pleasures of tyranny because of a document from Whitehall and the teachers could not so easily believe in a change of heart. The victim that was offered to the new order was the Rev. D. S. Stewart. He had been appointed in 1850 and had been a Chief Inspector for about twelve years at this time. He was hated by the teachers with peculiar passion. Pope, the president of the N.U.T., and Kekewich between them found a Minute under which they forced his resignation. The teachers were jubilant. Scorning the convention that one does not insult a fallen enemy, James Runciman wrote an article for the *Schoolmaster* of the bitterest abuse:[10]

When I think of the misery caused by that man I find it hard to restrain myself. His cynical contempt for fairness and common truthfulness make me indignant; and I know, only too well, how many fine young fellows have been hindered in life through his lazy and haphazard way of endorsing certificates. Why, that man would lounge round a school for 10 minutes, and then go away and write the same mechanical reports on the certificates of the whole staff.

How dare this insolent man talk to me, and at me, as if I were a spaniel? Is he my superior in blood, breeding or intellect? And yet, when I plead for a man at the crisis of his life, this government clerk takes it upon himself to jeer me.

The one example was enough. The Rev. Du Port, who was next on the teachers' list, allowed them to summon a meeting which he attended. He listened to their grievances—and promised amendment.

In another field Kekewich met the teachers' complaints. It was necessary every year to cancel or suspend the certificates of a few teachers for gross misconduct. The matter had been dealt with by the office—and there had been many doubts about the justice of the punishments. From now on, in every case, the Secretary of the N.U.T. went to the office, was shown all the papers, and invited to concur in the sentence. He almost always did. There was thus established a concordat with the teachers which was entirely beneficial.

The effects of the Code in the schools were also good. The teaching could be more interesting—there could be drill, cooking and science lessons and manual work at centres outside school. The evening schools no longer had to teach according to the standards, but might provide higher grade teaching. In fact, by general agreement, a great step in advance had been made in the cause of education, or as Sir Lyon Playfair said, 'It is a real revolution in the state of the education of the country. That revolution has been pending for some years.'

The final stage in this reorganization of Elementary education came in 1891 when arrangements were made to free the schools. For many years it had been clear that if education was compulsory it ought to be free. In 1885, when the matter was raised, the Conservatives opposed it strenuously, but it remained under consideration with questions asked in the House at intervals. By 1889 it was clear that action would have to be taken. The Scottish Education Department decided to use its share of the 'whiskey money'[11] to make all teaching under Standard V free. In England there was a different organization, and the money went elsewhere; but it was certain that something would soon be done. The education debates of 1890 are full of references to 'the Bill which the government intends to introduce next year', and it is mentioned in the Queen's speech outlining the forthcoming legislation. 'Your attention will be invited to the expediency of alleviating the burden which the law of compulsory attendances has in recent years imposed on the poorer portion of my people.'

The Prime Minister made speeches at Newport and Nottingham promising to 'assist education'. George Kekewich unkindly suggests that this was merely the manœuvre of a tottering Government to 'dish the Radicals', but it was quite clear that whoever held office would have to deal with the matter, and it might as well be the Conservatives.

The only real question was how best it could be managed. Any educational matter was still debated on sectarian grounds. The voluntary schools, staggering along in permanent inferiority to the Board Schools, were determined to resist any change that might harm them. The *Quarterly* in January 1891 deplored free education as a general principle: it might, it feared, destroy denominational schools, but it thought it useless to oppose it absolutely. The only thing to do was 'to try and influence the Bill so that it will do the minimum of harm'.

The plan which was produced in June was much more liberal than the Scottish measure, and of a charming simplicity and equality. Taking 3*d.* as the average fee charged in schools, it proposed to give to any school

379

that chose to accept it a grant of 10s. a year on average attendance for
children aged three to fourteen. If the school fees had been 3d. a week
or less, the school was now free—if the fees had been higher, the school
could still charge the difference. There were no conditions—except
those governing public elementary schools in general. There was, however, in the Bill a revolutionary proposal.

Section 5 gave to every parent an absolute right to free education—
and if no existing local school gave it, and refused to provide it, then
they must return to 1870 and call in a School Board. The clause attracted
little attention in the debates, but, in the event, in York and Liverpool
among other places very considerable building had to be done to meet
the parents' demands.

As with most educational matters the interest only extended to a few.
Halfway through the debate on the first reading the House was counted
to make sure forty were present, and the debate on the second reading
was hardly better attended. There was very little to urge against the
Bill. A few, like Talbot, the reactionary member for Oxford University,
saw in increased government help for education nothing but disaster
and a prospect of 'free meals, free clothes, free everything' as the
'natural consequences' of the Bill. But on the whole the tone of the
debate was well expressed by Picton, the opening speaker: 'The
peculiarity of this bill is that both sides of the House seem to compete
in eagerness to get it passed.' And passed it was, by an almost unanimous
vote in the Commons and with the blessing of the Archbishop of
Canterbury in the Lords.[12]

The results of the Act were generally agreed to be most beneficial.
When in June 1892 Sir William Hart-Dyke rose to make his report to
the 'sparsely filled benches' he could say:

The Act has been in all its operations a most conspicuous success. There
was a great influx of children into our schools . . . and the new Act has
worked admirably as regards attendance [and, perhaps more important
to a politician], no complaints have come from any part of the country.

Next year, Acland, the new Vice-President, had an even more
successful story to tell. The attendance in the year had increased by
120,000. The children were much more regular, and the schools were
thriving. He added the thought, new at this time, that 'if we want good
attendance, the schools must be happy and attractive places for the
children to go to'. It was worth the £6,200,000 for which he was asking.

380

In fact everyone was full of hope and confidence, and the teachers looked forward to a brighter future. 'Where are the 3 Rs now?' asked the *Schoolmaster*[13] jubilantly. 'No; the age of the 3 Rs is dead, buried and pulverized into invisible dust. We are gradually drawing the special subjects into the seine.'

Notes

1. P.P., 1889, LIX, 31.
2. P.P., 1888, XXXV, 122.
3. Hansard, CCCXXXV, 1656.
4. *Schoolmaster*, 20 July 1889.
5. Mr Yoxall, Nottingham; Mr Ernest Gray, N. W. Ham.
6. *The Education Department and After*, pp. 53 ff.
7. P.P., 1890, LC, 423.
8. Hansard, CCCXLIV, 626.
9. Minutes, 1889–90, p. 203; *Schoolmaster*, 12 April 1890, p. 533.
10. *Schoolmaster*, 10 January 1891, p. 65.
11. Under the Local Taxation Act, Customs and Excise (to be explained later).
12. Hansard, CCCLIII, 1834; CCCLIV, 1099.
13. *Schoolmaster*, 21 March 1891.

Chapter Eighteen

Secondary Education

The success of the primary schools meant that the great problem of the 1890s was the organization of Secondary Education. The pressure towards it came from two directions. For the first time in history nearly everybody could read; and the demand for literature passed to the book rather than the ballad; though at the beginning the subjects dealt with were much the same—tales of Maria Martin or Spring-heeled Jack, the Bad Boys Paper or stories of the ruin of poor girls 'told in the plainest words'—in fact, the typical 'penny dreadfuls'.

The multiplication of penny books was sufficient to attract attention. Both the *Edinburgh* and the *Quarterly* carried articles dealing with what one unkindly calls the 'Literature of the Streets', and said that the sales of these books ran into two million a week. 'This literature has done much', says the *Quarterly*,[1] 'to people our prisons, our Reformatories and our colonies with scapegraces and ne'er-do-wells.'

The religious publishers counter-attacked. The Religious Tract Society published the Boys' and Girls' Own Papers, and the Society for Promoting Christian Knowledge had its own Penny Library of Fiction. For those who could afford a little more there were sixpenny editions of *Westward Ho!*, *The Pilgrim's Progress* or *Oliver Twist*. Both the articles end with the hope that more and more good books will be published sufficiently cheaply for people to buy them.

There were also now free libraries; not many—only six in London—but the number and the use of them was increasing. The Museums and Libraries Act of 1850 allowed the councils in cities and boroughs to impose a halfpenny rate for the purpose of providing these amenities. By 1860 some twenty towns had adopted this Act, and the number

383

steadily increased. In Birmingham in the early 1870s out of a population of 343,000 some 10,000 people were using the library—and of these 7500 were under twenty-five—with a peak borrowing age of fourteen to twenty. The largest group were mechanics, with boys and apprentices next—the jewellers contributing 500.[2]

This reading public, of higher intellectual level than the readers of the penny fiction, shows that the spread of knowledge was taking place among the artisan classes, and that the younger generation were leading the way. The habit continued to grow, and by the 1890s had become one of the pleasures of life for many people. Naturally the demand was not confined to text-books, and fiction accounted for a large proportion, nearly 80 per cent, of the issues. In 1895, W. Roberts of 86 Grosvenor Road, S.W. felt that this excessive growth of novel reading constituted a social danger, and wrote to *The Times* (as well as to the *New Review*), saying that the free libraries were a complete failure from the point of view of their founders. They were '*not* intended to supply an unlimited quantity of fiction indiscriminately on the cheap'. They should be like the British Museum and only issue fiction when it was five years old.

At the other end of the scale the universities had developed in a remarkable way during the 1870s and 1880s. In 1869 Owen's College, Manchester, was refounded and began to flourish. It was followed by Armstrong College of Science, Newcastle-on-Tyne; the Yorkshire College of Science, Leeds; the University College of Nottingham; Masons College, Birmingham; Firth College, Sheffield; Bristol College; Liverpool College.

These colleges were founded by local effort to supply local needs, and they were staffed by men who felt themselves missionaries and spread their gospel of knowledge in all their districts. University extension lectures gathered people together—rich and poor—and led to a demand for greater facilities. In England this need was often met by the benefactions of the rich; in Wales by the pennies of the poor.

In the older universities women's colleges were founded, and over much of the country there was the open door of a university ready to welcome the student who was qualified to enter it.

Between the eager readers who had received a primary education, and the emergent universities was the gap that should have been filled by secondary education. Some attempts had been made, particularly in the education of girls. Miss Buss and Miss Beale had founded schools, and the Girls' Public Day School Company was providing a sound education in various cities after opening their first school in Chelsea in 1873. But such schools were few—and only for the more prosperous middle classes.

In England, on the whole, the firmly-held theory was that the state, as such, had no concern with secondary education, and that it should certainly not be paid for from public funds, central or local. If people wanted their children to have an education beyond the elements they must pay for it themselves unless, of course, there was an endowment which would provide it. England possessed a large number of educational endowments, and enquiry had shown both their size and the scandalous manner in which they were still wasted. In 1869, just before he passed his Elementary School Act, Forster passed the Endowed Schools Act which he hoped would enable these endowments to be put to their proper use. The plan was to empower the Endowed Schools Commissioners to prepare schemes for the different schools, and care was taken to overcome the schools' resistance and to prevent the matter getting lost in Chancery.

The Act did not accomplish all that was hoped. At first the Charity Commissioners had little educational experience. The foundations fought to retain their abuses; and, even when a scheme had been drawn up, there was no inspection to see that it was properly carried out. The work went on very slowly.

Even if all the schools had been reformed, there would still have been a most inadequate provision for secondary education. The existence of a school in any place was often an historical accident, and movements of population might change the character of a district, or leave a school without pupils. In spite of this obvious fact the English continued to hope that these schools might be enough, or that parents would be driven to provide for their own children through the agency of fee-paying schools.

In Scotland the Act of 1872 had explicitly given the School Boards the control of secondary education. This was in accord with the custom of the country which had always considered the higher grade burgh schools part of the public school system.

The hope of self-education could not be extended to Ireland. It was inevitable that some provision should be made in that country as soon as it was demanded. In 1878 the Irish Intermediate Education Act set up a Board of seven members, appointed by the Lord Lieutenant, to hold office during pleasure. The Board was an examining body which gave special scholarships, strictly on the results of examinations. The money to be provided by 'the Commissioners of Church Temporalities in Ireland who shall, out of property accruing to the Commissioners under the Irish Church Act, make available a sum not exceeding £1,000,000 a year'.

The organization was thus similar to that of the Department of Science and Art, but the scholarships were rather larger, held for two or three years, and the subjects of study more literary. 'Literature and history of Greece, Rome, Great Britain and Ireland, France, Germany and Italy—Mathematics, Natural Science', and for good measure— 'anything else that is approved'.

Wales at once made a claim for some similar provision for Secondary Education. A commission was appointed under Lord Aberdare to enquire into the matter and reported in 1882. It acknowledged that Wales was very lacking in Educational endowments, and, as what there were were Church of England foundations, they worked inequitably in a non-conformist country. The report recommended the establishment of higher grade Board schools, grammar schools and colleges. The only immediate result was that grants of £10,000 (rising to £12,000) were distributed to the three University Colleges.

The Government when pressed to say what action it meant to take on the schools pleaded that the matter was very difficult and contentious, and that it would rather leave it over for the present.

The difficulty was that there was, at the time, no body which could be entrusted with the control of secondary education. In Ireland, the Lord Lieutenant could be given the power of appointment and the bargaining for influence could take place in private. Moreover, as the Board was only an examining body it could hardly misuse its power for sectarian purposes. In Wales, where actual schools were desired, neither the Church nor the Nonconformist bodies could be given control without strife. It was much easier for the Government to do nothing.

The whole prospect for Secondary Education was changed by the Act of 1888 which established County and County Borough Councils. The Representation of the People Act of 1884 had extended the householder and lodger franchise, given to the boroughs in 1867, to the country; and had thus enfranchised larger numbers of industrial workers, miners and others, who lived outside the boroughs, as well as the agricultural workers. The Act of 1888 was the natural sequel, giving to the county a voice in local as well as central government. These new

County Councils provided the very type of authority that was needed for education. They were uncommitted to any party and they controlled considerable areas and populations.

Wales understood this at once, and the Welsh Intermediate Education Act followed immediately, being passed, as someone recalled, 'very late at night'. Under it Welsh County Councils were empowered to levy a halfpenny rate to which the Treasury would contribute an equal amount. The schools were to be controlled by Joint Education Committees of the County Councils, composed of three members nominated by the County Council and two persons nominated by the Lord President of the Council, who should choose persons well acquainted with Welsh needs, and preferably residing in the district. The Welsh completed the scheme, to the admiration of English reformers, by a Central Board for Intermediate Education which co-ordinated the work of the different counties and arranged for the best use of resources.

England was not yet prepared to use public funds for secondary education in general, but the permanent anxiety lest the superior technological instruction on the Continent should lead to a loss of British trade made the country more willing to provide technical schools. In 1884 the Royal Commission on Technical Instruction had stated:

> It is desirable that in the proposed reorganization of Local Government power should be given to important local bodies, like the proposed County Boards and the municipal corporations, to originate and supply secondary and technical schools. . . .
>
> Intelligent youths of the artisan classes should have easy access to secondary and technical schools by numerous scholarships, and the more promising students among them again to the higher technical colleges. . . .

Now that the 'local bodies' had come into existence, part at least of the recommendation could be carried out. In 1889, under the Technical Instruction Act, County and Borough Councils were permitted to levy a penny rate for technical and manual instruction, and by the further Act of 1891 they could give scholarships to enable poor boys to take advantage of it.

This was a good principle, but the cost of establishing the intermediate schools in Wales or the technical schools in England was high, and they might never have come into being except for a most extraordinary series of chances. In 1890, in the hope of encouraging temperance, a Bill was brought in raising the duties on spirits, and appropriating some of the resultant money to compensating publicans whose

387

licences were to be extinguished. The proposal for compensation met with the most determined opposition.³ The debate raged for twenty-five days, and, at last, the Government were glad to accept a compromise proposal that the 'whiskey money'—otherwise called the 'residue'—should be given to the County Councils to be used—if they saw fit—for education. If they did not wish to use it for education they might use it to reduce the rates. In Scotland, as we have said, it was used to remove school fees for children under Standard V. In Wales it was at once applied to the Intermediate Schools. In England, tentatively at first, and then more boldly, it was used for technical education in the towns and for agricultural schools in the country.

In the first year the amount available for England and Wales was about £800,000. The doubt in the minds of the promoters of schools was whether they could rely on a similar sum being granted each year. In reply to questions in Parliament the Government gave assurances that it would be a permanent grant and that the Councils could proceed with confidence. The County Councils thus had a considerable sum which they could devote to educational schemes under their own control, and they became, from that time, autonomous authorities in charge of a considerable part of the national education.

The confusion of educational agencies in England was now extreme. There were the School Boards officially charged with the provision of elementary education, but more and more intruding into the junior secondary stage. They and the Elementary schools were supervised and grant-aided by the Department of Education in Whitehall. There were the County Councils allowed to provide Technical education without any supervision. The Charity Commissioners were trying, with increasing success, to organize the endowed schools. The Department of Agriculture took an interest in rural education. The Department of Science and Art at South Kensington gave its grants impartially to whoever earned them, and asked no questions. The private schools, of all grades, struggled on, usually in poverty and squalor. All these were surveyed in a book, *Studies in Secondary Education*, published in 1892 under the editorship of Arthur Acland.

Acland was at the time engaged with an abortive Education Bill and next year became Vice-President of the Council, in charge of Education. It was natural that he should set up a Commission, under the chairmanship of James Bryce, to survey the whole field. It reported on 1 November 1895.⁴ The book and the Report of the Commission can be read together. They both give the same picture of confusion, duplication and inadequacy.

Said the Commission:

The problems which Secondary Education presents have been approached from different sides, at different times, and with different views and aims. The Charity Commissioners have had little to do with the Education Department and still less with the Science and Art Department. Even the borough councils have, to a large extent, acted independently of the school boards, and have, in some instances, made their technical instruction grants with too little regard for the parallel grants which were being made by the Science and Art Department.

Their isolation and their independence . . . will nevertheless prepare the observer to expect the usual results of dispersed and unconnected forces, needless competition between the different agencies, and a frequent overlapping of effort with much consequent waste of money, of time and of labour.

Not a single county in England could give a clear or even approximately comprehensive picture of all the schools in its area; there is no list, no register, no organization as far as secondary schools are concerned.

The result, as Matthew Arnold had pointed out some years before, was that 'our middle classes are among the worst educated in the world . . . and our body of secondary schools the most imperfect and unserviceable in civilized Europe'.

We may, perhaps, start at the bottom of this curious disorder of schools. The greater School Boards had a system of higher grade schools and organized science schools, both groups giving the rudiments of secondary education. The numbers of these higher grade schools or organized science schools had been growing in the towns. In 1894 there were in England—exclusive of London—60 of these schools which took the children after they had passed all or most of the ordinary standards. Some took the children after they had passed Standard VII, others when they had passed Standard IV. In the former case all the work done was for the examinations of the Department of Science and Art, in the latter, part was for the examinations held under the Code, and the rest for South Kensington. Of these 60 schools, 39 were organized science schools with laboratories and science lecture-rooms. A large proportion of the whole had manual workshops and cookery kitchens. These schools were almost all in large towns—48 in County Boroughs. Outstanding examples were the school in Deansgate, Manchester, and the Standard VII school in Birmingham.[5]

These schools met a need, and were eagerly attended, and their existence was most important as the general standard of education rose. Their finance was composite. For example the Birmingham Standard VII school in 1890 was supported as follows:

		£
By:	Grants from South Kensington	1062
	Grants from Whitehall	141
	Fees	175
	Books sold	4
By:	Rates	797
		£2179

The important thing in this statement, in view of later history, is the part of the cost borne by the rates. But, at the time, what most concerned the critics was the impossibility of classifying the school definitely:

That as the meaning and limits of the term 'elementary' have not been defined in the Education Acts, nor by any judicial or authoritative interpretation but depend only upon the annual Codes of the Department on whose power of forming such codes no limit has hitherto been imposed, it would appear to be of absolute necessity that some definition of the instruction to be paid for out of the rates and taxes should be put forward by the legislature. Until this is done the limits of primary and secondary education cannot be defined.

In fact the present system offers a temptation so to enlarge the curriculum as practically to convert primary schools into secondary schools in which a portion of the cost of the education of the children of wealthier persons would be defrayed out of the rates or Imperial funds.[6]

It recommended 'That the State should recognize the distinction between elementary and secondary education to a greater degree than had yet been attempted. . . . If the curriculum of higher elementary schools is restricted within due limits—they may prove to be a useful addition to our school machinery for primary education.'

There was even more ambiguity about the position of the evening continuation schools. After 1890 they were relieved from the necessity of making elementary education the major part of their work, and in later years were encouraged to attract students by higher-grade or recreational classes. A large proportion of their students were adults and few needed elementary instruction. They were even more dependent on the rates than the schools for younger children.

Above these were secondary schools of different types, including the technical schools. These latter the County Councils were specifically permitted to support. There was more doubt about their rights where more general secondary education was concerned, and various methods were adopted in different districts. Some Councils co-operated with the Charity Commissioners in the development of an endowed school, others gave grants to secondary schools which had been started by other agencies. For example, Cambridgeshire in 1890 gave £400, the West Riding £2611 and Northumberland £86 5s. By 1895 the Councils were feeling more confident of their rights, and in nine areas were in process of founding their own secondary schools. In other cases the County Councils made no contribution to secondary education and Bedford, Bucks, Middlesex and Dorset were among the eighteen who failed to do so.

Even where there were schools they were haphazard and conformed to no plan. Birmingham, with the great King Edward foundation, was unique in having schools arranged in an ordered system. London was unique in its Technical Education Board, which, instituted in 1893, included representatives from all the major educational agencies within the capital. The Board had twenty members drawn from the County Council and also representatives of the School Board, City and Guilds of London Institute, London Parochial Charities, the Headmasters' Association, the N.U.T. and the London Traders' Council. It was thus able to know what was needed, and to plan and institute schools of the right type, including special Trade Schools for localized industries, such as printing in Fleet Street and furniture-making in Shoreditch.

Apart from this tentative public provision of education were the ubiquitous private secondary schools which met the needs of lower middle class parents by providing a cheap education. These schools lived on the grants that they obtained from South Kensington and therefore taught only those subjects for which grants were given, and which did not involve expensive equipment. The literary subjects were therefore excluded and science was taught without practical work. The book *Studies in Secondary Education* gives an account of the Liverpool Institution to show the unsatisfactory nature of these schools. The buildings were bad, dark, cold and insanitary, and the children grossly overworked in taking a succession of unrelated subjects which were learnt parrot fashion.

Boys of 13 come at 8.15 and work 8 hours in ill-ventilated class-rooms and have 3 hours' homework.

The cause of this system is the custom of allowing the masters to receive ¾ of the grants received and paying them miserable salaries. The boys are farmed out to those masters who are lucky enough to teach science subjects to make what they can out of them. One boy earned 30 science certificates in less than 5 years, making £10 a year for his teacher when he was supposed to be getting an education.

The boys of 12 or 13 fresh from the elementary schools are sturdy, healthy and full of life, the older boys are in many cases ill-formed, narrow shouldered, stooping and suffering from weak eyesight.

The state of Liverpool Institute and College shows that Secondary Education for the poorer classes cannot be self-supporting. These schools will continue to fall below the average Board School until they receive some kind of public recognition and control.

Every fault in the Institute could be removed by proper endowment or State aid. At present it receives about £1000 from Imperial grants, but it is received in the worst possible way, and accompanied by all the worst evils of payment by results.

Even such provision as this was not universal. The *Studies* comments:

Many of the more backward districts have so little to show in the way of Secondary Schools that it would scarcely be worthwhile to describe the paltry provision that exists. If Birmingham is a specimen of a town with a large, well-ordered endowment, Liverpool is an equally large area almost entirely destitute of such foundations.

This was becoming well known and Acland summed up the general feeling in his resolution:

In the interests of technical, commercial and agricultural instruction, as well as of general education, it is indispensable that the attention of the Government should be no longer limited to primary education . . . but should be extended to the secondary education of the Country which should be under the supervision of a responsible minister.

Some attempt to organize secondary education was clearly due, but, while the Bryce Commission was still considering its report, a fresh crisis had arisen with the voluntary schools. This was precipitated by Circular 321.[7] Innocent-seeming and moderate in tone, it was nevertheless recognized as a serious threat. It was addressed to the inspectors and began:

'My Lords are desirous of obtaining a fuller and more detailed statement about the condition of the different schools'; and the inspectors were therefore asked to fill up a form about each of the schools in their districts.

It is, of course, not to be understood that, in every case where the school is to some extent defective, you are required to press for an immediate alteration. . . . In that matter you will, as heretofore, use your discretion.

The form then asked such questions as: 'Is the school dry, in good repair, well-ventilated?' 'Are the staircases adequate?' 'Are there cloak-rooms?'

No standards were laid down in the inquisition, and the inspectors were apparently supposed to judge as 'reasonable men'. The effect, however, of the enquiry was considerable. The Annual Report of 1895 states:

Owing in a large measure to the special reports which we instructed Your Majesty's Inspectors to make to us in 1892–3 on the buildings and premises of all schools in receipt of Government Grants the expenditure on structural alterations and extraordinary repairs has recently been very large.

This demand for increased expenditure brought into prominence the unsatisfactory state of the great body of voluntary schools. Since 1870 they had been gradually falling back as compared with the Board schools, both in premises and teaching staff; and there was now no doubt that the Board schools were very superior. They could ask what they wished from the rates, and the County Councils, which provided the money, had no power to control their expenditure. As a result the Board schools enjoyed, on the average, an income of 10s. per child per year more than the voluntary. From this inequality it followed that the teachers in the voluntary schools were less well paid—to the extent of about 9s. per child per year, and had 1s. per child less to spend in books and apparatus.[8] It followed also that as the less skilful teachers took posts in the voluntary schools, the standard of work was lower and the Government grant less. All this was freely admitted. In perhaps half of rural England the Church school had no competitor, but in the towns, or where a School Board ran a rival school, there was danger of the extinction of denominational education.

All through 1894 and the early part of 1895 *The Times* carried letters protesting about the plight of the voluntary schools and proposing schemes for their assistance. The voluntary schools were, of course, predominantly Church schools, but there were also Roman Catholic,

393

Jewish and Wesleyan, all of whom insisted on their own catechisms. The Government saw in their demand a means of strengthening their position, and on 20 September 1895 a clear hint was given that an agreed scheme for the help of these schools would be favourably considered. Unfortunately no scheme received general approval; and the frequent exhortations to the religious bodies to get together and plan produced only a very select gathering of churchmen.

The interest in this matter was diverted by the publication of the Bryce report.[9] The main provisions of the report were (1) the formation of a Central Education Authority consisting of a Minister, with control of all types of education and a unified secretariat, assisted by a small Educational Council; (2) the formation of Local Education Authorities which should be formed from the Councils of Counties or County Boroughs and should have a mixed membership. These would take charge of Secondary Education and be empowered to survey the present provision and supplement it where necessary. It was further proposed that higher grade schools should be acknowledged to be secondary, and should be detached from the School Boards and administered by the Local Education Authority. Otherwise the School Boards were left untouched. The commissioner felt that the matter was urgent:

> Of the loss incurred through the want of such coherence and correlation it is impossible to speak too strongly. Unfortunately, so far from tending to cure itself, it is an evil which every day strikes its roots deeper. The existing authorities and agencies whose want of co-operation we lament, are each of them getting more accustomed to the exercise of their present powers and less disposed to surrender them. . . .

All this was in accordance with the general opinion on the subject, and *The Times* said: 'The Commissioners' Report is an attractive one'— but before any action could be taken on it, while the Government might be thought to be considering their policy, the agitation in favour of the voluntary schools recommenced.

In the latter part of November 1895 a great deputation waited on the Prime Minister. There were the two Archbishops and many lesser dignitaries. The *Schoolmaster*,[10] rather jeeringly, records the occasion:

> Rather more than 200 persons, chiefly ecclesiastical dignitaries, but with lords, dukes and knights and members of parliament among them, gathered in a gloriously gilded apartment of the Foreign Office, and, after waiting for about a quarter of an hour, all rise and applaud as a door at the

end of the room swings open, and there appears Lord Salisbury, the chief figure in the ultimatum-while-you-wait epoch.

The demands, which the Archbishop presented, asked for—among other things—

An increase of contributions from public sources sufficient to meet the increased cost of education throughout the country—and a rearrangement of all Government grants so that poorer schools may share equally with richer schools in these grants.

They asked, moreover, that the rating powers of the School Boards should be subordinated to the control of some other body, and that arrangements should be made for special denominational religious instruction to be given in Board Schools on demand.

The Government expressed itself sympathetic, but there was criticism. Some of the more liberal clerics disowned their own body and argued that to ask for more public money without conceding full religious liberty was unreasonable. For example, the Bishop of Hereford, Dr Percival, wrote:

In all schools that are largely supported by public money the local public ought, in common justice, to have some share in the management and be consulted on the character of the religious instruction. There was a great deal of insincerity in the common use of this cry. The real object of the present struggle is to secure larger grants from the State and yet to hold on to the exclusive denominational appointment of teachers. . . . No voluntary school ought to receive larger grants from the public purse so long as its managers are prohibited by its Trust deeds from employing any teacher who is a Nonconformist.

The Dean of Ripon agreed with him.

The teachers considering the Archbishops' proposals noted that no increase in the total amount expended on education was contemplated, but only a rearrangement which took from the School Boards to support the voluntary schools. They argued that before any step be taken to give more money to the voluntary schools an audit must be established of their accounts. They also regarded the demand for denominational instruction in Board schools with great hostility.

The Government was more complaisant. When in the Spring of 1896 it introduced its Bill, it hoped first of all for Church support. In the speech which Sir John Gorst made on 31 March introducing the Bill he started with a long passage about the achievements and needs of the

395

voluntary schools.[11] He went on to recite the case of the smaller School
Boards which, with a rate of 1s. 6d. or more in the £, still could not pay
their teachers adequately or provide fittingly for their children, and
offered help.

Having proffered this bribe to his supporters, he set out the main
clauses of the Bill. Its first and most important said that every County
and County Borough should set up an Education Committee of which
the majority must be members of the Council, and the others co-opted
in various ways. This would take charge of education in its district, but
its function was 'to supplement what existed, not to supplant it'—The
Local Authority was to have charge of technical and secondary education and might establish and manage any secondary school and train
teachers. The Education Department might transfer to its charge any
school or department maintained by a School Board which 'in the
opinion of the Education Department is other than Elementary'. For
money it might use rates, administer the 'residue' under the Local
Taxation Acts and the grants from the Department and Science and
Art.

Where there was no School Board the Local Authority became the
authority for elementary education, taking the place of the Attendance
Committee, and any School Board which was in default lost its powers
to the Local Authority. Moreover any School Board which wished might
transfer its schools.

The Bill thus clearly threatened to deprive the School Boards of their
higher grade schools and suggested that in time the Boards might wither
away altogether. More immediately, clause 26 stabilized the School
Board rate at its present level and thus prohibited an extension of its
work.

In the next group of clauses it proposed a grant-in-aid to voluntary
schools and poor Board schools of 4s. per head per year. This money
was to be applied to improving the teaching staff, and be liable to audit.
Lastly, clause 27 decreed that in public elementary schools 'if parents
of a reasonable number of scholars attending the school require separate
religious instruction to be given to their children the managers shall as
far as possible provide it'.

The Bill passed its second reading by the large majority of 267, but it
did so with the aid of the Irish group whose support was only temporary; and thereafter the Bill was left with few friends—but as the
centre of much interest. For the first time, apparently, an education bill

was a matter of general public attention and the papers all commented on it.[12] Said the *Schoolmaster*: 'Scarcely a parliamentary candidate in the general election of 1892 mentioned education—scarcely a candidate in 1895 left it out.' The notices of the Bill in the papers followed the common lines of policy. *The Times* said it was 'a well-considered effort to save the voluntary schools'. The *Daily Chronicle* that it was 'a Bill for the destruction of the School Boards and for the State endowment of denominationalism'. The *Standard* treated it as 'a bold comprehensive and statesmanlike measure' and the *Leeds Mercury* as 'the most extraordinary scheme ever concocted out of Bedlam'.

The main opposition came from three parties, the School Boards who were determined to fight for their existence, the smaller boroughs who did not wish to be merged in the County Education Committees, and, most bitter of all, the opponents of clause 27—the Nonconformists who saw all their victories in the School Boards swept away, and the teachers who regarded it as threatening to reintroduce the sectarian strife that the Board schools had so happily transcended. Moreover they considered it unworkable. Their opposition was all the sharper because Athelstan Riley was once more threatening to block the promotion of all teachers who refused to promise to teach in accordance with his views.[13]

In the committee stage the Government was overwhelmed by amendments. The earliest, accepted by Arthur Balfour—against the wish of Sir John Gorst—provided that there should be an Education Authority in every borough over 20,000 inhabitants. This increased the number of projected authorities from 126 to 222. This, the Government said, destroyed the real point of the Bill, and, faced with an apparently endless fight, it withdrew it. But, if the Bill died, it died in glory. The announcement of the abandonment of the Bill on 22 June was made into a social occasion.

The scene in the House of Commons this afternoon was enthralling and will become historic. There was a great concourse of spectators. Never during this Parliament have the green benches and the members' galleries been so full. The Peers' Gallery was crammed. The Strangers' Gallery had not a seat to spare. The stone cage above the press gallery was full of gorgeous-hued 'birds', the ladies who preferred the scene to the terrace. . . .[14]

No one was sorry for the Bill's death, except the 'Church party' who were 'glum'.

Still, the Government did what it could for them; and in the course of the next year quietly arranged for the distribution of some £100,000 to the necessitous schools both voluntary and Board.

After this defeat, the Government changed its tactics. It realized, perhaps, that it had tried to do too much at once, and that it had chosen the wrong allies. In the next six years it worked continually, achieving one point after another, till it carried, in 1902, the Bill which set the whole education of the country on a new footing.

The teachers also had plans which they were hoping would be realized in the next Bill. In these years their two great grievances were the right their employers had of dismissal without appeal, and the extent to which managers, especially clerical ones, still demanded extraneous duties as a condition of employment. A teacher who taught all the week felt it a hardship to be compelled to spend the whole of Sunday playing the organ or teaching Sunday School—or he objected to his wife's unpaid work as sewing mistress being a condition of his retaining his post.

In regard to dismissal the Department had consistently refused to intervene, saying that it was not a party to the contract and therefore could do nothing. Instead the N.U.T. took its own action. Its Tenure Committee investigated every case reported. The smaller School Boards in rural districts were as bad offenders as voluntary managers, and most issues of the *Schoolmaster* in these years have something to report. The action taken was always energetic. If the Union's mediator was repulsed, the funds of the Union were made available. Sometimes in the case of a voluntary school the teacher was enabled to open a new school, as close as possible to the old one, and, if his children followed him, the offending school was deserted. If in a Board school an election was nearly due, all the energies of the Union were thrown into running candidates who would support the dismissed teachers. In most cases three or four of the teacher's supporters would be elected, and he would be reinstated. If the teacher decided to give up teaching, the Union would then run him for membership of the School Board—and he was frequently elected top of the poll.

This went on up and down the country, and kept the rights of teachers before employers and the public. In the same way, in Parliament, the teachers' case was continually put. There were now three teacher members, Gray, Yoxall and Macnamara, and they allowed very little to pass unnoticed that was of interest to their body. Thus when the time did come, the modifications which the teachers desired were accepted readily into the Bill.

The teachers themselves were changing. There is no doubt that they were more prosperous. At the suitable times of the year the *Schoolmaster* has pages devoted to holidays in the British Isles or overseas; the advertisement pages have pictures of smart suits. The Pension Bill finally passed in 1898 and there was something other than penury to look forward to.

The younger teachers had a rather wider outlook. The conditions for pupil teachers continued to improve and the training colleges had begun to change—perhaps as a result of the earlier scathing report. The inspector records in 1896 that more were providing recreation rooms (St John's, Battersea did so in that year) and other reasonable amenities: 'Many obsolete rules have been abolished, more liberty is allowed and the students are coming to be treated as grown up people not children.' Games were being played more frequently.[15]

The day training colleges, which had been proposed by the Cross Commission as a means of alleviating the shortage of teachers, had come into being.[16] They were managed by committees in close association with a university. The University supplied the academic teaching, and special lecturers were appointed to teach education and supervise the work in schools. At first their condition in many cases was not happy. The report on the one in Birmingham said:

The rooms in which the college is lodged form part of the Midland Institute, which is closely contiguous to Mason College. They are dingy, ill-lighted for the most part, and not comfortably or suitably furnished, and they are approached by two flights of steep stairs. The recreation is especially deficient. It is under consideration to bring the college into fuller connection with Mason College.

It was not long before the college crossed the road, and began the intimate association with the university which lasted till 1950. Other colleges developed in much the same way.

The universities also were taking a part in teachers' training—not only for secondary schools. 'All the University Colleges in England and Wales,' says the report of 1894, 'with Oxford and Cambridge, are now training teachers. The students, considering their previous education, have done very well. Some Universities treat them as equal students, some as inferior, but the best is very good.' Aberystwyth, in particular, allowed them to live in hall and did not segregate them in any way.

The day training colleges made one very important contribution—the idea that a university career could be pursued concurrently with training. This had been accepted since 1891[17] when the regulations for the Certificate Examination allowed the substitution, in each year, of a university examination in place of the academic part of the Department's syllabus. This permission was naturally more appropriate to the day colleges, which were in such close relation with a university, but some students in other colleges availed themselves of it. In 1896, 217 training college students passed approved university examinations, 86 from the resident colleges and the rest from the day colleges.

The Department was also sanctioning a third-year course, which might be spent abroad. For example in 1894 three girls from Stockwell and two men from the Borough Road had been to France and had written theses to show their progress.

There was also an attempt to introduce some philosophy and history of education to the course. In 1891 the prescribed books for the second year were Herbert Spencer's *On Education*, chapters 2 and 3, Locke's *Thoughts Concerning Education*, paragraphs 140–95, and in the third year two of the three following: *Life and Work of Thomas Arnold*, Quick, *Educational Reformers*, Bain, *Education as a Science*. Quick was the most popular choice. The Rev. R. H. Quick, Vicar of Sedburg, and formerly University Lecturer at Cambridge in the History of Education, published his book in 1874 and it went through many editions. It dealt with the schools of the Jesuits, Ascham, Comenius, Locke, Rousseau, Basedow, Pestalozzi, Jacotot, and Herbert Spencer. It was not well adapted to its purpose and the report on the certificate papers shows that methods of teaching had not greatly changed, even if the subject-matter was more advanced.

Quick's 'Educational Reformers'

The memories of many of the men must be very retentive, for they often reproduced the very sentences and in many cases too the very long German words used by Mr Quick which, as they probably did not understand the language, was the more remarkable.

The other subjects, too, had been learned in the same manner.

Report on Political Economy

[Papers] were one and all redolent of the text-book, and it was easy to trace in nearly every case the books—some unfortunately rather antiquated—which had been in use in the different colleges. As a consequence dogmatism appears everywhere from the very definitions to the discussion of such burning questions as bimetallism.

Salvation is still supposed to be found in a study of the text-book—and in that alone.

Report on Examinations in general

Wherever a 'book' question occurs, it is attempted by most of the candidates and generally with success. In those questions however where text-books give only an indirect form of aid . . . the answers show every variety of merit or demerit just as the candidate has observed and thought, or depended upon the suggestions of the text-book mainly or entirely.

The slight liberalization of the training colleges was concurrent with the slackening of tension in the schools. From 1895 onwards it was possible for a good school to escape altogether the annual inspection and to be judged and its grant assessed on the impression formed by the inspector in one or two unannounced visits. The system spread rapidly. By 1897, 88 per cent were excused annual inspections and the struggle to be ready for the great day was over. As one inspector wrote, 'The new system is in one sense an educational revolution.' But the schools were slow to make the most of the opportunities. He adds: 'Teaching has always been one of the most conservative of professions . . . and teachers are very loath to admit any change in their methods.' So we can imagine that over most of England the words of another inspector were true:

During the past 2 years the schools throughout the division have been making steady progress on the old lines. Few teachers have ventured to make experiments with the variety of course now available.

In accordance with this policy the inspectors were instructed to mitigate the severity of their questions.[18] They were warned when hearing reading not to ask too many questions on words and phrases in the reading book, 'it is difficult for young scholars to give the meaning of a word by a synonym or to paraphrase a passage in simple language'. In geography they were advised to visit a school at the beginning of the year and agree with the teacher just what the syllabus should contain. Grammar should be much simplified and history was *not* to consist simply of lists of names or authors and the 'Teaching of Science which consists in learning definitions or numerical calculations by heart is especially to be avoided'. In the best schools the daily grind was diversified by drawing, manual work, cookery, drill, games and swimming.

The scholarship system was also being developed. In London, from about 1893 there were 600 junior scholarships for children under thirteen for two years; 100 intermediate; 7 or 8 senior to be held at a university. Both boys and girls from the elementary schools went to Oxford or Cambridge, and the *Schoolmaster* published each year a list of the wranglers who had started their education in the elementary schools.

The final liberation of the schools came with the Code of 1900. All the piecemeal grants were swept away and the schools received capitation grants of 17s. for infant children, and 22s. for older. The inspectors were able to reduce the grants by only a shilling for defects, and the only additional payments were for cooking and manual instruction.

Notes

1. *Quarterly Review*, July 1890, p. 152.
2. J. A. Langford, *Modern Birmingham and its Institutions* (1873).
3. Hansard, CCCXLIV, 701 ff.
4. P.P., 1895, XLIII, Bryce Report.
5. P.P., 1888, XXXV, 179, 189.
6. P.P., 1888, XXXV, 241, 243.
7. 21 January 1893.
8. P.P., 1878–9, LVII, 179; Minutes, 1877–8, p. 372.
9. P.P., 1895, XLIII–XLVI.
10. *Schoolmaster*, 23 November 1895.
11. Hansard, XXXIX, 526.
12. *Schoolmaster*, 26 December 1896.
13. Gautrey, *Lux Mihi Laus*, p. 102.
14. *Schoolmaster*, 27 June 1896.
15. *Schoolmaster*, 19 July 1890, p. 81.
16. Report of Cross Commission, p. 98.
17. Minutes, 1890–1, pp. 536 ff.; 1896–7, p. vi.
18. *Instructions to H.M.I.s*, 1896.

Chapter Nineteen

The defeat of the School Boards

The failure of the Education Bill in 1896 left the Government as determined as ever to organize and unify education, and it also left them with a juster knowledge of the forces arrayed against them and of the value of the support of certain groups. It was clear that the time was not ripe for another large Bill, and the next five years were in consequence a period of preparation for the next attempt.

The first necessity was to destroy the power of the great School Boards who would resist any scheme of true organization. They were very powerful, especially as the Nonconformist sentiment of the country was fully behind them. They were also supported by the teachers, who had by now learnt to control their elections and consequently their policy. What the School Boards lost the County Councils must gain, and their development as an organizing force must be encouraged. Lastly, before any unified local control could be established, the Central Office must be so reorganized that a single body controlled all the educational activities at present scattered among so many different agencies.

The three men of power in these years were Sir John Gorst the Vice-President, Robert Morant of the Department of Special Enquiries and later Gorst's personal Secretary, and Dr. William Garnett, Secretary of the Technical Education Board of the London County Council. Gorst was a lawyer-politician who, like Lowe before him, had spent some time in the Antipodes (though this time it was New Zealand). He had returned with no love of democracy and a determination to impose order on his chaotic charge. Robert Morant had been the Victorian good young man, with high ideals and an interest in the welfare of boys. In 1886—twenty years after Anna Leonowens—he had gone out to Siam to continue the work of educating the royal family. In the eight years that he stayed in the country he dreamed of organizing a national system of education; but the British and French territorial ambitions made Europeans unpopular. In 1894 he was back in England, in poor health and without work. Fortunately for him, on 1 January 1895 the Department of Special Enquiries was formed by the Education Department under Michael Sadler, and Morant was appointed Assistant Director at a salary of £300, rising to £500. Morant was able, determined and a hard worker. He had the perfect bureaucrat's power of writing penetrating memoranda and devising ingenious regulations. If Gorst disliked the School Boards because they were democratic, Morant was concerned for their effect on the voluntary schools. Nor did he like the militant teachers, as the Holmes–Morant circular was to show later. Dr William Garnett was one of the dedicated band of educational missionaries, and, after a fellowship at Cambridge and a Whitworth scholarship, had been the chief creator of Nottingham University College and the College of Science at Newcastle-on-Tyne. In 1893 when the L.C.C. felt secure enough to turn its attention to education, he took charge of its Technical Education Board, which rapidly found itself in direct competition with many of the schools and evening classes run by the School Board. Thus each of the three had a more than official interest in destroying the School Boards. These were three very powerful men, and their only official opponent was George Kekewich, the Secretary, who, perhaps because he had once been offered the Secretaryship of the London School Board, still believed in the system. But he was nearing retiring age, and it was easy for Gorst to take Morant as his confidante and chief assistant, and by-pass the amiable elder.

These men had a good case—they were far too clever to accept a bad one. The School Boards had outlived their usefulness, and their boundaries fixed, inevitably, by the circumstances of the times, were now completely anachronistic. The great urban School Boards had done most valuable work, the smaller Borough Boards had been a great help, but the rural ones were in many cases a failure and completely obstructive. Moreover the School Boards did not cover the country. Of the 12,000 civil parishes in England, all charged with the duty of educating their own children, 2000 had School Boards, the remainder relied on voluntary effort. These 2000 School Boards controlled 4352 schools. As the bigger boards controlled several schools, the great number of the Boards could have had only one school in their charge. The small numbers of inhabitants in many of the districts made any efficient organization impossible. There were 151 Boards with from 1 to 250 inhabitants in their districts, 448 with 251 to 500, and 385 with 501 to 750. Nobody could seriously defend these minute districts, but, if they were to be extinguished, the great urban Boards could hardly, in logic, remain, now that the County Councils existed. The County Councils seemed to have other advantages beside their size. The anomaly by which the School Boards were allowed to demand any sum they liked from the rates, without the control of a larger authority, was felt to put a dangerous power in their hands. Secondly, as the School Boards were elected for the one purpose only, and as the elections aroused comparatively little general interest (the poll being often only 20 per cent of the electorate), it was easy for the teachers to gain control of them. How much safer to give the management of education to a body elected for a number of purposes and controlling all the finances of the district. The County Councils were likely to be less expansionist in education, and less open to the influence of interested parties. Considering these things, now that the legislative attempt to cripple or destroy the School Boards had failed for the time, the triumvirate turned to administrative action which could be taken without reference to public opinion.

As far as elementary education went the School Boards were in an unassailable legal position. They could only be destroyed by act of Parliament. However, much of the work of the greater School Boards was of a very different kind. The pride and weakness of these Boards were their higher grade schools and evening continuation schools. There is little doubt that both types of schools were of doubtful legality, there is no doubt that it had been the policy of the Education Department to encourage them, especially since 1890. For years the District Auditors had been surcharging items of expenditure in connection with these schools, and the Local Government Board had been consulting the Education Department as to policy. Sometimes at the request of the Department the decision had been given against the auditor, sometimes his decision had been upheld but the surcharge remitted. From 1890, when Cockerton succeeded the more militant Lloyd Roberts as Auditor in London, and Kekewich became Secretary, the policy was in favour of the School Boards, and the influence of the Auditor declined. In consequence, the higher grade schools increased and the evening continuation schools dealt more and more with adults, offering, on the one hand purely recreational classes, and, on the other, advanced work to a high

406

standard. It was against this part of the Boards' work that the attack was launched.

Both higher grade schools and evening continuation schools drew a considerable part of their revenues, as has been said, from the grants of the Department of Science and Art, which fell, like rain, impartially. In the big towns there was some central organization of grant-earning classes; but in the counties a great part of the work for these grants was done by classes here and there, organized by any body of managers which was willing to do it, and without any general direction. It was obviously expedient that some central body should be made responsible for the co-ordination of these classes. Consequently, in 1897 the Science and Art Directory contained a new Clause VII, offering the opportunity for organization:

> In Counties and County Boroughs which possess an organization for the promotion of Secondary Education, such organization, if recognized by the Department, may notify its willingness to be responsible to the Department for the Science and Art instruction in its area. In such cases grants will in general be made to the managers of new schools only if they are acting in union with such organization.

The 'organization for the promotion of Secondary Education' was clearly the Committee of the County Council charged with this duty, and the Clause would, if accepted, place all further development of higher grade and evening schools under its control. It was asserted that in the Counties the Clause was gladly accepted,[1] and that it served to bring the beginnings of order. The London School Board, on the other hand, saw the threat it contained, and promptly applied to be recognized as an 'organization for the promotion of secondary education' in opposition to the Technical Education Board of the L.C.C. The two bodies appeared to argue their case at South Kensington in the presence of Sir John Gorst with Donnelly in the chair. The decision, as had been predetermined, was in favour of the Technical Education Board; but it was recognized that the decision was of great importance, and, before it was published, it was submitted for Cabinet approval. During the discussion, the School Board claimed that under the Education Code (1890) Act they had the right to give education at any level to adults in evening classes, and to some, at least, of the children in higher grade schools. This Act, rushed through to legalize the Code of 1890 said, Clause I:

> It shall not be required as a condition of a parliamentary grant to an evening school that elementary education shall be the principal part of

407

the education there given, and so much of the definition of the term 'elementary school' in §3 of the Elementary Education Act of 1870 as required that elementary education shall be the principal part of the education given in an elementary school shall not apply to evening schools.

The Parliamentary taunt that the Education Department whether it was 'loquacious' or 'reticent' was always 'obscure' could have applied very well to this Act; and the claims which the London School Board based on it were so wide that the Government were alarmed. The decision which recognized the County Council as the organization for secondary education was a warning to the School Boards and served to prevent any expansion of their work, but it did not, of itself, invalidate their claim to the legal right to continue their more advanced work.

In general this check was felt to be necessary, for, as Sir E. Clarke had said in the debate on the 1896 Bill, 'If parliament would only leave secondary education alone for ten years, the elementary teachers and the school boards would have got the whole system into their hands.'[2] Sir John Gorst and his team, as well as Balfour, the Prime Minister, were not going to have secondary education organized from the bottom—they felt it could be done better and more economically from the top.

After this partial victory, Gorst was content to leave the London School Board for a while, and to turn to the next step—the organization of a central authority.[3] Till that had been achieved, no general plan for dealing with the actual conduct of schools was possible. In August 1898 the Duke of Devonshire introduced the Board of Education Bill to the Lords.[4] The Bill was to establish a central authority formed by the union of the Education Department at Whitehall and the Department of Science and Art at South Kensington under a head who could concern himself with all educational matters, and absorb the educational functions of the Charity Commissioners and the Board of Agriculture.

The organization of secondary education was given as the chief purpose of the Bill. The Duke explained that it was impossible to organize even secondary education under the Local Education Authorities if there were no central body to deal with problems as between School Boards, managers of Science and Art classes, endowed schools, private schools and County Councils.

It has never been the duty of any minister [he said] to attempt to place either before his colleagues or before Parliament any complete and well defined scheme of the objects to which the secondary education of the country ought to be directed. It is impossible to state with any approach to accuracy what amount of public money, derived either from the exchequer or from the rates, is now being applied by School Boards to what is practically secondary education.

New problems were always arising; for example, Chambers of Commerce were now asking for commercial education, and there was no authority in a position to provide it legally.

From the debate, it was clear that the Board of Education would concern itself with the whole field of education. Lord Reay made the point that technical and secondary education could not be separated, as the power to profit by technical instruction depended on a satisfactory secondary education, and that, in its turn, secondary education demanded a good primary grounding. There must be an overall authority to have the general supervision.

There was a wide measure of agreement, and the Archbishop of Canterbury expressed the feelings of his party when he said that he 'rejoiced, and rejoiced exceedingly' at the appearance of the Bill. By June of the next year the Bill passed its second reading in the Commons.

The new Board was to have a President, and be composed of the First Lord of the Treasury, the Chancellor of the Exchequer and the Secretaries of State for various Departments. The Board thus followed the precedent of other Boards and the now defunct Committee of Council, by having members who could never be expected to meet, but whose offices lent respectability to the responsible Minister. The Government also made it clear that this was only the first stage in the reorganization, and that the institution of Local Authorities for education would follow as soon as possible. As the central authority was not functioning till 1 April 1900 there was inevitably some little delay.

'The Bill,' said Mr Channing in the debate, 'though small is of enormous importance.' The *Schoolmaster*[5] agreed, commenting on it when it finally became law:

The Board of Education Act is a measure the ultimate importance of which it would be impossible to over-estimate. Its addition to the statute book is really an epoch in the history of English education, and therefore of the nation.

While the Board of Education Bill was making its way through Parliament, the attack on the School Boards was resumed. It was essential to test and, if possible, destroy the claim to legal justification for the education of adults. Gorst, Garnett and Sidney Webb, as Chairman of the Technical Education Board, arranged that Black, headmaster of the

Camden School of Art, acting as a ratepayer, should challenge the School Board's accounts at the next audit. Black brought in Hales, a solicitor and member of the Board of Governors, and behind Gorst stood Morant with his memoranda and the Department library files. Together they managed to uncover a sufficient number of precedents and shady practices.

The Audit cases were heard in April and May 1899, and Cockerton found against the School Board's provision of Science and Art schools and classes. He allowed the expenditure on evening schools. The School Board appealed to the High Court on the disallowal, and the Local Government Board, driven on by Gorst[6] (who afterwards denied any share in it[7]) engaged Lord Robert Cecil as counsel. The School Board was represented by H. H. Asquith and Llewelyn Davies. The appeal, which was heard in November 1900 and reported in the Law Reports of the Queen's Bench division in 1901,[8] was before Justices Wills and Kennedy. The legal point was quite simple: were the School Boards allowed to subsidize advanced education, particularly that earning grant from the Department of Science and Art, out of the rates, i.e. from the school fund? H. H. Asquith pleaded merely that the ambiguity of the 1870 Act and its successors, which left 'child' and 'elementary education' undefined, allowed the School Boards to do what they liked. Further, the practice of giving advanced education through the School Boards had been going on for so long with official approval that it had practically become a right.

On the other side it was argued either that the School Boards were not entitled to teach anything beyond the subjects of the Whitehall Code, or that they could teach what they liked so long as no part of the cost fell on the rates. As it was generally agreed that the classes under South Kensington could not be self-supporting, and must either charge fees or be subsidized from the school fund, the second contention was as fatal to the Board's advanced work as the first.

The judgment against the School Board was inevitable. Justice Wills said that the question was not whether the School Board had the right to give advanced education, but whether money from the rates could be used for it. Whitehall had the power to make what rules it liked for grants, and so might South Kensington; but

it is not the business of either department to enquire whether any particular school, voluntary or Board, is exceeding its rights . . . by giving education which has satisfied the condition and earned the grants.

410

To argue that such action sets the school board free to teach at the expense of the ratepayers to adults and to children indiscriminately the higher mathematics, advanced chemistry (both theoretical and practical), political economy, art of a kind wholly beyond anything that can be taught to children, French, German, history, I know not what, appears to me to be the *ne plus ultra* of extravagance.

After this hint of non-judicial prejudice, he continued:

Therefore the fact that grants have been paid for more than 20 years to schools of this class is immaterial. We must ask what and to whom did the Acts of 1870 and later authorize the School Boards to teach at the expense of the rates. It is clearly stated that children are to be given elementary education, and this cannot be held to cover teaching foreign languages and advanced science to adults.

But School Boards 'may of course, carry on such work provided the whole of the funds required for it are furnished from sources other than contributions from the rates'.

Justice Kennedy agreed with him, and added that in his opinion, any instruction given by the School Boards under the Whitehall Code could legally be subsidized by the rates, but not instruction under the Science and Art Directory.

A. L. Smith, Master of the Rolls, decided in the same sense on a further appeal:

In my opinion the many Acts which were subsequently passed—up to and including the year 1891—have no real bearing on the point I have to decide, except that they show that the leglislature was throughout dealing with the elementary education of children, and nothing else.

It was not within the power of the Board to provide Science and Art classes of the kind referred to in this case either in the day schools or in evening continuation schools out of the School Board rate or school fund.

This decision was accepted as putting an end to the greater part of the work of the higher grade schools and to the evening continuation schools. The enemies of the Boards received it with joy. The *School Guardian*, the organ of the National Society, was especially jubilant:

The wings of the London School Board have been mercilessly clipped, and we hope that our friends in the provinces will look round and see whether there are not other School Boards which want pulling up a bit.

Other, less-committed, papers looked forward to the end of the process of which the recent judgment was the beginning. 'Let us', said the

Guardian, 'have no further continuance of corrupting illegality. Let the Government use to the full its present opportunity. Let the Minister of Education do for local education authorities what he has already done for the central authority,—let him consolidate and unify.' In fact let him 'create local education boards which by delegation from the county and county borough councils shall possess not only the present educational powers of the School Boards and the County Councils, but the added power of dealing with local secondary education'.

The time for a real reform of education seemed to have come. There was a national optimism and buoyancy at this beginning of the century. Mafeking had been relieved in May 1900, in the same month Roberts entered Johannesburg and on 5 June Pretoria fell. The Boer War, which had caused such dissention and disgrace, was practically over; and, although the Conservatives were back in power, Lord Rosebery in December, speaking for the Liberals, called for a new effort from all parties:

We must be prepared to set our house in order, and cease to consider what has sufficed for the past will suffice for the future.

It behoves all friends of education to seize the psychological moment and to turn to solid practical advantage the feeling that is abroad that the foundations of our Empire must be strengthened if our supremacy is to be maintained.

Such words were a clear demand for an Act which should end the existing confusion, but the Government was not to be hurried. It meant to be sure this time. Just when the audit case was being tried before Cockerton, perhaps as an insurance in case the matter did not go well, one more blow was struck at the School Boards. The Higher Education Minute, of 6 April 1900, had been devised by Morant with more than usual bureaucratic subtlety. While it professed to legalize higher grade schools under School Boards it was so drafted that any school could be disqualified on any technicality that the office might devise. In any case, no pupils over fourteen could be taught, and the curriculum must be scientific—a fitting preparation for skilled artisans—and not the liberal secondary education that so many parents desired.

The Minute was administered in the spirit of its begetters. After a year, and 190 applications for recognition, Sir John Gorst declared in Parliament that about 'a dozen had been recognized', though his indignant questioner only knew of two.[9] Of the London School Board's 79 higher grade schools, four science schools had been conditionally recognized. In fact, the whole business was described by Yoxall as an 'administrative fraud'.

The outcome of the appeals on the Cockerton case created a new situation. It was generally accepted that the School Boards must now discontinue their evening schools as well as their higher grade teaching. Sir John Gorst speaking in Parliament tried on the one hand to minimize the disturbance caused to education, and on the other to denigrate the work of the School Boards. 'So far as the Higher Grade schools generally are concerned there is not one that is in danger of either extinction or of being seriously damaged by this judgment.' It is difficult to think that this was true, unless he meant that the schools had already been destroyed by the Minute. But he admitted that 48 schools had a 'science top' which would be cut off and some 900 children would be affected. As to the evening schools there was no doubt that large numbers of students, about 228,000, would be deprived of education. Sir John disposed of them by an attack on the quality of the education given in the Board schools. It was spasmodic, superficial, and included dancing.

But, bad as these schools were supposed to be, something must be done for their immediate continuance. The real aim of the Government was expressed by the Duke of Devonshire when he said, 'Aided by the Cockerton judgment we shall this year have made it perfectly clear that the School Boards are in future to be limited to duties connected with elementary education.'

At first it was proposed to do this by a large education act which would make the general settlement so much desired by all parties. Yet the Government hesitated on the brink. The Liberal Government was a bare five years in the future, and demands for reform were being heard in every constituency. Under these circumstances the Bill which was introduced on 7 May 1901 was a surprise and disappointment. Sir John Gorst started his speech by saying, 'I will ask leave to establish in every part of England and Wales a Local Education Authority which is intended to supervise education of every kind, and which it is hoped may ultimately have the control and supervision of all schools, whether elementary, secondary or technical.'[10]

These brave words were not reflected in the text of the Bill. There were to be Committees of the County Councils which would merely take over the duties and resources of the Technical Education Committees, leaving the School Boards in control of elementary education.

Naturally there was no enthusiasm. The *Westminster Gazette* said: 'The Bill contains nothing, or next to nothing. What happens to the School Boards? The answer is "Nothing". What happens to the County Councils? The answer is "Next to nothing". What happens to the Cockerton schools? The answer is that "Nobody knows".' All that the *Guardian* could suggest was that the Bill offered a trial run for the County Councils and that as soon as they knew the work they would oust the School Boards. However charitably interpreted the Bill was inadequate, and it was abandoned for the year.

But it was necessary to do something about the schools which the Cockerton judgment had declared illegal, and the Government saw the opportunity to advance one step more on its path without risking too general opposition.

The Bill which was to achieve this and allow the continuation of the more essential schools was an exceedingly ingenious document. Its purpose was stated as being 'to enable Local Authorities to empower School Boards to carry on certain schools, and to sanction certain expenses'.[11] It thus completely subordinated the School Boards to the County Councils, so far as a part of their work went, and it established the principle of an over-riding Local Authority. There were voices raised against it. When leave was asked to bring in the Bill in July 1901, James Bryce protested against the introduction of a 'highly controversial Bill' under the ten-minute rule: 'This measure is one which is intended to establish a very large and far-reaching principle. . . . They are seeking to snatch upon a temporary Bill the assertion of an important and far-reaching principle. . . . They are seeking to effect what amounts to an educational revolution in this country, and they are trying to do it by a mere side wind.' The Government accepted this interpretation: 'This is an authoritative declaration of the general line upon which we mean to proceed in our future Bill.'

Those who had been associated with the School Boards began to pity them, as great men fallen into adversity. Macnamara uttered the general feeling: 'I hope all interested in the School Boards will oppose to the bitter end this attempt to make the School Boards, before they are finally swallowed up, bow down and go cap in hand to local Councils, and beg to be allowed to carry out the work till they are abolished by the new Bill. It is adding insult to injury.'

But the Government feared that the School Boards still had power. When it was suggested that it would be less wounding to their self-respect if the schools to be preserved were licensed by the Board of Education rather than the County Councils, Sir John Gorst opposed it; and gave, in a memorandum, the illuminating reason that the Board of Education would never be able to withstand the pressure that would be brought to bear in favour of the schools: 'The power would be exercised under the influence of the School Boards and the National Union of Teachers. It would afford no practical check on the School Boards who would at once occupy the whole field of secondary education in the great towns.'

In spite of the humanitarian opposition, the Bill was passed, and the defeat of the School Boards was now complete. As the *Schoolmaster* inelegantly expressed it, 'The claim has been jumped and the whole thing prejudiced.' There was nothing to come now but the final Bill.

The Bill was introduced in March 1902.[12] After the first week it could be said that the debates were 'remarkable for good temper, moderation and a genuine desire to promote educational progress'. The second reading passed with a majority of 237, aided by the unreliable Irish vote. In the Committee stage, however, the mass of amendments threatened to swamp the Bill. But, this time, the Government were determined, and after 39 days it forced it on by the use of the closure. Yet, even so, the Duke of Devonshire could say, reviewing the passage of the Bill,

This Bill has occupied in the other House a length of time almost equal to that ever devoted to any measure, and has occupied in committee more time than any measure ever submitted to parliament. The Education Act of 1870 occupied 22 days in the House of Commons; the Irish Home Rule Bill of 1893 occupied 78 days of which 46 days were committee. The present Bill occupied 58 days of which 46 were on details of the Bill and two of financial resolutions.

The result of all this work was satisfactory; and in its final form the Bill did what its friends hoped.

The Bill had three main parts. Part I established Local Education Authorities: 'The Council of every County and every County Borough shall be the Local Education Authority. Provided that the Council of a Borough with a population of over 10,000 or an Urban District with a population of over 20,000 shall be the Local Education for Part III of this act.'

The Government thus bowed to the local pride of the smaller boroughs and assured their neutrality towards the Bill. If it multiplied the number of authorities that was a lesser evil than opposition.

415

Part II gave all secondary education to the County Councils. In the final form of the Bill they were charged with the duty of surveying the existent provision and consulting with the Board of Education on the needs of the district. They could spend all the Local Taxation money and a rate up to 2*d.* in the £, or more with the sanction of the Local Government Board. Among the types of secondary education, the training of teachers is specially mentioned.

Part III dealt with elementary education, and in this section most important changes were made in committee. The first draft said, 'This section shall apply only with-in the area of a Local Education Authority for which it is adopted', and thus left the Local Authorities and the School Boards to fight it out in hundreds of skirmishes all over England. The final version, more boldly and more wisely, said, 'The Local Education Authorities shall throughout the country have the powers and duties of a School Board.'

The next section provided for the maintenance of all schools by the Local Authority. Voluntary schools, in return for maintenance, must accept one-third of their managers on the nomination of the Local Education Authority, must abandon religious discrimination and submit to the Authority's control of the appointment and dismissal of teachers, except on religious grounds. The managers were still liable for structural repairs to the fabric.

This arrangement preserved the voluntary schools as part of the educational system of the country, and it removed their chief disadvantages. They would no longer be starved and hopelessly inferior (though their buildings might become antiquated) nor would the teachers be left unprotected from the vagaries of the less satisfactory managers. It was to this preservation of the voluntary schools that the opposition of the Nonconformists was directed.

The power of the County Councils was to be exercised through an Education Committee. This was to be composed in such a way that the majority of the members were always members of the Council, but there must be co-opted members. Some of these must be women, for women were not yet eligible for membership of the Councils.

This was the scheme which in December 1902 was launched on the country. We may perhaps sum it up in the words of Sir Richard Jebb on the third reading:[13]

This Bill embodies a great national reform, and before it leaves this House it seems well that some of us should attempt to state the broad effects of the Bill on the educational prospects of the country as we see it. . . .

Why was the Bill brought in? The first cause was that elementary education was in an unsatisfactory state. This was so because some of the voluntary schools were leading a precarious existence, and some of them were more or less inefficient through poverty. Then as to our secondary system: it was in a chaotic condition. . . . There is a third defect, and that is the want of proper linking between primary and secondary education. . . . This Bill makes it possible for the first time, that every public elementary school shall be maintained in a state of satisfactory efficiency. Then as to secondary education. In Clause II the Local Authority is charged to take a survey of the educational needs of its area and to supply or aid the supply of education other than elementary.

Next as to linking primary and secondary education. This can be done largely by a judicious system of scholarships, but also by the adjustment of curriculum of schools of different kinds and grades.

The training of teachers is now expressly named. The Local Authorities can establish Training Colleges and aid institutions already existing . . . and thus remove the grievances of non-conformists. . . .

When the machinery of this Bill is in full operation I hope that in most localities of England there will grow up a real living interest in education . . . and this Bill will prove, what its framers have intended it to be, a far-reaching and salutary measure of reform.

The Act of 1902 did all that its friends hoped, and rather more than some of its sponsors desired: it made possible the whole future development of education. The County and Borough Councils were powerful and stable bodies sensitive to local pressure. What a district wanted it could have, provided it was prepared to pay half the cost; Whitehall supervised and helped, but it did not initiate. The principle of diversity was thus continued in English education.

The Local Authorities received their primary schools from the School Boards; their main work of creation was at first directed to secondary and technical education. The provision to begin with was scanty, and most of it was fee paying; but year by year all types of education expanded. In some ways local freedom brought good results. The district could provide the type of education that suited it, and institute art or technical schools which taught the local trades. On the other hand, there were 'residential' districts which saw little need to provide education for the lower classes. It was not till after the 1944 Act that Whitehall began to demand 'development plans' and try to force expansion in the more backward areas.

417

This local variation also showed itself in the treatment of the teachers, and it was many years before a national salary scale was instituted.

The Act did not remove the distinction between the state and the voluntary schools. A denominational school received grants for maintenance, but not for capital expenditure. The result was a continuance of the sub-standard schools, resisting change on the grounds of expense, and often recruiting the less-well-qualified teachers. In the great re-organization which followed the Hadow Report the denominational schools, as a body, changed far more slowly than those controlled by local authorities; and some slum and village schools continued into the 1950s with arrangements which were unsatisfactory even at the beginning of the century.

The idea that an education beyond the elements was a privilege that must be bought, or at most granted free to a minority of clever children, lasted till 1944 when it was decreed that 'aptitude and ability' should be the test of the type of education offered to a child, and that all children had the right to something more than the bare tools of knowledge. Long before that, the relationship between primary and secondary education had been a source of concern to the authorities. As the school-leaving age was raised and as more children passed to the secondary schools the position of the older children in the primary schools became more and more unsatisfactory. The Local Authorities devised many solutions to the problem, but its increasing urgency made some general re-organization necessary. The Act of 1944 offered a solution to the problems that had been understood up to that time; we are now trying to solve those which that Act itself created.

The framers of the English educational system have gone on trying to solve each problem as it has arisen, with varying degrees of success. But education does not stand alone, it is part of the general life of the community. A cynic might note that most English Education Acts have followed a war in which we have discovered the importance of physical and mental efficiency. The demand for education has also been closely associated with technical development. The age that needed the ceaseless simple toil of children has long passed away. The demand now is for technicians of a high order to control the complex machines that do our work for us. The history of education since 1800 can be seen largely as the history of the machines which have set children free to receive learning and have made their elders anxious to impart it to them. The acceptance of the dignity of all men springs from a materialistic as well as a religious source.

418

Notes

1. For all this chapter, see Eric Eaglesham, *From School Board to Local Authority* (1956).
2. Hansard, XL, 1030.
3. P.P., 1899, VIII, 515, Report of Standing Committee on Law.
4. Hansard, LXIII, 666.
5. *Schoolmaster*, 30 December 1899.
6. Eaglesham, p. 120.
7. Hansard, XCIII, 984.
8. Queen's Bench Division, 1901, 1, 322, (C.A.) 726.
9. Hansard, LXXXVIII, 505; XC, 601 ff.
10. Hansard, XCIII, 970.
11. Hansard, XCVI, 609.
12. Hansard, CV, 846.
13. Hansard, CXV, 1080.

List of the chief official publications referred to in the book

Minutes of the Committee of Council on Education, 1839–1898.
Reports of the Department of Science and Art, 1852–1898.
Reports of the Board of Education, 1899, 1902.

These volumes contain the General Report, Statistics, Reports of H.M.I.s, Minutes, Instructions, Code, Correspondence, etc. for each year.

They are most easily consulted in the Library of the Ministry of Education.

Education Acts

1836. To facilitate the conveyance of sites for schools.
1868. Public Schools Act. To make further provision for the good government and extension of certain public schools in England.
1869. To amend the law relating to Endowed Schools.
1870. To provide for public Elementary Education in England and Wales. Amending and extending Acts, 1872, 1873, 1876, 1880.
1872. To amend and extend the provisions of the Law of Scotland on the subject of Education.
1878. Act to promote Intermediate Education in Ireland.
1889. To facilitate the provision of Technical Education.
1889. To promote Intermediate Education in Wales.
1890. For the purpose of making operative certain articles in the Education Code of 1890.
1899. Board of Education Act.
1902. Education Act.

Reports—Parliamentary Papers

1816, IV, 1; 1818, IV, 1. Reports on the Education of the lower orders of the Metropolis.
1818, IV, 55. Report on Eton and St Bees.
1819, IX, A, B, C. Digest of Parochial Returns.

1820, XII, 341. General table showing the state of Education in England.

1825, XII, 1. Education in Ireland.

1826, XVIII, 1. Parochial Education in Scotland.

1829, IV, 443. Education in Ireland.

1834, IX, 1. Report on state of Education.

1835, VII. Report on Education in England and Wales.

1837, VII. Report on Education of the Poorer Classes in England and Wales.

1837, VII, 437. Report on state of Education in Scotland.

1837, VII, 345, p. 347. Report on schools of public foundation in Ireland.

1837, VIII, pt I, 1. Report on progress and operation of plan of Education in Ireland.

1841. Training and Education of Pauper Children, Poor Law Commissioners.

1847, XXVII, I, II, III. Report on Education in Wales.

1851, XLIX. Education and training of Pauper Children.

1861, XXI, pt I, 1. Royal Commission on state of Popular Education in England. Newcastle Commission.

1864, XX, 1. Royal Commission in Revenues and management of certain schools and colleges.

1865, VI. Report of Select Committee on constitution of Committee of Council.

1866, VII. Report of Select Committee on Education.

1867, XXVIII, pt 1. Royal Commission on schools not comprised with in the two recent Commissions on Popular Education and Public Schools.

1881, XXVI, 153. Report on Technical Education.

1881, XXXIII, 1. Report on Intermediate and Higher Education in Wales and Monmouth. Aberdare Report.

1884, XXIX. Royal Commission on Technical Education.

1886, XXVI. Report of Royal Commission on the Elementary Education Acts. Cross Commission.

1895, XLIII, 1. Royal Commission on Secondary Education. Bryce Commission.

List of official publications

HANSARD, *chief Education debates*

19 February 1807, VIII, 865
24 April 1807, IX, 538
Whitbread. Poor Law Bill.

21 May 1816, XXXIV, 633
20 June 1816, XXXIV, 1230
Brougham, Education of the Poor in the Metropolis.

9 April 1829, XXI, 608
Petition of Irish Bishops.

9 September 1831, VI, 1249
Stanley on reform of Irish Education.

30 July 1833, XX, 139
Roebuck on National Education.
17 August 1833, XX, 732
Vote of £20,000 for Education.

19 May 1835, XXVII, 1199 and Appendix
Wyse on Education in Ireland.

1 December 1837, XXXIX, 425
Lord Brougham's plan for a Board of Education.

12 February 1839, XLV, 273
Lord John Russell on plans for Education.
4 June 1839, XLVII, 1377
Lord John Russell abandons the Normal School.
14 June 1839, XLVIII, 227
Start of debate on Committee of Council on Education.
The debate continued for several days.
11 July 1839, XLIX, 128
The Queen's answer to the Lords' petition.

24 March 1843, LXVII, 1411
2nd reading of Factories' Education Bill and debate.
15 June 1843, LXIX, 1567
Bill withdrawn.

5 February 1847, LXXXIX, 858
Lord Lansdowne explaining the Minute of 1846.

19 April 1847, XCII, 952
Lord John Russell on the 'Government plan of education'.
Debate and continued.

4 April 1853, CXXV, 522
Lord John Russell asking leave to introduce Education Bill.

2 May 1855, CXXXVII, 2112
Sir John Pakington introducing an Education Bill and debate.
11 June 1855, CXXXVIII, 1784
Adjourned debate.

8 February 1856, CXL, 449
Bill for Vice-President of Committee of Council for Education introduced in Lords.

6 March 1856, CXL, 1955
Lord John Russell's Resolution on Education.

11 February 1858, CXLVIII, 1184
Sir John Pakington moves for the appointment of a Commission to enquire into state education.

22 July 1859, CLV, 313
Lowe on Education Estimates.

8 July 1861, CLXIV, 484
Debate in Lords on Newcastle Report.
11 July 1861, CLXIV, 699
Discussion in Commons and debate on estimates.
Lowe's speech, 719 and following.

13 February 1862, CLXV, 191
Lowe's speech and debate on Revised Code.
25 March 1862, CLXVI, 21; 27 March, 137
Debate on Revised Code.
28 March 1862, CLXVI, 240
Lowe gives way.
5 May 1862, CLXVI, 1204
Further debate.

12 April 1864, CLXXIV, 897
Inspectors' reports and censure on Lowe.

12 May 1864, CLXXV, 368
Select Committee appointed to enquire into the 'mode of conducting
the business of the Education Department'.

15 March 1869, CXCIV, 1356
Endowed Schools Bill. 2nd reading, debate.

17 February 1870, CXCIX, 438
Elementary Education. Leave to introduce the Bill.
14 March 1870, CXCIX, 1919
Debate on 2nd reading. Debates continued till 1 August.
Royal Assent 9 August.

10 March 1871, CCIV, 1788
Debate on New Code.

15 June 1876, CCXXIX, 1897
Elementary Education Bill (compulsory attendance).
Debate on 2nd reading. Continued till Royal Assent 15 August.

8 August 1881, CCLXIV, 1210
Mundella on Revised Code.
11 August 1881, CCLXIV, 1511
Lord Spencer on Revised Code.

29 June 1883, CCLXXX, 1933
Debate on whether a Minister of Education is necessary.
16 July 1883, CCLXXXI, 1465
Debate on insanity and over-pressure. Debates at other times particularly:

11 March 1884, CCLXXXV, 1184

17 June 1886, CCCVI, 1723
Statement on progress of education.

27 April 1888, CCCXXV, 813
Debate on Technical Education.

5 April 1889, CCCXXXIV, 1681
Debate in Lords on Education Code.
11 April 1889, CCCXXXV, 204, 1657
Further questions and observations on the Code.
18 July 1889, CCCXXXVIII, 653
Code withdrawn.

15 May 1889, CCCXXXVI, 121
2nd reading Intermediate Education (Wales) Bill.
14 August 1889, CCCXXXIX, 1248
Final stage of 2nd reading of Technical Instruction Bill.

12 May 1890, CCCXLIV, 641
Lords' observations on Education Code.
6 June 1890, CCCXLV, 162
Debate on Education Code on the Estimates.

8 June 1891, CCCLIII, 1834
Debate on Elementary Education (Fee Grant).
22 June 1891, CCCLIV, 1099
Debate on 2nd reading.
16 July 1891, CCCLV, 1329
Elementary Education (Fee Grant). 2nd reading in Lords.

16 June 1892, 4th Series, V, 1355
Statement of effect of Fee Grant and Code of 1891.

29 March 1895, XXXII, 445
Lords debate on Code.

31 March 1896, XXXIX, 526
Sir John Gorst asks leave to introduce Education Bill.
5 May 1896, XL, 555
Debate on 2nd reading, continues for several days, and then in committee.
22 June 1896, XLI, 1572
Bill withdrawn.

11 February 1897, XLVI, 188
Voluntary schools Bill. Additional capitation grant.
16 February 1897, XLVI, 534
2nd reading.
5 April 1897, XLVIII, 539
Elementary Education Bill. Increased grant.
Bill introduced: debated several days.

1 August 1898, LXIII, 666
Board of Education Bill introduced in Lords.

24 April 1899, LXX, 321
2nd reading in Lords.

1 August 1899, LXXV, 1066
Board of Education Bill. Debate and Bill passed.

3 May 1900, LXXXII, 596
Discussion on Code of 1900.

5 March 1901, XC, 594
Debate on Education on Supply.
8 July 1901, XCVI, 1170
2nd reading of Bill to legalize certain evening classes.

5 May 1902, CVII, 638
2nd reading, Education Bill. Debates continue many days till Royal
    Assent 18 December 1902.

Index

Place, Francis, 54
  evidence to Commission
    (1835), 105
Prussia, state system of education, 51
Pupil teachers:
  used in Holland, 89
  instituted and regulations,
    179ff.
  training and progress, 191
  numbers, 193
  overworked, 194
  difficulties in teaching them,
    195
  centres, 365

Quarterly Review:
  on Minutes of 1846, 186
  on Revised Code, 249
  on certificated teachers, 251
Queen's Scholars, 181

Reading, methods of teaching,
  166, 217
Religious dissension dying out,
  298
Roberts, Robert:
  at Amlwch, 36
  going to school, 123
  goes to Caernarvon, 155
  troubles with his Rector, 200
Roebuck, speech on education
  (1833), 66
Runciman, James:
  his life at Borough Road, 368
  The Ritualist, 370
Russell, Lord John:
  initiates Committee of
    Council, 77
  pays special attention to sub-
    ject of education, 177
  speech on education (1853),
    207

introduces trial resolutions
  (1856), 240

Sandford, R. F., Secretary, 344
School Boards:
  in Forster's Act, 304
  types and members, 307
  finance, 316
  religious instruction, 322
  try to compel attendance, 325
  bargains with teachers, 330
  equip the schools, 331
  provide secondary education,
    389
  defeated by County Councils,
    404
Schools:
  advanced elementary, 358
  charity, 6
  common day, 39
  dame, 38
  finance in 1840s, 161
  methods and conditions:
    in 1840s, 165
    1850s, 212
    1860s, 260 (whole chapter)
    1870s and '80s, 343
    1890s, 376
  monitorial, 31, 35
  Scottish parochial, 46
  specifications for buildings,
    126
  time-tables, 170
Simpson, James, evidence on
  popular education, 73
Snell:
  Evidence to Newcastle Com-
    mission, 199
  views of *Quarterly* on him,
    251
Sneyd-Kinnersley:
  on examinations, 264
  on parishes, 306